The Color Factor

NBER Series on Long-Term Factors in Economic Development

A NATIONAL BUREAU OF ECONOMIC RESEARCH SERIES
Edited by Claudia Goldin

Also in the series:

Understanding the Gender Gap: An Economic History of American Women (Oxford University Press, 1990)
Claudia Goldin

Height, Health and History: Nutritional Status in the United Kingdom, 1750–1980 (Cambridge University Press, 1990)
Roderick Floud, Kenneth Wachter, and Annabel Gregory

Race and Schooling in the South, 1880–1950: An Economic History (University of Chicago Press, 1990)
Robert A. Margo

Fatal Years: Child Mortality in Late Nineteenth-Century America (Princeton University Press, 1991)
Samuel H. Preston and Michael R. Haines

Golden Fetters: The Gold Standard and the Great Depression, 1919–1939 (Oxford University Press, 1992)
Barry Eichengreen

The Federal Civil Service System and the Problem of Bureaucracy: The Economics and Politics of Institutional Change (University of Chicago Press, 1994)
Ronald N. Johnson and Gary D. Libecap

Insider Lending: Banks, Personal Connections, and Economic Development in Industrial New England (Cambridge University Press, 1994)
Naomi R. Lamoreaux

In Pursuit of Leviathan: Technology, Institutions, Productivity, and Profits in American Whaling, 1816–1906 (University of Chicago Press, 1997)
Lance E. Davis, Robert E. Gallman, and Karin Gleiter

The Evolution of Retirement: An American Economic History, 1880–1990 (University of Chicago Press, 1998)
Dora L. Costa

Yankeys Now: Immigrants in the Antebellum U.S., 1840–1860 (Oxford University Press, 1999)
Joseph P. Ferrie

Wages and Labor Markets in the United States, 1820–1860 (University of Chicago Press, 2000)
Robert A. Margo

A Prelude to the Welfare State: The Origins of Workers' Compensation (University of Chicago Press, 2000)
Price V. Fishback and Shawn Everett Kantor

Straining at the Anchor: The Argentine Currency Board and the Search for Macroeconomic Stability, 1880–1935 (University of Chicago Press, 2001)
Gerardo della Paolera and Alan M. Taylor

Water, Race, and Disease (MIT Press, 2004)
Werner Troesken

The Democratization of Invention: Patents and Copyrights in American Economic Development, 1790–1920 (Cambridge University Press, 2005)
B. Zorina Khan

Heroes and Cowards: The Social Face of War (Princeton University Press, 2008)
Dora L. Costa and Matthew E. Kahn

The Changing Body: Health, Nutrition, and Human Development in the Western World since 1700 (Cambridge University Press, 2011)
Roderick Floud, Robert W. Fogel, Bernard Harris, and Sok Chul Hong

Economic Development in the Americas since 1500: Endowments and Institutions (Cambridge University Press, 2012)
Stanley L. Engerman and Kenneth L. Sokoloff

Political Arithmetic: Simon Kuznets and the Empirical Tradition in Economics (University of Chicago Press, 2013)
Robert William Fogel, Enid M. Fogel, Mark Guglielmo, and Nathaniel Grotte

Well Worth Saving: How the New Deal Safeguarded Home Ownership (University of Chicago Press, 2013)
Price Fishback, Jonathan Rose, and Kenneth Snowden

The Color Factor

The Economics of African-American Well-Being in the Nineteenth-Century South

HOWARD BODENHORN

OXFORD
UNIVERSITY PRESS

OXFORD
UNIVERSITY PRESS

Oxford University Press is a department of the University of
Oxford. It furthers the University's objective of excellence in research,
scholarship, and education by publishing worldwide.

Oxford   New York
Auckland   Cape Town   Dar es Salaam   Hong Kong   Karachi
Kuala Lumpur   Madrid   Melbourne   Mexico City   Nairobi
New Delhi   Shanghai   Taipei   Toronto

With offices in
Argentina   Austria   Brazil   Chile   Czech Republic   France   Greece
Guatemala   Hungary   Italy   Japan   Poland   Portugal   Singapore
South Korea   Switzerland   Thailand   Turkey   Ukraine   Vietnam

Oxford is a registered trademark of Oxford University Press
in the UK and certain other countries.

Published in the United States of America by
Oxford University Press
198 Madison Avenue, New York, NY 10016

Cataloging-in-Publication data is on file at the Library of Congress
ISBN 978-0-19-938309-2 (hbk.); 978-0-19-938310-8 (pbk.)

For Pam

RELATION OF THE DIRECTORS TO THE WORK AND PUBLICATIONS OF THE NBER

1. The object of the NBER is to ascertain and present to the economics profession, and to the public more generally, important economic facts and their interpretation in a scientific manner without policy recommendations. The Board of Directors is charged with the responsibility of ensuring that the work of the NBER is carried on in strict conformity with this object.

2. The President shall establish an internal review process to ensure that book manuscripts proposed for publication DO NOT contain policy recommendations. This shall apply both to the proceedings of conferences and to manuscripts by a single author or by one or more coauthors but shall not apply to authors of comments at NBER conferences who are not NBER affiliates.

3. No book manuscript reporting research shall be published by the NBER until the President has sent to each member of the Board a notice that a manuscript is recommended for publication and that in the President's opinion it is suitable for publication in accordance with the above principles of the NBER. Such notification will include a table of contents and an abstract or summary of the manuscript's content, a list of contributors if applicable, and a response form for use by Directors who desire a copy of the manuscript for review. Each manuscript shall contain a summary drawing attention to the nature and treatment of the problem studied and the main conclusions reached.

4. No volume shall be published until forty-five days have elapsed from the above notification of intention to publish it. During this period a copy shall be sent to any Director requesting it, and if any Director objects to publication on the grounds that the manuscript contains policy recommendations, the objection will be presented to the author(s) or editor(s). In case of dispute, all members of the Board shall be notified, and the President shall appoint an ad hoc committee of the Board to decide the matter; thirty days additional shall be granted for this purpose.

5. The President shall present annually to the Board a report describing the internal manuscript review process, any objections made by Directors before publication or by anyone after publication, any disputes about such matters, and how they were handled.

6. Publications of the NBER issued for informational purposes concerning the work of the Bureau, or issued to inform the public of the activities at the Bureau, including but not limited to the NBER Digest and Reporter, shall be consistent with the object stated in paragraph 1. They shall contain a specific disclaimer noting that they have not passed through the review procedures required in this resolution. The Executive Committee of the Board is charged with the review of all such publications from time to time.

7. NBER working papers and manuscripts distributed on the Bureau's web site are not deemed to be publications for the purpose of this resolution, but they shall be consistent with the object stated in paragraph 1. Working papers shall contain a specific disclaimer noting that they have not passed through the review procedures required in this resolution. The NBER's web site shall contain a similar disclaimer. The President shall establish an internal review process to ensure that the working papers and the web site do not contain policy recommendations, and shall report annually to the Board on this process and any concerns raised in connection with it.

8. Unless otherwise determined by the Board or exempted by the terms of paragraphs 6 and 7, a copy of this resolution shall be printed in each NBER publication as described in paragraph 2 above.

CONTENTS

Acknowledgments   xi

1. Introduction   1

2. Legal Constructions of Race and Interpretations of Color   19

3. Race Mixing and Color in Literature and Science   34

4. The Plantation   50

5. Finding Freedom   70

6. Marriage and the Family   98

7. Work   123

8. Wealth   144

9. Height, Health, and Mortality   167

Epilogue   188

Appendices   199
Notes   263
References   289
Index   315

ACKNOWLEDGMENTS

The Color Factor is based on 17 years (1998–2014) of research into the social, political, and economic construction of race in the early nineteenth century. Eighteen years ago, I was not thinking much about race and color, certainly not about color in the nineteenth century. My finding this path was serendipitous and my travels down it have been glorious. One summer afternoon in 1998, I was in the Library of Virginia looking for some information on Virginia's early nineteenth-century banks. As I scrolled through rolls of microfilm, I happened upon some documents titled "Free Negro and Mulatto Registers." When I looked more closely, I noticed that the records included brief descriptions of free-born and manumitted African Americans, including their ages and heights. At that time, I had some passing familiarity with anthropometric history and made the fateful choice to gather the registers from a dozen or so counties to see if average heights might shed light on African-American well-being. It was only much later that I paid much attention to the color designations in the registers. A preliminary investigation revealed a marked height advantage for those described as mulatto, and more so for those described as bright or light mulatto. Whence this height differential? Was it real? Was it a statistical anomaly? Was there evidence of light-dark differences in other measurable dimensions? I read a bit and discussed this preliminary finding with my friend and colleague Fluney Hutchinson. He thought I was on to something. I have been thinking and writing about color ever since.

Many people have helped me as I worked my way through the project. My friends, colleagues, and coauthors, Susan Averett and Chris Ruebeck, helped me translate my thoughts into formal economic models and testable hypotheses about color and racial identity in the modern world. Our joint work, which appeared in *B. E. Journal of Economic Policy and Analysis* (2009) and a pair of National Bureau of Economics Research working papers, focus on the circumstances under which a mixed-race person will self-identify as white, as black, or as mixed race. It is a perplexing problem and I think we offer some insight into the connection between the economics and psychology of identity. Although analytical tools developed in our working paper and published article on modern mixed-race youth do not appear here, they shape the discussion at several points and I thank Susan and Chris for making me think more clearly about some important issues.

Participants at professional conferences and seminars provided invaluable comments and insightful criticisms. During presentations at two NBER Summer Institutes, Claudia Goldin, Price Fishback, and Eugene White pushed me to think more and better about the connections between color and outcomes. Participants in the MacArthur Network on Social Interactions at the Brookings Institution (2003) pushed me to connect the color designations in the Virginia registers to the 1860 census. The result, as they predicted, is a better understanding of nineteenth-century racial nomenclature and racial identity. Patrick Mason deserves special thanks for an invitation to present at a miniconference at Florida State University. The other participants invigorated my research and deepened my conviction that a wide-ranging exploration of color differences within the black community would contribute to the ongoing debate on race in America. An article coauthored with Chris Ruebeck that appeared in a special issue of the *Journal of Population Economics* (2007) was an outgrowth of the paper we presented at that conference, and I thank Heather Antecol and Deborah Cobb-Clark for including it. My thinking has evolved some since Chris and I wrote that paper, but its influence on the discussion in Chapter 8 is evident. Frank Lewis pushed me to think more clearly about manumission. My analysis is much better for his prodding, and I thank Springer for permission to reproduce some of the material from my *Cliometrica* (2010) article in Chapter 5, which expands on the earlier discussion of manumission. Kyle Kaufmann, then editor of *Advances in Agricultural Economic History*, read an early version of my study of rural African-American wealth holding and asked me to submit it for publication. Because the data underlying that study were lost in the transition between computers, I am grateful to JAI Press/ Emerald for permission to reproduce several tables from my "Complexion Gap" (2002) article in Chapter 8, though my thinking about some of the issues has evolved considerably since 2002.

Seminar participants at Duke, George Mason, Lafayette, Lehigh, Michigan, Northwestern, SUNY-Binghamton, Wake Forest, and Wesleyan (twice); conference participants at the Allied Social Science Annual Meetings, the Economic History Association, and the Southern Economic Association meetings; and several generous referees all deserve special thanks for participating in my voyage of discovery. I am particularly grateful to Raymond Cohn and Tomas Cvrcek for reading an early draft of the manuscript and offering many helpful comments. Ray convinced me to scrap the first iteration of the introduction and start over; Tomas offered valuable advice in my study of marriage markets. Four anonymous readers also pushed me to rewrite substantial parts of this manuscript, and the book is better for their thoughtful comments. I cannot thank Claudia Goldin enough for including my monograph in the National Bureau of Economic Research's economic history series.

William "Sandy" Darity and Greg Price deserve special mention. Their support and encouragement sustained the project at several critical junctures. Sandy's belief that historical understanding might illuminate and influence modern discussions of color has not wavered, even when others were skeptical. His invitations to conferences and panels introduced me to a circle of scholars—notably Darrick Hamilton, Rhonda Sharp, Art Goldsmith, Tiffany Green, Patrick Mason, Sam Myers, and the late Linda Datcher Loury—with whom I might otherwise have not interacted. I benefitted greatly from my discussions with them. It was discussions with them that pushed me to explore the contemporary legal, literary, and science literature to better understand how people in the nineteenth century thought about race and color.

Over the years I had the privilege of working with some terrific research assistants who diligently entered data and shared their own experiences with race and color: Shivani Malhotra, Veronica Hart, Martha Osier, Keming Liang, Qiong Wu, Chutima Tontarawongara, Mrittika Shamsuddin, and Adam Pié. Lafayette College and the National Science Foundation (grants SES-0109165 and SES-0453995) generously underwrote their support.

I thank Scott Parris and Cathryn Vaulman at Oxford University Press. Scott's enthusiasm for the project saw me through the final push. And Cathryn's help marshaling the manuscript through the editorial process made that process relatively painless. I also thank her for helping me identify and obtain permissions for the cover art.

Greg Price was instrumental in my securing funding from the National Science Foundation at an early date, which helped get the project off the ground. I am grateful for funding from several other organizations that supported the collection of the data that underlay my arguments throughout the book. The Ewing Marion Kauffman Foundation supported an extended visit to the Baker Library at Harvard University, which led to a deeper understanding of nineteenth-century African-American entrepreneurship and self-employment discussed in Chapter 7. The Earhart Foundation supported the collection of wealth data from tax records and the federal censuses discussed in Chapter 8. Grants from the Economic History Association and Lafayette College supported the collection of height data analyzed in Chapter 9. Financial support from the Irish-American Cultural Institute and Lafayette College funded the collection of ancillary data that influences the discussion at several points in the manuscript.

I would be remiss if I did not mention Lou and Jean Kolek for their support and for letting me use their home as a crash pad when I needed some time away to play some golf and clear my head. Thanks, too, to my parents, who generously lent me their guest room on my many visits to the Library of Virginia and looked after my dogs while I labored in the archives.

No one played a larger part in this project than Pam. She spent countless hours traveling to and working in archives, entering data, and listening to me talk about color. I cannot thank her enough for her unwavering encouragement, support, and patience. With love and appreciation, I dedicate this to you.

The Color Factor

Introduction

In September 1852 John Scott Bailey petitioned the Henrico County, Virginia court asking for legal certification of his non-negro status.[1] In support of his petition, Bailey provided an affidavit from Sarah M. Burton and Frances C. Burton, which traced Bailey's ancestry back four generations. The Misses Burton claimed to have known the Bailey family for "20 or 30 years," attested that John Scott Bailey had a black great-great grandfather and an Indian grandfather on his paternal line, and a one-quarter black, three-quarter Indian great-great grandmother on the maternal line. To the best of the Burtons' knowledge, all of Bailey's other ancestors were white, though they could not attest to the race of his great-great grandfather on the maternal line. On September 8, 1852, the court found that the petitioner, by Virginia's statutory definition, was "not a negro." Figure 1.1 reproduces the court's order to the clerk to enter its decision in the record and provide a copy of its decision to Bailey. The following year, Braxton Smith petitioned the same court with the same request. Smith's mother, Milly Smith, was a white woman with four other children considered white, but the petition was silent about the racial makeup on the paternal line. The court denied Braxton's petition and refused to issue a certificate legally recognizing his non-negro status.[2]

The two cases reveal that racial classification in late antebellum Virginia was about, among other things, physical appearance and what was known or could be proved about a family's racial history. Unlike Bailey, Smith was not legally white, but he was not black either. Smith inhabited a racial middle ground; he was mulatto. In the 1850 manuscript census, in fact, Braxton Smith was classified as a mulatto; there were two adult John Baileys enumerated in the Henrico County-Richmond City area and one John S. Bailey in Westmoreland County (40 miles from Richmond), all of whom were classified as white. It appears that Bailey and Smith presented sufficiently similar physical characteristics that some people considered them white, while others considered them non-white. In petitioning the Henrico County court, both were pursuing the same objective—to be legally classified as non-negro. Both men presumably petitioned for legal non-negro status because some authority contested their legal whiteness,

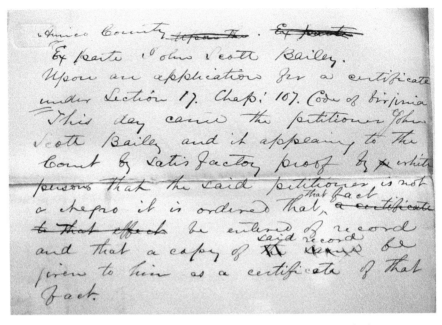

Figure 1.1 Henrico County, Virginia Court Decision in John Scott Bailey's Petition.
Source: Free Negro and Slave Records, Henrico County, Box 2 (1852), Library of Virginia.

which they were then required to prove. Perhaps they wanted to avoid paying the $1 annual capitation tax imposed on free African-American men; perhaps they wanted to own firearms, a right not extended to nonwhite residents; perhaps they wanted to avoid the possibility of being auctioned for a term of labor if they were unable to pay their annual property taxes. Even if Bailey's neighbors or some bureaucratic authority were aware of his part-African heritage, the court's determination that he was not black had potentially profound effects on the economic, social, and political opportunities open to him and his children. He was freed from the many legal proscriptions imposed on free African Americans.

Understanding the Bailey and Smith cases—and the thousands of similar court proceedings dating to the early eighteenth century in which people of part-African heritage contested their racial designations—requires an appreciation of contemporary American social and economic order as it applied to people of African descent.[3] This is such a study, the broad-brush outlines of which appear in the Bailey and Smith cases. The defining characteristic of that era's social and economic ordering is that it was organized around subtle differences in skin tone and other physical markers of European or African ancestry. Briefly stated, this study shows that relative to dark-skinned African Americans, light-skinned, mixed-race men and women achieved higher levels of economic well-being in nearly all measurable dimensions. Light-skinned men and women were more likely to escape the bonds of slavery; they were more likely to have received some education and to work at a skilled occupation; light-skinned men and women lived in larger, more stable families; they were healthier and wealthier.

Returning to the Bailey and Smith cases, this book is not about race in the modern sense, at least as it is commonly discussed in North America; it is not about differential outcomes between whites and blacks, or people of (mostly) European and (mostly) African ancestries. That racial gulf was wide and is well documented.[4] Thus I do not trace the different life paths traversed by Bailey, who after 1852 was legally white, and Smith, who after 1853 was not. Rather, this study documents the difference between the mixed-race, presumably light-skinned Braxton Smith and his neighbor Daniel White. Braxton Smith, as his affidavit shows, was the son of a white woman. His 1850 census entry reveals that he was a 35-year-old mulatto, employed as a carpenter who could read and write; he owned $500 in real estate.[5] Daniel White, who resided in Smith's racially integrated neighborhood, was an illiterate, 36-year-old black man employed as a common laborer; White rented a room in what is probably best described as a tenement with nineteen other mostly unrelated, mostly illiterate laboring-class adults. Two instances do not reveal systematic differences, but they are consistent with the large-sample results reported throughout the remainder of this study. Even though color-based differences in any single dimension were not always great—certainly not as great as the difference between black and white—small differences in several dimensions cumulated to profoundly different life experiences between light and dark African Americans. Modestly better realizations in one or more dimensions made a person's life more rewarding, more productive, and more enjoyable. Light-skinned men and women consistently reported one or more better realizations than did their dark-skinned neighbors.

If this study is about the consequence of a racial and color ordering, it is imperative to begin with an explanation of the nineteenth century's racial and color order and what it implies. Any social and economic ordering is a society's generally accepted system of beliefs, practices, and laws that coordinate relationships between members of different race-color groups.[6] In applying this to the nineteenth-century United States, it is useful to start with Jennifer Hochschild and Brenna Powell's five components of a racial ordering—(1) a definition of races; (2) a categorization of individuals into unique and mutually exclusive races; (3) a hierarchical ordering of races; (4) a delineation of acts that are prohibited, permitted, forbidden, and obligatory by race; and (5) appropriate social relations within and across races—and connect it with Alice Walker's notion of colorism, that social and economic status, even within races, is determined by skin color.[7]

Modern studies of colorism contend that race and color are conceptually distinct, in that colorism is defined as preferential treatment of same-race people based on their color.[8] In nineteenth-century America color and race were inextricably linked. Color could be, and sometimes was, construed narrowly as one of various shades such as chocolate, mahogany, copper, and gingerbread, among others. But color was also shorthand for a complex of physical features, including skin tone, hair texture, and the shape of an individual's nose, that signified something about a person's place in society's color ordering. Different mixes of European and African ancestries yielded people of different colors and other physical features, and contemporary Americans struggled as much with how best to categorize people as with how to treat people of different colors. In the end, light-skinned African Americans were considered to be different from their dark-skinned brethren, received preferential treatment, and realized better outcomes in several measurable dimensions.

Although the US census bureau adopted a tripartite classification scheme in the mid-nineteenth century, there is abundant evidence that contemporary thinking about race was color-based and operated along a continuum from light to dark. Thus in his court-supplied freedom papers, Wager Rix, the 17-year-old son of Polly Rix of Petersburg, Virginia, was described as being of a light complexion, "a freckled face and long waving hair."[9] Sisters Mary Elizabeth (18 years) and Virginia Ann (15 years) Boasman were each described as a "mulatto girl with long straight hair."[10] Mid-nineteenth-century Virginians had fairly consistent expectations about mixed-race people's features. They expected to see light or "bright" complexions, lightly freckled faces, and long, curly hair.[11] In fact, deviations from these combinations sometimes became a person's most notable feature. A dark mulatto runaway slave's signature feature was "knotty" hair, "more so than is common for one of her color." A bright mulatto runaway woman's hair was described as "not as long as usual for one as bright as she is."[12] If contemporary Virginians did not share conceptions concerning the stereotypical markers of racial heritage, skin color, and hair, including phrases like "more so" and "not as long as" would not have been particularly helpful in distinguishing the runaway in question from the local population of free blacks and slaves.

Blacks, those with presumably little European ancestry, shared their own common physical traits, at least in the eyes of whites. Seventeen-year-old Daniel Stewart, for example, was described as "of black complexion . . . has thick lips."[13] Between the mid-1820s and the mid-1830s, the clerks of the court in Fauquier County, Virginia described dark-skinned people with flat noses, broad mouths, thick lips, dark eyes, and "tolerable large" teeth "tolerably far apart."[14] Their hair was variously described as bushy or woolly, but occasionally "long for one of her color." Similar depictions occur throughout the registers and runaway advertisements. Spare as they are, registers and advertisements provide a window into the defining physical characteristics of black and mulatto census categories, which were color, hair, and facial features.[15]

Regional variations notwithstanding—definitions, categorizations, and intergroup relations differed somewhat in the Upper and Lower South—the social order constructed by nineteenth-century Americans was less like the modern North American practice of classifying anyone with any African heritage whatsoever as black and more like the modern Brazilian ordering practice of categorizing people by color.[16] In modern Brazil, the Portuguese *cor* (color) is roughly the equivalent of *raça* (race).[17] And color (*cor*) is based on a complex evaluation of skin tone, hair type, and the shape of one's nose and lips, among other physical attributes. Some scholars contend that color is preferred to race in Brazil precisely because it captures nuance and is better suited to capturing social position as a continuous rather than binary descriptor of an individual.[18] In 1963, sociologist Marvin Harris documented 40 distinct terms used to describe people's color in one Brazilian fishing village; a 1976 national survey revealed the use of 100 different color terms, though six accounted for more than 90 percent of all responses.[19] Harris considered the Brazilian census authority's mid-twentieth-century attempt to collapse that country's complex color ordering into three categories—*branco, pardo*, and *preto*, or roughly the equivalent of the US census bureau's mid-nineteenth-century adoption of white, mulatto, and black—"a lamentable surrender to non-Brazilian concepts of racial identity," of questionable usefulness in capturing color-based differences.[20]

Intrigued by the Brazilian bureaucracy's attempt to map many colors into two nonwhite racial categories, three teams of geneticists have found, using a variety of genetic markers, that there is no significant ancestral difference between Brazil's intermediate racial class and its black class.[21] Box-and-whisker plots of the individual proportions of African component of ancestry reveal much more variation within the group of Brazilians than in separate samples of Portuguese and West Africans. There is also substantial overlap in the box plots for *pardos* and *pretos*. One study found that Brazilians inhabiting the "black" category had, on average, 48 percent non-African ancestry; those inhabiting the "intermediate" class had 55 percent non-African ancestry.[22] At the individual level, skin color, even when determined by systematic physical evaluation, was a poor predictor of genomic ancestry as revealed in various genetic markers.[23] This does not make color any less important a determinant of Brazilian's opportunities and life chances; it simply means that color provides less precise information about ancestry than is commonly believed. Some nineteenth-century Americans recognized this, but nonetheless used color to infer race, at least when color mattered, as in John Bailey's and Braxton Smith's appeals for nonblack status.

It is impossible to conduct the same sort of genetic analysis on the long-deceased individuals around whom this book is centered, but contemporary sources can be used to conduct an analysis in the same spirit for the nineteenth-century Chesapeake region. The 1850 and 1860 US censuses categorized African Americans into two groups: black and mulatto. Between the 1790s and the mid-1860s county courts also provided free African Americans with freedom papers, and clerks provided reasonably precise descriptions of people's colors.[24] For 1,250 Virginians appearing in the court records who were positively identified in either the 1850 or 1860 census, the court documents include 35 different color designations ranging from "very black" to "copper" to "gingerbread" to "light" to "nearly white." Those 35 designations are combined into the six color groups reported in Table 1.1. The category Black, for example, includes individuals described as light black, black, and very black.

Table 1.1 shows that the six broad color designations appearing in the court documents consistently map into the two racial categories used in the decennial censuses. Fully 92 percent of individuals described as "black" and 91 percent of those described as "dark" in the court records were categorized as black in the census. Approximately 70 percent of individuals described as "yellow" or "light" in the Virginia free registers were classified as mulatto in the census. Statistical analysis reveals that individuals described as "black" and "dark" in the registers were about 15 to 17 percent *more* likely than others to be labeled black in the census. Individuals described as "light," "yellow," and "nearly white" in the records were 45 to 60 percent *less* likely to be labeled black in the census.[25] The concordance between Virginia's court records and the federal census provides some assurance that the census' racial classifications were not random with respect to color, although little is known or can be inferred about an individual's actual ancestry. Moreover, statistical analysis shows that money did not lighten in mid-nineteenth-century Maryland and Virginia. Controlling for other characteristics, literate, land-owning African Americans working in high prestige occupations were not more likely to be identified as mulatto by census marshals.[26]

Both modern Brazilians and nineteenth-century America's color ordering reveals what anthropologists and human biologists have long recognized: race

Table 1.1 Virginia Registration Colors and Census Races[a]

Registration Description	Black in Census	Mulatto in Census
Black	192	16
Dark	210	21
Brown	207	68
Yellow	33	73
Light	28	66
White	1	5

[a] *Notes:* Register descriptions are color designations in Virginia registers of free blacks. Thirty-five separate color designations were combined into six categories. Black includes light black, black, and very black. Dark includes dark and very dark. Light includes bright, light, very bright, and very light. Yellow includes bright yellow, dark yellow, olive, and tawny. White includes fair and nearly white. Brown includes all other colors, including light brown, dark brown, chestnut, copper, and gingerbread. Thirty-seven matched individuals had no color designation in the registers and are not included here. *Sources:* Virginia Register Sample and manuscript censuses of 1850 and 1860 federal decennial censuses. See References and Appendix 4.1 for the details of the Virginia Register Sample.

is partly social construct and partly biological datum.[27] Referring, again, to the modern Brazilian case as a point of reference, one study found that young people tended to incorrectly estimate their genomic ancestries (they underestimated European and overestimated Amerindian ancestry based on genetic markers), but third-party observers consistently sorted the youth into the three broad racial categories (white, brown, and black). More interesting, perhaps, is that when faced with genomic evidence that contradicted the students' self-identified race, the students showed remarkably little interest in redefining their racial selves. Brazilian students believed that their color and the social constructs surrounding color would continue to define their lives. Nineteenth-century Americans were similarly disposed to have color order people's lives.

To better illuminate the gulf between thinking about color and race then and now, consider Hochschild, Weaver, and Burch's five-part characterization of the United States' racial order in the first half of the *twentieth* century, or roughly one hundred years after the period studied here.[28] In defining races, most Americans agreed that there were four races: white, black, Asian, and Amerindian. In categorizing them, most Americans would have agreed that even if a person was racially mixed, they belonged to a single racial group. Assignment to that group was fixed and, presumably, determined at birth. Early twentieth-century categorization intersected with the social hierarchy through the rule of hypodescent, under which racially mixed people were assigned to their ancestral group occupying the lower social rank. Whites, who had more economic resources and political power than any other conventionally defined racial group, were at the top of the racial order; blacks occupied the lowest rung. Thus the intersection of the hierarchy and hypodescent meant that a child of mixed black and white parentage was black, immutably and indelibly black. The racial order proscribed certain interracial acts. About a third of US states prohibited interracial marriage; residents in the other two-thirds of the states frowned on it. Segregation was pervasive and, in the Old Confederacy, institutionalized. The formal rules of Jim Crow, enforced by the extralegal practice of lynching, assured black deference and that certain lines were rarely crossed. Finally, relations between the racial groups were distant and typically hostile.

Compare this to the Upper South a century earlier, or in the mid-nineteenth century. There was little agreement about how many races there were. Definitions were unclear. Contemporary American's most prominent racial theorists disagreed: based on his analysis of the sizes and shapes of human skulls, Samuel George Morton identified six races; Josiah Clark Nott further subdivided Morton's categorization into ten races.[29] John Van Evrie divided mankind into five races.[30] Others argued that Jews were almost certainly a distinct race; some thought the Irish were.[31] Lacking bright-line definitions, categorization was similarly fuzzy, and the John Scott Bailey and Braxton Smith cases show that race was not immutable and indelible. For many mixed-race people it was contestable, and the more so the lighter the person's skin tone. Intermediate categories were constructed; hypodescent was not society's default way of thinking about race. Whites inhabited the highest place in the racial and social ordering, but European ancestry and white skin did not guarantee being placed at the top of the hierarchy, as many nineteenth-century Irish immigrants could attest.

Fuzzy, color-based boundaries between races blurred the boundaries between acceptable and unacceptable interracial acts. While interracial sexual relations were frowned on in polite society, and interracial marriage was prohibited in most states, interracial cohabitants were more likely to be shunned than prosecuted. It was widely known, for instance, that US Vice President Richard Johnson (1837–1841) had two children with a former slave whom he considered his common-law wife, and while his "indiscretion" cost him the support of some southern politicians, his political career did not suffer until he took up with a 19-year-old mixed-race mistress during his vice presidency.[32]

While African Americans might be barred from schools and some other public places, residential segregation was uncommon. In the South's major cities whites, blacks, and mixed-race people shared neighborhoods in relative peace.[33] And while relations across the races were chilly, they were typically not as distant and openly hostile as they would become after the American Civil War. In short, it is simply incorrect to project the modern racial order onto the nineteenth-century American South. Race relations mark an instance where L. P. Hartley's oft-repeated adage holds—"the past is a foreign country: they do things differently there."[34]

The Nineteenth-Century Algebra of Color and Mixed Race

Modern social-science scholarship contends that there is "little connection between social race and genetics [or biological race]," though this notion has recently been challenged by modern, statistical mappings of the human genome.[35] Imagine then the struggles nineteenth-century Americans faced, without the benefits of modern genetics testing, in making sense of race in the presence of markedly different phenotypic features occurring among African Americans with different proportions of European and African ancestries. It is their thinking and their struggles that determined how contemporary people of color were treated, so it is useful to understand how they thought about and classified ancestry, color, and other traits into a coherent racial scheme.

Concerned as they were with proper classification into the black and mulatto categories, nineteenth-century Americans devised several mechanisms to trace an individual's genealogy so that he or she could be correctly categorized. Some commentators, such as traveler and chronicler Frederick Law Olmsted, offered verbal descriptions that often became quite confusing. To make matters worse, there were few common usages across cultures (with the exception of negro and mulatto), and different categories might sound similar (compare scatara and saltatra) and be easily confused by the uninitiated. Table 1.2 provides the most commonly reported nineteenth-century terminology, with secondary usages in parentheses. As the table makes readily apparent, keeping track of mixed-race people was complicated. English language categorizations employed terminology based on blood fractions—mulatto (½), quadroon (¼), octoroon (⅛), and so on. Spanish and French speakers, on the other hand, categorized people based on the number of generations a person was removed from the original interracial moment—tercerón (three generations), quarterón (four generations), and quinterón (five).[36] Making matters worse, the terms, though developed with classificatory precision in mind, were often used imprecisely. When precision was unnecessary or the ancestry unknown or unclear, nineteenth-century Americans simply used the term *mulatto* as a catch-all category for all people of mixed descent. The term *quadroon*, in common usage, was used to describe individuals who were reasonably fair-skinned and were of mostly European ancestry, but retained some vestige of African ancestry. Octoroons may have retained a few barely discerned traces of stereotypically African features that were evident only on close physical inspection.

At those moments when precision was desirable but confusion likely, nineteenth-century writers sought ways to explain the subtleties of race mixing in compact, convenient, and less confusing ways. Legal historian George Stephenson, for example, provided a standard family tree diagram.[37] Suppose the investigator wanted to provide a racial classification for John Scott Bailey, whose ancestry was documented by the Misses Burton. Start with the first the generation immediately above the person in question, or his parents. If either was black, Bailey would have been one-half black and one-half white, which, in the mid-nineteenth century, made him mulatto. Neither of Bailey's parents was black, strictly speaking, so it was then incumbent on the investigator to consider Bailey's grandparents. If any of them was black, then Bailey would have been one-quarter black and, according to contemporary categorizations, a quadroon. To the best of the Burtons' knowledge, none were black. But a legally complete accounting of race in 1850s Virginia demanded that the court consider the race of Bailey's great-grandparents. If any one of them was black, then Bailey was an octoroon. Based on the Burtons' account and, accepting their assumption that Bailey's maternal great-great-grandfather was white, John Scott Bailey's father, Joseph, was an octoroon and his mother, Edith, was white. Bailey was, at one-sixteenth white, a meamelouc (see Table 1.2) and, therefore, legally white by Virginia's statutory one-eighth rule.

Table 1.2 Nineteenth-Century Racial Designations and Definitions

Racial Mix	Southern United States	Caribbean	Blood Fraction
All African	Negro	Negro	All
Griffe-Negro	Sacatra		Seven-eighths
Negro-mulatto	Griffe (Sambo)	Grifo (Cabro) (Zambo)	Three-fourths
Griffe-mulatto	Marabon		Five-eighths
Negro-white	Mulatto	Mulatto	One-half
Mulatto-mulatto	Mulatto	Mulatto	One-half
Griffe-white	Mulatto	Mulatto	Three-eighths
Mulatto-quadroon		Saltatra	Three-eighths
Mulatto-white	Quadroon	Terceron (Morisco)	One-fourth
Quadroon-white	Octoroon (Metif)	Quarteron (Ochavon) (Alvino)	One-eighth
Octoroon-white	Meamelouc	Quinteron	One-sixteenth
Meamelouc-white	Quarteron		One-thirty second
Quateron-white	Sang-mele		One-sixty fourth
All European	White	White (Creole)	Zero

Notes: Principal usages with less common usages in parentheses. Among people in the Caribbean and, to a lesser extent, along the Gulf Coast, whites born in Europe were distinguished from people born in the Americas. The latter were labeled Creoles. Nicholson claims that Caribbean observers did not generally classify beyond Ochavon because people with such a small fraction of black heritage "retain no traces of African original." *Sources*: US definitions: Olmsted, *Cotton Kingdom*, 294. Caribbean definitions: Nicholson, *British Encyclopedia*, Vol. IV (1809). See also Heck, *Iconographic Encyclopedia*, III, 438; Winterbottom, "Account of the Native Africans," 197, for other variations.

The Bailey case is notable because up to the Civil War and beyond, most investigators would have stopped at the third generation back because persons less than one-eighth black would have presented few of the stereotypical markers of blackness—dark complexions, broad noses, thick lips, and woolly hair—and would have approached, if not crossed, the line into legal whiteness (see Chapter 2). Stephenson's insistence that a full racial accounting go back three generations was based on two factors: if only one of a person's eight great-grandparents was black or part black, the person in question was in all likelihood legally white; and, absent official marriage and birth records, going back more than three generations stretched most people's memories and led courts into the realm of hearsay.

A genealogical chart simplified racial classification when searching for a single black progenitor up to three generations removed, but it was less helpful if there were multiple nonwhite progenitors. If there had been black ancestry in both branches of Bailey's family, perhaps such that a mulatto had married an octoroon, Bailey may not have passed into legal whiteness. It would have been incumbent on the investigator with "a mathematical turn of mind," wrote Stephenson, to "take these three generations and work out the various other combinations."[38] Stephenson, however, failed to provide a general mathematical approach.

In 1815 one contemporary observer with a mathematical turn of mind, Thomas Jefferson, offered such a mathematical approach. Because the offspring of any two parents, he wrote, "has one-half of the blood of each parent, and the blood of each of these may be made up of a variety of fractional mixtures, the estimate of their compound in some cases may be intricate."[39] Jefferson provided a convoluted explanation of how to accurately attribute a mixed-race individual to the appropriate category, but his algebra is easily explained. Let W signify a pure white (European) parent and N a pure Negro (African) parent, setting aside the question of racial purity. If these two people mate, the offspring will have one-half white and one-half Negro blood, which can be written mathematically as $M = \frac{1}{2}W + \frac{1}{2}N$. Suppose now that person M (mulatto) mates with a white (W). Person M's offspring's blood quantum can be written as $Q = \frac{1}{2}(\frac{1}{2}W + \frac{1}{2}N) + \frac{1}{2}W = \frac{1}{4}N + \frac{3}{4}W$. Suppose further that person Q (quadroon) mates with a white in the third generation. His offspring's blood quantum can be written as $O = \frac{1}{2}(\frac{1}{4}N + \frac{3}{4}W) + \frac{1}{2}W = \frac{1}{8}N + \frac{7}{8}W$.

The complications arising from the mixing of people of mixed-race background referred to by Stephenson can be easily accommodated by Jefferson's blood quantum algebra. Suppose that person of type O (octoroon) mates with a person of type M (mulatto). That offspring's blood quantum can be calculated as $\frac{1}{2}(\frac{1}{8}N + \frac{7}{8}W) + \frac{1}{2}(\frac{1}{2}W + \frac{1}{2}N)$, which equals $\frac{5}{16}N + \frac{11}{16}W$. Because this person's Negro blood fraction exceeded one-quarter but was less than one-half, she would have been legally considered a mulatto, though it is not hard to imagine a set of physical features that might lead casual acquaintances to label her a quadroon. As was typical in the nineteenth century, Jefferson believed that any mixture that yielded less than one-eighth black blood yielded whiteness. "Our canon," he wrote, "considers two crosses with the pure white, and a third with any degree of mixture, however small, as clearing the issue of the negro blood."[40] The resulting offspring would be white, partly because the law said she was (see Chapter 2) and partly because it was difficult to discern blackness when blackness constituted less than one-eighth or less of a person's heritage.

Jefferson's algebra worked when a person knew—or truthfully revealed—the racial makeup of his or her progenitors to three generations. This asked a lot of a person's knowledge, memory, and veracity. So contemporaries looked for alternative markers, and they often turned to hair. Good hair was hair that grew long, lay mostly straight, and exhibited a tendency to curl. What separated whites, blacks, and mixed-race people, in the popular mind anyway, was hair.[41] Peter A. Browne, a polymath and sometime professor at Lafayette College, believed he could identify ancestry through a close analysis of someone's hair. He invented an instrument known as the trichometer for analyzing animal hair and wool, but soon after turned to the study of human hair. He observed that hair was not all the same: Europeans had hair that was oval; Amerindian hair was cylindrical; African hair was eccentrically elliptical.[42]

Of direct interest here, Browne claimed that the hair of racial mixtures retained the racial characteristics of the parents' hair. A black-white racial mixed person's hair was both oval and eccentrically elliptical, and close measurement could reveal the extent of the mixing. Adopting the term "mulattin" to denote a degree of mixing, Browne developed a fractional classification scheme every bit as precise as Jefferson's blood quantum. A Hepta Mulattin, for example, was 14 parts white and 2 parts black (or 14:2). He labeled other mixes as Hexa Mulattin (12:4), Penta Mulattin (10:6), Tetra Mulattin (8:8), Tria Mulattin (6:10), Di Mulattin (4:12), and Mono Mulattin (2:14). Compound hybrids led to such tongue-twisters as Hepta-hypo-mono-mulattin. Although Browne's researches did not capture a wide scientific audience, his publications elicited so many donations that he was reputed to have owned the world's largest collection of human hair. Indian agents sent hair from across North America; he was sent hair from Africa; he owned strands of George Washington's, Napoleon's, and Andrew Jackson's hair; he even had hair from an Egyptian mummy. Scientists largely ignored him, but the general populace paid attention.

Jefferson's and Browne's algebraic approaches embody the Enlightenment principles of scientific investigation, principles of formalization, and precision that, while perhaps comfortable to modern social scientists, discomfit some modern humanists. Jefferson's calculations could have extended "to the point of delirium"[43]—one sixty-fourth, one-one hundred and twenty-eighth, and so on—but Jefferson understood his peers and the limits of contemporary science. Jefferson also knew how his peers responded to race mixing. He knew that once the stereotypical markers of blackness—dark skin, kinky hair, a broad nose—were barely evident, somewhere around one-eighth African ancestry, early nineteenth-century men and women stopped looking for them. Pushing the calculation of blood or hair fractions to the point of delirium was not of Jefferson's or Browne's "canon." What was of their canon was classification based on skin tone, hair length and texture, and facial features. Their objective, like that of the Brazilian geneticists, was to better understand the association, if any, between ancestry and contemporary color-based categorization. Categorization mattered then (and matters now) because color structured social, economic, and legal treatment of the person.

A Digression on Word Choice

If race and color are contentious and complicated, the words used to describe them are no less so. In my lifetime the preferred appellation for Americans of African ancestry has changed from Negro or colored to black, to Afro-American to African American to Black. Just as the word *negro* morphed into *Negro*, some writers transform the word *black* into *Black* (and *white* into *White*) when using these words to describe ancestry, in an effort to underscore the continuing power of race in American life. Even as scholars discuss their abhorrence of racial or color-based distinctions and argue that classifications are without merit, they capitalize, underscore, italicize, and place quotation marks around racial and color designations. This hardly seems the way to strip words of power. I resist the urge to cede these words more than simply descriptive power through capitalization or other means.

The word *mulatto* was derived, by common account, from the Spanish and Portuguese words for the mixed-breed, hybrid mule. Although the term is experiencing a renaissance, objections to the term as a race or color designation follow from the implicit association of people (mixed-race individuals) with animals (mules). Given that some slave owners treated their slaves little better than their mules, the zoological analogy is unfortunate. Alternative etymologies attribute *mulatto* to a medieval Spanish variation on the Arabic word *muwallad* (mixed), which referred to the progeny of Moors and Spaniards, and therefore indicates cultural more than racial mixture.[44] By the latter etymology, the racial designation loses its zoological association, but it is not clear that the recent interpretation is anything other than revisionist history. Regardless of its origin nineteenth-century Americans, as discussed in Chapter 3, freely acknowledged the traditional mulatto-as-hybrid usage, if not the literal mulatto-as-hybrid interpretation. Nineteenth-century Francophone Louisianans adopted the more polite *gens de couleur libre* (free people of color), which was sometimes applied in other parts of the South to light-skinned people of mixed racial backgrounds who distinguished themselves from black slaves in manners, deportment, and accomplishment.

After more than a decade of reading and writing about color, an appropriate, simple, and inoffensive terminology remains elusive. There are words that always offend, words that sometimes offend, and words that rarely offend. Two difficulties in writing about skin tone is that there are so many colors and combinations; one word or another in any descriptive list is likely to offend someone, and nearly all word choices, at least implicitly, reference blackness or imply blackness's subordinate status.[45] To minimize the potential for offense, I adopt the following terminology: *African American* refers to every American resident of African descent, regardless of proportion; black, except where it is used in its precise historical sense, as in Chapter 2, refers to dark-skinned African Americans of (presumably) mostly African heritage; *mixed, mixes,* or *mixed-race* refers to light-skinned African

Americans with discernible Europeans and African ancestry. Archaic terminology, such as *Negro, mulatto, quadroon, octoroon,* and *yellow,* appear only when used in their historical context or when other words fail. Hereafter, when they appear they are not capitalized or italicized or otherwise set apart. They are words, and they stand or fall depending on the context and the user's intent.

When the archaic terms are used it is because to understand the history of color, colorism, and race mixing in the United States, historical actors must be allowed to speak in their own voices. To strip historical actors of their own vocabulary is to strip them not just of their power, but of their power of observation. Absent astute observation, 24-year-old Charles Cooley of Petersburg, Virginia might have slipped into history as Negro rather than the far more intriguing bright mahogany complexion described in his freedom papers. A clearer portrait of 16-year-old Seraphine Gilchrist, unusually short for her age at just four feet and eleven inches, emerges when we are told that she was not just light, but nearly white.

Edward Byron Reuter's 1918 study of the place of mulattoes in America elicited harsh criticisms not least because his definition of mulatto was so expansive that it excluded few African Americans of any color that served his purpose, which was to demonstrate the greater social and economic accomplishments of the mulatto relative to blacks.[46] To his critics, Reuter's error was in placing people like Charles (bright mahogany) and Seraphina (nearly white) in the same category; his taxonomy was too crude and too unscientific to yield useful insights. I am led to ponder whether modern empirical social scientists are not equally guilty of classificatory imprecision when they treat race as a binary variable (black and white). Individuals who consider themselves black are not just black; they are every shade of brown from nearly white to dark mahogany. Can we truly understand the consequences of color in an increasing color-sensitive society when we treat all colors just the same? One objective of this study is to push social scientists beyond the convenient black-and-white dichotomy and ask them to think more clearly and deeply about the meaning of race and color in an increasingly mixed-race, multihued world.

In matters so fundamental and yet so easily misconstrued as race, it is important to heed Carlo Cippola's admonition: "We all tend to be parochial, intolerant and ethnocentric, and hence all need continuously to strive to be informed and sensitive about lifestyles, values and behaviours that differ from our own."[47] If I fail at any point to demonstrate proper sensitivity in my word choice, it is not for lack of striving or sensitivity.

Plan of the Work

This study investigates the extent to which color-based differences manifested themselves in the first half of the nineteenth century. Although its focus is on economic issues—work, wealth, incomes, and so on—it also investigates a wider range of topics, including definitions, family structure, and health, than are common to many economic studies. It compares color-based differences across several dimensions in slavery and in freedom during the period before the Civil War.

One issue of continuing interest to modern scholars remains the emergence or adoption of the one-drop rule. In his 1971 Pulitzer-Prize winning comparative study of race relations *Neither Black Nor White*, Carl Degler concluded that there are only two races in the United States: black and white. "A person," he wrote, "is one or the other; there is no intermediate position."[48] Degler's conclusion reasonably captured the racial realities of late-1960s America, but the world Degler described was even then disappearing. Werner Sollors's 1997 book riffed on Degler's title with *Neither Black Nor White Yet Both* and concluded that the intermediate space afforded the mixed-race person "has been sacrificed to black-white dualism."[49] Across the four centuries that blacks and whites have mingled throughout the Americas, black-white dualism prevailed mostly in the United States and mostly in the twentieth century.

Chapter 2 discusses nineteenth-century approaches to racial definition and shows that society opened an intermediate space for light-skinned, mixed-race people. Legislatures provided statutory definitions of black and white that did not conform to the one-drop rule. A person could be statutorily white even with known and discernible African ancestry. Moreover, before the Civil War the trend was toward wider rather than narrower definitions; that is, mixed-race men and women with greater black ancestry who were presumably of darker skin tone were increasingly accepted as legally—if not socially—white. Courts became the battleground on which statutory definitions were contested, and holdings contributed to the fuzziness of contemporary definitions of race and its social fluidity. Race and color were not synonymous, but they informed one another at law.

After considering legal contestations of race, the third chapter turns to early nineteenth-century literary and scientific considerations of mixed race and color. Through the literary trope of the "tragic mulatto," early American novelists created mixed-race women to expose the inequities of slavery. Where the comparable treatment of a black woman might not have elicited much sympathy, portrayals of a part-white heroine stripped naked and inspected on the auction block evoked visceral responses among white readers. Scientific explorations were contentious too, but the one point of agreement was that light-skinned, mixed-race people differed fundamentally from their parent races. Some scientists produced statistics demonstrating mixed-race inferiority (work capacity and reproductive fertility were lower), while others provided statistics demonstrating the light-skinned, mixed-race people's superiority (intelligence and morality). In retrospect both arguments were problematic, not least because the statistical associations were spurious. Nevertheless, these scientific studies shaped contemporary discourse about race mixing and color.

Chapter 4 begins with an exploration into race mixing and color on the plantation. Race mixing was the nearly inevitable product of two sexes, two races, proximity, and time. Satisfying all four conditions, the southern plantation provided an
amenable environment for race mixing. But the now-traditional account of slave
owners forcing themselves on unwilling slave partners is overly simplistic—and
often, though certainly not always, false. On the earliest Chesapeake farms, race
mixing occurred most often between white servant women and enslaved black
men. Some white men preyed on slave women, but some slave women enjoyed
enough self-agency to use sex to their own advantage; slave women sometimes
exchanged sex for favors. Although the conditions of exchange were asymmetrical, an economic approach to sex on the plantation shows that neither consensual
nor forcible sex on the plantation was costless to the slave owner. It was a disruptive force that raised the cost of operating a plantation, and, though some planters
labored to limit its incidence, interracial sex occurred with greater frequency on
larger plantations. Interracial sex produced mixed-race children, and the chapter concludes with an investigation into the extent to which mixed-race slaves
received preferential treatment on the plantation. Mixed-race, light-skinned
slaves were more likely to be assigned to less onerous tasks and to be taught skills;
light-skinned slaves disproportionately worked in the kitchen, in the master's
house, or at a craft. Despite these privileges, light-skinned slaves did not monopo-
lize the Big House.

Chapter 5 explores how color interacted with slaves' exit from the plantation.
Some left through manumission, others by running away. Studies of New World
slavery provide compelling evidence that selective manumission was more often
granted to light-complected, mixed-race slaves than to dark-skinned blacks. This
is consistent less with the contention that mixed-race slaves were the sons and
daughters of masters and more with the economic approach, which predicts that
mixed-race slaves were more readily accepted into free society and were better
prepared to negotiate freedom. Slave owners were also more likely to advertise
light-skinned than black runaway slaves. This regularity, too, is consistent with
what might be labeled "rational running." The mixed-race proportion of the free
African-American population was larger than the mixed-race slave population,
so that mixed-race slaves could more readily slip into the free African-American
neighborhood without raising undue suspicions among inquisitive whites.
Whether by running or manumission, mixed-race slaves were more likely than
black slaves to escape bound servitude.

The sixth chapter explores how color intersected with the family. Families
played a central role in African-American life, and this chapter provides and
tests an economic model of color-based matching in the marriage market. The
available data, drawn from several contemporary sources, demonstrate a powerful tendency toward color-based marriage homogamy. Light men married light
women; dark men married dark women. One measure of household success is

the number of members its can support. The second section of the chapter shows that homogamous light-light households were systematically larger than homogamous dark-dark households. Color influenced family formation, reproductive success, and family size.

One reason homgamous light-light marriages could support larger households was because light-complected men and women worked in more lucrative jobs than black men and women. Mid-nineteenth-century Americans of all races and colors—white, black, and mixed-race—met with drudgery, marginality, and poverty. Chapter 7 shows that realizing economic success was hard for all, but African Americans had to overcome disabilities not faced by whites. Light-hued men and women more readily overcame them, and found modestly more remunerative employment than blacks. Taking into account several factors likely to influence employment choice, black men were, however, more likely than mixed-race men to enter into "petty" self-employment, such as huckstering or carting. In the rural South, black men were less likely to become tenant farmers or owners; unlike mixed-race men, black men were overwhelmingly employed as farm laborers. Mixed-race men were considerably more likely to climb up a rung or two on the agricultural ladder, though farm ownership eluded most.

Chapter 8 documents household wealth. The available evidence shows that households headed by a black male or female were about 5 to 10 percent less likely than households headed by a mixed-race person to own real estate. When black households owned real property, they owned considerably less. Because household wealth is skewed, a focus on mean holdings hides important dimensions of property ownership, but regardless of whether means or medians are the relevant measure, black ownership lagged. The nineteenth-century African-American experience can be discussed from two perspectives. A gloomy case might focus on low rates of home and farm ownership—one-fifth of black and one-third of mixed-race households—among the South's African Americans. Moreover, property owners owned small, relatively unproductive plots. A more hopeful case stands on the same fact—in the shadow of slavery, one-fifth of black and one-third of mixed-race households owned the land they tilled. These are not trivial proportions considering the legal, social, and economic hurdles standing between African-American households and property ownership. Historian Luther Porter Jackson contends that this achievement deserves recognition. It speaks to the unremitting striving of black and mixed-race people in America.

The final chapter considers the health and nutritional advantages enjoyed by light-complected Americans. Since the mid-1980s, a large body of literature uses human heights to document the nutritional well-being of various groups. The nineteenth-century concern with differentiating slaves from free African Americans generated a trove of information on heights. Free African Americans were required to register with local county clerks, who provided dark- and light-skinned men and women with freedom papers. Those papers typically included a description of color and height. The data point toward taller and, presumably, healthier light-skinned people. By contemporary world standards, Americans were tall. It turns out that light-skinned men and women were taller than blacks.

The weight of the evidence points toward a decided light complexion advantage in the nineteenth-century South. Regardless of how well-being is measured—employment, health, or wealth—light-skinned men and women were privileged. Before turning to the evidence on well-being, the next chapter provides insight into contemporary Americans' legal definitions of blackness and their thinking about mixed-race people of different colors.

2

Legal Constructions of Race and Interpretations of Color

In his classic study of the color line in early twentieth-century America, the noted muckraker Ray Stannard Baker recognized that before he could write about the color line he had to answer the "seemingly absurd question: What is a Negro?"[1] He was confident at the outset that he knew the answer, but he found it was not evident on visual inspection. Baker spoke with men and women with black complexions, thick lips, and kinky hair who were "unquestionably Negroes." He also met with Negroes who were Negroes in "defiance of the evidence" of his senses. He interviewed blue-eyed Negroes, Negroes with thin noses, and Negroes with soft, straight hair. The more he traveled and investigated the color line, the more confused he became about race in America. Skin color and physical features were not the defining characteristics of race; ancestry was. A fundamental issue, as Baker soon realized, was the method by which society categorized people into races.

By the time Baker published his study, Americans on both sides of the color line were comfortable with society's working definition. Mixed-race people, even light-skinned ones, were socially and economically black and were treated as such. After reviewing the statutory law of every state circa 1900, Gilbert Stephenson concluded that "it is safe to say that in practice one is Negro or is classed with that race if he has the least visible trace of Negro blood in his veins, or even if it is known that there was Negro blood in any one of his progenitors."[2] Anthropologists call this hypodescent; most Americans know it as the "one-drop rule." The rule, as it is used in the United States, means that any known (or knowable) black ancestry, regardless of how little and how far removed, makes a person black. More generally, hypodescent implies that racially mixed people are assigned to the subordinate racial group. This is the modern approach to racial definition in the United States. It emerged in the postbellum South and found gradual acceptance across the nation.[3]

It is difficult to date when the one-drop rule became generally accepted, but it was well on its way to wide acceptance in 1896. *Plessy v. Ferguson*, as every

American historian knows, marks the court's endorsement of the constitutionality of separate-but-equal. An underappreciated feature of historical accounts of *Plessy* is that Homer Plessy—the man ejected from the whites-only railroad car—was seven-eighths white and one-eighth black, and "the mixture of colored blood was not discernible in him." On appeal, Plessy's attorney argued that given his client's evident whiteness, he should have been afforded the rights, privileges, and immunities afforded to all white citizens, including the right to sit in the whites-only car. The Supreme Court's opinion held that state statutes that drew arbitrary legal distinctions between white and nonwhite did not threaten equal treatment of the races, and were therefore constitutional. Moreover, the court was willing to accept local differences in definitions of race.[4]

In the twenty-first century, it is convenient to believe that such legalities are relegated to a distant, racist past and are no longer relevant in an enlightened, post-civil rights America. But consider Suzy Phipps.[5] In 1977 Suzy applied for a passport and, as part of the application, she needed a copy of her birth certificate. She obtained one from the Louisiana Division of Vital Records. The certificate listed her parents as colored. Suzy was shocked. Raised as white, Suzy believed she was white and that her parents were white. When she asked that her birth certificate be corrected, she was informed that no error had been made, that her birth certificate would not be changed, and that so far as the state of Louisiana was concerned, she was the daughter of two colored parents.

Suzy and her siblings filed suit seeking a mandamus that would compel the Louisiana Department of Health and Human Services to correct the erroneous birth certificates.[6] The court refused to issue the writ because the state had a duty to change the birth certificates only if the Phippses could show that white was the correct designation. A voluminous trial record included photographs, descriptions of physical appearance, and depositions of friends and family attesting to the family's whiteness, but the critical piece of evidence was a detailed official genealogical chart constructed by the state health department, which showed that one of Suzy's great-great-great grandmothers was a black slave. Under Louisiana's 1970 law (repealed in 1983), any individual with one-thirty-second part or more Negro blood was legally colored. By law at least one of Suzy's parents was colored, but she was not.[7] The state appellate court upheld the lower court's ruling, but in dissent, Judge Armstrong argued that the mandamus remedy should be awarded on equitable grounds. Although Suzy's birth certificate did not classify her as colored and her having been raised as white notwithstanding, the society in which she lived was one in which racial assignment followed "ancestral designations." Now that it was known that one of her parents was nonwhite, Suzy would be considered black by some Louisianans.[8]

Suzy Phipps's story is remarkable in several regards. Suzy's zeal in seeking legal remedy speaks volumes about the importance of public and self-perceptions of race. Moreover, it speaks to the modern American approach to race, which is that race and color can be separated. Even more remarkable is the state's perseverance in maintaining a specific racial designation based on a minute trace of African ancestry revealed by an official genealogist. The state's defense of its classification is noteworthy "in a country where for about a generation there had been official racial equality under the law."[9] Finally, the state appellate court's willingness to maintain the bureau's classification is curious when federal courts hold official racial classifications subject to strict scrutiny, because official classifications provide the mechanism by which the state might violate equal protections guaranteed by the Fourteenth Amendment.[10]

Plessy and *Phipps* were litigated in a long tradition of contested racial classifications. Trials of racial determination date to eighteenth-century Maryland, when people of racially mixed ancestry sought to escape slavery or some other legal or social disability of blackness. Those eighteenth-century trials are not just legal and historical curiosities: they are an integral part of America's racial past; they reveal a great deal about the construction of race when race, as Americans now understand it, was being constructed; and they shine a bright light on the mechanics of racial definition that culminated in the one-drop rule. The evolution toward and the eventual adoption of the rule was not inevitable. It was the consequence of legislative choice and public acceptance. A study of the history of trials of racial determination focuses attention on the lines separating black, mulatto, and white and the legal space afforded mixed-race people throughout the nineteenth century.

The Law of Race and Mixed-Race in the Early Nineteenth Century

Homer Plessy's argument before the Supreme Court of the United States should resonate with lawyers and economists, because he offered a subtle legal and economic argument. Plessy argued that whiteness was a valuable form of property, and the ability of an employee to deprive a customer of his or her property without due process was unconstitutional. The Court sidestepped the issue, partly because Plessy had not offered this challenge in earlier proceedings and partly because under Louisiana law, Plessy was not denied his property. He was not legally white. Still, the Court's decision left the door open for anyone rightfully denied his whiteness to pursue such a case: "If he be a white man and assigned to a colored coach, he may have his action for damages against the company for being deprived of this so called 'property.' "[11] But such a case would turn on whether the hypothetical plaintiff was white by legal definition. The court let existing local definitions stand because statutory delineations fell within the general police power of the states.[12]

Although some may think that too much is read into the Court's decision, the fact is that by 1896, Americans had been creating statutory definitions and delineations of race for nearly two centuries, and mixed-race Americans had been contesting their racial classifications in court for at least a century. They sought, as Homer Plessy unsuccessfully sought, to claim the property in whiteness they believed rightfully theirs. The documentary evidence surrounding these trial of legal definition is remarkably deep and of inherent historical interest in its own right. Ultimately, however, these cases shed light on the construction of race in the eighteenth and nineteenth centuries, which was when race and racial classification became momentous in America.[13] Lines were drawn between white and black, but they were sometimes drawn so as to leave a fuzzy middle ground of mixed race in between that often turned on a person's color. In other words, the law created a distinguishable group of people who were white and black and neither.

Statutory Definitions of Race

To fully appreciate racial classification and the unique status of mixed-race people in North America between the late-seventeenth and the late-nineteenth centuries, it is important to begin at the beginning. The need for creating statutory definitions of race in early America resulted from two issues: Determining which people of which races would have the privileges of civic participation, including voting, jury duty, and mustering in the militia, among others, and to which race would mixed-race individuals be assigned.[14] Not surprisingly the Chesapeake colonies, where Africans were first introduced in the North American colonies, were the first to wrestle with racial definition. Virginia indirectly initiated a type of racial classification with its 1662 law that contrary to English tradition established *partus sequitur ventrem*, or that the child's legal status (slave or free) followed from his or her mother's status. The offspring of a slave woman was a slave regardless of color or racial heritage; the offspring of a free woman was free regardless of color or racial heritage. Thus a child of a black father (whether slave or free) and a white mother would be afforded basic civil and civic rights, having been born free.

Although the 1662 law did not assign mixed-race children to one or another racial category, it established certain presumptions based on the mother's color. Having a white mother carried a presumption of freedom (which equaled whiteness), while having a black mother carried a presumption of enslavement (which equaled blackness). Freedom suits brought by slaves with free black mothers complicated this simple dichotomy, which forced Virginia to revisit its racial definition.

In 1705 Virginia barred blacks and mulattoes from holding any civil, military, or ecclesiastical office. Although later judicial interpretations (discussed below) sometimes accepted the strict definition of a mulatto as the offspring of one white and one black parent, Virginia's 1705 statute followed the custom of using the term *mulatto* to signify mixed-race people generally. The act specifically defined the offspring of a white and an Indian, or anyone with at least one black great-grandparent, as a mulatto under the law.[15] Any person of completely African or black ancestry was Negro and any person with between one-half and one-eighth black ancestry was legally mulatto, at least as the term was used in statute law.

Given that African servants had been introduced into the Chesapeake colonies only in 1620, and initially only in small numbers, Virginia's lawmakers at the time were confident that a rule encompassing three generations of race mixing would cover any conceivable case of racial definition. Any lesser mixture was unlikely, and in the improbable event that such a person even existed, his or her legal status would probably not come before a court because contemporaries observed that beyond one-eighth black ancestry "the distinction of colour [sic] is hardly perceptible," and crossing for four generations was "sufficient to render a negro [sic] white."[16] Leon Higginbotham argues that the import of the 1705 act lay in its creation of a white-mulatto boundary, rather than a white-black boundary.[17] In the early eighteenth century, a one-eighth rule effectively disqualified all people of black heritage from legal whiteness and the possibility of civic participation.

Without explanation, Virginia amended its definition of mulatto in 1785. After that date, all people with one-fourth to three-fourths black ancestry (between one and three black grandparents) would be classified as mulatto. By implication, people of one-eighth black ancestry previously considered mulatto were now legally white. Whereas the 1705 law had excluded anyone with any black ancestry from citizenship, the 1785 law created an intermediate class of people. Joel Williamson states that the new legal definition was such that: "People who were significantly black, visibly black, and known to be black, but by the law of the land . . . had the privileges of whites."[18] It might be more accurate to state that the law created a category of people who were significantly mixed -race, visibly mixed-race, and known to be mixed-race, but had the privileges of whites.

James Hugo Johnston claims that the 1785 act simply aligned the legal definition with existing social practice.[19] Higginbotham speculates that the law removed the possibility that prominent men with some remote "taint" of black ancestry might be exposed and unable to exercise the rights and privileges of whites.[20] Alternatively, though Higginbotham recognizes it as an unlikely explanation, the law may have responded to a fear that a growing class of disfranchised one-eighth black men might politically align themselves with free blacks and mulattoes and challenge the existing political order. In offering seventh-eighths white men the franchise and other basic rights, Virginians may have adopted the Caribbean practice of establishing a buffer class of privileged, light-complected mixed-race men who would align themselves with property owners rather than property-less slaves and free blacks in the event of insurrection. All existing explanations remain speculative, however, because the act itself is silent on it motivations and no systematic political economy study of the 1785 act exists.

If the import of Virginia's 1705 law lay in its creation of a white-mulatto boundary, the import of its 1785 statute law was twofold. First, it created two racial boundaries. Although it moved the line, it maintained a line between whites and mixed-race people at one-fourth black ancestry. Second, it established a demarcation between blacks and mixed-race people. It was no longer the case, as Joel Williamson notes, that an individual of discernible African ancestry necessarily fell within the purview of the state's ever expanding black code.[21]

Figure 2.1 provides a diagrammatic exposition of the 1705 and 1785 Virginia laws, as well as Louisiana's 1970 law, which approximates the one-drop rule. Panels A and B depict why race was contestable in the eighteenth and nineteenth centuries. Racial certainty existed only for those of all European or all African ancestry. But anyone of mixed racial heritage was considered to be a member of a particular group—black, mulatto, or white—depending on blood fraction. Two notable features emerge from a close examination of Figure 2.1. First, eighteenth-century law created, by definition, an intermediate class that was black and white and

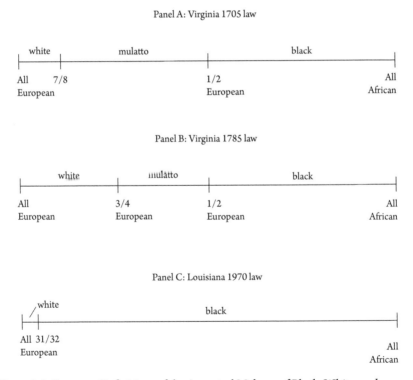

Figure 2.1 Statutory Definitions of the Ancestral Makeup of Black, White, and Mixed-Race in Eighteenth-Century Virginia and Twentieth-Century Louisiana.
Source: Author.

neither. The 1785 amendment narrowed the racial mixtures considered mulattos, but clearly retained the designation for a not insignificant proportion of the population. Second, eighteenth-century law recognized as white individuals who were not, strictly speaking, all white. Under all versions of the law, any individual with more than one-half African (black ancestry) was black, so that the law thus created a relatively broad class of people of black heritage. Anyone with two or more black grandparents, for example, was legally black.

Virginians may have created racial definitions that were meaningless if people did not observe or act on them. The definitions were meaningful, however, in that they separated African Americans of different colors and ancestries into different groups. Court records described in Appendix 5.1 recorded colors and heritages and reveal that 53.6 percent of individuals appearing in the records were considered black, 45.5 percent were mulatto, and the remaining 0.9 percent was legally white despite having known African ancestry. It is possible to further subdivide the categories, which reveals that 39.3 percent of blacks were considered "light" and 20.9 percent of mulattos were considered "dark." These "dark" individuals occupied the area encompassing the black-mulatto divide and may have socially, if not legally, crossed it on occasion. Similarly, 44.5 percent of mulattos were considered "light" so that a nontrivial number of people—far more than the 0.9 percent satisfying the legal definition—may have occasionally crossed the line into social whiteness. This is not *passing* as the term is commonly used, because these light-skinned mixed-race people were not hiding their African ancestries, but they used their European ancestries to their advantage when they could.

Until sometime after the Civil War, there were individuals who were of mixed heritage who were not legally black. Some were legally mulatto and some were legally whites. Those considered mulatto labored under many of the same civic disadvantages as blacks. They were subject to the same discriminatory head taxes, were excluded from civic privileges such as voting, and were subject to the restraints imposed by an ever-expanding black code. They were not, however, socially black. In the same way, a small group of men of women of African ancestry were legally white. Although they were legally white they were not necessarily socially white, but, as will be shown in later chapters, light-complected mixed-race people were privileged in several dimensions compared to blacks and dark-skinned mixed-race people.

Virginia's 1785 law was important as well, because it proved durable and exportable. Kentucky copied Virginia's act nearly verbatim; Florida, Mississippi, and Arkansas adopted the one-fourth definition. Tennessee and Georgia adopted a one-eighth rule; North Carolina one-sixteenth. Delaware and South Carolina did not create a statutory definition prior to the Civil War.[22] Ira Berlin contended that these statutory definitions disconcerted those whites who believed that they blurred the boundaries between the races and allowed mixed-race people of various complexions and ancestries to scoot under the color line.[23] Definitions that

classified some people of known and visible black ancestry as white surely bothered some whites, but legislatures had ample opportunity to amend these laws.
That they did not until after the Civil War suggests that the majority of white
Southerners remained comfortable with statutory definitions adopted in the late
eighteenth and early nineteenth century.[24] Statutory definitions did not, as Berlin
contended, "push too many people of both colors to the wrong side of the color
line and create social chaos."[25]

Freedom Suits and Judicial Implementations of Statutory Definitions

Social chaos did not follow, but trials of racial determination did. Once statutory
definitions of race had been created it was only a matter of time before people
of color began challenging their racial classifications in court. Because whiteness was privileged and blackness was not, light-skinned, mixed-race people in
the fluid borderland between white and black brought suit to be declared white
so that they could reap the privileges of whiteness. Faced with the issue of racial
determination, antebellum courts followed one of three paths in settling the
issue: genealogy (the inexact construction of family histories); science (the dis-
cerning of ancestry by physical markers); and performance (prior social and
political behaviors, included but not limited to voting, militia duty, or public
acceptance at events attended exclusively by members of one or the other race).

In a world without birth and death certificates, marriage licenses, or much of
any kind of centralized recordkeeping genealogy was problematic, mostly because
it relied on hearsay evidence about the ancestry of people long dead. Courts were
rather lenient in allowing hearsay, but only when offered by witnesses with close
familiarity with the petitioner's family history.[26] The science of race, such as it
was in the early nineteenth century (discussed in the next chapter), created more
confusion than clarity. But the high stakes of racial determination drove courts
to adopt fairly liberal rules of evidence concerning racial markers, features, and
ancestry. Performance emerged as the central narrative of many trials of racial
determination. Because evidence of community treatment of the petitioner,
including the social activities and civic rights he or she exercised, often took center stage, existing interpretations hold that cases turned on a petitioner's racial
performance.[27]

The sheer number of trials of racial determination in the antebellum era
(Ariela Gross identifies 69 that reached state appellate courts; an unknown number were decided at trial and not appealed) precludes relating more than a few to
reveal the fuzzy separation of white from mixed from black.[28] Read one way, these
cases can be used to show that the line separating white and nonwhite was historically contingent. Read another way, they also show that the line separating black
and mixed was also historically contingent. In short, although several existing

interpretations dismiss the possibility, many of the cases identified and discussed by critical race theorists demonstrate that whites were willing, sometimes eager, to afford people of known and visible black ancestry some of the privileges of whiteness without necessarily embracing them as social, political, or economic equals.[29] Like their Caribbean contemporaries, nineteenth-century Americans recognized a racial middle ground. Grouped together in the mulatto category, the inhabitants of this racial middle ground ranged widely in skin color, hair texture, and physical features, yet had one feature in common: they has at least one black ancestor, probably within living memory.

Consider, for example, *Gobu v. Gobu*, decided in North Carolina in 1802, in which the petitioner claimed that when he was just eight days old some unknown person left him in a barn. The defendant, then a 12-year-old girl, discovered him, raised him, and claimed him as her slave. Described by the court as olive in color ("between black and yellow"), with long hair and a prominent nose, the petitioner argued that his physical features suggested white parentage, which carried with it a presumption of freedom. In its holding, the supreme court of North Carolina accepted the premise that every black person was a slave because all blacks brought to North Carolina had arrived as slaves. Blacks and their descendants must continue as slaves until manumitted by proper authority. It was incumbent on any black person claiming his or her freedom to establish that right. The court was "not aware that the doctrine presuming against liberty has been urged in relation to persons of mixed blood, or to those of any color between the two extremes of black and white."[30] It was just as likely that a mixed-race person was descended from a free white as an enslaved black woman, and given the "many probabilities" in favor of the person's liberty, he or she "ought not be deprived of it upon a mere presumption." Gobu's (part) whiteness—his olive skin, long hair, and thin nose—established the basis for his freedom.

Gobu was not anomalous. Similar arguments appeared (and prevailed) in freedom suits litigated to state supreme courts in Maryland, Virginia, Tennessee, Kentucky, Arkansas, Texas, and Louisiana.[31] In 1810 a light-skinned slave named Adelle petitioned for her freedom, and the Louisiana court cited *Gobu* in arriving at the same conclusion. Judge François-Xavier Martin held that unless definitive proof of their legal enslavement could be produced, light-complected, mixed-race individuals were presumed free because they might be descended from Indians, whites, or free mixed-race parents. A Virginia slave owner lost title to an adult female slave and her children because he had imported them from North Carolina, and when they petitioned for their freedom he could not provide documentary or even circumstantial evidence to show that the light-skinned, adult female was related in her maternal line to a slave.[32] Where the Virginia slave owner failed, Texan George Gaines offered proof of a woman named Ann's descent from a slave in the maternal line, and the Texas appellate court returned her to slavery despite her being the descendant of a quadroon and a white, which made her one-eighth black and, therefore, legally white.

Ann's was not an unusual case. Ariela Gross and Walter Johnson show that the so-called white slave troubled many contemporaries, even hardened slave owners.[33] It was not uncommon, in fact, for juries to ignore *partus sequitur ventrem* and liberate light-complected slaves, especially fair-skinned women with white features.[34] Sometime before 1835 a light-complected young woman with straight hair, a thin nose, and other markers of European descent moved into Sevier County, Tennessee, and for a time found employment with and lived as free in the home of one Mr. Miller. When a Mr. Denman arrived from Georgia and claimed Harriet as his runaway slave, all three parties appeared before the local justices of the peace. In an astonishing result in a slave society, the justices released Harriet and jailed Denman, during which time Harriet fled the area in the company of a young white man.[35]

Alexina Morrison's story parallels that of Harriet's. Alexina was a slave. In 1857 she escaped a Jefferson Parish, Louisiana plantation, and took refuge in the parish jail. She told the jailer that she was white and illegally sold into slavery after being kidnapped in Arkansas. Because she had blue eyes and straw-colored hair, the jailer took her into his home and accompanied her to dances and other community activities. She became so popular that when James White came to claim her as his slave, he was "surrounded and threatened by a lawless mob."[36] *Morrison v. White* was tried three times. Alexina's attorneys asked the jurors to trust their eyes and the first trial ended with a deadlocked jury. James White petitioned for and received a change of venue for the second trial. The second trial included the testimony of several doctors who testified to Alexina's whiteness. Alexina prevailed in the second trial. White refused to relent, successfully appealed, and a third trial again ended in a hung jury. He again appealed to the Louisiana Supreme Court in 1862, but the trial was delayed during Federal occupation and ultimately dismissed after the war.

Modern Interpretations of Nineteenth-Century Law

Between Reconstruction and the 1980s, cases of racial determination fell off the scholarly radar until they were rediscovered by a group of legal scholars engaged in a program known as "critical race theory."[37] Critical race theorists employ these cases to show, among other things, that race is historically contingent and socially determined. The new bottom-up approach of critical race theory investigates the operation of law on the ground—that is, how slaves and slave owners or free blacks and free whites interacted through the law. Trial-level records are critical to these studies, because it was in the courtroom that members of society's lowest orders—slaves suing for freedom, or free persons of color suing for privilege—appear in the historical record and speak for themselves. Because this bottom-up approach emphasizes the importance of spatial and temporal distinctiveness, critical race studies offer a richness of detail concerning the nuances of racial determination in the nineteenth century.

Ariela Gross, for example, argues that cases such as Alexina Morrison's demonstrate a deep ambivalence toward race and racial definitions. From the vantage point of the early twenty-first century Alexina's racial identity and status is obvious: she was descended from at least one black ancestor, most likely in the maternal line, and she probably lied about being abducted and sold into slavery. There were statutory definitions of race (one-eighth) and status (*partus sequitur ventrem*), and there were social understandings of race and status. The compelling evidence to a majority of three sets of jurors in Jefferson Parish, Louisiana—an unapologetic and unrepentant slave society—was not the testimony of a respected white, planter, and slave owner.[38] Rather, the compelling evidence was Alexina's visible whiteness: the color of her eyes, her hair texture and color, the shape of the arch in her foot, how well she comported herself at dances and balls populated by whites, the sexual interest shown in her by white men of character, and how comfortably she lived as white in a white household. Outward appearances and social performance convinced local whites that she was white and deserved the privileges of whiteness.

What is a social scientist to make of these stories? Critical race theory is a decidedly postmodern literature, which emphasizes the centrality of individual narrative. Its recurring themes are race as social construction, race as performative identity, and race as endogenous to the individual's circumstances.[39] None of these are original ideas: constructivist notions about how people frame their world cropped up throughout the twentieth century.[40] The illogic of bright-line racial definitions was recognized at least two decades before critical race theory emerged.[41] And the attention paid to the specifics of particular cases makes generalizations difficult. If not handled with great care, collections of individual narratives quickly cross the line into just so many "just-so" stories. Despite critical race theorists' contention that whiteness is legal property, they have not explored how their arguments might intersect with the foundational texts of the economics of law literature.[42] Such an endeavor would extend the appeal of this subject to economists and social scientists more generally. What follows is not a theoretical integration of the two literatures, but a brief demonstration of how the law and economics literature offers some insights into the trials of racial determination.

A straightforward economic model of litigation in the spirit of Paul Rubin's classic formulation offers a handful of predictions consistent with nineteenth-century freedom suits (Appendix 2.2 provides the derivations).[43] First, the greater a slave's value out of slavery, where self-valuation included potential market earnings plus the subjective value of freedom, the more likely a slave was to bring a freedom suit. To the extent that mixed-race or light-complected slaves had higher earnings prospects in the market out of slavery, more freedom suits would have been brought by mixed-race or light-complected slaves. Light-complected slaves were more skilled, on average, than dark-complected slaves, so we would expect to see more light- than dark-complected slaves initiating freedom suits (see Chapter 4).

Second, if light complexion or mixed-race ancestry improved the slave's odds of prevailing at trial, more freedom suits would have been brought by mixed-race slaves. The available narratives provided by critical race theorists are consistent with this prediction. When physical descriptions are offered in the trial records, they overwhelmingly describe individuals with fair complexions, straight hair, prominent noses, and other traditionally European physical features. The second prediction is also consistent with Ira Berlin's contention that following the successful prosecution of freedom suits by two Maryland slaves in the 1790s, the state's county courts were swamped with such suits. In 1797 Maryland's attorney general complained that "hundreds of negroes [sic] have been set loose upon the community" with little more than hearsay testimony as evidence.[44] An improvement in the odds of a slave winning at trial invited the initiation of freedom suits.

A third prediction of the model is that the higher the slave owner's costs to defend their rights in freedom suits, the more likely out-of-court settlements were to occur. Recall the substantial costs borne by slave owners such as Denman (who spent time in jail in pursuit of his slave) and White (who bore the costs of three unsuccessful suits, an uncertain appeal, and the prospect of staring down a belligerent mob). Faced with these kinds of costs, slave owners with a light-complected slave threatening to prosecute a freedom suit may have been amenable to settlement through manumission, hiring out, or other accommodation. An economist might think of this as a type of Coase Theorem of slavery: the ultimate allocation of rights is invariant to the initial allocation when bargaining is possible.[45] It is not surprising that states known for the liberal treatment of slaves in freedom suits were also the states with relatively liberal manumission laws (i.e., Maryland, Virginia, and Louisiana). Had states with liberal rulings in freedom suits prohibited manumission, slave owners would have been forced into costly litigation rather than the opportunity to resolve the dispute through private negotiation and settlement.[46]

Opportunities for fruitful lines of theoretical and empirical research into the statutory and common law of race are manifold, and much less is known about the law of race and mixed-race than the existing state of critical race theory would lead us to believe. The existing literature emphasizes physical appearance and the performance of race. Statutes defined black, mulatto, and white by proportion nonwhite ancestry rather than physical appearance or performance, but poor recordkeeping meant that determining exact proportions was problematic. It was so difficult that, in fact, "no one seemed to try."[47] But this did not mean that no one tried to sort out white from black from mixed, or that no one struggled to categorize people who straddled precisely defined ancestry boundaries that were often contested on fuzzy color lines.

The central premise of critical race theory is that race is legally, socially, and economically constructed, and therefore fluid across time and space, and most such scholars try to identify the line separating white from nonwhite at particular places at particular times. They tend to overlook a wide zone separating white from black. Daniel Sharfstein recognizes this oversight. Southern courts, he contends, understood the contemporary "artificiality of the color line," but preserved it in "all its contradictions" because it afforded them opportunities to fit the law to the circumstances, sometimes to the advantage of the mixed-race person.[48] Carl Degler, too, observes that the "presence of the mulatto . . . literally blurs and thereby softens the line between black and white."[49] Statutory law was not a weapon employed solely in the service of white supremacy; neither was it designed to push all people of African ancestry into blackness.

Without a doubt, most whites were white and most blacks were black, but there were many people of mixed racial heritage not pushed into blackness; some were even pushed into whiteness when white sensibilities considered it equitable to do so. The equivalence of mixed-race and black is a twentieth-century interpretation consistent with the one-drop rule. Nineteenth-century Southerners did not divide the world into neat categories of white and black; they appreciated—even embraced—ambiguity. Mixed-race peoples were often included with blacks in the polis (voting, jury duty, mustering into the militia); many of the era's black codes, in fact, explicitly stated that the codes applied to mulattoes as well as blacks.[50] By itself, the imposition of the same disabilities on mulattoes as blacks in some instances is not evidence that the two groups were considered or treated the same by society writ large. In 1833, for example, Virginia's legislators granted the members of the Wharton family a dispensation from an 1806 act that required all manumitted blacks and mulattoes to emigrate from the state. The dispensation was granted because they declared the Whartons white because they were only "remotely descended from a colored woman." The Whartons, to paraphrase Joel Williamson, were significantly mixed, visibly mixed, and known to be of mixed race, but by special legal dispensation were not to be treated as being part black. This was not an outcome we would expect to observe in a dichotomous, two-color society. Virginia's political elite were willing to carve out a racial middle ground.

The same legislative session that granted special dispensation to the Whartons passed an act that opened the door for many mixed-race people to escape the disadvantages of legal mulatto-ness (those one-half to one-fourth black). The act authorized county courts "upon satisfactory evidence . . . to grant to any free person of mixed blood . . . not being a white person nor a free negro [*sic*] or mulatto, a certificate that he or she is not a free negro or mulatto, which certificates shall be sufficient to protect and secure such person from and against the pains, penalties, disabilities and disqualifications, imposed by law upon free negroes and mulattoes, as free negroes and mulattoes."[51] The inclusiveness of Virginia's definitions of Negro, mulatto, and white leaves little apparent room for a free person of

African heritage to be not white, not mulatto, and not black. A reasonable interpretation of the act is that the legislators were creating a general class of dispensa-
tions like the one granted specifically to the Whartons. Whenever a county court
saw fit to grant such an exemption, the nonwhite, nonblack, nonmulatto individual in question was relieved of, among other disabilities, the duty to register with
a county clerk every five years, the need to apply to a county court for permission
to move across a county line within Virginia, the payment of a special capitation
tax levied only on free blacks and mulattoes, and, upon failure to pay the annual
tax, the possibility of being hired out involuntarily for a period sufficient to defray
the unpaid tax.[52] Importantly, the law did not inhere the privileges of whiteness to
free persons of mixed blood; it relieved them of the disabilities of being mulatto,
even though they presumably were mulatto by a strict reading of the 1785 statute.

Conclusion

It is important to understand whether the authorities saw or knew race and color
when race and color were not evident. Evidence from the marriage registry maintained at St. John's Episcopal Church in Richmond, Virginia suggests they did.
Among the many marriage registers are several for "free persons of color."[53] James
and Nancy Booker (née Harris) were both black; Patrick and Sophia Maxwell
(née Lazenberry) were both mulatto; Peter Logan was mulatto; and Aggy Cole
was black. There is nothing particularly noteworthy about the Bookers and the
Maxwells other than that they were enumerated in both the parish's marriage
register and the federal decennial census. What is surprising but, in light of the
Wharton case, plausible is that Jonathan and Lucy Ann Smith (née Davenport),
William and Eliza Green, and Abram and Lavinia Bailey (née Bee)—free persons
of color in the marriage registry—are enumerated in the 1850 census as white!
Here are individuals whose minister recognized (or knew) them to be people of
color, but census marshals who relied on little more than visual and social cues
classified them as white. They lived in white neighborhoods, worked as clerks or
farmers, and owned some property, all of which made them white so far as the
census taker was concerned. It is not known, however, if they ever exercised any
of the legal privileges of whiteness or whether they, like the Whartons, escaped
the disabilities of mulatto-ness. In either case, they had, as Berlin noted, scooted
under the color line.

   It is not clear whether these six people were passing, which presumes that they
purported to be white, lived as white, and concealed their blackness. Given the
marriage registries, it would have been simple enough for anyone with an interest
in exposing them to do so. All we can conclude is that they were of sufficiently fair
complexion that they were considered white in some contexts by at least some

segments of the white population, but they were of sufficiently well-known black ancestry to be considered mulattoes in other contexts.

Perhaps no cases stand in starker contrast in revealing the fundamental shift from antebellum mixed-race middle ground to postbellum one-drop rule than a comparison of *Plessy* (1896) and *State v. Kimber* (Ohio 1859). Though seven-eighths white, Plessy was legally ejected from a whites-only railroad car. In 1859, Sarah Fawcett paid her fare and stepped on a Cincinnati streetcar. Henry Kimber, a conductor for the streetcar company, ordered her off. She refused; having paid her fare, she claimed her right to ride. Kimber forcibly ejected her from the car and Fawcett charged him with assault and battery. Kimber's attorney offered a two-prong defense: first, he did not use excessive force; and, second, because Fawcett was a person of color, it was his duty to expel her from the car. The Hamilton County court ruled that Fawcett—a woman "about as much white as African race"—had a right to ride in the same streetcar as whites. The well established duty of a common carrier, the court wrote, was to receive all well-behaved passengers ready to pay the fare. It was not legal for them to make "unreasonable discriminations . . . on account of personal dislike, . . . complexion, [or] race."[54] The defendant was fined $10 and costs. We are left to wonder how American history may have unfolded had the *Plessy* court ruled like the *Kimber* court. We are also left to wonder whether the *Kimber* court would have been as accommodating had Sarah Fawcett been less noticeably white, but taking the court's observations at face value Fawcett's light complexion mattered even if it was not determinative.

The statutory and case law is clear. Contemporary whites carved out a legal racial middle ground, one that did not give people of mixed racial ancestry all the civic and legal rights of whiteness, but one that protected them from the more severe legal handicaps imposed on blackness. Virginia's 1833 act was a remarkable piece of legislation; it specifically opened the door for sympathetic courts to create a special class of people, one that fell outside what appears to be an inclusive definition of black, mixed, and white. If legislators respond to the median voter, as modern political theory holds, the law implies that the typical Virginian was not conflicted by a racial middle ground. In fact, the typical Virginian asked for and was granted the freedom to relieve some of the inhabitants of that middle ground of the civic disabilities associated with it. It is imperative that Virginia not be conflated with the South writ large, but Virginians were among the first to face the issue of categorizing mixed-race people, and Virginians' choices influenced choices made elsewhere. There were notable differences, of course. Virginia provided precise racial definitions; South Carolina eschewed statutory definitions and allowed courts wide discretion in making racial determinations. Still, legal traditions originating in the Chesapeake reveal that the one-drop rule was not the law of the land in the pre-Civil War South, a fact that other features of antebellum southern society also make clear.

Race Mixing and Color in Literature and Science

Critical race theorists use nineteenth-century case law to identify the legal line between white and nonwhite. Theirs is an interesting question, because whiteness provided a host of legal and civic privileges including jury duty, muster in the militia, the ability to testify in court, and the right to vote that were denied to those considered black or mulatto. If the court found a person was mulatto, that person lost an essential element of his or her whiteness. But critical race theorists and other legal scholars lose sight of a second important point: that while mixed-race people may not have been legally white, they were not socially black. The same neighbors who would deny the mixed-race person the civic privileges inhering to whiteness allowed that same person—perhaps even encouraged them—to participate in other aspects of white society. Mixed-race people danced at white dances; they sometimes attended white churches and sent their children to white schools; they occasionally assembled at white assemblies. In most social circumstances, known mixed-race people were not white, but they were not black either. White society carved out an intermediate space for light-skinned African Americans.

Consider the case of Joseph Nuñez, the son of a white woman and a dark-complected man variously described as Spanish, Portuguese, Indian, or mulatto. Joseph died without descendants shortly after he sold slaves to Seaborn Bryan, a white man. The court-appointed executor of Nuñez's estate sued for the return of the slaves because, as a man of African ancestry, Nuñez had no right to convey title to slaves. The Nuñez case was tried on three separate occasions before Georgia's highest court found for the executor and ordered the return of the slaves. Ultimately, the case turned on the court's determination that neither Joseph Nuñez nor his father ever engaged in the civic rights of white men. Neither man had ever voted nor served on a jury. The court interpreted these men's failures to participate in these acts of citizenship as evidence of their blackness. Nuñez then was not legally white.

But a number of witnesses for both the plaintiff and the defendant reported to have seen or heard about Nuñez's attendance at any number of white functions. Mary Rogers testified that Nuñez was never treated as a man "having any negro [*sic*] blood, but as a respectable . . . white blooded man." Nuñez, she continued, was "always among the respectable white people in the neighborhood in their dances, parties, &c."[1] Two other witnesses who were similarly disposed to accept Nuñez as a white man testified that he "never kept low, trifling or rakish company." Rather, he associated with whites at parties, assemblies, and gatherings, all events to which blacks were neither invited nor welcomed. Even witnesses who believed Nuñez was part black described him as an intelligent, educated gentleman with whom they were happy to associate. Few antebellum southern white men would have described a black man—no matter how intelligent and gentlemanly—as intelligent and gentlemanly. Even among the witnesses disposed to accept Nuñez as a mixed-race man, which disqualified him in their eyes from citizenship, he was not so black as to be disqualified from the social benefits of (part) whiteness. The social fiction of his Portuguese heritage was widely accepted even if the legal fiction was not.

Trial transcripts such as Nuñez's must be handled with care. While it is tempting to read contemporary attitudes into them, we cannot be certain that the narratives reflect popular beliefs. Plaintiffs argued one side, defendants the other. Witnesses may or may not have literally believed what they were saying. They were making statements with a purpose; they were trying to advance a cause at trial and offered interpretations they believed would resonate with judges and juries.[2] Because attorneys and witnesses on opposing sides thought theirs was the resonating narrative, it is difficult to know which narrative was more widely accepted. Were mixed-race people more white or more black in popular conception? Did whites view mixed-race people as distinct from blacks? Did they treat them differently? While there is no uniformity of opinion, the weight of the evidence suggests that mixed-race people were considered more white than black and were treated as such.

The courtroom was just one arena in which mixed-race people established their racial space. They interacted with whites at work, at play, and at home. Contemporary observers were not blind to the social ambiguities of race. Travelogues, novels, and scientific investigations present complex assessments of the place of mixed-race people in early nineteenth-century society. Astute observers recognized and commented on the racial middle ground afforded mixed-race people. Generally, men and women with some white ancestry were held in higher esteem than those of purely African heritage. They were viewed as more intelligent, educable, and attractive. In short, mixed-race people were different. They were black and white and neither.

Mixed-Race Melodrama

The mixed-race stereotype that gained wide currency in prewar abolitionist literature came to be known as the "tragic mulatto." Her story, briefly summarized, is that of a beautiful, young, mixed-race woman with only the slightest outward appearance of African heritage that she herself is often unaware of. Her complexion is, as Lydia Marie Childs describes her, "scarcely deeper than the sunny side of a golden pear," and she is "graceful as an antelope, and beautiful as the evening star."[3] Her situation takes a tragic turn when her father unexpectedly dies and it is revealed that she is in fact a slave of part-black ancestry. Creditors of her father's estate seize her to be sold at auction. Condemned to suffer the vulgarity of the slave pen—surrounded by scoundrels "laughing, joking, swearing, spitting and talking"—she stands alone and disgraced.[4] Sold to a brutal slave driver, like Harriet Beecher Stowe's Simon Legree, who either takes sexual advantage of her himself or puts her out as a prostitute, she is doomed and almost invariably dies, often by her own hand.[5]

The titillation and melodrama common to nineteenth-century romance stories are so obvious and the character such a trope that the tragic mulatta is considered nearly irrelevant by modern critics, though there is evidence of her reappearance.[6] The tragic mulatto fell from favor partly because her plight was "hardly the paramount evil of slavery," and the practice of making the tragic heroine all but white points to the racial prejudices of abolitionists themselves.[7] It was the mixed-race person's whiteness, rather than her circumstances per se, that evoked the reader's sympathies. Tens of thousands of black women were yanked away from families, friends, and all that was familiar and forced to suffer the traumas and indignities of public auction, yet they rarely appeared in abolitionist literature or antislavery fiction.

Fictional portrayals of mixed-race people bear on the issue of separate mixed-race identity because, as Monique Guillory contends, social conventions shape literary conventions, and nearly every contemporary novel with a mixed-race character draws sharp distinctions between the mixed-race individual and his or her black compatriots.[8] Male mixed-race characters were typically cast as violent or rebellious or both; mixed-race men denounce their white ancestry and are of "restless, tempestuous, rebellious, patricidal or fratricidal disposition[s]."[9] Consider George Green, a character in William Wells Brown's Clotel (1853), loosely based on Thomas Jefferson and his relationship with Sally Hemings.[10] George, whose "hair was straight, soft, fine, and light; his eyes blue, nose prominent, lips thin, his head well formed, forehead high and prominent," is brought before the court as a defendant in a slave revolt. He commands the scene as the most gifted orator in the courtroom, invoking Jefferson's Declaration of Independence as a justification for slave defiance. George ultimately achieves his freedom not from his oratorical powers—his defiance, in fact, earns him a capital sentence—but by disguising himself as a woman during a jailbreak.

Mayne Reid, too, draws sharp distinctions between black and mixed-race men. His serialized novella Oçeloa (1859) juxtaposes Black Jake and Yellow Jake. Black men like Black Jake are "hideously ugly, with thick lips, low retreating foreheads, flat noses, and ill-formed bodies."[11] Yellow Jake, on the other hand, is handsome, but sullen and morose, resentful and cruel, in part because the object of both

Jakes' affections—a beautiful quadroon slave—favors Black Jake. Because he believes she has turned the quadroon slave girl against him, Yellow Jake lures the planter's daughter to an alligator pond. The planter's daughter is rescued, literally from the reptile's jaws, by Black Jake. Reid's narrator informs us that Yellow Jake's resentment and cruelty are "more common among mulattoes than negroes" and follow naturally from the mulatto's greater intellectual and physical gifts, which yield a "keener sense the degradation of his [slave] position." The "pure negro," the narrator explains, rarely acts the unfeeling savage because "he has been accustomed to play the part of the sufferer."[12] Yellow Jake is blessed with the lighter skin, but Black Jake has the lighter heart. The mixed-race man is more intelligent and physically capable, but he is disagreeable, dangerous, and diabolical.

No literary juxtaposition of black and mixed is more regularly invoked than Harriet Beecher Stowe's George Harris and Uncle Tom. George is of mixed ancestry and possesses "gracefulness of movement and gentlemanly manners."[13] Like many fictional mixed-race men, George inherits his (part) black mother's emotional sensitivities and his white father's intellectual capacities. It is this combination of empathy, intelligence, and physical prowess that makes the mixed-race man so dangerous. Stowe contrasts George's independence and defiance to Tom's "gentleness . . . lowly docility of heart . . . childlike sympathy of affection, and facility of forgiveness." Young Eva, in fact, asks her father to allow Tom to be her personal attendant and escort, due in part to his "instinctive gratitude" for the many kindnesses previously shown him by the master's family.[14] The master agrees, but assigns Tom to the horse stalls when Eva has no need of him, though his posting is more sinecure than assignment. Stowe's characterizations fit squarely in what George Frederickson labels the romantic racialist tradition, a genre in which blacks are presented as simple people possessing nearly inexhaustible Christian charity.[15] Mixed-race men, by comparison, are restless and less forgiving.

Unlike their male counterparts, tragic mulattas are rarely rebellious and embrace their white ancestry. They are beautiful and, because their racial mix disqualifies them from full social equality, they are invariably "sad, melancholy, resigned, self-sacrificing, or suicidal."[16] Along with her grace, the mulatta's striking physical beauty defines her. Walt Whitman's Margaret was "of that luscious and fascinating appearance . . . [with] large, soft, voluptuous eyes, and beautifully cut lips, [which] set off a form of faultless perfection."[17] Stowe's octoroon Emeline—"soft, dark eyes, with longer lashes, and her curling hair is of a luxuriant brown"—and Brown's equally attractive Clotel suffer the tragic mulatta's fate. Reid's mustee woman—"the very wonder of beauty: her eyes liquid and full of fiery love—long lashes; lips luscious as honeycombs; figure tall; bust full; lips like those of a Cyprian goddess; feet like Cinderella's—in short perfection"—escapes Emmeline's and Clotel's untimely demises, but when the young white man's parents become aware of their son's infatuation with her, he is sent to study at West Point and beyond the reach of her charms.[18] Fictional portrayals of blacks and mixes cast them in different roles. If these accounts resonated with contemporary readers, art must have followed life. The reading public readily accepted portrayals the emphasized fundamental differences between black and mixed-race people.

Chroniclers, Travelers, and Color

Nonfiction writers of all stripes, too, commented on light-skinned, mixed-race men and women. In travelers' chronicles and other nonfiction accounts, the archetypal mixed-race woman is not the tragic mulatta of contemporary fiction, but the exotic and desirable *placée*. Unlike the tragic mulatta, the *placée* loses her virtue not at the hands of a brutal slave owner or overseer, but as part of a *plaçage* agreement consummated at a quadroon ball. Available young, fair-skinned, mixed-race women and young white men in search of mistresses attended quadroon balls. Chaperoned by their mothers, the fair-skinned, mixed-race women were "gracefully dressed, and conducted themselves with much propriety and modesty."[19] Dances were danced and when the music stopped some of the men and women who had paired off entered into *plaçage* agreements.

Under a *plaçage* contract a light-skinned woman became a single white man's mistress in return for a cash payment to the young woman's family. In addition, the man promised financial support for the mistress and any children produced during the relationship. The man typically provided his mistress with an apartment, furnishings, clothing, and an allowance. Some relationships were passing fancies that lasted only a short time; others were based on genuine sentiment and lasted for years. Sometimes the women inherited property, and, rarely, fortunes.[20] Some relationships ended tragically with the woman's abandonment at an inopportune moment, as in John Stedman's famous—if disguised—account of his five-year *plaçage* with a light-skinned woman in Surinam.[21] Most ended when the gentleman simply tired of his mistress or became engaged to a white woman, which almost always brought a *plaçage* agreement to an end.

Placées represented a tiny fraction of the mixed-race female population, and because the many contemporary descriptions reveal a prurient fascination with unconventional relationships not unlike the modern fascination with the intersection of celebrity and money and sex, depictions of *placées* may not provide an accurate portrayal of contemporary opinion. But travelers and other contemporaries revealed their thoughts about the differences between blacks and mixed-race men and women in offhand comments as well as detailed descriptions of the people they encountered as they passed through the South. Thomas Jefferson, for example, compared blacks to Europeans and Native Americans and found blacks wanting in both physique and personality. Blacks lacked both "flowing hair" and "elegant symmetry," and their perspirations exuded a "disagreeable odour."[22] Jefferson said little about mixed-race people, other than to repeat a report that they were "enterprising and intelligent," and to recommend a quadroon to the governor of South Carolina as a man of "tall fine figure."[23]

Other contemporaries, however, drew sharp distinctions. While Harriet Martineau considered blacks "sleek, intelligent, and cheerful looking," at one point she declared them "desperately ignorant" and nearly uneducable at another. In her lone commentary on mixes, Martineau labeled the woman "beautiful" and the girls "pretty."[24] Similarly, Fannie Kemble, an English woman who lived for a time on a Georgia plantation, described blacks as "childish human beings, whose mental condition is kin in its simplicity and proneness to impulsive emotion." Mixed women, while pretty and graceful, were "always serious, not to say sad and silent... [with] an air of melancholy." Mixed-race men, on the other hand, were "mutinous," "spying and secretive."[25] Although Edward Sullivan found that blacks "sometimes possess an intellect, and that too of a very high order," he was mostly alone in this assessment in describing one mulatto woman as the "ugliest girl I ever saw."[26]

Unlike Sullivan's nearly singular experience, most observers described mulattoes and quadroons as handsome or pretty, with "fine eyes and expressive features," "graceful and elegant," and of "gentle deportment."[27] While often "ready to frolic," blacks were "dull, idiotic, brute-like" creatures that moved about with "besotted expressions"; they were "indolent" and had a tendency "to intemperance and petty dishonesty."[28] The fact that most such chroniclers interacted with blacks as slaves engaged in exhausting labor, while they were more likely to see and interact with mixed-race men and women as free people moving about at their leisure in urban markets, should not be discounted. Had the circumstances been reversed—enslaved mixes and free blacks—travelers may have drawn different portraits. But the circumstances were as they were, and accounts of black dullards, pretty mulattoes, and refined quadroons resonated with contemporary audiences partly because such descriptions were consistent with casual observations and reinforced existing beliefs and prejudices. More importantly, such descriptions reinforced the tendency among whites to carve out a separate racial space for light-skinned, mixed-race men and women, because blacks and mixes were believed to be inherently different.

The Saddest Book: Scientific Interpretations of Color and Race Mixing

By the seventeenth century the term *race*, as it was used in contemporary scientific circles at least, connoted groups of people originating in particular geographical places (i.e., northwestern Europe) who shared common physical characteristics (i.e., fair complexions).[29] Most of the time, natural history's geography-physiognomy link could be easily employed in scientific and popular discussion. People of western European descent were readily assigned to one group, while people of West African descent were assigned to another. When American natural historians confronted complexity, they either threw their hands in the air or they relied on experience to derive "truths," which they treated as axioms derived from a priori reasoning. Mixed-race people presented one such instance of complexity, and nineteenth-century science followed both paths, which complicated and brought into question the very notion of race.

Nineteenth-century debates concerning the origin of the races were complicated by the fact that they had to contend with the biblical creation story. Many contemporary scientists were reluctant to contradict Genesis. That reluctance defined the boundaries of the debate. At one extreme was the view that Adam and Eve were both white, which meant that blacks were of an entirely different species. The other extreme accepted the single genesis of a common race; different complexions followed from later adaptations to climatic conditions. Neither interpretation was completely satisfactory, however. The separate race theory should have eliminated the possibility of interspecies mating and reproduction. And the climate adaptation story was inconsistent with the available empirical evidence—namely, that subsequent generations of whites living in tropical climates were not growing ever darker; blacks living in temperate climates were not becoming lighter.

The mid-nineteenth-century debate over poly- and monogenesis can be viewed as the quaint, unscientific speculations of an earlier era, or they can be taken as serious expressions of contemporary attitudes toward the varieties of mankind.[30] Confronted by the "other" for the first time, a white man might see in a black man a common humanity. Or, he might, like the respected Harvard zoologist and naturalist Louis Agassiz, be struck by, even repulsed by, the differences between them.[31] And once the differences became the object of debate, the issue was whether they were differences of kind or degree, whether they were immutable or acquired, whether they were fixed or fluid. If they were fixed and immutable differences of kind, polygenesis logically followed even if it was difficult to reconcile with the scriptures.

The scientific debates generated speculative alternative hypotheses. In an essay published in the 1744 edition of the Royal Society's *Philosophical Transactions,* John Mitchell posited that "Noah and his sons were of a complexion suitable to the climate in which they resided," which was a swarthy complexion midway between black and white and most likely about the color or the Tatars of the lands of eastern Europe and north-central Asia. As people migrated out of the Fertile Crescent, they became lighter or darker depending on whether they traveled west and north toward Europe or west and south toward sub-Saharan Africa.[32] In 1759 John Winthrop IV, a mathematics professor at Harvard, offered a similar hypothesis.

In his satirical novel *Adventures of Captain Farrago,* Hugh Henry Brackenridge offered a nearly heretical alternative interpretation of the creation, one that made all descendants of Adam and Eve mulattoes.[33] "I am of the opinion," says the narrator, "that Adam was a tall, straight-limbed, red-haired man, with a fair complexion, blue eyes, and an aquiline nose; and that Eve was a negro woman." For Brackenridge beauty in nature followed from diversity and variety. Human beauty was no different. Thus, "as God made Adam in his own likeness, so it is to be supposed, that Adam begat some in his, and these were red-haired, fair-complexioned, blue-eyed, proportionately featured boys and girls, while on the other hand, some took after the mother, and became negro men and women. From a mixture of complexion, the offspring, at other times, might be a shade darker, in one case, than the father; and a shade lighter, in another case, than the mother, and hence of diversified progeny, with a variety of features."[34] Brackenridge's conception of an interracial progeny was clearly a parody of contemporary science, but it illuminates the wildly different views—popular and scientific—toward the science of race mixing and color.

The central issue was whether blacks and whites were different species or different varieties of the same species. Eighteenth- and nineteenth-century naturalists provided no unequivocal answers. Writing in 1822, William Lawrence noted "those forms, proportions, and colours, which we consider so beautiful in the fine figures of Greece, in contrast the woolly hair, the flat nose, the thick lips, the retreating forehead and advancing jaws, and black skin of the Negro . . . the ruddy and sanguine European with the jet-black African."[35] He asked whether these were brethren; did they descend from a common ancestor? Or, was there more than one Adam? And, if more how many?

In thinking about the issue, Lawrence applied the existing classification scheme, which held that species were identified by fixed external forms perpetuated across generations through within-group sexual reproduction and a powerful aversion to intercourse with other groups (species). In the wild state, Lawrence observed, very similar animals did not interbreed: hares did not mix with rabbits; mice did not breed with rats; horses did not breed with asses.[36] Thus separate species (mice and rats) differed from simple varieties (breeds of dogs) in that varieties copulated and generated offspring that were equally healthy and prolific; species did not.

Once Lawrence admitted this definition of species, the puzzle of monogenesis or polygenesis of a man was resolved: "all the races breed together; and their offspring is prolific, either with each other, or with any of the original races." Lawrence continued: "Indeed, we know no difference in productiveness between such unions and those of the same race."[37] But Lawrence could not help but identify some known exceptions: she-mules were known to conceive, if rarely; the offspring of a billy goat and a ewe was capable of reproduction, as were some hybrids of domesticated birds. What linked the known exceptions was that they were all domesticated animals and the hybrids tended to reproduce only when humans intervened. Applying this logic to man, Lawrence could draw no other conclusion than that the separate races were varieties of a single species. He deftly avoided the religious implications. "Whether the species originated with a single pair," he wrote, "is a question which zoology does not possess the means of solving."[38]

In the United States the question of monogenesis versus polygenesis took on a new life as the abolitionist debate intensified. It was no longer enough to argue that slavery was humane because it was a civilizing device moving blacks toward eventual social equality; whites had a right, perhaps even a duty, to exercise control over blacks because blacks were a subordinate species. Proving that blacks were a separate species was a tough row to hoe, given that blacks and whites readily copulated and their offspring appeared, at first blush, to be healthy and prolific. Moreover, the claim that the races were separate species implied polygenesis, which placed its advocates at odds with religious orthodoxy.

A number of prominent American scientists and clerics weighed in on the subject, but two of the more notable were Josiah Clark and his occasional collaborator George R. Gliddon. Gliddon is described by William Stanton as a "name-dropper, a sponger, a swinger on the shirttails of the great, a braggart, pretender, and scatologist."[39] Reginald Horsman, Nott's biographer, offers a less scathing assessment of Gliddon, but describes his writing (without exaggeration) as dense, disorganized, confused, and nearly unreadable.[40] Gliddon lived for a time in Egypt, employed in his father's business and then as US vice-consul. Carvings on the ancient Egyptian tombs convinced Gliddon of two things: the date of the creation calculated from biblical sources was too recent; and the races appeared in their current form at least as early as the Egyptian dynasties. Gliddon interpreted these two observations as compelling evidence of polygenesis. He spent much of his career collecting evidence in support of polygenesis and waging war with religious writers who defended the biblical monogenesis story.

Gliddon and Nott were friends and collaborators, but Nott was less combative, capable of appreciating nuance, and, while convinced that the races were separate species rather than simple varieties, welcoming of scientific debate on the issue.[41] Born in Columbia, South Carolina, Nott attended South Carolina College, medical school at the University Pennsylvania, and a year of private medical lectures in Paris. In 1842, with an established medical practice in Mobile, Alabama, Nott's imagination was captured by an anonymously published article titled "Vital Statistics of Negroes and Mulattoes" that appeared in the *Boston Medical and Surgical Journal* and argued that mulattoes were a degenerate mixture because they were shorter-lived than whites or blacks.

Later that year Nott published his first anthropological study, "The Mulatto A Hybrid," in the respected *American Journal of the Medical Sciences*. Nott understood that many readers would be skeptical of mulatto hybridity, but he asked that readers consider certain facts that he had uncovered during his practice. Having lived for some time in cosmopolitan Mobile, where the races had been mixing for several generations, his observations led him to conclude that (1) mixed-race men and women demonstrated intellectual capacities intermediate between whites and blacks; (2) mixed-race men and women were shorter-lived and less healthy (less "capable of endurance"); (3) mixed-race men and women were "particularly delicate"; (4) mixed-race women were "bad breeders and bad nurses," so that many of their children died young; and (5) mixed-race men and women who interbred were less prolific than mixed-race men and women who mated with either of the parent races.[42]

Based on his personal observations, Nott concluded that blacks and whites were not varieties; they were separate species. It followed that mixed-race people were hybrids. Nott read widely, and his essay reveals that he was familiar with William Lawrence's *Lectures*; his argument follows Lawrence's, except for the conclusion. Nott's characterizations of the races are not unlike Lawrence's, and Nott's list of the exceptions to the rule of infertile hybrids follows Lawrence. Where Lawrence considered the exceptions to be rare instances inapplicable to the study of human races, Nott saw the exceptions as a way to classify mixed-race people as one of the exceptions. If the interspecies breeding of certain hybrids, such as the Chinese and the common goose, occurred in contradiction to natural "laws," it was not unreasonable to conclude that black-white hybrids were similarly "governed... by peculiar laws." Although mixed-race men and women were capable of breeding among themselves, Nott asserted that the offspring of such intrabreeding were a "degenerate, unnatural offspring, doomed by nature to work out its own destruction."[43]

According to Horsman, Nott was a gifted physician and his medical training had instilled a deep respect for the empirical approach to scientific inquiry. He rejected bleeding and purging as a course of treatment, for example, because his own experience taught him that it tended to weaken already physically stressed patients. In most cases, rest and good nursing care did more good by doing less. When others attributed yellow fever to miasmas, Nott suspected but could not prove an insect-borne animalcular vector.[44] In medical matters, when evidence contradicted one of Nott's theories, he abandoned the theory. For whatever reason, Nott failed to bring this empirical sensibility to his racial theorizing. His writing on race, and especially on race mixing, was a particularly egregious case of special pleading: he invoked exceptions to generally accepted rules to make his point without justification, and he regularly invoked anecdotes as proof. As George Stocking notes, Nott's (and he was not alone in this) evidence on hybridity often took the following form: "I received information from a well-informed gentlemen in that place, and he assured me that . . .."[45] Contradictory anecdotal evidence was dismissed because it either did not come from a gentleman (a notion of deep importance to Nott the Southerner) or was unreliable for some other reason.

For Nott, as for other nineteenth-century biologists, the ability of two animals to produce fertile offspring was prima facie evidence that were of the same species. Humans obviously satisfied this criterion, so that the polygenesis theory could only be maintained either by redefining what it meant to be a species or by showing that the apparent fertility of mixed-race people was not real. Polygenists did both, but Nott, like many others, emphasized the latter.[46]

What was the degenerate mixed-race people's path to destruction? Nott claimed that it was indiscriminate interbreeding between blacks, whites, and mixes, which would yield a mongrel race. Nott was convinced that a population of mixed-race mongrels would eventually die out. His argument turned on the mix's presumed shorter life expectancy. Life expectancies would continue to decline with each increasingly mongrelized generation until there were too few adults remaining to reproduce. But was the contention that mixed-race men and women were shorter-lived than blacks or whites correct? This was the one piece of evidence that seemingly supported Nott's hypothesis. The 1860 census, in fact, reveals a significantly lower proportion of mixes than blacks at older ages (see Appendix 3.1). Mixed-race life expectancy, too, was lower than for blacks. At nearly every age, black life expectancy, both male and female, exceeded mixed life expectancy by two to three years. However, the fundamental evidence on which the mongrel disappearance-cum-degeneration hypothesis was based was problematic, because it was based on unwarranted assumptions about stable cohort sizes and that both populations had achieved an equilibrium, neither of which held.

The existing evidence of shorter mixed-race life expectancy, combined with the mixes' presumed inferiority as a "common subject of remark" in the South, convinced Nott that mixed-race people would become more degenerate with successive generations. He opined at one point that if one hundred white men and one hundred black women were sent to an isolated island, the island would be left unpopulated in a few generations. There was no other conceivable result of "breeding from a faulty stock," a stock that existed in violation of nature's fundamental law of species. For Nott and his followers, the very rarity of the quinteroon (one black progenitor four generations removed) was evidence enough of the "death and sterility" that followed from successive generations of racial interbreeding.[47] It didn't appear to trouble Nott that casual observers might easily mistake quinteroons for white (and regularly did), which would lead to an undercount of quinteroons, or that five generations of race mixing was itself rare. It also did not appear to trouble Nott that reports from the Pitcairn Islands, where about 20 Bounty mutineers and Polynesians settled in 1790, that the mixed-race children were "in good condition, and of excellent figures," and that the population was increasing at a sufficient pace to reach the estimated population limit of around 1,000 inhabitants in the not-too-distant future.[48]

Nott and Agassiz met at a meeting of the American Association of the Advancement of Science meeting in Charleston, South Carolina in 1850. Nott delivered a paper outlining his case for polygenesis; Agassiz, in the audience, jumped to his defense. Their sympathetic views led to friendship. Christophe

Irmscher, Agassiz's biographer, notes that the trip to Charleston had a lasting influence on Agassiz's hastily drawn belief in polygenesis. After the conference, Agassiz was taken on a tour of plantations around Columbia, South Carolina, introduced to slaves originating in different parts of Africa, and shown the conditions under which they labored. Agassiz's southern perambulations left him convinced that blacks and whites were fundamentally different. After Agassiz departed Joseph T. Zealy, a local daguerreotypist, took pictures of several slaves at sessions organized by Dr. Robert W. Gibbes. The daguerreotypes, many of which are now available on the Internet, were to provide Agassiz with the documentary evidence necessary to connect fundamental physical differences between blacks and whites to their ostensibly separate origins, which he attempted to do in two articles appearing in *Christian Examiner* in 1850.[49]

Despite its internal inconsistencies and its failure to square with the evidence, Nott's—and now Agassiz's—hypotheses found favor, which were repeated and expanded on in their chapters appearing *Types of Mankind* (1854) and *Indigenous Races of the Earth; or New Chapters of Ethnological Inquiry* (1857). Ever the empiricist, Nott knew that he had not and could not then provide a definitive tests of his polygenesis and hybridity-degeneracy hypotheses, but he remained convinced that when the right data became available it would support his thesis. In the meantime he relied on Samuel G. Morton's *Crania Americana* (1839), which reported that the internal capacity of black skulls was lower than the capacity of white skulls. The implication, refuted in the twentieth century, was that black brains were smaller, which was consistent with inherent differences, including black intellectual inferiority.[50] Nott relied, too, on Agassiz's equally poorly formed speculations on polygenesis and black inferiority, which were given more weight than they deserved because they were offered by Harvard's Agassiz. Morton and Agassiz were less ready than Nott to draw sweeping scientific conclusions and less ready than Gliddon to antagonize clerics. Agassiz was convinced by Nott to contribute to *Types*, which also included some of Morton's previously unpublished work. Agassiz's and Morton's statures as scientists gave the volume its intellectual heft, but *Types* undoubtedly is, as Irmscher states, "one of the saddest books in the canon of nineteenth-century racial thinking."[51]

Other writers took Nott's and Agassiz's polygenesis hypothesis and ran with it. The influential *DeBow's Review* reprinted part of John Campbell's "Negro-Mania" in which he contended that no mixed-race population was self-perpetuating. The survival of a mixed-race society demanded repeated injections of the parent races' blood. General amalgamation of the races was impossible; the only conceivable outcome was extinction.[52] John Wilson, a Georgia physician, argued that mixes were shorter-lived than blacks due to the "want of congeniality" in the mixing of white and black blood; Dr. Samuel Kneeland claimed that it was widely known, among physicians at least, that mixes were "frail, diseased," and rarely lived to ripe old ages; and, in reviewing the results of the 1860 census Joseph Kennedy, the superintendent of the census, was comfortable in stating that the 1850 and 1860 censuses revealed that "the mingling of the races is more unfavorable to vitality, than a condition of slavery."[53] Repeated as fact by US Congressmen, doctors, newspaper editorialists, and literary critics with proslavery sentiments, the mixes' physical inferiority was widely accepted, though more article of faith than proved fact, in southern scientific circles by the time the South seceded.

Even without access to systematic evidence, natural scientists did not let polygenesis go unchallenged. John Bachman, minister at Charleston, South Carolina's St. John's Lutheran Church and collaborator with John J. Audubon on *Birds of America*, attacked Nott and Agassiz in his *Doctrine of the Unity of the Human Race*. Bachman was a good enough naturalist to recognize that Agassiz's and Nott's ruminations were unscientific nonsense.[54] They could not have it both ways; the scientific idea of interspecies infertility was either true or it wasn't.[55] Bachman labored to expose the fallacy of Nott's special pleading. While Bachman readily accepted the hypothesis of black inferiority, he considered them the same species. Blacks and white did not sexually repulse one another, as would be expected of different species. Rather, blacks and whites attracted and living in close quarters in the Americas offered a familiarity that bred not contempt, but comingling born of consanguinity. Just look around, he wrote; mulattoes were abundant enough and prolific, too. Thus Bachman's argument against amalgamation arose from moral rather than scientific concerns. Amalgamation was natural, but immoral.

Just as Nott and Agassiz had their following, Bachman had his own. George Tucker acted the scientist and turned to the evidence when he analyzed racial statistics from Connecticut and Louisiana, as well as New York City and New Orleans, reported in the 1850 census. He concluded that the data disproved the inferiority hypothesis. Virginian Moncure Conway was "firmly persuaded that the mixture of blacks and whites [was] good; that the person produced [was], under ordinarily favourable circumstances, handsome, and intelligent."[56] North Carolinian Moses Ashley, too, criticized Nott's inadequate training as a naturalist. Nott failed to grasp several fundamental zoological ideas, not least of which was the sexual repulsion exhibited by separate species. In reply to Nott's assertion of eventual mixed-race infertility, Ashley also pointed to reports of Pitcairn Island where, he asserted, the offspring of English sailors and Polynesian women had been successfully reproducing since the *Bounty's* grounding.

The era's naturalists and scientists could not find much common ground on the question of hybridity and the place of mixed-race people, but public opinion tended toward one of two conclusions: either mixed-race people occupied an intermediate space between that of whites and blacks, a conclusion usually supported by reference to the mixes' superior intellectual abilities; or mixed-race people were not fundamentally different, physiologically at least, from blacks. An anonymous contributor to *DeBow's Review* asserted that the "mixed race [individual] exhibits powers more susceptible of cultivation than the pure African," which was why planters assigned their mixed-race slaves to different duties than their field slaves.[57] By 1853 even Nott was willing to concede that a small trace of white blood "improved" the blacks' morals and intelligence.[58] Perhaps the most compelling piece of evidence on the question of mixed-race intelligence for nineteenth-century commentators was Samuel Morton's (now discredited) finding that the average white cranium had an internal capacity of 85 cubic inches, the mixes' 80, and the blacks' just 71.[59] For nineteenth-century naturalists brain size and intelligence went hand-in-hand, and that the mixes' cranial capacity was closer to the whites' than the blacks' was unmistakable biological evidence of the mixes' intellectual advantages. Following the contemporary naturalists' own logic, Morton's skulls suggested that mixed-race people were more white than black. Although Morton's studies were discountenanced in the twentieth century, he was widely respected among nineteenth-century scientists.[60] His findings provided intellectual heft to the notion that mixed-race men and women were neither black nor white. Rather, they were an intermediate race—intermediate in color, physical features, and intelligence. For Nott, intermediate implied hybrid. For others, it implied only variety. In either case, Morton's science established a scientific foundation for the differential treatment of mixed-race people, though it did not allay concerns with amalgamation and fears of mixed-race degeneracy.

Of course, even an unsophisticated modern statistical analysis of the 1860 slave census shows that claims of mixed-race physical degeneracy are not evident (see Appendix 3.1). The census identified slaves by sex, color (black or mulatto), age, and disability (blind, deaf, idiotic, insane), if any. Linear probability estimates reveal that mixed-race men and women were no more likely than blacks to demonstrate a physical or mental disability. If anything, mixed-race slaves were marginally less likely to be identified as being blind or idiotic, but the proportion of people so identified is very small.

But observant contemporaries knew this, too. As a member of the American Freedmen's Inquiry Commission, Samuel Gridley Howe surveyed doctors, politicians, and others with first-hand knowledge of blacks and mixed-race people. One recipient of the survey was Frederick Law Olmsted, then in Norfolk, Virginia. Gridley attached to the survey a request that he speak to the managers at a southern life insurance company that insured slaves. Howe wanted to know whether insurers charged different rates for "sicklier mulattoes." One local company that had underwritten such contracts, mostly on house servants, mechanics, and steamboat hands, had not charged different rates.[61] Southerners, especially those with some skin in the game, did not then view black and mixed-race men and women as different statistical risks. Evidence discussed in Chapter 5 in this volume, in fact, suggests that mixed-race slaves commanded higher prices, which is inconsistent with a presumed greater sickliness among those of mixed race.

Nott and his intellectual followers condemned race mixing, if not mixed-race people themselves, based on their insistent belief in race mixing's tendency toward

physical inferiority.[62] Without irrefutable (or even good) evidence, hybridity theorists accepted that mixed-race people were delicate, fragile, short-lived, less capable of long hours at hard labor, and less able to endure exposure to harsh climates
(their reproductive success in the Caribbean notwithstanding). The hybridity
camp, Nott included, did not condemn race mixing or mixed-race people, based
on its moral implications or the intellectual inferiorities of mixed-race people.
For those outside the hybridity camp, their principal objection was moral. Even
Agassiz was forced to step outside the science and condemn amalgamation on
moral grounds. Halfbreeds, he wrote, were "as much a sin against nature as incest
[was] . . . a sin against purity [of] character."[63] Many whites, Nott included, viewed
mixed-race people as more intelligent and more educable than blacks. Observant
whites could not help but notice that mixed-race people became leaders, entrepreneurs, physicians, and publishers; that is, mixed-race people were more accom-
plished than blacks. But for some mid-nineteenth-century whites, the mixed-race
person's intellectual capacity was not an unmitigated good. Mixed-race people
also became the "stirrers-up of strife," demanding privileges and encouraging
blacks to aspire to more than many whites were prepared to offer.[64] Mixed-race
people were anomalous and dangerous even if they were worthy objects of scientific inquiry. It is hard not to believe that some whites took comfort in Nott's belief
that the disruptive mongrel would disappear if the races would just stop mixing.

Conclusion

Both radical abolitionists and more mainstream opponents of slavery were
forced to tread carefully around the issue of race mixing. Proslavery advocates
often labeled antislavery and abolitionists as amalgamationists. Lincoln famously
blunted this criticism in one of his debates with Stephen Douglas when he denied
that "because I do not want a negro woman for a slave I must necessarily want her
for a wife."[65] Lincoln was shrewd enough to distance himself from race mixing
even while portraying his opponents as paranoid. Still, Lincoln's opposition to
slavery invited criticism, especially from the paranoids. The term *miscegenation*
was coined by two journalists in an 1863 pamphlet, which, although a hoax, purported to reveal Lincoln's amalgamationist agenda.[66] That the pamphlet garnered
such attention shows that only by distancing one's self from race mixing could a
Civil War era politician maintain mainstream support. Distance mattered for the
most of the next century, as well.

   Although his fiction appeared three decades after the Civil War, as the nation
was racing toward the one-drop rule, William Dean Howells offered his interpretation of the tragic mulatta. Rhoda Aldgate is the daughter of a white doctor and
an octoroon woman. When her parents die, Rhoda is taken in by the Merediths.
The Merediths do not intend to keep Rhoda's racial heritage a secret, but they

never find quite the right moment to tell her. When they learn that Rhoda—by now a tragic beauty of olive complexion and inky black hair—is about to accept a marriage proposal from a young white minister, Mrs. Meredith make telling Rhoda her imperative duty. Before revealing her secret to Rhoda, however, she confesses it to Rhoda's putative uncle, Dr. Olney. Olney's initial reaction is to find his previously beloved Rhoda repulsive, but compassion for his adopted niece compels him to come to terms with her secret. Still, Olney cannot believe that her life will unfold as he, or any of the Meredith's, had hoped. Once her racial heritage is exposed, her life will change forever because, as Dr. Olney previously observed, "one would be quite as likely to meet a cow or a horse in an American drawing room as a person of color."[67]

In terms of that kind of personal interaction, probably not much had changed between 1840 and 1890. In the earlier era, whites had been willing to carve out a separate social space for mixed-race people. Along some margins, mixed-race men and women were treated better than blacks: they escaped some legal disadvantages that blacks labored under; they were considered more attractive than blacks, a trait modern economics has shown to be valued in the marketplace; they were generally considered more intelligent—or, at least, more educable—than blacks; and to many, mixes were simply more human than blacks, which meant that they were more humanely treated.[68] As Dr. Olney's cutting observation makes clear, however, mixed-race people were not white, not even remotely so. Few found acceptance or friendship in any white American's drawing room, north or south, Joseph Nuñez notwithstanding. That whites could not imagine having a mixed-race friend does not mean that they could not relate to them—at arm's length perhaps—differently than the way they related to blacks. The remaining chapters document the consequences of this differential treatment.

4

The Plantation

Slave patrollers in Louisa County, Virginia were out on a November night in 1825 searching the quarters for some stolen leather. When they approached slave Edmund's cabin on John Richardson's plantation, the patrollers caught Dorothea, a neighboring planter's young white wife, fleeing the scene. A subsequent investigation revealed that Dorothea and Edmund had an ongoing illicit relationship. They had been discovered in Dorothea's bed a few weeks before. One witness later testified that Edmund and Dorothea had practically lived together as man and wife for some time. Another described Edmund as "bright in color" and "more likely" than Dorothea's much older husband. Publicly embarrassed by Dorothea's sexual escapades with Edmund, her husband petitioned the legislature for a divorce. His petition asserted that Dorothea and Edmund's "illicit intercourse" had produced a mixed-race child that stood as "living evidence of her guilty and dishonorable course of conduct."[1]

Dorothea and Edmund's relationship was not the sexual relationship most commonly attributed to the southern plantation. More emblematic are the familiar stories of Sally Hemings and Frederick Douglass. The facts of the Hemings-Jefferson saga, as originally revealed by James Callender in September 1802, are now believed to have been largely correct.[2] Sally was the mixed race daughter of Jefferson's father-in law, James Wayles, and Wayles's slave Betty Hemings, which made Sally the half-sister of Jefferson's wife Martha. Sally came to Monticello when Martha inherited from her father's estate. Sally later accompanied Jefferson's daughter to Paris while he served as American minister to France. It is believed that Jefferson and Hemings's liaisons began during their time in Paris. Sally returned to Virginia with Jefferson, even though she might have readily obtained her freedom under French law. Sally did not take advantage of her right to freedom in France because she wanted to go home, but did so only in return for a promise of preferential treatment for herself, her family, and any children she and Jefferson might produce. Moreover, she is believed to have negotiated for the manumission of her children by Jefferson, all of whom eventually found freedom.[3]

Douglass, born Frederick Augustus Bailey circa 1818 on Maryland's eastern shore, was convinced from a young age that he was the son of an unknown white man, perhaps his master. He considered himself "yellow," or of a muted complexion less dark than his copper-colored grandparents and considerably lighter than his deep black mother.[4] Raised by his grandmother at Tuckahoe until he was six years of age, he was then taken to Wye House plantation to serve Edward Lloyd, former Maryland governor and United States senator. The white residents of Wye wanted for little and were served by a bevy of house servants, some of whom were light-skinned and "delicately formed," and performed their duties in the hand-me-down dresses of Lloyd's daughters. Douglass endeared himself to Daniel Lloyd, Edward's son, and became Daniel's playmate and companion—a not uncommon elevation in condition for an intelligent, likely, light-complected slave on a large plantation.[5] Although it was not the path Douglass was to take, it was not unusual for these mixed-race childhood playmates of the planters' sons to become the privileged and educated house servants or the skilled artisans on the plantation. Instead, at age seven Douglass was sent away from the plantation to serve as house-boy to the Baltimore relatives of his owner. He spent the next six years of his child-hood as the "light-colored slave boy living with a family that owned no slaves."[6] He was allowed to roam Baltimore's streets and wharves, learn of a wider world, and return in the evening to the home of a woman who taught him to read. The preferences shown him—whether due to his ancestry, his color, or his precocious talents—shaped the youngster that was to become Frederick Douglass in ways that a youth spent at hard field labor would not have, could not have.[7]

The familiar stories of Sally Hemings and Frederick Douglass, as well as the lesser-known one of Dorothea and Edmund, bring into focus several features of color on the eighteenth- and nineteenth-century plantation. Dorothea and Edmund make clear that interracial sexual relations on the plantation (or in the South more generally) "did not uniformly involve white men and black women."[8] This is not to deny that white planters did not take advantage of female slaves. It raises questions, however, about the too-convenient connection between mixed-race people and white-on-black sexual assault. In addition, Sally Hemings's experience highlights the advantages given to mixed-race slaves: they were often given less onerous jobs, provided with skill training, and generally treated less harshly than blacks on the plantation. Sally's experience also reveals that many slaves retained some measure of agency on the plantation. Although they did not negotiate with planters as equals, they nonetheless negotiated some of the terms of their enslavement. Given that mixed-race slaves were favored in training and employment, it seems likely that they had more say in the terms of their bondage than unskilled black field hands.

Sex and Race Mixing

Miscegenation or racial amalgamation requires two sexes, two races, proximity, and time.[9] Chesapeake colonists learned that it did not require many people or much time. White colonists settled Jamestown in 1607. Africans arrived in 1619.

The first reference to a black person appears, but only indirectly, in Virginia's court records on September 17, 1630 and it involves interracial sex: Hugh Davis was ordered "soundly whipt" for "abusing himself to the dishonor of God and the shame of Christians by defiling his body by lying with a Negro."[10] Ten years later Robert Sweet was required to do penance in church for getting a Negro woman pregnant. The woman was whipped. Colonial Virginians were clearly concerned with race mixing and were willing to punish both parties to reduce its incidence.

By modern standards the punishments for interracial sex appear severe indeed. Virginians imposed substantial penalties for fornication generally—loss of civil rights (1645), 500 pounds of tobacco or whipping (1657), time at the pillory (1691)—but the penalties for sex across the race line were particularly severe. Interracial marriage was prohibited in 1662. Any white person who dared marry a Negro was to be banished from the colony, and any English woman who gave birth to a mixed-race child was to pay the parish church a £15 fine or, if she could not, be sold by the church wardens into five years of indentured servitude. The innocent mixed-race child was to be bound out until thirty years of age.[11]

Maryland (1661), Massachusetts (1705), North Carolina (1715), Delaware (1721), and Pennsylvania (1725) also prohibited interracial marriage, provided for similar penalties, and instructed church wardens to bind out mixed-race bastard children.[12] The church vestry book of one Virginia parish documents white and African-American children born out of wedlock, including 15 of mixed race, bound out according to law. Children were typically bound out to male planters—such as Dol and Bidde, who were bound to Godfrey Ragsdail in July 1727.[13]

With only 15 (identifiable) mixed-race children bound by church wardens in Bristol Parish, Virginia between 1720 and 1789, the evidence suggests that the laws were only intermittently enforced, which would likely vitiate any practical effect they might have had in deterring socially undesirable sexual behavior. Moreover, with the most severe punishment imposed on the children born out of wedlock, the law would deter only the purely altruistic parent whose principal concern was his or her child's welfare, and then only if three decades of indentured servitude generated a discounted stream of costs to the child greatly in excess of the benefits received. Studies of slavery suggest that the cumulative returns to slave owners from working slaves covered the cumulative costs of raising them from birth at about age twenty-eight.[14] Planters were notably less able to beat, mistreat, expropriate, and exploit servants than slaves, so it is not evident that 30 years of service imposed an inordinate economic cost on illegitimate children. Planters provided food, shelter, clothing, and training in return for labor after age 10 or 12 and hard labor beginning during or after adolescence.

Because the penalties for interracial sex were not so punitive to effectively deter, the law's purpose was to keep illegitimate children off the parish roles and to compensate planters for the costs imposed on them by their servants' promiscuity.

Then as now, children born out of wedlock were more likely than children born into two-parent households to live in poverty. The local parish was legally responsible for the care of the indigent, and binding out poor children reduced the parishioner's assessments. Further, planters were legally responsible for maintaining the offspring of their female servants during the woman's remaining years of service. By extending the woman's term of service and binding the child to the planter for 30 years, the law allowed planters to recoup their costs. Thus, Henry Royall informed the Bristol Parish that "he hath two Moll. [mulatto] Children born in his house" and petitioned that they be "bound to him & his heirs." The church wardens agreed. The parish also bound mixed-race children born in their household to Butler Herbert, Geoffrey Rags-Dail, and Henry Randolph. Scores of white children, too, shared these mixed-race children's fate.

Although legal sanctions against unwanted sexual behavior—fornication, prostitution, or interracial sex—are not "totally ineffective," it is unrealistic to think that law can eliminate the incidence of victimless crimes, especially in the sexual sphere.[15] In the case of interracial fornication on the eighteenth-century Chesapeake plantation, a law extending the female servant's term of service by five years in the event that sexual activity generated a child and imposing 30 years of indentured servitude on the child seems particularly quixotic effort to influence male sexual behaviors.

When a man produces a child outside marriage, his cost of parenthood is ordinarily less than the cost of parenthood inside marriage. He will typically devote less time or other resources to the child, which lowers his expected costs of fornication. In the extreme, he may choose to sire all his children outside of marriage and push the costs on to the mother, or the taxpayers (parishioners) if the mother cannot adequately support the child. The more completely the social safety net protects children and the lower the probability of being held to account for paternity, the greater the incentive for men to roam sexually. To the extent that unmarried men were not purely altruistic toward their offspring, they did not bear the full costs of their sexual liaisons. Moreover, the law binding children born outside marriage to masters with the wherewithal to care for and train them in farming or other occupations may have driven the costs of children to the unmarried father to near zero. Thus the connection between the preamble of Maryland's 1661 antiamalgamation law—"a great damage doth befall the master"—and the thousands of bastard children of all races bound out by colonial church wardens.[16]

The foregoing presumes that the mixed-race offspring was not that of the planter himself. Existing historical interpretations of the early days of racial amalgamation suggest that they were not. Historians agree that interracial sex in the early colonial period occurred mostly between black slave men and white female servants. Black slaves and white servants lived, worked, ate, played, and slept together on seventeenth- and eighteenth-century Chesapeake plantations.[17] There were few racial boundaries between servants and slaves, so there were few meaningful barriers to race mixing.[18] One historian estimates that in the seventeenth and early eighteenth-century Chesapeake region, more white women than black women gave birth to mixed-race children.[19] Ann Wall's case may have been emblematic. She was convicted in an Elizabeth City County, Virginia court for "keeping company with a negro." She and her two mixed-race children were bound to a planter in Norfolk County. If she ever returned to Elizabeth City County, she was to be banished to Barbados forever.[20]

Public concern with race mixing among the lower orders was not confined to the Chesapeake, however. David Lewis, a constable in colonial Haverford, Pennsylvania, for example, brought a black man and a white woman before the court for having produced a mixed-race child. The black man testified that the white woman enticed him and promised to marry him; she confessed to having made the promise. The unnamed woman received 21 lashes and the slave was admonished not to have anything more to do with white women "uppon paine of his life."[21] A Maryland law of 1728 that imposed the same servitude penalties on free black and mixed-race women who gave birth to children sired by white men as that imposed on white women who associated with black men was belated recognition that sex across the color line occurred in nearly every conceivable combination. Such laws stemmed but did not eradicate interracial sex or its consequences. The Maryland census of 1755 enumerated 3,592 mixed-race people, or 2.5 percent of the colony's population.[22] Sex across the color line was not rampant in the colonial era, but occurred with sufficient frequency to elicit public concern and governmental regulation.

Interpretations of the colonial era and its laws concerning interracial sex have cast the laws as measures designed to establish sexual barriers between black men and white women while leaving sex between white men and black women unsanctioned. Law created an asymmetric regime that, as Carter Woodson described it, left "women of color without protection against white men, who might use them for convenience."[23] Popular accounts hold that asymmetric legal treatment of interracial sex put in place in the eighteenth century led to asymmetric behavior in the nineteenth. Abolitionists, for example, portrayed the slave quarters as little more than a harem kept for the pleasure of dissipated and degenerate white men. An anonymous speaker at an Ohio Anti-Slavery Convention listed the many sins of slavery, including "lust emboldened by impunity; concubinage encouraged by premium."[24]

In recounting his experience to an English abolitionist, a Virginia field hand named Madison Jefferson told of "unbridled licentiousness" of planters and of black women "who refuse to submit themselves to the brutal desires of their owners, [and] are repeatedly whipt to subdue their virtuous repugnance."[25] J. W. Lindsay, a Tennessee slave, told of planter Ben Kidd, who was "desperate mean" and owned one slave woman that "he used whenever he saw fit." If any of his female slaves ever failed to submit, he made "nothing of knocking them right down" with his cane. Kidd was, according to Lindsay, the "worst man I ever saw."[26] Some white men surely preyed on slave women, while men like Virginia's William Byrd II, openly pursued slave and servant women alike rather indiscriminately and without legal consequences.[27] Sexual exploitation surely occurred on the nineteenth-century plantation.

Mid-twentieth-century interpretations, probably in response to abolitionist exaggeration, swung in the opposite direction and downplayed the extent of sexual assault without denying its existence. Kenneth Stampp, for example, contends that planters were not sexual predators; they were not even the principal sexual partners of slave women on the plantation.[28] Rather, it was the lower order of white men who resided on or near the plantations.[29] Like their colonial predecessors, late antebellum planters regularly complained of their overseers' and local white men's sexual escapades undermining slave discipline. Charles Manigault, for example, sometimes hired young men as assistant overseers on his Gowrie Plantation in the Georgia low country. By 1848 he expressed his dissatisfaction with most of them, not least because the young men's friends often came around for the opportunity to "slip off" with one of Manigault's female slaves.[30] Although sexual assault was not unheard of among the planter class, the plantation was "hardly ... the harem of abolitionist fancy," and the frequent charges that planters had their way with attractive young slave women were exaggerated and represented an "injustice to blacks as well as whites."[31] Stampp spoke for some of his generation of scholars when he wrote that when members of the planter class engaged sexually with slaves, it was mostly the "casual adventures of adolescents engaged in sexual experimentation."[32]

To many twenty-first-century scholars, earlier interpretations sound too much like the imaginings of middle-aged professors equating the actions of nineteenth-century planters with the "concupiscent larks" of college students.[33] The antebellum slave quarters was not the mid-twentieth-century fraternity house. For most modern historians, the archetypal interracial sexual relationship of the mid-nineteenth century is no longer Sally Hemings, but Celia. In 1850, Missourian Robert Newsom traveled from Callaway County to Audrain County to purchase Celia, a 14-year-old slave.[34] On the return trip, Newsom raped Celia. His sexual assaults continued over the next five years, and she bore at least two mixed-race children by him. When she could no longer bear the repeated abuse, she murdered Newsom. Although represented by three prominent local attorneys, Celia was convicted and hanged.

Modern interpretations hold that the Sally Hemingses, or those with enough agency to negotiate some of the terms of their bondage, were the rare exceptions. The best the Celias could hope for was to be left alone. More realistically, however, they could anticipate of life of ongoing physical and sexual abuse. Late twentieth-century interpretations hold that interracial sex occasionally involved asymmetrical exchange between slave and master, but was mostly exploitation "born of trauma, dependence, and constraint": interracial sex was rape—full stop.[35] Slave women presented "tempting prey," and accounts of consensual relationships between planter and slave are mere apologetics.[36] Bernie Jones speaks for many of his generation when he contends that "slave women were sacrificed" for the short-term sexual pleasures of white men and for the long-term value generated by the children they produced. The common wisdom, in fact, is that one of the motivations for sexual exploitation was the children it generated. *Partus sequitur ventrem* only encouraged the sexual exploitation of slave women because any planter who raped and impregnated his slave women added "at no additional cost" a mixed-race slave to work or sell for profit.[37] Among postmodernists, Celia's is a powerful narrative due to the clarity with which it pits the slave protagonist against the planter antagonist.

An Economic Approach to Interracial Sex

The economic approach to sex differs from the postmodern approach (and the abolitionist approach, for that matter) in that it finds less compelling narratives of power, assault, abuse, and exploitation than narratives of costs, incentives, opportunities, and constraints. The differences in these approaches are not trivial.[38] Because only a handful of studies have investigated the economics of sex inside slavery, it is useful to discuss some basics.[39]

An economic approach assumes that the preferences of whites and blacks over inter- and intraracial sex are determined exogenously (outside the model) by culture, religion, and other social, familial, and personal factors.[40] Some people will have stronger and others weaker preferences for sex generally, and within each group some will have preferences for intraracial sex while others will have preferences for interracial sex. When discussing preferences, to quote a famous dictum, *non est disputandum.*[41] To consider whether any sexual behavior is rational in the economic sense—cost-minimizing means necessary to achieve some well-defined ends—it is necessary to define the ends (benefits) of sex. Richard Posner labels the possible ends *procreative, hedonistic, sociable,* and *dominance.*[42] The *procreative* end needs no elaboration. The *hedonistic* end can either satisfy the prosaic "scratching an itch," or advance the more poetic "cultivation of the faculty of pleasure." The *sociable* objective is the use of sex to cement intimate bonds, such as sex within companionate marriage. And the *dominance* objective typically manifests itself as rape, in which the sexual aggressor expresses his or her physical dominance over the victim. In discussing sex on the plantation, postwar-era historians emphasized the *hedonistic* objective ("adolescent experimentation"); abolitionists and, more recently, postmodernists emphasize *dominance* (rape), but give the *procreative* (children as profit center) objective a prominent supporting role.

People also have limited resources—time, money, and the physical capacity for sex, among others. People also face different prices (costs) for inter- and intraracial sex. The price of sex generally includes the risks of acquiring a sexually transmitted disease, the risk of unwanted pregnancy, time, and any direct or indirect monetary expenses incurred in the pursuit of sex. In addition, there are social stigmas attached to certain kinds of sex; sex outside of marriage, for instance, is frowned on in some cultures, as is promiscuous behavior, homosexual sex, and so on.

Costs imposed on the planter for sex in the slave quarters emanated from three sources: the home, the slave quarters, and the community. At home, Mary Boykin Chestnut's oft-quoted assessment "any lady is ready to tell you who is the father of all the mulatto children in everybody's white household but her own" surely captures some measure of truth, but the evidence suggests that whites wives were not so obtuse.[43] Frederick Law Olmsted was taken aback by the alleged extent of interracial fraternizing, and one woman informed him that the effects of white men's sexual escapades in the slave quarters were most keenly felt by the South's white women. It dashed their hopes of "domestic happiness." The many divorce petitions from white women citing their husbands' infidelities with slaves attest to the household disruptions created by interracial sex on the plantation.[44] Short of divorce, sexual liaisons between planter and slave could not but infuriate white wives. Jealousy and strife surely adversely affected the philandering planters' home lives.

Sexual adventures, whether forced or consensual, also took a toll in the slave quarters, disrupting the slaves' private lives and reducing their productivity. Jealous white women, enraged by their husbands' infidelities, sometimes took revenge on the slave women involved.[45] Slave men, too, took revenge on sexual interlopers. Harriet Martineau discussed the case of two slaves burned alive outside Mobile, Alabama, for having avenged themselves of their planter's sexual assaults on their wives by killing the master's white children.[46] She recognized that this was an extreme case, but black men did strike back, sometimes violently, when the planters' depredations became intolerable. Recall, too, that Celia's case ended in the master's death at Celia's hand. Slave women were not without recourse as the victims of repeated abuse. Even historians willing to attribute much interracial sex as adolescent larks recognized that it required a "special variety of obtuseness" to overlook the psychological impact of sexual abuse on the slaves, which often became a "personal crisis of major proportions."[47] It could not but have negatively affected slave productivity.

Even planters who resisted sex in the quarters had to concern themselves with the activities of other white men in the neighborhood. Planters regularly instructed their overseers, for example, to resist the temptations of the slave quarters because fraternization diminished the overseer's authority and undermined discipline. Haller Nutt of Natchez, Mississippi instructed his overseers: "Above all things avoid all intercourse with negro women. It breeds more trouble, more neglect, more idleness, more rascality, more stealing & more lieing [*sic*] ... & more everything that is wrong on a plantation than all else put together."[48] Lapses in discipline might be the least of the planter's worries. One Georgia planter fumed that during a brief four-month tenure, his former overseer had transmitted a "highly virulent disease" to every slave woman on the plantation.[49]

Communities mattered, too, because neighbors established and enforced local behavioral norms and punished those who breached them.[50] Southerners' attitudes toward interracial sex followed from their dislike of blacks, their concerns over fornication generally, and their uneasiness with the disposition of mixed-race children.[51] The law held that the child's condition followed the mother's (*partus sequitur ventrem*), but pragmatically accepting a law and being comfortable with it are not the same. Interracial sex was frowned upon throughout the South and one cost of engaging in it was the "opprobrium heaped upon both parents and offspring."[52] The worst that discrete interracial fornicators might expect was the clucking of tongues among local gossips; those who openly violated the norm were infamous and not always accepted into polite society. In the small communities of the South it was difficult to keep secrets, and local whites knew who did and who did not fraternize with their slaves. Elite, land-holding planters rarely faced angry mobs, but laboring-class white men who openly cohabited with black women faced the prospect of organized violence by groups of men bent on upholding community norms.[53]

Finally, it must not be forgotten that one of the most significant costs of sex are the costs of children. Jones asserts that planter-on-slave rape generated "costless" children, but it is hard for any parent to conceive of such a thing as a costless child.[54] From the slave woman's perspective, pregnancy and childbirth in the nineteenth century was not without substantial risks. While White writes that the "jury will have to remain out" on the extent to which slave women practiced birth control and abortion, there is evidence that at least some slave women were familiar with natural abortifacients.[55] From the master's short-term perspective, pregnancy and nursing reduced the female slave's productivity. In the medium term, planters had to bear the costs of raising a child to the age at which she started to pay her own way. In the long term, the planter had to sort out the child's legal disposition. Southern law held that the child's status followed the mother's—*partus sequitur ventrem*—and some planters were comfortable with their mixed-race offspring serving in lifelong bondage.[56] Many were not, however, and some went to great lengths and bore substantial costs in efforts to manumit and provide for their enslaved mixed-race children. Thomas Wright, a planter in Campbell County, Virginia, bequeathed his house and all its furnishings to his slave mistress Sylvie and 370 acres of land to his mixed-race son Robert. John Stewart of Petersburg, Virginia, bequeathed his entire bank account ($19,500) to his mixed-race daughter. Philip Henshaw, of Essex County, Virginia had a daughter by a slave woman owned by another man. Henshaw purchased the daughter and bequeathed her half of his estate. Henshaw's sister was to receive the other half of his estate so long as she did not contest the will.[57]

Whether these men and others like them freed and provided for their children from reasons of conscience, guilt, or genuine affection, even their last acts were not costless. As they prepared for death, they wrestled with troubled consciences, unhappy families, and unsympathetic courts. White heirs regularly challenged wills that provided for slaves, a fact not lost on white men who went to extraordinary lengths in life to provide for their children after their deaths. In 1813, for instance, William Kendall petitioned the Virginia legislature asking to manumit his mixed-race son. Kendall felt "great concern for his [son's] future welfare and liberty," and was uneasy with the prospect of his being another man's slave. Troubled with deep concerns over their children's future welfare, men like Kendall could not have gone unconcernedly into the long good night.[58] Sharon Block advocates for a multiplicity of approaches in understanding sex and rape in early America even if doing so provides a "messier story than we may prefer."[59] An economic approach adds some useful complications and improves our thinking about sex on the plantation. The issue, of course, is whether the approach can explain the reality observed on the plantation.

Testing the Economic Approach

The economics of interracial sex generates a straightforward prediction: the higher the costs of interracial sex, the less likely its incidence. A higher price of sex does not, of course, preclude its occurrence, but it seems likely that interracial sex was subject to a downward sloping demand curve. A decline in the price will encourage increased consumption, but economists are often interested in how that increase can be decomposed into income (lower price is equivalent of increase in effective income) and substitution (lower price increases opportunity cost of consuming alternative goods) effects, which will depend on the relative strength of an individual's preferences for intra- and interracial sex. The historical evidence points toward interracial sex as reasonably own-price elastic and an inferior good, which implies that the substitution effect of lower prices of interracial sex would overwhelm the income effect.[60] Rothman's study of sexual behaviors in antebellum Virginia reveal men ready to cross the sexual color line when African-American prostitutes were more readily available than white prostitutes, but his discussion suggests that the elite were less likely to do so or, at least, they were less willing to be seen doing so.[61] An exception, of course, was the *plaçage* tradition among the very wealthy in antebellum New Orleans. The bottom line, however, is that because different men had different sex drives and faced different opportunities and costs, they engaged in different amounts of interracial sex.[62] Sex was not free, not even sex taken by force from those with a limited capacity to resist.

The federal decennial censuses of 1850 and 1860 can be explored to better understand sex on southern farms and plantations. Each census collected and reported detailed information on the age, sex, and race of slaves on each slave holding unit. The issue is how to measure race mixing. The census, of course, provides no direct measure of sex on the plantation, but affords an indirect measure. Sex produces offspring with some regularity, so a reasonable proxy of recent interracial sex is the presence of young mixed-race children on the plantation. The empirical problem is that children appear only sometimes after sex and then only with a lag. Moreover, plantations were fluid environments—slaves were born, died, bought, and sold; overseers came and went; planters and their sons, nephews, and neighbors altered their behaviors over their life cycles; and so on—so any proxy should focus on a reasonably brief period. The measure adopted here is the presence of a mixed-race child two years of age or younger, which is effectively a proxy measure of the occurrence of interracial sex in the previous 33 months.[63]

Holding all else constant, the variables most likely to correlate with race mixing are the size, structure, and location of the plantation or other slave holding. The size of the slave holding may have offsetting effects. Richard Steckel, for example, posits that amalgamation was negatively related to the size of the slave holding, because personal interactions between whites and blacks decreased with plantation size. With the exception of domestic servants, planters owning dozens, even hundreds of slaves may have had little personal interaction with them. Moreover, the opportunity costs of potentially disruptive sexual relations between the races were greater on larger holdings because per capita slave productivity was higher on larger plantations.[64] On the other hand, economic theories of mating and marriage suggest that the probabilities of finding an acceptable sexual match increases (at a decreasing rate, perhaps) with the size of the available pool of potential matches. With more sexually mature women from which to choose, a larger plantation held the potential for assortative sexual matching not available on small plantations with fewer potential matches.

There is no best way to control for the effects of plantation size. Steckel, for instance, included a linear term (number of slaves) in his regression, but there is no a priori reason why the incidence of interracial sex should increase linearly in plantation size. If the opportunity cost-productivity effect mattered, it seems reasonable to segregate plantations into the productivity classes identified in the economics of slavery literature (1–5 slaves, 6–15, 16–50, and 51 or more). Such a classification also captures any potential nonlinearity in assortative matching, although other specifications might also capture nonlinearities. Preliminary analysis suggests nonlinear effects and Appendix 4.1 provides the details of the empirical analysis, including alternative specifications of plantation size, as well as the effects of other variables included in the regressions.

Using the same productivity-based plantation size categories as Fogel and Engerman, Figure 4.1 presents the unconditional probabilities of observing a

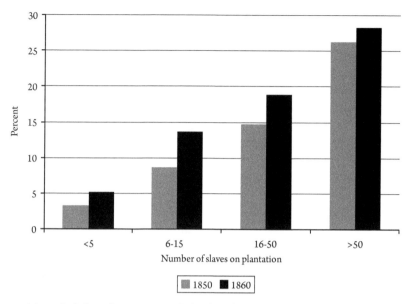

Figure 4.1 Probability of Census Marshals Identifying a Mixed-Race Infant on a Plantation. Sources: Author's calculations from data in Menard et al., Public Use Microdata Samples.

mixed-race child on farms and plantations of different sizes. In 1850, for instance, census marshals identified mixed-race children two years of age or younger on 3.3 percent of southern farms with less than six slaves. The proportion steadily increased in the number of slaves on a plantation; 8.7 percent of plantations with 6 to 15 slaves had a mixed-race infant; 14.8 percent on plantations with 16 to 50 slaves did; and 26.3 percent of plantations with more than 50 slaves. Census marshals in 1860 were more likely to count some light-skinned individuals as mixed-race than they had been in 1850, so the percentage of farms on which marshals identified a mixed-race child increased across all farm sizes, but the same pattern emerged a decade later. Marshals identified a mixed-race child on 5.5 percent of small slaveholding, whereas they identified a mixed-race child on 28.4 percent of the largest plantations.

The data are consistent with economic models of assortative mating markets.[65] This does not imply that white men searched for like-minded slave women with whom they might establish a household and exploit any advantages in the household division of labor. Rather, it recognizes that sexual attraction is idiosyncratic, and an individual's preferences are more likely to be met when the pool of potential sexual matches increases. Even sexual aggressors are presumably more likely to become aggressive when a close, but unaccommodating, match presents itself. Absent documentary information on sexual race mixing on plantations, historians are left to search for indirect measures to understand interracial sex on the plantation. The presence of mixed-race children is one measure, albeit an imperfect one. Nevertheless, mixed-race children were more likely to be identified by census marshals on larger plantations, and the likelihood nearly doubled at each step in plantation size category. Some female slaves may have benefitted from the greater anonymity afforded by a large plantation, but it appears that local white men—whether planters, overseers, or neighbors remains unclear—were more likely to find an acceptable sexual match on a large plantation.

W.E.B. Du Bois described interracial sex on the plantation as "stark, ugly, painful, beautiful," which is a fairly timeless characterization of sex generally.[66] It is too convenient to characterize sex on the plantation as being of one type. Sex was complicated on the nineteenth-century plantation, just as it is complicated in the twenty-first-century suburbs. Sex was not always rape, it was not always the physical manifestation of love, and it was not always the consequence of the sexual experimentations of young men. Sex on the plantation was "characteristic of any commodity where subject women are controlled by men . . . [who are] neither entirely good nor entirely bad."[67]

Interracial sex was sometimes an expression of dominance and unequal power. It surely was in Celia's case. But it was not always thus. Though Harriet Jacobs's tale is cast as one of slave owner sexual aggression, a critical element of her life's story is that she was able to deflect the unwanted advances of her owner for years before she escaped.[68] Without minimizing the emotional stress of nearly constant threat, hers is an expression of slave agency, imperfect as it was. Was interracial sex sometimes had within a long-term relationship? Surely it was. The thousands of wills in which planters directed the manumission of their slave mistresses and their children with provisions for their legacy stands as testimony of love or commitment or guilt, or something of all three.[69] Interracial sex was sometimes about young white men exploring their sexuality. And it was also about young black women exploring theirs. It is a happy state of affairs that slavery studies are in flux. On one side are scholars who maintain that slaves had some agency and some measure of control over their lives. On the other are scholars who maintain that slaves, especially slave women, were powerless against the onslaught of white male dominance. These approaches establish the boundaries of inquiry, but both surely disguise the reality of the plantation. Relations, especially sexual relations, were almost certainly more complex than either approach posits. Economics does not always provide the desired answers—the sources of people's preferences are often taken as given and left unexplored—but in the case of interracial sex on the plantation it offers a new level of nuance to existing historical interpretations. People respond to incentives, regardless of whether they consciously acknowledge it, and any discussion of interracial sex demands a careful accounting of the costs and benefits of engaging in it to both parties.

Mixed-Race Advantages on the Plantation

Even as a youngster Frederick Douglass recognized preferential treatment afforded mixed-race slaves, especially when the mixed-race slave was the planter's offspring. The slave known as William Wilks on Colonel Edward Lloyd's plantation was a "fine looking man . . . about as white as anyone on the plantation." He bore, to Douglass's eye, a striking resemblance to Colonel Lloyd, who granted him freedoms not enjoyed by any of his other slaves.[70] Such preferences were not lost on travelers either. One Englishman noted that quadroons were generally selected to serve as domestics. They were more attractive and "their constitutions were too delicate" for field labor.[71]

Sometimes the link between race mixing and preferential treatment of the delicate mixed-race female was obvious to everyone involved. In 1854, the mixed-race slave Dolly was taken on as the 26-year-old bachelor Louis Manigault's cook. Manigault's father still ran the family's plantations, but Louis wintered on the low-country rice plantation and split his summers between an inland plantation and the family home in Charleston, always with Dolly in tow. She remained Louis's cook until he married in 1857, at which time she was sent away to cook at the family's low-country plantation despite her own and the overseer's protestations that her delicate constitution was ill-suited to the low-country summer climate. Louis's marriage did not appear to permanently disrupt his relations with Dolly, however. In April 1859, Charles Manigault informed his son that he was allowed only one servant at the crowded Charleston summer residence. Charles presumed "no doubt [it] will be 'Dolly' as She can wash, & do other things for you."[72] It is not hard to conjure up what those other things might be, but Charles's attitude toward mixed-race slaves suggests that he did not disapprove of Louis's presumed dalliances.

Charles Manigault believed that mixed-race slaves should be treated differently. He considered them a third caste, neither black nor white, so long as they kept their distance from blacks. And so long as they carried themselves with "respectful Deportment," Charles Manigault provided them with some skill training and they generally avoided the most onerous tasks and field work.[73] Charles's wife, probably not without reason, discouraged the preferential treatment shown mixed-race slaves, even mixed-race men. Like Mary Chestnut, Elizabeth Heyward Manigault saw mixed-race people as a scourge on the honor of the South's black women. During one of the family's extended European vacations, Elizabeth would not even allow her son to remain in a Paris school that admitted two mixed-race Cuban children.

The place of the light-complected mixed-race slave on the plantation has been reinterpreted several times since the nineteenth century. Contemporary observers remarked on the preferences shown and demanded by mixed-race slaves. John

Benwell observed that quadroon slaves were generally employed as domestics because their constitutions were too delicate for field labor.[74] Frances Kemble's exchange with one of the slaves on her husband's Georgia low-country rice plantation reveals how mixed-race slaves attempted to use their heritage to their advantage. Kemble recounted:

> The mulatto woman, Sally, accosted me again to-day, and begged that she might be put to some other than field labor. Supposing she felt herself unequal to it, I asked her some questions, but the principal reason she urged for her promotion to some less laborious kind of work was, that hoeing in the field was so hard on her on *account of her color*,'and she therefore petitions to be allowed to learn a trade. I was much puzzled at this reason for her petition, but was presently made to understand that, being a mulatto, she considered field labor a degradation; her white bastardy appearing to her a title to consideration in my eyes . . . the faintest admixture of white blood in their black veins appears at once, by common consent of their own race, to raise them in the scale of humanity (emphasis in original).[75]

Unlike her neighbor Charles Manigault, who favored his mixed-race slaves, Kemble was not swayed by Sally's argument, mostly because Sally's father had been a low-class white man hired to work on the plantation. As the daughter of a laboring white man, Sally was not deserving of special dispensation. Yet another pair of mixed-race children elicited a more compassionate response from Kemble. "Because of their color," she wrote, "it is almost impossible to resist the impression of unfitness of these two forlorn young creatures for the life of coarse labor and dreadful degradation to which they are destined."[76] The preferences shown them followed, according to John D. Paxton, a Virginia minister, because mixed-race slaves were the "neatest, the best looking and, for the most part, the most intelligent and active."[77] Paxton's observation is consistent with white attitudes toward light-skinned, mixed-race peoples.

Among twentieth-century scholars tales of mixed-race advantages fell from favor, if mixed-race peoples were discussed at all. Frazier's hostility to the so-called mulatto elite is evident, though he acknowledged that white planters *sometimes* showed their mixed-race concubines and light-skinned offspring some advantages.[78] Blasingame's and Gutman's studies of black folkways and families contain few mentions of mixed-race people and offer no discussion of mixed-race advantages. Jordan and Genovese dismissed them altogether. Jordan contended that "mulattoes do not seem to have been accorded higher status than Negroes in actual practice."[79] More colorfully, Genovese wrote that "however much the quadroon and mulatto servants . . . dominated the Big House of legend, they did not dominate the Big House of reality."[80] A preference for mixed-race may have developed in Charleston and New Orleans, but by Genovese's telling, it did not translate outside a small circle of urban sophisticates.

Systematic evidence collected as part of the economics of slavery project reveal the merits of each side of the debate. Using the records of New Orleans slave sales, the results in Figure 4.2 reveal modest advantages shown light-skinned, predominantly mulatto and quadroon men. While light-skinned men represented 10.2 percent of the sample, they made up 13.8 percent of semiskilled slaves, 16.7 percent of artisans, 20.6 percent of domestics, and just 9.7 percent of field hands.[81] Similarly, light-skinned females represented 13.5 percent of females put on the New Orleans auction block, but they made up 22.9 percent of domestics sold. Light-skinned men were overrepresented in semiskilled, skilled, and domestic service and light-skinned women were overrepresented in domestic service, but in no case did mixed-race people represent anything close to a majority of the more advantageously employed. Still, the proportion of mixed-race domestics was twice their proportion of the overall slave population. It would have been hard for contemporary observers not to have taken notice.

One problem with this analysis of the New Orleans slave sale data is that it reports only raw averages and fails to control for other features. Regression analysis of the same data shows that light-skinned, mixed-race slaves were not overrepresented in domestic service once other slave and slave-owner characteristics are controlled for.[82] Working with a sample of former slaves who reported their slave occupations when they crossed the lines and enlisted in the Union Army, Robert Margo found that while light-skinned slaves made up just less than 10 percent

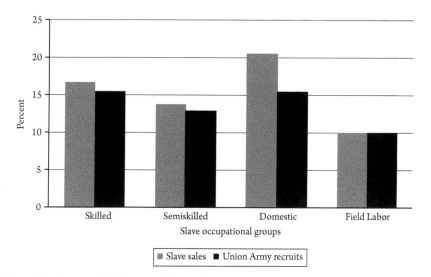

Figure 4.2 Percent of Male, Mixed-Race Slaves By Occupational Group on Southern Plantations. Sources: Olson, "Occupational Structure," and Margo, "Civilian Occupations."

of enlistments, they represented more than 15.5 percent of skilled recruits and domestics, and 13 percent of semiskilled recruits.[83] Logit regressions that control for characteristics of the former slaves, year and region of enlistment, and local crop mix reveal that (all else constant) light-skinned recruits were 3.5 percent more likely to be domestics, 3.1 percent more likely to have had skill training in slavery, and 7.6 percent less likely to have been a field hand in slavery. Potential selection bias is likely to understate the extent to which light-skinned recruits represent the underlying slave population from which they were drawn. Recruits tended to be young, and many skills were acquired with age; recruits had to pass a physical exam and able-bodied slave men were more likely to have been assigned field work; and well-treated slaves may have been less likely to cross the lines and join the Union Army.

Eugene Genovese downplayed or dismissed mixed-race preferences, but contemporary observations and modern statistical analysis point toward modestly favored treatment. Planters preferred mixed-race men and women as house servants, and gave them more skill training. Mixed-race slaves were more likely than blacks to receive some education, to eat from the Big House's kitchen, to be better clothed and shod, and have greater freedom of movement on and off the plantation.[84] Frederick Law Olmsted was so impressed with the responsibilities heaped on one mixed-race driver on a rice plantation that it warranted description. The driver supervised the plantation's skilled slaves, carried the keys to the storehouses, and rationed provisions to the other slaves. In some respects his authority was nearly as great as the overseer's.[85] As Toplin notes, the mixed-race slave's significance in antebellum plantation life "relates not to their numbers but to the special attention" given them.[86] Many southern whites preferred mixed-race slaves and provided them with opportunities not given to black men and women. The preferences shown light-skinned, mixed-race slaves on the plantation carried over into freedom. It was these same advantaged former slaves who emerged as leaders of the African-American community in the antebellum and postbellum eras.

Color and Slave Prices

For an economist the proof of a preference is revealed in a willingness to pay to indulge that preference. The issue, then, is whether white preferences for mixed-race slaves showed up in slave prices. Four independent econometric studies of sale prices include controls for racial background and color, but have not focused on them. Using data on slave sales in New Orleans between 1804 and 1862, Laurence Kotlikoff finds that light-complected females sold for higher than average prices; light-skinned men also sold for a premium, albeit smaller than the female premium.[87] In revisiting these estimates, he finds that the female mixed-race premium peaked between 1810 and 1819, when it reached 19 percent. A 14 percent premium, relative to the price of a dark-skinned slave, persisted into the 1820s and declined thereafter.[88] A subsequent study using the same data confirms Kotlikoff's basic result: over the era of United States control of Louisiana, light-skinned female and male slaves sold at a modest premium in the New Orleans market over otherwise comparable dark-skinned slaves.[89]

Shawn Cole investigates the New Orleans slave market between 1770 and 1820, during which administrative control over the city changed hands three times.[90] Because the Spanish, French, and Americans adopted different rules governing the conditions of slavery, it is possible that slave prices may have differed across regimes. Cole's findings are remarkable in that they reveal a persistent 25 to 30 percent price premium for light-skinned males, relative to the comparison group of dark-skinned females. Because Cole controls for and finds a premium for the male sex generally, the light-skinned male coefficient is capturing a mostly color effect. A light-skin, female price premium is evident, but it is considerably smaller than that for males.

Cole's and Kotlikoff's findings counter the traditional explanation that the preference for mixed-race female domestics followed from the sexual preferences of male planters. The data do not support it. If sex were the motivation, the mixed-race preference, however large, would have been greatest for sexually mature women but not old women. When the antebellum New Orleans sample is divided into three groups—girls less than 12 years, women 12 to 40 years, and women over 40 years—on the hypothesis that planters would not find the young and the old attractive sexual partners, we find that the color preference was most pronounced for the young and the old.[91] Sexually mature, prime-age, light-skinned females were *not* preferred as domestics. On reflection, this is not as incongruous a result as it may first appear. Slave owners regularly brought in young slave girls as playmates and teens as nannies for their young daughters, and older women to cook and clean. Charles Manigault, for example, made a gift of a "fine Mulatto woman" Martha to his son Louis to care for Louis's newborn son. Louis was quickly impressed with her abilities as seamstress and pastry cook, and she displayed proper deference for one so smart.[92] Slave owners were governed by the same prejudices observed among the general public, so it is not surprising that they brought light-skinned and mixed-race girls and women into their homes as domestics, cooks, and personal servants.

Nineteenth-century observers commented on sales of light-skinned, mixed-race people. Edward Sullivan, for example, reported that quadroons regularly fetched $1,000 or $1,500 at auction; fancy girls fetched a "fancy price."[93] But just as people who openly engaged in interracial sex risked opprobrium, slave holders who bought and sold slaves with fair complexions risked their reputations. For many contemporaries the sale of fair-skinned, mixed-race people was one of the more disgraceful aspects of slavery. Sullivan observed that "although it is not actually worse to buy or sell a man or woman who is nearly white, than it is to sell one some shades darker, yet there is something in it more revolting to one's feelings."[94] Even hardened slave traders were sometimes reluctant to buy and sell the fairest mixed-race slaves. In 1821 the public auction of a fair-skinned woman and her children scandalized Louisville, Kentucky. No one would bid for them because, as a local newspaper explained, there was "something so revolting to the feelings at the sight."[95] Mixed-race slaves sold at a premium, but only so long as their African heritage was obvious. Experienced traders found the nearly white slave nearly impossible to sell, partly because few Southerners wanted to own a slave as fair as themselves and partly because nearly white slaves stood a better chance of legally challenging their enslavement or running away and making space for themselves in the anonymity of a city.

It is not unreasonable to conjecture that the price premium paid for light-skinned mixed-race women originated in sexual motives. Popular accounts focus on the sale of mixed-race "fancy girls" to serve as concubines and prostitutes.[96] There is probably some truth in the popular accounts, but Kotlikoff's finding that the largest percentage premiums were paid for girls under 12 years and women over 40 suggests that the premium was not driven solely or even mostly by the demand for mixed-race concubines and prostitutes. Rather, it may have been driven by free African Americans purchasing family members.[97] The light-color premium was highest when free African Americans were among the most active buyers. The motive underlying the fair-female premium was that of light-skinned men buying their light-skinned daughters and wives. There may have been a sexual component to the purchase of wives and girlfriends, but it was not the sexual motive ascribed to buyers in popular accounts.

Conclusions

Light-skinned, mixed-race slave men and women routinely received privileges and favors withheld from black slaves. Mixed-race slave John Izard, for example, was trained as a carpenter and was the most favored slave on the Gowrie plantation in the 1840s and 1850s. He was allowed to travel alone on errands between the plantation and Savannah, eight miles down river; he was paid cash for extra work; he was trusted with the keys to the building in which the plantation's rice threshing machine was kept. But possibly more than any other privilege, John Izard had the privilege of a surname, which was an unusual symbol of respect paid by a low-country planter to one of his slaves.[98] John Izard leveraged his talent and his acquired skills to obtain privileges unavailable to other slaves, just as Sally Hemings may have leveraged the sexual favors she bestowed on Thomas Jefferson into life in the Big House for herself and eventual freedom for her children.

History has not been particularly kind to the privileged mixed-race slaves who curried favor. The work of the plantations would not have proceeded so efficiently in the absence of the special privileges afforded the domestics and cooks, the carpenters and the drivers, the animal tenders and the coopers. To some, the privileged mixed-race slave is the epitome of Harriet Beecher Stowe's Uncle Tom. He was too deferential, too obedient, too quick to curry favor, and too ready to abandon his black brothers and sisters to advance his own place on the plantation. But William Dusinberre's account of plantation life reveals a world in which the privileges bestowed on favored slaves were impermanent and often fleeting.[99] A servant house built especially for the plantation's domestic servants apart from the field hands' quarters was about all that separated the privileged from the unprivileged. Cooks and coopers alike were regularly ordered into the fields, sometimes because they fell from favor and sometimes just simply to get the harvest in on time. In other cases, privilege accrued to those who simply outlived their peers—and their usefulness in the fields. The job of overseer's cook or plantation nurse usually fell to an older female, sometimes light-skinned, sometimes not, who rated as a quarter-hand or less in the fields. The line dividing field hand and privileged slave was fine indeed. Privilege accrued not to those fortunate enough to have acquired a skill, or to those who adopted the planters' culture and speech patterns. It accrued to those with leadership abilities, and to those who survived long enough to take on some responsibilities on the plantation. Skin color and ancestry surely influenced skill acquisition and longevity itself, so they are not unconnected. The evidence of job assignment and slave prices reveal a preference for mixed-race slaves, but it was not the case that light-skinned slaves worked the house and dark-skinned slaves worked the fields. There were dark nannies and light field hands. But when privileges were granted, they were more often granted to the light-skinned slaves.

5

Finding Freedom

Frederick Douglass's owner, the shopkeeper Thomas Auld, hired out Douglass to a local farmer for the 1835 season. After having spent much of his youth in Baltimore under the direction of Thomas Auld's sister-in-law, Douglass bristled at the harsh conditions and hard labor on the sandy soils of Maryland's eastern shore. Douglass and four fellow slaves hatched an escape plan, but he was betrayed practically on the eve of the attempt by one of his own. As the members of the white posse were taking the would-be runaways to the local jail, the elderly mother of the planter to whom Douglass had been hired accused him of being the ringleader. "You devil! You yellow devil!" she shouted, "It was you that put into the heads of Henry and John to run away. But for *you*, you *long legged yellow devil*, Henry and John would never have thought of running away."[1] Old Mrs. Freeland's assessment—that only the yellow devil could have hatched an escape plot—demonstrated white concerns with mixed-race people generally, and intelligent, literate mixed-race slaves more specifically. Douglass was the instigator, but Mrs. Freeland did not know that and because the slaves were savvy enough to have destroyed their forged passes when they saw trouble coming, there was no proof of the conspiracy or Douglass's instigation of it.

The other slaves' owners retrieved their slaves from the county jail soon thereafter, but not before slave traders had put the fear of sale south to a rice, sugar, or cotton planter into the conspirators' heads. Thomas Auld let Douglass cool his heels in the jail for a week while he struggled with what to do with his increasingly troublesome slave. Auld considered selling Douglass south, and was probably encouraged to do so by his domineering, ill-humored wife. But Auld made a different choice. He sent Douglass back to Baltimore and promised him his freedom at age 25 if he stayed out of trouble and worked diligently at a trade in the meantime. By Douglass's account, Auld was convinced that he would lose his slave either way. He could profit by the loss and sell Douglass south, or he could follow his conscience and hope that the promise of freedom in exchange for good behavior would redirect Douglass's energies long enough that Douglass's departure would not be a total loss. Like many of his contemporaries, Thomas Auld used the carrot of future freedom when the stick of punishment seemed unlikely to properly motivate his slaves. It was no coincidence that the medium-complected, mixed-race Douglass was offered the carrot rather than threatened by the stick. Color factored into the selection of slaves for manumission.

Color also influenced which slaves ran and how masters dealt with run-aways. Mixed-race slaves were more likely than blacks to run, and slave owners offered rewards for the recovery of runaways commensurate with the mixed-race slaves' greater market value, but the greater rewards offered for the recovery of mixed-race runaways did not differentially improve the likelihood of having a mixed-race slave returned. Light-complected, skilled, and literate slaves were better positioned to negotiate the obstacles standing between a would-be run-away and freedom. Light-skinned, skilled, and literate runaways were also in a more favorable position to take advantage of the opportunities open to slaves achieving freedom.

Whether through manumission or escape, the evidence makes it clear that mixed-race slaves were more likely than their black brethren to achieve free-dom. Whereas just 10.4 percent of the South's slaves were of mixed race in 1860, 40.8 percent of the slave South's free African Americans were.[2] Where vibrant free African-American communities emerged in the South before the Civil War—mostly in cities such as New Orleans, Charleston, Richmond, and Baltimore—the communities were decidedly mixed. New Orleans' free com-munity was 78 percent mixed in 1860; Charleston's was 84 percent mixed, and Richmond's was 43 percent. Subsequent chapters investigate the relative condi-tion of black and mixed-race people in freedom. This chapter investigates how that hard-won freedom was achieved by a lucky few.

Color and Manumission

In 1778, Virginian Landon Carter confided to his diary that "slaves are devils, and to make them otherwise than slaves will be to set devils free."[3] In this Carter's thinking paralleled Thomas Jefferson's, who famously compared slavery to hold-ing a wolf by the ears.[4] Not much good would come to the slave owning class from holding on *or* letting go. Other champions of freedom were equally loathe to manumit slaves: John Marshall manumitted only one of his 90 slaves; George Mason, who spoke out against the continuation of slavery at the Constitutional Convention, never manumitted a single slave; and Patrick Henry's will allowed his wife, if she saw fit after his passing, to manumit just two of his 100 slaves. The con-tradiction of slave owners as champions of liberty was not lost on contemporaries.

Samuel Johnson famously pondered: "How is it that we hear the loudest yelps for liberty among the drivers of negroes?"[5]

But prominent, much-studied men were not alone in their concerns with manumission. Nearly every state that allowed slavery at some point, north or south, imposed various restrictions on the slave owners' freedom to manumit. Some states allowed manumission only by special legislative enactment, which, in South Carolina after 1800, was almost never granted. Others, like Maryland, raised few barriers. Most states fell somewhere in between. Table 5.1 provides selected state regulations and limitations on manumission. Age restrictions were common, as were requirements that the newly freed slave emigrate from the state.

Table 5.1 Manumission Restrictions in Select Southern States

State	Year	Eligible ages	Security bonds	Forced emigration	Emigration exceptions
Maryland	1750	<50 years	no	no	n/a
	1796	< 45 years	no	no	n/a
Virginia	1782	18–45 females 21–45 males			
	1806			yes	none
	1815			yes	merit
	1837			yes	good behavior
	1849	no age limit			
North Carolina	1741	no age limit		yes	merit
	1777			no	n/a
	1801		$250		
	1831		$1000	yes	merit
South Carolina	1722	no age limit		yes	none
	1735			yes	legislature
Tennessee	1801		variable		
	1831			yes	none
	1842		$500	yes	merit
	1849			yes	none
Louisiana	1804	18–45 females 21–45 males			
	1830		$1000	yes	merit
	1852			yes	none
	1857			yes	jury

Source: From information reported in Klebaner, "American Manumission Laws."

Equally common, however, were laws allowing for exceptions to the emigration mandate, and the available evidence suggests that exceptions were freely made where allowed.[6]

Table 5.1 also reveals that southern states revisited and tinkered with their manumission laws. In 1806 Virginia, for example, required that manumitted slaves emigrate from the state within 12 months of receiving their freedom. No exceptions were anticipated. In 1815 the legislature amended the law. Freed slaves still had to emigrate within a year, but might be granted an exception if the ex-slave petitioner could demonstrate some meritorious act to the legislature. In 1837 exceptions could be granted by county courts if the petitioner provided evidence of past good behavior. The right to remain was made conditional, as well, on continued good behavior. Tennessee, alternatively, required immediate emigration, and there was only a brief regime between 1842 and 1849 when exceptions could be granted.

With manumission, Southerners walked the fine line between the libertarian right to own and dispose of property and the conservative impulse to regulate. The Supreme Court of the United States pronounced on this in 1834, when Justice Thompson wrote that as a "general proposition" an owner of property was "at liberty to renounce his right to it, either absolutely or in any modified manner he may think proper."[7] That is, the right to abandon property existed without explicit sanction at law, but the right could be denied by legislation. And states legislated extensively on the practice of manumission. Why? States have a deep and abiding interest in the composition of their citizenry. Just as that concern now provides a justification for immigration controls, the state's interest in the nineteenth century provided a justification for regulated manumission. Manumission implied, as the Tennessee high court acknowledged in 1834, that the state was "adopting into the body politic a new member," which was a "vastly important measure in every community."[8] So while slave owners might retain a right to manumit, that right was not absolute. In most places, an act of manumission could be consummated only with the assent of the community, typically through the agency of the legislature or the court.[9]

States employed their regulatory police powers to ensure that unproductive slaves, whether due to age or other infirmity, were not abandoned and left for taxpayer support.[10] But concerns with infirm slaves feeding at the public trough appear to have been a minor contemporary concern. Southerners expressed deeper—if less justified—concerns, including the social ills that would arise from perceived free African-American sloth and criminality, the potential for free African Americans to make their still-enslaved kith and kin restive, and fear that free African Americans might openly incite insurrection.[11] But Jefferson may have captured one of his generation's principal concerns with the practice when he wrote that manumission, absent removal of the newly freed African American "beyond the reach of [race] mixture," was anathema because the races would not long remain pure.[12] Race mixing remained a perennial concern. Colonization, much discussed but never garnering broad support, offered a way for manumission opponents to reconcile black slavery, manumission, and white racial purity. Though whites might be favorably disposed toward mixed-race individuals, they did not encourage race mixing itself.

A slave society's approach to manumission speaks to a broader understanding of the nature of its slavery, because the terms and conditions by which individuals passed from chattel property to personhood speak to the condition of slavery. It speaks to whether slavery was considered a permanent or temporary condition; whether it was heritable; whether slaves might transition into personhood or citizenship. Manumission was therefore not an act but a process, "and one laden with significance" for those slaves fortunate enough to achieve it.[13] For the slave, manumission might arrive by deed, by will, by purchase by friend or family, or by self-purchase. A multitude of factors such as sex, age, urbanization, and the local or regional profitability of slavery all influenced manumission. Table 5.2 presents information from a representative sample of manumission studies on the characteristics of freed slaves. Most slaves attained freedom between 14 and 45 years of age; the majority were female; mixed-race slaves were overrepresented, as were skilled urban slaves. The available data makes it hard to generalize on self-purchase. The characteristics of manumitted slaves reveal something about contemporary beliefs toward the worthiness of certain individuals for freedom.

Traditional portrayals of manumission cast it as an act of benevolence, mercy, or conscience.[14] Modern portrayals, even among historians, begin from the premise that manumission served to support, rather than undermine, the peculiar institution.[15] Steven Whitman and Eva Sheppard Wolf, for example, contend that manumission was the product of ongoing negotiations between slaves and slave owners concerning the terms under which slaves would labor and owners would direct.[16] Manumission served slavery because the ability to manumit inhered great power in the master—the power to set a slave free as well as the power to hold the slave in bondage. Manumission served slave owners because it cleared a path to freedom in return for the slave's obedience, diligence, and good behavior. Manumission, in other words, provided masters negotiating leverage because owners ultimately held the keys to freedom. Holding out the possibility of freedom provided slaves with incentives to do as instructed. From the individual slave's perspective, the master was the monopoly seller of manumission.[17]

Slaves actively negotiated several dimensions of their employment, including the terms by which they might achieve freedom.[18] In her study of Surinamese manumission records, Rosemary Brana-Shute finds evidence that slaves were active participants in and contributors to their conditions of labor and paths to freedom.[19] Manumission required negotiations that balanced the desires of

Table 5.2 Characteristics of Manumitted Slaves in the New World[a]

Place	Dates	Age (average)	Female %	Mixed-race %	Urban %	Skilled %	Self-purchase	Sample size
New Orleans	1770–1820	20	63%	39%	76%	24%	30%	4,060
New Orleans	1827–1846	young	68	over	n/a	n/a	n/a	1,770
South Carolina	1737–1785	adult	66	33	n/a	n/a	28	379
Virginia*	1782–1806	26	half	n/a	n/a	n/a	8	n/a
Virginia†	1782–1806	33	50	25	n/a	n/a	n/a	421
Virginia‡	1795–1865	26	45	26	13	n/a	n/a	863
Suriname	1760–1826	young	63	60	over	over	n/a	1,346
Curaçao	1740–1830	n/a	60	54	n/a	n/a	n/a	n/a
Argentina	1776–1810	14–45	59	49	n/a	n/a	60	1,356

Notes: [a] over=overrepresented relative to the relevant characteristic among the overall slave population. Sources: New Orleans (1770–1820): Cole, "Capitalism and Freedom"; New Orleans (1782–1806): Kotlikoff and Rupert, "Manumission of Slaves"; South Carolina: Olwell, "Becoming Free"; Virginia* (1782–1806): Wolf, "Manumission and the Two-Race System"; Virginia† (1782–1806): Babcock, "Manumission in Vigirnia"; Virginia‡ (1795–1865): see Appendix 5.2; Suriname: Brana-Shute, "Sex and Gender"; Curaçao: Klooster, "Manumission in an Entrepôt"; Argentina: Johnson, "Manumission in Colonial Buenos Aries."

slaves, slave owners, and their families.[20] Slaves wanted their freedom; masters wanted productive workers. Promises of freedom might encourage productivity. At the same time, slaves desired family stability, while masters were concerned with legacies and bequests to children and grandchildren. A slave owner might view manumission as a mechanism of labor control, but was forced to consider how manumission might alter the family dynamic—both his own and that of the slave's—over the longer term. Manumission involved, not surprisingly, a complicated economic calculation.

Common forms of negotiated manumission in the Chesapeake region were delayed manumission and term slavery. Delayed manumission was as it sounds: the slave was promised freedom at some future date, presumably in return for continued good behavior and diligent service. A deed of manumission was filed with the county court specifying the future date of manumission. The delay varied from a few months to several years. Some manumission deeds put off freedom until the slave reached his or her majority (21 for men, 18 for women). Some wills released the slave only after the death of the manumitter's spouse or other heirs. One study of wills and deeds from Virginia between 1782 and 1806 found that the average delay (when a delay was specified) was nine years, but ranged between one and 31 years.[21]

Term slavery operated differently—a slave owner sold his or her slave to another, but the bill of sale specified that the slave would be freed after a certain term of good service. Term slavery also served to *support* rather than weaken slavery. Term sales, like delayed manumission, were made conditional on good behavior, diligent effort, and not running away, practices that benefitted the manumitter as much as the slave. In 1805, when Virginia's legislature contemplated restricting manumission, Richard Drummond Bayly raised the rhetorical question: "Will not such a law make servants relax in their endeavour to please when they know that the great Reward which probably prompts them to the faithful discharge of their duty can never be bestowed upon them?"[22] Bayly feared not just the dissipation of effort, but of the increased threat of insurrection once slaves learned that one door to liberty had been slammed shut.

If slavery was social and civic death, manumission gave social, if not civic, life. Because the manumitted slave was transformed from chattel property to legal person, it is almost certain that society was selective about who might be granted personhood: the productive, the beautiful, and the fair-skinned all seem likely candidates. Whether these were the groups so favored is an empirical question.

Agency, Incentives, and the Economics of Manumission

Manumission in the Upper South expanded dramatically in the immediate post-Revolutionary era. Estimates of manumissions vary widely, but the median estimate of 18,000 freed between 1782 and 1795 in Virginia alone is defensible, given the available evidence.[23] In their explanations of the large-scale manumission of slaves in the post-Revolutionary Upper South, historians have attributed to slave owners a combination of republican principles, religious scruples, general antislavery sentiment, and economic motives. The economic factors most commonly identified with the post-Revolutionary, Upper South wave of manumission were the declining price of slaves, soil depletion, and falling tobacco prices.[24] While these explanations may partly explain the unprecedented number of manumissions in the Upper South in the post-Revolutionary era, they do not explain the ubiquity of manumission in nearly all slave societies at all times.

The economic problem of slavery is that the peculiar institution is, like every other worker-employer relationship, plagued by agency costs. The principal-agent problem emerges when one person (the agent) working on behalf of another person (the principal) makes choices that effect the payoff to the principal. Problems arise when the agent's and the principal's incentives are not aligned, and asymmetric information limits the principal's ability to monitor the agent's actions. In a worker-employee relationship, for example, the worker engages in actions that increase his utility at the expense of his employer's. It is possible to align the worker's and the employer's relationship through piece rate payment systems, efficiency wages, or other practices. Unlike other labor agreements, however, slavery relies on, among other incentives, coercion to elicit productive behaviors from the worker, which is optimal (for slave owner-principals) only under certain labor market conditions.[25]

Daron Acemoglu and Alexander Wolitzky extend a standard principal-agent employment model to circumstances in which the principal can coerce. The standard interpretation of coerced labor holds that coercion occurs under labor scarcity, but the Acemoglu-Wolitzky results shows that scarcity need not be the driving force, especially when the coerced workers' productivity is high outside the slave sector. It may be that coercion persisted in the American South because slaves were more productive in cotton than in noncotton production.[26] Their model is consistent, however, with two features of American slavery: coercion increases the agents' effort, and workers with a lower outside option are more coerced and provide higher levels of effort in equilibrium. It is well known that slaves labored long hours, under grueling conditions that noncoerced labor refused to accept at prevailing market wage rates.

Coercion mitigated but did not resolve the agency problem. Slave owners regularly complained that slaves shirked, feigned illness, broke tools, mistreated livestock, filched food, and engaged in other forms of covert resistance. George Washington often expressed his desire to "get clear" of slavery; he believed that slavery undermined the slave's incentives to "establish a good name" because slaves received small rewards from hard work and good behavior.[27] Coercion was integral to slavery, but it was not the slaveholder's only method of eliciting effort. Slave owners employed various carrots and sticks to limit the extent to which slaves shirked, feigned, broke, mistreated, and filched. Slave owners sometimes offered payments in excess of subsistence. In return, slaves consumed the excess or they saved enough by forgoing current consumption to purchase their freedom at some future date. Manumission was, to many slaveholders' thinking, the ultimate carrot. Washington used it, though not as selectively as many of his peers.

For masters and slaves that enter into an implicit or explicit manumission agreement, the fraction of a slave's life spent in slavery is a function of the slave owner's estimate of the future slave output he can expropriate, the amount of output in excess of subsistence paid the slave, and the strength of the slave's preference for freedom captured by his or her savings rate.[28] If we assume slaves cannot borrow, they must accumulate their purchase prices prior to manumission.[29] A stylized, graphical depiction of the slave's decision calculus is provided in Figure 5.1. Assume, for simplicity, a constant positive marginal product over her working life, which is an oversimplification that reasonably applies to skilled slaves or domestics; it was not true for field hands, whose productivity as part of slave gang surely exceeded their productivity as independent farm workers.[30] Because skilled slaves and domestics were more likely to be manumitted, the assumption of common marginal product in and out of slavery is a not unreasonable simplification. This lifetime trajectory of marginal product is represented by the w line in Figure 5.1. Assume further that the slave owner expropriates a constant amount e of slave output in every period of the slave's working life. The residual $(mp - e = c_s)$ represents the slave's potential consumption in each period.

A slave whose taste for current consumption and future freedom are such that current consumption is preferred will follow consumption path c_s, in which she consumes the (constant) difference between her marginal product and the slave owner's expropriation. Because she does not save, she will remain enslaved to the

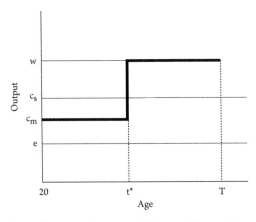

Figure 5.1 Life Cycle Productivity, Saving, and Time to Manumission. Source: Bodenhorn, "Manumission in Nineteenth-Century Virginia," *Cliometrica* (2007). Used by permission.

end of her days. On the other hand, a slave whose tastes are such that future free-dom is more desirable than current consumption will follow lifetime consump-tion path c_m where $c_s - c_m$ at each period up to time t^* equals savings in each period in slavery. At time t^*, the slave's cumulative savings equals her market price, equal to the discounted present value of the slave owner's expected future expropria-tions, and she buys her freedom. In freedom, the slave receives the whole of her marginal product and does so until the end of her working life at time T.

Manumission by self-purchase is well documented across the South and else-where in the New World. Between and 10 and 20 percent of manumitted slaves achieved their freedom through self-purchase.[31] Slaves raised the money in nearly as many ways as there were slaves: Denmark Vesey of Charleston, South Carolina won a lottery; Robert Clark of Petersburg, Virginia saved the tips he earned as a hostler; George Horton, of Chapel Hill, sold poems for 25 cents each to University of North Carolina students.[32] Another 10 to 20 percent were purchased by previ-ously freed family members.

Only a small fraction of manumissions resulted from a slave owner's moral misgivings over slavery.[33] In the majority of manumissions, no money changed hands and the basis of freedom was the slave owner's "affection" for the manu-mitted slave. This fact can be reconciled with the economic model if we think about saving more broadly than accumulated money. Faithful and diligent ser-vice built up a stock of goodwill with slave owners. Particularly dutiful slaves may have accumulated a stock of nonpecuniary wealth that could be exchanged for freedom. The foregone current consumption in these cases was in not shirking, feigning, breaking, and filching (or at least not getting caught). The high propor-tion of manumissions for good service implies that incentives schemes were at work. Promises of manumission *in futuro* were made to solve the agency problem and were the result of extended negotiations between slave and slave owner.

It was in the practice of self-purchase and the promise of future freedom that Southerners wrestled with whether implicit contracts between slaves and slave owners were enforceable. As chattel property, slaves had no right to own property and rarely had standing before the law.[34] Two exceptions were gener-ally recognized: slaves prosecuting freedom suits, and slaves seeking to enforce manumission agreements. For the promise of manumission to have the desired agency effect in eliciting slave effort, agreements needed to be credible and bind-ing. Failing to enforce such agreements would have undermined the incentives provided the slave as agent, and threatened slave productivity and peaceableness. While hundreds of owner-slave contractual cases made their way into courts in the antebellum South, two stand out. In *Waddill v. Martin*, for example, the Supreme Court of North Carolina determined that the slaves of a testator could continue their ongoing practice of keeping a share of the profits from the plan-tation's cotton crop, some of which was grown on private plots assigned to the slaves.[35] The slaves' savings were held by the executor, and the court refused to distribute the slaves' monies to the estate. Although it goes unstated, the court clearly understood that the estate's reneging on the agreement would create management problems for the executor.

In *Guardian of Sally, a Negro v. Beaty*, a slave, with her owner's blessing, used her free time to work in a nearby town, but only after she had put in her day's work for her owner. She saved her wages and accumulated enough savings to purchase and manumit a slave girl named Sally. The slave's owner, Beaty, sued to recover Sally, claiming that slaves had limited rights to property and no right to alienate it. His slave's purchase of Sally made Sally his property. Sally's case was tried in equity rather than law, and Sally's attorney argued that the slave had paid her master what was owed him. Further, the slave had acted with such frugality and generosity that basic notions of justice argued for Sally's freedom. The jury found in Sally's favor without leaving the box to deliberate. Chief Justice of South Carolina, Justice John Rutledge, wrote that it did not take the state's high court long to decide in Sally's favor either. What connected the courts' decisions in both *Waddill* and *Guardian of Sally* was the courts' recognition that encouraging effort and maintaining peace on plantations depended on honoring agreements. Taking away the slaves' option of deferring current consumption in hopes of purchasing their own or a loved one's freedom would have significantly undermined slavery itself.

Manumission rates in the American South were low compared to other slave regimes, and skeptics might argue that the rates were too low to provide slave agents with the appropriate incentives within the principal-agent relationship. Estimates of manumission rates, even in the Upper South where manumission was more common than elsewhere in the South, range from a low of one per thousand slaves (0.1 percent) to a high of forty per thousand slaves (4 percent). Carefully constructed estimates are more on the order of six to twelve per thousand (0.6 – 1.2 percent).[36] The long odds of achieving freedom through manumission appear unlikely to have elicited good behavior and extra effort. But the ability to elicit good behavior even for long odds may have followed from prospect theory, one of behavioral economics basic tools. Unlike expected utility theory, which is based on the assumption of rationality, prospect theory is consistent with persistent choice mistakes, especially when a low probability event offers a potentially large payoff. People tend to overestimate the probabilities of salient outcomes (manumission) and underestimate the probabilities of undesirable outcomes (failing to save enough to purchase freedom).

Colin Camerer and Howard Kunreuther argue that such biases may emerge from, among other sources, optimism ("It *can* happen to me!"), or from an excessive focus on much-discussed low-probability adventitious outcomes relative to less discussed, but more likely undesirable outcomes.[37] If slaves were optimistic or were convinced that manumission was within reach, they may have overestimated their odds of achieving freedom.[38] And they may have offered more effort than they would have had their expectations been more realistic.

Finally, some manumitted slaves were the offspring of the person manumitting them. Although southern men were reluctant to admit paternity—just three percent of manumitting slave owners in Anne Arundel County, Maryland and between four and twelve percent in New Orleans, Louisiana recognized paternity in official manumission records—it was not uncommon for manumitted slaves to be fair-haired, blue-eyed, light colored, and of mixed race.[39] In some cases, the freed mixed-race slave was the slave owner's offspring; in other instances, the mixed-race slave was freed because some slave owners were uncomfortable enslaving people who so closely resembled whites. Even "gratuitous" mixed-race manumissions were consistent with the predictions of the economic model. As Table 5.2 makes clear, few achieved freedom before reaching their mid-twenties or early thirties, or about the age at which the slave owner had recouped the cost of raising and sustaining the slave into adulthood. Further, mixed-race slaves tended to be more skilled, and therefore more productive than black slaves in slavery and freedom. The higher productivity of skilled, mixed-race slaves meant that they were better positioned than blacks to save and faced the prospect of higher incomes in freedom, both of which increased the likelihood of manumission.

Color and Age at Manumission

On November 16, 1818 James Jackson of Southampton County, Virginia registered a deed of manumission in which he freed eight slaves between 2 and 40 years old because he believed it "injust [sic] for one human being to enslave another man [and] deprive [him] against his will of the profits of his labor."[40] Arthur Whitehead freed six slaves because he was convinced "of the odiousness of slavery."[41] By comparison, Thomas Vaughan's deed of manumission of February 14, 1806 simply stated that "for diverse good causes," he freed "a Negro man Kit aged 50 and a Negro girl named Fanny abt 9 yrs of age."[42] In March 1857, Meriwether L. Anderson, the executor of Mary J. Oldham's estate, emancipated Sachel simply because Oldham requested that her slave be set free after her death (see Figure 5.2), offering no specific reason for her benevolence. Thousands of such deeds document the manumission of tens of thousands of slaves. Trying to make sense of who was freed and why is difficult to ascertain from close readings of manumission texts that recount the owners' reasons or from purely counting the number and types of slaves freed and slave owners who freed them.

Given the myriad reasons cited by slave owners—religion, politics, conscience, love, paternity, or simply "diverse good causes"—and the myriad contractual conditions agreed on by slaves and their owners, a purely textual study that focuses on details is unlikely to capture the central tendencies of manumission. Much can

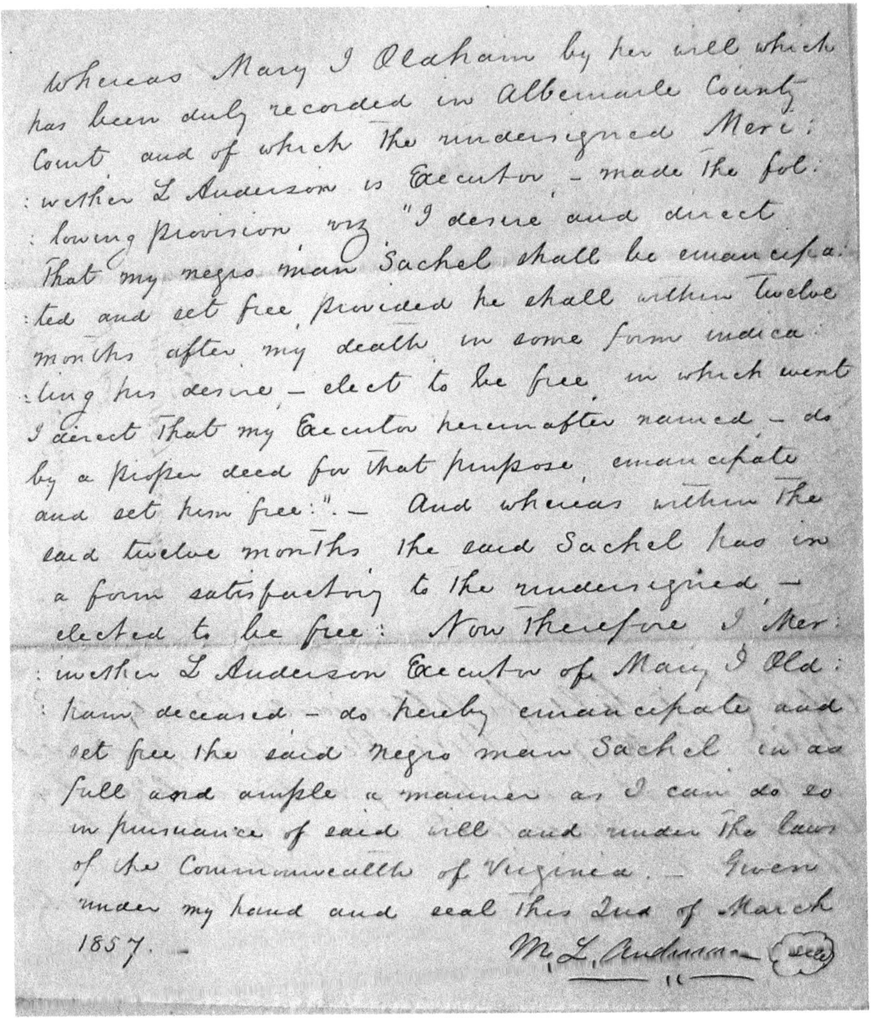
Whereas Mary I Oldham by her will which
has been duly recorded in Albemarle County
Court and of which the undersigned Meri:
:wether L Anderson is Executor, - made the fol:
:lowing provision, viz, "I desire and direct
That my negro man Sachel shall be emancipa:
:ted and set free, provided he shall within twelve
months after my death in some form indica:
:ting his desire, - elect to be free, in which event
I direct That my Executor hereinafter named, - do
by a proper deed for that purpose, emancipate
and set him free:". - And whereas within the
said twelve months the said Sachel has in
a form satisfactory to the undersigned, -
elected to be free: Now therefore I Mer:
:iwether L Anderson Executor of Mary I Old:
:ham deceased - do hereby emancipate and
set free the said Negro man Sachel in as
full and ample a manner as I can do so
in pursuance of said will and under the laws
of the Commonwealth of Virginia. - Given
under my hand and seal this 2nd of March
1857. - M. L. Anderson (seal)

Figure 5.2 Meriwether L. Anderson Manumission Affidavit. Source: Free Negro and Slave Records, Albemarle County, Box 1 (1857), Library of Virginia.

be learned about its central tendencies from statistical analysis of manumission in Virginia.

The basic statistics are themselves illuminating (see Appendix 5.2 for details). Table 5.2 shows that manumissions in Virginia were similar to manumissions elsewhere in the New World. The average age at manumission was 26 years; slightly less than half of manumitted slaves were women; approximately one-fourth of manumitted slaves were of mixed race; slaves—as is apparent in all three of the Southampton manumission documents discussed above—tended to be freed with kith and kin; slaves residing in urban areas were overrepresented among manumitted slaves; and manumission by deed and will were about equally likely, though a small fraction of slaves attained their freedom through the intervention of the courts.

While these facts are interesting, regression analysis can add nuance to understanding who was manumitted and when (though not necessarily why). The economic model discussed earlier offers two variables of interest: the proportion of an eventually manumitted slave's life spent in bondage (t^*/T); and the age at manumission (t^*). We know that the average age at manumission among manumitted slaves was 26 years. But this statistic includes all manumitted slaves, including children manumitted with one or both of their parents. The latter sort of gratuitous manumission may not have been driven by the agency relationship between slave owner and manumitted slave, though it was surely driven by negotiations between slave owners and the manumitted child's parents. It is useful, then, to consider only adult slaves to determine whether there is a systematic relationship between the manumission of adult slaves and the characteristics of the slave, most notably whether the slave was of mixed race or light color.

The unconditional mean proportion of life spent in slavery was 54 percent for eventually manumitted mixed-race slaves and 61 percent for eventually manumitted black slaves. After controlling for other features, regression analysis shows that mixed-race slaves, in fact, spent nearly nine percent less of their lives in bondage. Absent some reference point, it is difficult to place the nine percent difference in context. Figure 5.3 provides some comparative context for several factors likely

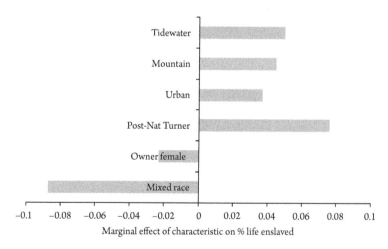

Figure 5.3 Marginal Effects of Slave Characteristics on Percentage of Life Enslaved. Notes: The predictions show the percentage change in the fraction of a slave's life spent in slavery, conditional being manumitted, attributable to that characteristic. For example, mixed-race slaves, conditional on being manumitted, were enslaved for approximately 8 percent less of their life than eventually manumitted black slaves. Source: Author's calculations from data described in Appendix 5.

to influence manumission and the age at which it occurred. Male slaves served about four percent more of their lives enslaved than female slaves.[43] Slaves manumitted by female slave owners served about two percent less of their lives in bondage compared to slaves eventually manumitted by male slave owners.

Compared to slaves in rural places, urban slaves served about four percent more of their lives enslaved. Given the overrepresentation of urban manumissions across New World societies this result appears counterintuitive, but it is consistent with the economic model. Although urban slaves were more likely to receive some cash payments and were better positioned for self-purchase, urban slaves also tended to be more productive in urban employments relative to rural slaves in rural employments, and afforded their owners greater expropriation possibilities.[44] Thus urban slaves would be forced to save more prior to self-purchase or have less left after the masters' expropriations, which is consistent with longer terms in slavery. Slaves residing in the Tidewater and the mountains also spent a larger fraction of their lives enslaved than did slaves in the Piedmont. Given the poor, sandy soils of Tidewater and the rocky terrain of the mountains, it simply took longer for slaves in these regions to accumulate their purchase price. Finally, social concerns with slave discipline and policing the free black population after Nat Turner's Southampton insurrection in 1831 extended the fraction of a slave's life in bondage by about eight percent relative to slaves at risk for manumission before that year.

Kaplan-Meier survivor charts presented in Figures 5.4a and 5.4b can be used to investigate age at manumission (t^*) and provide additional compelling evidence of the preferences shown mixed-race slaves. The unconditional mean age at

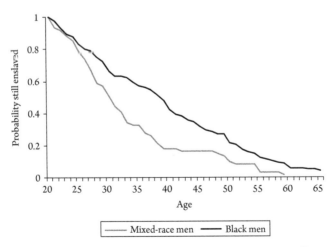

Figure 5.4a Probability of Remaining Enslaved at Age Among Eventually Manumitted Men, Black and Mixed-Race Slaves. Source: Author's calculations from data described in Appendix 5.

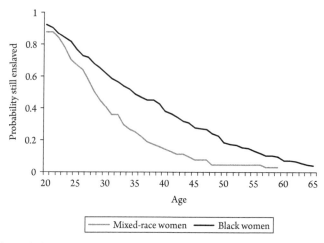

Figure 5.4b Probability of Remaining Enslaved at Age Among Eventually Manumitted Women, Black and Mixed-Race Slaves. Source: Author's calculation from data described in Appendix 5.

manumission for eventually manumitted mixed-race (adult) slaves was 32 years, compared to 39 years for blacks.[45] When we divide the races by sex, interesting patterns emerge. Up to around 25 years, black and mixed-race men were about equally likely to remain in bondage. After that the manumission experiences of the two races diverge. About half of all eventually manumitted mixed-race men are free by age 30; half of all eventually manumitted black men are free at age 39. Fully 75 percent of eventually manumitted mixed-race men are free by age 38; it is not until age 50 that the 75-percent mark is reached for black men. The survivor patterns for mixed and black women are similar. Half of eventually manumitted mixed-race women are free by age 28; black women do not reach the 50-percent mark until age 35. While several other factors are statistically important in explaining age at manumission—region of residence, time period, and sex of slave owner, among others—color has the single largest influence on age at manumission (see Appendix 5.2).

Color mattered for manumission, too. Mixed-race men and women were manumitted earlier in life, which meant they spent a considerably smaller fraction of their lives in bondage. Given the centrality of parentage in manumission, the question of color arises. Did color play a comparable role? In short, yes. One advantage of the Virginia register sample is that it provides detailed color descriptors of manumitted slaves. Thus a slave was not just black; he was dark black or perhaps very black. Similarly, a slave was not just mulatto; she might have been described as light or bright mulatto. Figures 5.5a and 5.5b present survivor charts by color within race (black or mixed-race). Among blacks, for example, the figure reveals that 50 percent of eventually manumitted light-skinned blacks were free by age 33,

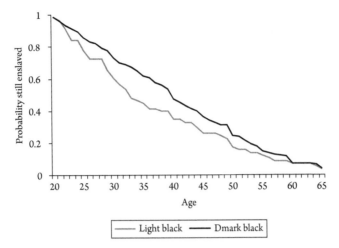

Figure 5.5a Probability of Remaining Enslaved at Age Among Eventually Manumitted Women, Light Black and Dark Black Slaves. Source: Author's calculations from data described in Appendix 5.

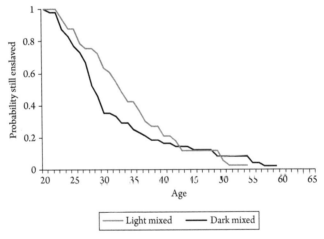

Figure 5.5b Probability of Remaining Enslaved at Age Among Eventually Manumitted Women, Light Mixed-Race and Dark Mixed-Race Slaves. Source: Author's calculations from data described in Appendix 5.

whereas 50 percent of eventually manumitted dark-skinned blacks were free only at age 40. Thus, the 50 percent mark of 39 years for all black men combined conceals notable within-race differences in age at manumission based on color. Moreover, given that the additional life expectancy of a 30-year-old slave was an additional 30 years, a seven-year differential in manumission age represented 23 percent of a slave's remaining life. The within-race color difference was not inconsequential. A comparable pattern is apparent among mixed-race slaves as well. At every age up to about age 45, light-skinned, mixed-race slaves were more likely to be manumitted than dark-skinned, mixed-race slaves.

This last finding—that color mattered as much as ancestry in preferential manumission—adds considerably to an understanding of slave life. Several studies of New World slavery note that one of the most common manumissions was a black or mixed-race adult woman freed with one or more of her mixed-race children. The eight slaves manumitted by James Jackson mentioned at the top of this section fall into this category. Jackson manumitted Pat, a 40-year-old black woman, and seven mixed-race children: William (16 years), Tom (14 years), Chloe Matilda (12 years), Peter (9 years), Willis (7 years), Dick (5 years), and Eliza (2 years). It is not unreasonable to infer that this was an instance of a white father freeing his slave concubine and his mixed-race children.

A common interpretation of the manumission of black woman and mixed-race children is that freedom was the white man's reward for the sexual favors provided by the black woman. Black Pat may have been Jackson's concubine and the seven mixed-race children may have been his, but Rosemary Brana-Shute argues that the inference of sex-for-freedom oversimplifies reality and muddies interpretations of manumission.[46] One problem with the sex-for-freedom interpretation is the unstated assumption that interracial sex was so extraordinary that it induced white men to manumit their mistresses in gratitude. Given the power structure on the plantation, and the discussion of sex on the plantation in Chapter 4, gratuitous manumission seems unlikely, though sexual favors were one source of goodwill.

A second and more salient problem with the sex-for-freedom interpretation is that there were many fewer manumissions than sexual relationships. Promising freedom in the pursuit of sexual gratification and failing to deliver would have undermined both the practice of voluntary concubinage and the freedom-for-effort promise that underlay slave productivity. Slaves were uneducated; they were not stupid. They would have quickly understood the emptiness of freedom-for-sex promises. A third and equally important consideration is that white men represented a declining proportion of manumitting owners over time. One-fifth of manumitting owners in antebellum Virginia were white women. Free blacks and mixed-race men and women, too, became numerically important grantors of freedom over time. Like Patty X, a free woman of color, who "in consideration of natural love and blessings of freedom" freed her husband in February 1819, an ever increasing proportion of manumission deeds were filed by the already free African-American man or woman with the wherewithal to purchase his or her spouse.[47]

Edward Long's observation concerning manumission in the West Indies is probably a more accurate portrayal of the manumitted slave than the bastard, mixed-race child upon whom the white father bestows a great favor. The slaves most commonly granted their freedom were "Domesticks, in reward for long and faithful service . . . Those, who have been permitted to work for themselves . . .

many of them find means to save sufficient from their earnings, to purchase their freedom . . . [and] Those who have effected some essential service to the public."[48] Mixed-race people were more likely than blacks to have served in the owner's household, to have a marketable skill, and to have performed some essential public service. In some instances, paternity explains the preferences shown mixed-race slaves, but the greater rewards accruing to color within race suggests that relatively fair-complected African Americans more closely approached the somatic preferences of white slave owners, and were more likely to receive favors from their owners.[49] Working in the owner's house or independently contracting to provide services to whites acculturated skilled, urban, light-skinned, mixed-race people to the norms of white society and the marketplace generally. Such acculturation placed them in propitious positions for freedom.

Runaways

On September 3, 1838 Frederick Bailey escaped from slavery. By Bailey's own telling, his escape was precipitated by an argument with his owner's brother, to whom he was required to submit his weekly earnings as a ship caulker. One Friday in mid-August Bailey failed to deliver his weekly earnings, choosing instead to attend a weekend religious camp meeting. Bailey delivered his weekly earnings promptly on Monday morning, but a quarrel ensued, which convinced Bailey that it was a good time to go. After two weeks' planning, he did so. Dressed as a sailor, he took a series of trains and ferries between Baltimore and New York. His girlfriend, the mixed-race and light-complected Anna Murray, met him there. They were married and traveled to New Bedford, Massachusetts, where Bailey hoped to find work as a ship caulker. Racial prejudice among New Bedford's white caulkers forced him into common labor.[50] Though he faced prejudice and discrimination at nearly every turn in the North, life as a free man in the North was far superior to being a slave in the South, even in a reasonably progressive Upper South city like Baltimore that afforded slaves like Bailey far more freedoms than nearly any low-country rice plantation or Delta cotton plantation slave might envision. Needing a new identity and a new name, Frederick Bailey adopted the surname Douglass, taken from the hero of Sir Walter Scott's *The Lady of the Lake*. Douglass was exceptional among runaways, not least because he successfully navigated his way north to freedom.

Recall that a few years earlier Douglass had come to an agreement with Hugh Auld: if Douglass minded his business and caused no trouble, he would be freed. Auld and Douglass's agreement was a relatively common one, at least among slaves savvy enough and productive enough to negotiate for their freedom.[51] Many slave owners believed that promises of future freedom, conditional on good behavior, encouraged good behavior, but not all slave owners were convinced. In

1791 Harry Dorsey Gough placed an advertisement in the *Maryland Journal and Commercial Advertiser* seeking the return of his runaway slave, Will Bates. Bates's running clearly infuriated his owner. Gough condemned his slave as a "very ungrateful Young Rogue who was born a Slave and Manumitted by [*sic*] only to serve a few years."[52]

Delayed manumission was designed to reward diligent effort, but some slaves ran anyway. Running among hired-out and self-hired slaves, like Douglass, was not uncommon. Slave owners demanded a large fraction of the slaves' weekly earnings. Frustrated with the disconnection between work, wages, and consumption, hired-out slaves were wont to run away.[53] Other slaves simply lost patience with their enslavement as the date of their promised freedom approached and chose to risk their future freedom by running away sooner. Doing so represented a breach of contract, so that courts usually considered delayed manumission agreements void even if the runaway returned on his or her own. That slaves nearing the end of their term ran suggests that they were no less subject to hyperbolic discounting than other market actors.[54] Cases like Will Bates's notwithstanding, the weight of evidence is consistent with term slavery encouraging good behavior. It is not causal evidence, of course, but the expansion of term slavery and a concurrent decline in runaways is suggestive.

In other cases, running substituted for delayed manumission when negotiations did not provide an escape hatch for slaves who considered themselves worthy of freedom. In 1827 slave Anthony Chase ran away because his mistress refused to entertain Chase's offers to purchase himself. Chase proposed hiring his own time for two or three years and paying a premium over his market value in return for his freedom. His owner rebuffed his offers and hired him out. After 11 years of faithful service Chase considered himself deserving, and because his owner was unwilling to negotiate, he ran.[55] For critics of the practice, Anthony Chase was the poster child of the social ills of manumission. Not only did manumission create jealousies among the still-enslaved, which undermined plantation discipline, but the ever-increasing population of free African Americans made it easier for runaway slaves to slip unnoticed into distant—usually urban—labor markets where they might hide in plain sight for weeks, months, even years.

Slaves ran away because they were obdurate, tired out and in need of rest, tired of brutal treatment, tired of too little food, tired of a repetitive diet, tired of their "ordinary condition of subjection," tired of being threatened with sale, enticed away by whites, or simply because the opportunity presented itself.[56] While contemporaries and modern scholars agree that running away was so common that few planters failed to complain of the practice, informed modern estimates imply that circa 1860 about 50,000 slaves ran away at some point during the year, which implies that only about one percent of slaves ran in any given year.[57] Stated another way, on any given day about 140 slaves in the southern United States went AWOL, a minuscule fraction of the nearly four million enslaved persons.[58]

The Economics of Running Away

Understanding the economics of slave runaways demands that the act be considered from the perspective of the slave and the slave owner, and how those points of view interacted with color. Start with the prospective runaway slave's calculus.

One way to approach this is with a Roy-type model of occupational choice, the details of which are provided in Appendix 5.3. Essentially, if each slave's utility depends on his or her compensation (or wage plus in-kind payments) in slavery and in freedom, and slaves have different (dis)tastes for slavery, the model shows that some slaves will run and some will not, even when they find themselves in similar circumstances. Color becomes a factor in the decision to run if compensation in slavery and in freedom is a function of color—either because slaveholders or employers, based on their prejudices, reward color, or if slaveholders or employers believe that color reveals something about productivity. Light-skinned slaves and free people, for example, may be more literate or more skilled on average than dark-skinned slaves and free people, so that employers are willing to offer them more compensation per hour.

The formal model presented in Appendix 5.3 shows that the decision to run is based on a comparison between the difference between some baseline compensation (perhaps "subsistence," which might mean something different to a slave owner than a slave) and the differences in the returns to characteristics in slavery and in running net of punishment costs. If the returns to slave activity (e.g., picking cotton) are higher with running, all else being equal, the slave will run. If the taste for running is higher than the taste for staying, all else being equal, the slave will run. But most importantly for present purposes is that the higher the returns to color in running relative to staying, the more likely slaves of favored colors are to run. If the characteristics are distributed according to some known distributions and certain features, such as color and productivity, are correlated, it is possible to generate a model of color-based selection into running.[59]

Just as the criminal justice system aims to reduce crime through a combination of increasing the likelihood of detection (deterrence) and increasing the cost of conviction (punishments), slave owners reduced the incidence of running away through deterrence and punishment. But just like the criminal justice system's inability to eliminate crime, slave owner's deterrence and punishment mechanisms did not eliminate running away, though it did reduce it to low levels. Even with the privations suffered under slavery, only about one percent of slaves ran at some point each year. This suggests that either the likelihood of success was very low, or the punishments imposed on captured and returned runaways were sufficiently draconian relative to the consumption afforded slaves who stayed put, or both, that few slaves expected running away to make them better off either in the short- or long-term.

There were individual and neighborhood features, however, that might tilt the calculus in favor of running. Proximity to a free state, as Jeremiah Dittmar

and Suresh Naidu show, may have improved the likelihood of success sufficiently to raise the number of runaways enough to reduce the optimal size of the
mean slaveholding.[60] This is consistent with contemporary accounts and historical interpretations of slavery and running away in border states. The proximity
of the Pennsylvania border and the relatively high rates of successful runaways
forced slave owners in Upper Maryland to expropriate less and generally offer less
harsh, less punitive terms of servitude.[61] Slaves from the Deep South ran—for
freedom anyway—only under special circumstances, such as David, the slave of a
Mr. Beardslee, who was hired out to work as a fireman on a Mississippi River
steamboat. When the steamboat docked at St. Louis, David ran and was believed
to have made it to Cincinnati. He was never recovered.[62]

Other features also tilted the calculus enough in the prospective runaway's
favor to induce running. Literate and skilled slaves probably had a better chance
than uneducated slaves of making it to a free state or a city where they might
blend in with free blacks, mostly because they were better prepared to interact
with inquisitive whites and had a clearer appreciation of the direction and distances they needed to travel to freedom.[63] Particularly productive slaves, or those
for whom expected consumption in freedom greatly exceeded consumption in
slavery, were also more likely to run, especially if they could make it to a city,
find employment, and pass for free.[64] Mixed-race slaves, too, were more likely
to successfully abscond. It was no coincidence that the Beardslee's absconding slave David was described as nearly "white, with blue eyes and light sandy
hair."[65] In 1850 less than one in ten slaves, but more than one in three free African
Americans, was of mixed race. A light-complected runaway with good hair and
good employment prospects was better positioned to evade detection and apprehension and slip into an urban free community.

Understanding who ran, why, and when is complicated by the absence of
systematic evidence. Much of the extant information on runaways is either
anecdotal—accounts from slave owners' diaries or recollections of former slaves.
Slave recollections provide vivid accounts of the perils and pitfalls facing runaways.[66] Virginia slave Madison Jefferson, for example, ran for Canada when
he was 16 years old. He got as far as Zanesville, Ohio, when he was betrayed by
some whites who offered to help. They betrayed his trust and carried him back to
Parkersburg, Virginia, where the white captors collected their reward; Jefferson
was returned to his owner, received 39 lashes, chained about the ankles, and forced
to chop wood by day; he was chained to a block and held in solitary confinement
by night.[67] The problem facing the historians is that it is hard to know how authen-
tic, reliable, and realistic such accounts are. Without diminishing the significance
of stories like Jefferson's or the horrors faced by slaves, memories get hazier with
time and storytellers and their publishers faced incentives to exaggerate.

The second commonly used source of information is runaway advertisements.
Found in nearly every southern newspaper, the advertisements announced

a reward and contained the relevant information about the slave and the slave owner. While the advertisements provide details about slaves—color, height, hair type, wardrobe, personality, skills, and literacy, among others—they are subject to unknowable selection bias. It is well known that not every runaway slave was advertised. Slave owners who believed their slave was just "lying out" in the neighborhood rarely advertised their missing slaves. Placing an advertisement was also costly in time and treasure. Not only did the slave owner have to post a reward for the capture and return of his slave, but placing an advertisement required traveling to town and paying the printer.[68] Given the costs involved, slave owners were probably more likely to place advertisements for slaves who were more likely to successfully abscond or for more valuable slaves. Thus advertisements do not provide a representative sample of slaves, or even perhaps runaway slaves. The advertised slaves are representative of no other group than runaways that warranted an advertisement. Runaways were a select subset of slaves, and advertised runaways were a select subset of runaways.

Recognizing that reliable inferences cannot be drawn about the overall slave population from the information included in runaway advertisements, the advertisements yet reveal interesting features about the class of advertised runaway slaves. Franklin and Schweninger concluded, from their sample of 2,000 runaways from five southern states, that about 80 percent of runaways were male and 75 percent were between 13 and 29 years.[69]

Appendix 5.3 describes a sample of nearly 2,500 advertised runaways from Virginia and North Carolina. More than 85 percent of these runaways were male, and while the ages of runaways ranged from 10 to 61 years, the average age of runaways was 27 years. Nearly 15 percent of runaways were mixed race, compared to 7.7 percent of the overall slave population in 1850. The selection on mixed race is consistent with rational running, however. More than one-third of the free African-American population was mixed race in 1850, so mixed-race runaways could more readily find refuge in free communities. Similarly, nearly 14 percent of advertised runaways had a skill worthy of mention in the reward notice. This proportion exceeds the proportion of skilled slaves in the general population. Finally, among the 1,146 notices that reported the height of adult males (21 years and older), the average height was 68.2 inches. Advertised runaways' average height is more than half an inch taller than free-born African Americans and more than one inch taller than slaves entering the interstate slave trade, a comparison group that may itself exhibit positive selection on height.[70] Runaways were tall, smart, skilled, and light. They were not typical slaves.

Although runaway advertisements can tell us relatively little about the underlying slave population, the characteristics of runaways suggest systematic differences—runaways were lighter complected, more skilled, more literate, and taller than other slaves—consistent with an economic model of rational running. The runners' characteristics improved their odds, relative to the general slave population, of successfully running away. Light complected, skilled, strong, and tall men would have blended in with free blacks and found ready employment in southern cities like Baltimore, Norfolk, and Petersburg with sizeable free African-American communities.[71]

The Economics of Runaway Advertising

It is also useful to think about the economics of runaway advertisements from the planters' perspectives. Planters and overseers tracked runaways themselves, but most could not afford more than a few days off their farms without risking the further breakdown of slave discipline. After a local search, the owners of runaways informed neighboring planters and the captain of the slave patrol to be on the lookout. They alerted local and county officials—sheriffs, justices of the peace, and jailers, among others—or placed advertisements in local newspapers. The lag of a few days to a few months between the date a slave ran away and the placement of ads suggests that slave owners waited to ensure that the slave was not just lying out in the neighborhood. It was not unusual for slaves to spend a week in the woods and return famished. When slaves absconded, most planters were less concerned about permanent escape than the slave's death by misadventure and the loss of the owner's investment.[72] Advertisements appeared only after the slave owner or overseer was convinced that the runaway slave had traveled beyond his reach.

State laws established the basic framework for the capture and return of runaways. In South Carolina, for example, every planter was required to have at least one white man eligible for slave patrolling (18–45 years) on the plantation at all times. Moreover, it was the duty of every white male to take into custody any black person reasonably believed to be a runaway and deliver that black person to the county jail. The jailer was required to pay the captor 7¢ per mile (up to 25 miles per day), plus 50¢ per day spent delivering the slave to the jail, plus $2.14 as a reward for capturing and delivering the slave. The jailer later recovered these sums from the runaway's owner. If the slave went unclaimed for 12 months, the jailer was to put the slave up for auction, reimburse himself for costs, and hold any excess in the event that the slave owner appeared to claim his or her runaway slave after the 12-month period.[73] Figure 5.6 reproduces a court order instructing the Henrico County, Virginia sheriff to conduct the sale of an unclaimed runaway slave.

It is useful to think about retrieving runaways from the slave owner's perspective as a problem of recovering lost property. The law can establish either of two regimes: finders keepers, or original owners retain property rights. Steven Shavell shows that when the owner of lost property retains ownership and is better positioned than others to be aware of the approximate time and place that the property went missing, recovery efforts will be economically optimal because the

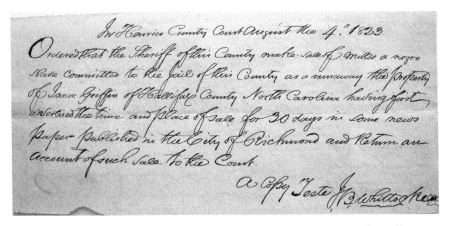

Figure 5.6 Court Order Instructing the Henrico County, Virginia Sheriff to Sell an Unclaimed Runaway Slave. Source: Free Negro and Slave Records, Henrico County, Box 2 (1823), Library of Virginia.

owner is the most efficient searcher and engages in search on his own.[74] Others will not search unless hired by the owner to do so. At the same time, the original ownership rule creates incentives for the owner to exercise optimal care to prevent loss, because the owner alone bears the loss and search costs.

Shavell's analysis of optimal prevention and recovery under an original ownership rule holds when runaway slaves were believed to be lying out—hiding on neighboring plantation or in a surrounding secluded area. The economics is more complicated when the runaway was believed to have traveled outside the slave owner's search radius. When the owner retains title but no longer has a reasonable opportunity to recover the slave, a runaway will often not be recovered. When finders of runaways have a positive duty to return it, the owner's incentive to search and recover is reduced. Southern lawmakers tried to counter the reduced incentive effects when they made it a legal duty for white males to recover runaways when presented with as reasonable opportunity. It was a patroller's legal duty to patrol daily, interrogate all African Americans encountered off a plantation, and apprehend any suspected runaway. Moreover, southern law made it the duty of anyone apprehending a suspected runaway to turn that slave over the county jailer within a few days of capturing the runaway or be subject to a punitive fine—a law consistent with the efficiency of returning adventitiously discovered property to its original owner.[75]

Southern property rules imply that rewards were offered only when slave owners were convinced that the probability their property would be recovered or returned was inefficiently low and the reward would induce search and recovery. From the slave owner's perspective, the optimal reward equaled the product of the increased probability of recovery following from the reward and the potential loss from the slave's permanently absconding (i.e., *reward = $\Delta p \cdot$ slave* *value*, where Δp is the change in the probability that the runaway slave would be returned). For a given change in probability of recovery following the offer of a reward, the calculus predicts that greater rewards would be offered for more valuable slaves.

The optimal reward rule can be restated as: $\Delta p = reward / slave\ value$. There is information on rewards from the advertisements, and slave values can be estimated for slaves by age, sex, and race/complexion from studies of eighteenth- and nineteenth-century slave markets (see Appendix 5.3 for details). By using the available information, it is possible to test whether slave owners were economically rational in that the rewards they offered equalized the probability of recovery and return across all slave types. Inflation-adjusted rewards for mixed-race slaves ($34.50) exceeded the rewards for black slaves ($29.43), but comparing the means of the reward-slave value ratio by color shows that the implied change in the probability of recovery and return was higher for black (0.042) than mixed-race (0.040) slaves. Analyses that control for runaway characteristics, as well as year and county in which the runaway absconded, reveal that the implied increase in the probability of return from offering a reward was nearly 5 percent (0.049) for all slaves. More interesting, perhaps, is that the marginal effects are virtually nil for observable slave characteristics: −0.003 percentage points for females; −0.2 percentage points for slaves who ran in groups; −0.04 percentage points for skilled slaves; 0.8 points for literate slaves; and, of particular interest in the current context, −0.2 percentage points for mixed-race slaves. The evidence implies that offered rewards approximately equalized expected recovery probabilities across slave characteristics.

The statistical analysis of information contained in runaway slave advertisements is consistent with rational behavior on the part of both slaves and slave owners. Given the punishments suffered for failed runaway attempts and the apparently low probability of success for most, few slaves ran away. The best available estimates imply an annual runaway rate of about one percent. While slave owners complained about the incorrigibility of slaves and their inclination toward absconding, most stayed put. Those with a better chance of success or with more attractive prospects in freedom (or particularly poor prospects in slavery) were more likely to run. Thus young, tall, skilled, literate, and mixed-race slaves were overrepresented among the class of advertised runaways. Slave owners responded rationally to absconding slaves. If the slaves were believed to be lying out, slave owners relied on local authorities to recover and return those slaves who did not return of their own accord after a few days away. Once slave owners became convinced that slaves had likely run beyond the limits of ready recovery, they took other steps to assist in recovery, including advertising. Eliciting extra recovery effort demanded an economic payment and slave owners offered rewards. Slaves and slave owners, to outward appearances anyway, behaved as if they were responding to economic incentives.

Conclusion

Runaway advertisements are replete with "gruesome references to twisted limbs, missing fingers and toes, burn marks, and scars, as well as poignant descriptions to people unable to look a white man in the eye or to speak to one without stuttering and trembling."[76] It is remarkable that more slaves did not run. What seemingly kept them in place was that unsuccessful running only made life harder. Returned runaways were whipped, shackled, collared, chained to heavy blocks, locked in cellars, put on short rations, or any of several other punishments. Up to now, our understanding of runaways has been provided by the analysis of narratives from which two prominent historians conclude that runaways were "young and old, black and mulatto, healthy and infirm, female and male, skilled and unskilled, urban and rural."[77] Their point is that runaways were drawn from the entire population of slaves. But such a statement provides few insights. In this instance, a little counting offers some fresh insights. If, for instance, we define "old" as 60 or more years old, then old runaways among advertised runaways were a rare breed. Only eight such runaways appeared in the nearly 2,500 advertisements studied here. Old slaves either stayed put, or they were of little economic value, or they were so easily recovered that their owners did not bother to advertise them. Statistical analysis also reveals that women ran at younger ages than men, and few ran in groups. While there are undoubtedly counterexamples, this observation suggests that as a rule, mothers did not run with their young children. Similarly, statistical analysis reveals that not only were mixed-race slaves overrepresented among advertised runaways, but they ran at earlier ages than black slaves. In this regard runaways resembled manumitted slaves. Mixed-race slaves sought and received freedom at younger ages, whether by manumission or absconding. Both facts are consistent with the economics of freedom.

Runaways were, in several observable ways, more like manumitted slaves than previously appreciated. Recall, for example, the hard-working Anthony Chase, who ran only after his master refused to entertain his entreaties to purchase himself. Chase's choice came down to flight or rebellion, or negotiation. When negotiation failed, Chase opted to run. Which path a slave followed—flight, rebellion, or negotiation—depended on the particulars of his or her condition. The consideration of the ways in which slaves achieved freedom suggests that negotiation was at least as common as running, even if it failed in Chase's case. Approximately one percent of slaves ran in any year in the late antebellum era; about one to two percent of slaves were manumitted. The path to freedom was trod at least as often by negotiators as by fugitives.

In 1860 more than 250,000 free African Americans lived in the slave South. Though this represents a modest six percent of the approximately 4 million African Americans (free and enslaved combined) in the South, the emergence of a free population of any consequence in the face of wide antipathy to manumission and ongoing efforts to deter and recover runaways testifies to slaves' unflagging efforts to free themselves and their loved ones.[78] Viable, even vibrant, communities of free people of color emerged in the Upper South and a handful of urban places, such as Charleston, Mobile, and New Orleans, in the Deep South. These free communities were disproportionately mixed race and light skinned, but the disproportion is not unexpected given the differential likelihood of mixed-race slave achieving freedom through flight or negotiation. It is to the mixed-race persons experiences in freedom that we now turn.

6

Marriage and the Family

In 1928 Ida Mae Brandon, then not yet sixteen years old, was courted by two young men, each in his early twenties. Well dressed, talkative, and charming, David McIntosh came courting on his tall red horse after Sunday services; the taciturn and serious George Gladney walked more than three miles to her house, his shirt soaked in sweat by the time he arrived. Ida Mae's mother wasn't "particular about either one of them. . . . they were too old for Ida Mae . . . and both of them were too dark." Ida Mae was "nut butter" in color with dark brown hair, and her mother expressed concerns over her daughter's future and hoped for "the more favorable economic prospects of a lighter man."[1] To her mother's dismay, the quiet and dark-skinned George won the heart of the lighter complected Ida Mae.

Family dramas such as Ida Mae's played out in many African-American homes and long predated her early twentieth-century experience. In 1854 a contributor to the *National Era* disputed the contention that "every one of African descent values himself in proportion to the degree of white blood he has in his veins, and it is rarely the case that mulattoes are willing to form matrimonial alliances with persons having less."[2] He labeled the assertion of color-based marriage matching a slander, but historians believe that such race- and color-based matching was more common than not. Tommy Bogger shows that in Norfolk, Virginia, "mulattoes showed a strong preference for other mulattoes."[3] Of 30 Savannah, Georgia couples studied by Whittington Johnson, he finds that 25 African-American couples matched on color.[4] And of the nearly 350 Baltimore marriages studied by Christopher Phillips, 80 percent of mixed-race males married mixed-race women and 90 percent of black men married black women.[5] Whether labeled complexion homogamy or positive assortative mating, the existing historical evidence is, so far as complexion is concerned, consistent with like matching with like.

In fact, the social convention toward assortative matching held such power that some light-complected African Americans roamed far outside their locality in search of suitable partners. Nancy Fuller, a free-born mixed-race woman from Norfolk, Virginia, married Alexander Jarrett, a light-complected black from Petersburg and the son of one of the wealthiest free black men in Virginia.[6] Richard

98

Cowling, a light-complected Norfolk native and reporter for the *Southern Argus*, traveled to Washington, DC to find a suitable light-complected bride. Unable to find an acceptable light-complected spouse in New York City, Willis Augustus Hodge traveled to Norfolk to court two eligible mixed-race women. Finding neither acceptable, he returned to New York unmarried. Given the risks associated with and the restrictions placed on interstate movements, the lengths to which free African Americans at mid-century went in search of light-complected spouses speaks volumes about the strength of color-based matching.

One issue of enduring interest is the stability of marriage matches. Concerns with the modern African-American family have led several researchers to inquire into its historical roots to determine whether the early African-American family resembled its modern incarnation. Extant historical evidence is inconsistent with the notion that modern dysfunction followed from slavery and emancipation.[7] John Alvord, a Freedmen's Bureau officer, observed in 1866 that African Americans liked to "congregate in families."[8] Alvord's impressions were undoubtedly based on observing the thousands of recently freed slaves who sought to legitimize their marriages by recording them with the Freedmen's Bureau. Still, those same records reveal that slave marriages were impermanent.[9] Nearly half of slaves recording their marriages with the Freedmen's Bureau reported a previous marriage that ended with the spouse's death. Another third declared that a previous marriage ended because the spouse was sold or moved away with a master. One in six slave marriages ended in desertion or simple mutual consent in an average of just 4.6 years.

A one-in-six voluntary marriage failure rate among slaves appears exceptional, but it was not out of line with a one-in-ten failure rate for all marriages contracted in the United States in the mid-1860s.[10] It was low compared to a one-third voluntary failure rate among all US marriages contracted in the 1940s. Context is vital in understanding marriage markets among slaves, ex-slaves, and free-born African Americans. The realities of dating and mating on the plantation may have made one-sixth of slave marriages unsuccessful not because former slaves eschewed marriage or because slavery failed to prepare people for the complexities of married life, but because desirable marital partners were hard to come by and poorly matched partners temporarily paired off rather than live alone.[11] The number of potential mates on the plantation, even a large plantation, was limited at best. The result was poor and, sometimes, short-lived matches. Poorly matched slaves often engaged in a type of serial monogamy.

It may have been the difficulty of successful matching on the plantation and elsewhere in the rural South that led to a second, oft-noted feature of nineteenth-century black life: the high rate of free black urbanization. It was not uncommon for recently manumitted slaves to relocate to a nearby city or town. Free African Americans, in fact, were one of the most urbanized groups in the early to mid-nineteenth century.[12] In Louisiana, for instance, 23.8 percent of the state's population lived in New Orleans in 1860; 57.3 percent of the state's free African Americans lived in the city. Comparable disparities in urbanization rates by race are evident in Louisville, Kentucky; Charleston, South Carolina; St. Louis, Missouri; and Petersburg and Richmond, Virginia.[13] Historians typically attribute this rural-to-urban movement as a means of escaping plantation drudgery or the long shadow cast by their former masters, or the deference expected of them even in freedom or to the desire to experience an alternative lifestyle available in cities and towns.[14] It is not unreasonable to posit yet another motivation: namely, that free African Americans preferred urban life because cities and towns offered a more vibrant dating life and much better opportunities for a propitious marriage match.

Color and Marriage Markets

Economists, sociologists, anthropologists, psychologists, and mathematicians have contributed to an extensive literature on matching and sorting in marriage markets. This literature demonstrates that marriage is not random; potential marriage partners sort along any number of observable attributes, including age, education, height, weight, attractiveness, religion, political persuasion, and race.[15] Theory indicates that the observed pattern of sorting can arise from either search frictions or preferences. A search friction explanation for matching on, say, education is that independent of preferences, people with similar education levels tend to interact frequently, either at school or at work. An individual may prefer someone with different educational characteristics, but is unlikely to meet and match with a person markedly unlike herself. A dishwasher in a diner has a small chance of meeting and marrying a Harvard MBA.

Preference-based sorting in what is known as a vertical ordering, in the absence of search frictions, will generate a matching equilibrium. A vertical order emerges in a heterosexual marriage market when each potential male mate ranks all women, all women rank all men, and the rank orderings are identical. That is, in a matching based on physical attractiveness, all men rank all women similarly and all women rank all men similarly. The most attractive male-female pair matches, the second most attractive male-female pair matches, and so on.[16]

Several scholars have developed formal matching models that emphasize either search frictions or preferences, and the choice of which to use depends on the question at hand. In the present case, our interest lies in matching on complexion. A model developed by Ken Burdett and Melvyn Coles, as extended by Theodore Belding, provides a useful formalization of the problem that can be explained using Figure 6.1.[17] Suppose that all men and all women can be ranked from lightest to darkest; that every man and every woman agree on the complexion rankings, and that all men and all women use this common complexion metric

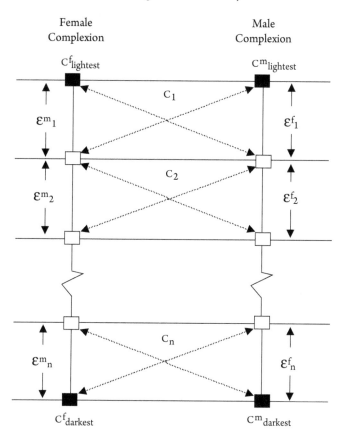

Figure 6.1 Color Class Formation Under a Color-Based Assortative Matching Regime.
Source: Author's rendering adapted from Belding, "Nobility and Stupidity," 6.

to evaluate potential partners. In the figure, women (left side) and men (right side) are ordered from lightest (top) to darkest (bottom). Some versions of matching models predict that the lightest man will match with the lightest woman, the second lightest pairs will match, the third lightest will match, and so on. But search frictions of various types might interfere with such perfect assortative matching. In response to these frictions, the lightest female is willing to match with the first man within a range of the lightest complexions who proposes to her. In the diagram this set of men considered an eligible partner by the lightest complected woman is defined by her selection criterion, represented by ε_1^f. That is, the lightest complected female will accept the first proposal arriving from a man in the group comprising the lightest complected man occupying the interval defined by $C_{lightest}^m - \varepsilon_1^f$. Assume that men behave similarly.

The complexion group C_1 is formed by the lightest complected female's and male's preferences. The lightest-complected female is a taste-maker for her peer group (light complected females) in the sense that any male within the range of acceptable colors for the lightest female is an acceptable partner for any female of darker color.[18] The lightest-complected male is a taste-maker for his peer group (light complected males) in the same way. Matching occurs within the group of light complected women and the group of light complected men.

To form the next lightest complexion group, remove those members of C_1^m and C_1^f and repeat the process beginning with the female just excluded from the group $C_{1'}^f$ or the last woman rejected by the men in complexion set C_1^m. Similarly, begin with the male just excluded from the group C_1^m. The process continues until sets of the darkest complected men and women, C_n^m and C_n^f (where n represents the ultimate number of sets), form. The result is assortative mating on complexion (homogamy), as demonstrated in Figure 6.1.

A more formal version of the model (explained in Appendix 6.1) generates a prediction not of perfect assortative matching on color, but of close correspondence in complexions between men and women. Search frictions, such as those created by pairing off on plantations by slaves or in small towns by free people of color, which limited the range of available choices, will generate apparent exceptions to complexion-based assortative mating. Any test of the model must recognize less than perfect complexion matches and that color was just one feature over which individuals had preferences.

Evidence on Color and Marriage

Intermarriage can be calculated from the stock of marriages at a point in time (prevalence) or from the flow of people who marry during a given period (incidence). Scholars prefer flow (or incidence) measures, because they afford the possibility to investigate trends and because partners may tend to look more alike the longer they are married. Marriage partners may switch faiths after marriage, so that a point-in-time (prevalence) measure may overstate the initial incidence of religious assortative matching. Although temporal changes in changeable traits may introduce biases into studies of assortative matching on education, body mass index, or other changeable personal characteristics, they present less cause for concern when studying less readily altered physical characteristics such as height, race, or color.

Several alternative measures are used to characterize the extent of intermarriage.[19] To explain the more common measures consider Table 6.1, which provides information on the prevalence of marriages by race reported in the 1860 census for all married African Americans in Baltimore, Maryland. Define the number of marriages between pairs of people by sex and race as N_{ij}, where i (= black or mixed-race) is the man's race and j (=black or mixed-race) is the woman's race. Thus, N_{bm} counts the number of marriages between black men and mixed women. (Whites are not discussed here because the incidence of black-white and mixed-white marriages was infinitesimal.) Panel A of Table 6.1 provides the number of mixed male–mixed female matches in the upper left corner, the number of black-black marriages on the lower right diagonal, and the black-mixed and mixed-black marriages in the off-diagonal cells. Given that blacks outnumbered mixed-race individuals, it is not surprising that marriages involving blacks dominated and that black-black marriages were the most common.

Panel B of Table 6.1 presents the same information as the percentage of all marriages and illustrates one of the most common measures of the extent of intermarriage: $(N_{bm} + N_{mb}) / N$. The prevalence of intermarriage within mid-century Baltimore's African-American community was a mere 9.2 percent. The table also reveals that 9.5 percent ($0.075 / 0.785$) of mixed-race females intermarried while

Table 6.1 Alternative Measures of Assortative Mating

Panel A: Number of marriages by color in Baltimore (1860)

		MEN		
		Mixed	Black	Total
	Mixed	238	90	328
WOMEN	Black	21	855	876
	Total	259	945	1204

Panel B: Fraction of marriages by color in Baltimore (1860)

		MEN		
		Mixed	Black	Total
	Mixed	0.198	0.075	0.273
WOMEN	Black	0.017	0.710	0.727
	Total	0.215	0.785	1.000

Panel C: Actual marriages / marriages predicted by random matching by color in Baltimore (1860)

		MEN	
		Mixed	Black
	Mixed	238 / 71	90 / 257
WOMEN	Black	29 / 188	855 / 688

Panel D: Log odds ratio for color-based assortative matching for three cities
Baltimore, Maryland: 4.7 (0.25)
Norfolk, Virginia: 3.3 (0.78)
New Orleans, Louisiana: 4.1 (0.56)

Notes: Panel D, standard errors in parentheses. See footnote 20 for standard error formula. *Sources*: US Census Office, Eighth Census (1860), Population manuscripts for Baltimore, Norfolk, and New Orleans.

7.9 percent (0.017 / 0.215) of mixed-race men intermarried. African-American women appear slightly more likely to intermarry than African-American men, but the differential is not large. Although percentages are easy to interpret, they provide relatively little information about the strength of assortative matching. Is an intermarriage rate of 9.2 percent notably large or small? There is no reference point by which to answer that question. Percentages also fail to account for the fact that when matching is random, members of small groups are less likely to match with other members of their group compared to members of large groups.

Panel C of Table 6.1 provides one way to account for the small group matching problem. Each cell of Panel C reports the actual number of marriages by each combination and the expected number of marriages if matching on race was purely random. The first value, N_{ij}, is the same value reported in the corresponding cell in Panel A. The second value is R_{ij}, where the subscripts are defined in the same way, which is the expected number of marriages under random matching. The ratio of actual to expected race-based matches reveal something about the strength of assortative matching (or the weakness of intermarriage). There were 3.35 times more mixed-mixed marriages and 1.24 times more black-black marriages in mid-nineteenth-century Baltimore's African-American community than would be expected under random matching. The impulse toward intermarriage was muted, too, because there were only 27 percent (=119/445) as many color intermarriages as expected under random matching.

Comparing the actual and expected number of intermarriages reveals something about the strength of assortative matching, but they are not amenable to statistical interpretation (especially concerns with statistical significance). This problem is overcome with the so-called odds ratio or log(arithmic) odds ratio. The odds ratio is defined as the odds that a mixed-race man marries a mixed-race woman divided by the odds that a black man marries a mixed-race woman. Mathematically, the odds ratio is calculated as $O = (N_{mm} / N_{mb}) / (N_{bm} / N_{bb})$, and the log-odds ratio is simply $\ln(O)$. If there are more than two groups, the log odds ratio can be calculated for each possible combination. If N_{mx} represents matches between mixed-race men and women of other races and N_{xx} represents marriages between all other types that do not involved mixed-race individuals, the log odds ratio is calculated as $\ln[(N_{mm} / N_{mx}) / (N_{xm} / N_{xx})]$.

As measures of assortative matching, log odds ratios offer four advantages over other measures. First, they provide a reference point by which to judge the strength of assortative mating. A value of the log odds ratio greater than zero (or a value of one for the odds ratio) indicates that there is more assortative matching than expected under a random matching regime; the larger the value, the more powerful the tendency. Second, odds ratios are useful for comparing matching across groups because they are independent of the relative sizes of the group. Third, it is a relatively simple matter to calculate the standard error of the log odds ratio to determine if the calculated log odds ratios are statistically significant, recalling that statistical significance and economic or social importance are not the same thing.[20] And, fourth, the odds ratio can be used with either ordered (e.g., income or education) or nonordered (e.g., race or religion) characteristics.

Panel D of Table 6.1 shows that the log-odds ratio and standard error for African-American marriages in 1860 Baltimore, Maryland; Norfolk, Virginia; and New Orleans, Louisiana. In each case the log odds ratio is statistically significant, but more importantly the values themselves indicate a powerful contemporary impulse toward color-based assortative matching. In Baltimore the odds of a black-black marriage was about 110 times ($e^{4.7} -1$) the odds of a black-mixed marriage. The odds of a black-black (or, equivalently, mixed-mixed) marriage were somewhat smaller in New Orleans (60 times) and Norfolk (27 times), but still large and indicative of a powerful tendency toward color matching among nineteenth-century African Americans.

The prevalence of assortative matching on color is evident in three southern cities with sizeable free African-American populations. Previous studies of these cities have revealed color-based outcomes, including strong preferences for marriage within one's color. Although Norfolk and Baltimore had substantial and vibrant African-American communities, neither was known at the time (or since) for a notable preference for light complexions and white heritage. Several historians, in fact, doubt whether light-skinned African Americans considered themselves different from dark-skinned blacks or whether Upper South whites considered them as different and treated them as such.[21] Whether mixed-race people received preferential treatment by whites is the subject of subsequent chapters, but evidence from historical marriage markets reveals a tendency toward assortative matching. African Americans of different color appear to have considered themselves different in some dimension correlated with color. New Orleans is typically treated by historians as a world apart, because light-skinned, mixed-race people were more readily accepted into polite white society and the light-skinned African-American elite insulated itself from the black masses. The tendency to assortative matching in New Orleans is not unexpected. What is unexpected is that assortative matching in color-conscious New Orleans was no stronger than in the supposedly less color-conscious Upper South cities of Baltimore and Norfolk.

A second important source of information on African-American marriages is found in records kept by the Bureau of Refugees, Freedmen, and Abandoned Lands, better known simply as the Freedmen's Bureau. The bureau was established in March 1865 as part of the War Department. Congress assigned the bureau responsibilities previously held by military commanders, including the supervision of black and white refugees, as well as all abandoned and seized real and personal property.[22] In many ways, the bureau acted like an aid agency: it issued rations to indigent freedmen, established hospitals, operated and maintained order in refugee camps, worked with various religious and benevolent associations in establishing schools, supervised the writing of labor contracts between former planters and slaves, adjudicated labor disputes, and offered limited legal advice and representation.

Besides relief and assistance, the bureau took on the task of solemnizing slave marriages, which had no prior legal standing under slave law. In May 1865 the bureau's commissioner issued a circular instructing assistant commissioners to designate officers to record any marriage conducted by any ordained minister within that assistant commissioner's jurisdiction. The commissioner's circular was not new policy; different departments of the Union Army had issued special orders recognizing marriage rites between contraband slaves dating back to 1861. Despite the general nature of the circular, observance of the order by regional commissioners was highly idiosyncratic. Some commissioners encouraged marriage ceremonies and kept meticulous records, while others simply informed former slaves of their marriage rights and kept few records of the marriages that did occur. Three sets of records are particularly good, however. Records from the areas surrounding Memphis, Tennessee and Vicksburg and Natchez in Mississippi provide details on thousands of marriages. The records include the name and ages of couples, their color, the color of their parents, and other partner-related information. In short, the Freedmen's Bureau marriage records are acknowledged to be "some of the most important records for the study of black family marital relations before and after the Civil War."[23]

The marriage records are particularly well suited to the study of color-based assortative mating, because each marriage pair listed their own color as well as the racial heritage or color of their parents. In total, the Tennessee and Mississippi record groups provide details on 9,426 individuals, and most of the records provide usable information on the color of the partner's parents. The marriage records afford an unusual opportunity to evaluate marital sorting based on alternative classification schemes.

In addition to the usual Deep South color descriptors for contemporary African Americans—black, brown, yellow, light, dark, and so on—the two Mississippi marriage registers record a large number of individuals according to their fraction of white blood. Thus Isaac Chambers, a 63-year-old man married in Natchez on April 10, 1865, was recorded as ¼ white; his father was black, his mother ½ white. Eliza Chambers, Isaac's wife, was recorded as ½ white; her father was black and her mother was white. Southern law and the evidence on so-called white slaves discussed in Chapter 3 suggests that Eliza's mother was not, strictly speaking, white, but was probably indistinguishably so by blood fraction. When the observations reporting precise blood fractions are augmented with blood fractions associated with contemporary racial terminology (black = 0 percent white, griff=¼ white, mulatto=½ white; quadroon=¾ white; octoroon=⅞ white, white=100 percent white), there are 7,168 pairs identified by racial heritage.

While the results need to be interpreted cautiously, they are indicative of a strong contemporary impulse toward color-based assortative mating.[24] Table 6.2 presents a husband-wife racial matching table categorized by the 11 blood fractions

Table 6.2 Assortative Matching By Racial Heritage Log-Odds Ratios for African-Americans Partners' Parents

	Mother's race										
		1/16	1/8	1/4	3/8	1/2	5/8	3/4	7/8	15/16	
	Black	white	white	white	white	white	white	white	white	white	White
Father's race											
Black	4.04*	−1.17	−1.77*	−1.61*	−2.82	−0.12	−1.98	−0.90	−3.15	—	0.22
1/16 white	−0.63	8.07*	4.08*	—	—	0.18	—	—	—	—	—
1/8 white	−1/78*	—	6.70*	0.76	1.81	−0.86	—	0.76	—	—	—
1/4 white	−2.00*	—	0.21	5.26*	0.51	−0.17	—	1.63*	0.17	—	−0.24
3/8 white	−2.86	—	1.79	−0.33	7.69*	—	5.58*	—	—	—	—
1/2 white	−0.35	—	−0.41	0.40	0.62	3.19*	0.72	0.27	0.28	1.13	−0.12
5/8 white	—	—	—	1.10	4.22*	—	7.78*	—	—	—	—
3/4 white	−0.95	—	—	0.39	—	1.30*	—	4.59*	2.94*	—	2.05
7/8 white	−2.38	—	1.54	—	—	—	—	2.23	7.49*	3.79	—
15/16 white	—	—	—	—	—	0.87	—	2.99	—	9.10*	—
White	1.39*	—	—	−0.19	—	0.97	—	0.81	0.20	—	2.30*

Notes: 7,169 marriages. Cells with "—" imply no marriages between relevant pairs. * implies p<0.05 (two-tailed test); critical z-value is 3.49 (not the usual 1.96). See footnote 20 for standard error formula. The value in each cell is interpreted as the odds that a man of color j marries a woman of color j relative to the odds that a man of color not-j marries a woman of color j. The value of 4.04 in the upper left-hand cell implies that the odds of a black-black marriage was 4.04 times more likely than a not-black–black marriage. *Sources:* Bureau of Refugees (Freedmen's Bureau), Series M826, Reel 42 (Natchez and Vicksburg, Mississippi); Bureau of Refugees, Record group 105.2 (Memphis, Tennessee).

appearing in the Freedmen's Bureau marriage records. The value 4.04 in the upper left-hand cell is interpreted to mean that a randomly observed black man was 56 times (= $e^{4.04}$ −1) more likely to marry a black woman than a nonblack man was. The notable feature of Table 6.2 is the large, positive (and statistically significant) values of the log-odds ratio along the principal diagonal from the upper left to the lower right cell. Thus, a ¼-white (commonly referred to as griff) male was nearly 200 times more likely to marry a ¼-white female compared to a non-¼ white man. Relative to men outside their racial group, men of ½-white heritage were more than 24 times more likely to marry ½-white women; they were also significantly more likely to marry a ¾-white (quadroon) women, 2.7 times (= $e^{1.30}$ −1) more likely to marry a ⅞-white women (octoroon), and 1.6 times more likely to marry a nearly white women.

Matching on racial heritage was not as perfect as a frictionless, preference-based model would predict. Search frictions or preferences on a potential mate's nonracial features meant that some black men matched with nonblack women. But the extent to which men of one-half or more white heritage matched with women of one-half or more white heritage, seen in the positive values in the lower-right corner of Table 6.2, is unmistakable. The magnitude and statistical significance of the values along the principal diagonal are simply too large to have been driven by chance. Similarly, the consistently positive values in the lower-right quadrant of the table appear sufficient to reject the alternative of random matching of marriage partners.

The information collected on fractional racial heritage is unique among records of African Americans, but it is open to criticism. When asked, people tend to exaggerate certain characteristics that are viewed positively by society at large. Thus it is well known that people overreport the number of years of school completed and other measures of educational attainment.[25] Given the tendency toward exaggeration, it is not unreasonable to think that mixed-race African Americans exaggerated their own and their parents' white heritage because whiteness was valued in mid-nineteenth-century white and black communities.

As an alternative to using blood fractions, Table 6.3 categorizes marriages using a combination of complexions (black, dark, brown, yellow, light) and traditional racial nomenclature (griff, mulatto, quadroon, and octoroon). Although the racial nomenclature had precise fractional definitions, its component parts—mulatto, quadroon, and so on—were often loosely used to identify persons of known mixed heritage of unknown fraction. Thus a visibly mixed person with medium brown complexion might be labeled "mulatto," while people of light brown complexions might be labeled "quadroons," and those nearly white as "octoroons" even if the observer was unsure of the precise racial mix. Despite their imprecision, labels such as "quadroon" or "octoroon" likely capture broadly defined contemporary racial categorizations.

As in the previous table, the large and positive values along the principal diagonal in Table 6.3 provide evidence of complexion-based matching. Black men were more likely to marry black women than a nonblack man was. Dark men were more likely to marry dark women than their nondark peers. Men labeled mixed were considerably more likely to marry mixed women than nonmixed men. While the large positive values on the principal diagonal indicate a powerful impulse toward complexion homogamy, the off-diagonal elements are equally informative. Compared to the rate at which they married black men, a consideration of values in the first column reveal that black women were much less likely

Table 6.3 Assortative Matching By Color Log-Odds Ratios for African-Americans Partners' Parents

Father's race	Mother's race										
	Black	Dark	Griff	Brown	Yellow	Light	Mixed	Mulatto	Quadroon	Octoroon	White
Black	3.34*	-3.10*	-1.61*	-1.51*	-0.75	-1.59	-1.98*	-0.19	-0.92	-3.17	0.33
Dark	-3.02*	6.60*	—	0.87	0.41	2.16*	—	—	—	—	1.00
Griff	-2.00*	—	5.34*	-1.78	—	-3.15*	-0.20	1.63*	0.17	—	-0.45
Brown	-1.83*	1.02	—	5.04*	0.73	0.75	—	-0.68	—	—	1.24
Yellow	-1.23*	0.48	—	1.07	4.66*	0.03	-3.33	—	—	—	0.07
Light	1.21	2.26*	—	1.97*	0.66	5.80*	—	—	—	—	—
Mixed	-2.37	—	-3.88*	—	—	-1.03	6.46*	-1.87*	-1.11	—	-0.99
Mulatto	-0.39*	-0.67	0.41	-2.09	-2.80	—	-2.12*	3.13*	0.26	0.28	-0.34
Quadroon	-1.05	0.41	0.12	—	—	—	1.30	—	4.63*	2.79*	1.86
Octoroon	-2.35*	—	0.21	—	—	—	-1.04	—	2.27	7.62*	—
White	0.92*	-0.57	-0.30	0.01	-0.07	0.16	-1.25*	0.81	0.69	0.09	1.87*

Notes: 8,644 marriages. Cells with "—" imply no marriages between relevant pairs. * implies $p<0.05$ (two-tailed test); critical z-value is 3.49 (not the usual 1.96). See footnote 20 for standard error formula. The value in each cell is interpreted as the odds that a man of color j marries a woman of color not-j relative to the odds that a man of color not-j marries a woman of color j. The value of 4.04 in the upper left-hand cell implies that the odds of a black-black marriage was 4.04 times more likely than a not-black–black marriage. *Sources*: Bureau of Refugees (Freedmen's Bureau), Series M826, Reel 42 (Natchez and Vicksburg, Mississippi); Bureau of Refugees, Record group 105.2 (Memphis, Tennessee).

to marry dark, brown, mixed, and octoroon men compared to dark, mixed, and octoroon women.

Several concerns can be raised with the racial and complexion classifications reported by the Freedmen's Bureau officials. It is possible that northerners were unfamiliar with the South's racial taxonomy and generated imprecise records. The records themselves provide few clues about who determined the marriage partners' race or complexion. But if the bureau officials asked the presiding ministers, most of whom were locals, about the appropriate designations, the records should reflect contemporary local usage. The racial blood fractions used in Table 6.2 also belie the notion that bureau officials imposed their own opinions: How was the official to determine the blood fraction of marrying couples' parents when the parents were not generally present? This still leaves the problem that recently freed slaves may have overreported their own and their parents' whiteness. A second concern is that if the recording official recognized what he thought to be complexion or racial homogamy, the records may be biased in that the officials' preconceptions led them to record marrying couples as similar in color even when they were not. Perhaps only instances of exceptional color differences appear nonassortative, when in fact nonassortative marriage was more prevalent than the data suggest.

The nature of the Freedmen's Bureau data does not offer any easy resolution to issues of biased or inaccurate reporting of racial heritage or color. One way to assuage concerns with bias in a single source is to turn to alternative, independent sources as a check. Information from the mid-nineteenth-century censuses, discussed earlier, provides one independent check. That data, too, provides evidence of a powerful tendency toward assortative matching on color on the encompassing black and mulatto categories. Consistent patterns across the two sources offer some assurance that assortative matching on race and complexion was at work in the African-American community, but census marshals may have been as prone to a type of confirmation bias in reporting race as Freedmen's Bureau commissioners. That is, they expected to see complexion matches within households and were more likely to record the same color than they might have had they encountered husbands and wives separately.

A third source of evidence on color-based matching is Virginia's free African-American registers, which also report the colors of marriage partners. Unlike the Freedmen's Bureau commissioners and the census marshals who observed the married pairs together, the Virginia court clerks who recorded the colors of Virginia's free African American sometimes observed partners together and sometimes apart. Such separation in recording married couples' colors should mitigate any tendency on the part of contemporary observers to record partners' colors as more alike than they may have been. More than 200 matches of husbands and wives were identified in the registers and they are consistent with assortative matching.[26]

Table 6.4 reports the log-odds ratios for six broad color groups. To make the table manageable, the complex color nomenclature is combined into a half-dozen broad categories: therefore, *black* includes individuals identified as "black" and "very black"; *mulatto* includes individuals identified as mulatto in addition to those identified as "dark mulatto," "light mulatto," and "bright mulatto." Support for race and complexion-based assortative matching is evident in the large and statistically significant log odds ratios along the principal diagonal. The odds that a black man married a black woman was more than 12 times ($=e^{2.59}-1$) the odds that a nonblack man married a black woman. The notable result seen in the table is that the odds of assortative matches are large, and that odds of nonassortative mating are quite small. For instance, a mixed-race man was 76 percent less likely ($=e^{-1.42}-1$) to marry a black woman as a black man was. Racial and complexion homogamy was a powerful force across the early nineteenth-century South. It is evident in cities, in rural areas, in the mixed farming regions of the Upper South, and the in the Mississippi River basin where King Cotton reigned supreme.

One advantage of the Virginia register sample is that it encompasses residents in rural and urban Virginia (Norfolk, Petersburg, Lynchburg, and Richmond), and provides evidence on features of the couples other than their race, including the individuals' heights, ages, year of measurement, and status at birth (slave or free-born). Regression analysis (see Appendix 6.2 for details) shows that after controlling for other characteristics, more than one-half of all marriages were color homogamous and that couples registering in one of four urban places

Table 6.4 Assortative Matching By Color Log-Odds Ratios for African-American Partners

	Black	Dark	Brown	Yellow	Mulatto	Bright
			Wife's color			
Husband's color						
Black	2.59*	−1.03	0.49	0.04	-0.03	−0.09
Dark	—	2.30*	−1.26	−0.53	0.31	0.53
Brown	0.04	1.02	1.55*	—	0.48	—
Yellow	0.45	−0.58	0.92	2.17*	−0.90	−0.32
Mulatto	−1.42	−0.35	0.35	−0.09	1.97*	−0.05
Bright	−0.75	−0.48	−1.44	0.60	−0.31	2.40*

Notes: 215 marriages. "—" signifies no observations between relevant pairs. * implies p<0.05 (two-tailed test); critical z-value is 3.20 (not the usual 1.96). Value in each cell is interpreted as the (log) odds that a man of color j marries a woman of color j relative to the odds that a man of color not-j marries a woman of color j. The value of 2.59 in the upper left cell is interpreted to mean that the odds of a black-black marriage is 13.3 times ($e^{2.59}$) more likely than a not-black-black marriage.
Source: Author's calculations from Virginia Free Black Register sample.

(Lynchburg, Norfolk, Petersburg, and Richmond) were 22 percent *less* likely to be color homogamous. This negative urban coefficient cannot be considered a causal effect; nevertheless, it shows that although color was an important factor influencing a choice of marriage partner, it became less important in larger marriage markets.

The result raises several interesting questions. Did partners in noncolor-assortative marriages selectively migrate to cities? Or were free African Americans who migrated more open to the possibility of noncolor-assortative marriages? Cities may have afforded individuals a level of anonymity that encouraged alternative choices. Alternatively, urban living, perhaps away from one's place of birth, relaxed familial or peer pressure to marry by color. Did cities, with their larger dating and marriage markets, allow preferences in other dimensions to trump color? Larger marriage markets surely afforded men and women the opportunity to match more precisely on other important characteristics (attractiveness, personality, earnings, and so on) that smaller, rural markets generally precluded. The Virginia register sample is too small and does not provide sufficient information on enough variables to untangle the relative importance of the many factors that influenced the choice of marriage partner. The preliminary results suggest that color was a powerful, but not lone determinant of one's mate.

Color and the Family

By the mid-nineteenth century, companionate marriage was the norm. Marriages were not arranged, at least not formally, so potential partners had substantial latitude in whom they married. Among historians marriage was about love and sex and procreation. It was also about responsibility; it was about struggle, work, worry, and the raising of children. One historian of the nineteenth-century American family, Brenda Stevenson, contends that contemporary marriage was about "coming of age in the eyes of one's family and community; it meant adulthood and its attendant responsibilities."[27]

Among economists, marriage is about subjective economic well-being (or utility). An economic model of the married household begins from the premise that the household is the basic production unit. The family produces a large fraction of the goods and services it consumes. A key consideration behind the decision to marry (up to the mid-twentieth century at least) is whether the man will be good provider and the woman an effective housekeeper.[28] Marriage emerges as a contractual relationship between production units subject to economies of scale in production and consumption. That is, marriage establishes partnerships that are more productive than other contractual alternatives, because the contractual relationship encourages marriage-specific investments that simple cohabitation may not. Investments encourage the sexual division of labor, which enhances productivity. Off the farm at least, the division of labor was such that the man's sphere was outside the home; the woman's was inside it.

Independent spheres of action did not imply independent spheres of concern. Contemporary correspondence and diaries reveal men agonizing over the expense of establishing a marital household; the cost of food, clothing, shelter, fuel, medical attention, travel, and entertainment weighed heavily on them. It was an "awesome burden," even for privileged white men with some means and promising or established careers.[29] It must have been doubly so for African-American men. A white man's failure to adequately provide for his family invited criticism, ridicule, and pity. A black man's failure to adequately provide invited a legally mandated forced breakup of the family. Maryland and Virginia law, for example, required local overseers of the poor or justices of the peace to remove minor children from poor African-American families and bind them as pauper apprentices to respectable whites capable of providing for them and training them for later employment.[30]

Men expected to find relief from the grinding labor and relentless concerns in a warm home overseen by a welcoming wife. Such expectations left women no less troubled than men about how best to create the warm and welcoming environment when they had so little control over their married lives. Often with limited support from family and friends and with limited means, women were expected to go to market, cook, clean, manage whatever domestic help there was, and raise the children. Children, too, fundamentally changed a woman's life and typically defined her marital existence. Mid-nineteenth-century women usually started having children shortly after marriage. And children took an emotional and physical toll on wives and mothers. In 1830 Nancy Conrad confided to a relative that family obligations and motherhood had come at the cost of her youth and one of her front teeth.[31]

Herbert Gutman long ago recognized that one subject "essential to an enriched and deepened understanding" of the African-American experience was the history of the African-American family.[32] Classic studies of African-American families include E. Franklin Frazier's two volumes, in which he tries to understand the historical roots of the mid-twentieth-century black family.[33] A number of famous studies followed.[34] The dynamics of the twentieth-century black family are set aside here; the focus is on the structure of the free African-American household prior to Emancipation. But existing evidence does not reveal systemic dysfunction. Theodore Hershberg's study of antebellum Philadelphia found that between 77 and 80 percent of the city's African-American households were traditional, two-parent families. Gutman found similar proportions in such disparate places as Mobile, Alabama (1860), rural Virginia (1865–1866) and Buffalo, New York (1855), as did Stevenson in Loudon County, Virginia (1860), Nicholls in Lunenberg County, Virginia (1814–1820), and Paul Lammermeier in seven Ohio River Valley cities (1860).[35] The majority of African-American households were *not* made up of nontraditional or broken families.

The existing research, although demonstrating a remarkable consistency in the proportion of traditional, two-parent African-American families across the mid-nineteenth-century South, does not provide any insight into whether family structure differed by partners' colors. Frazier thought that it did, and attributed the differences he observed to long-standing traditions that emerged in the South prior to Emancipation.

The issue at hand is whether families headed by black and mixed-race men and women differed in systematic ways. To investigate this issue, samples of black, mixed, and white households drawn from the 1860 population manuscript censuses of Baltimore, Maryland and New Orleans, Louisiana are analyzed. These two cities were chosen because they should be indicative (if not fully representative) of urban African-American experience in the Upper and Lower South. The samples were originally drawn to study differences in child school attendance (see Chapter 8); therefore the samples are not representative of these city's households, but they are representative of households with school-age children. Because the focus is on the family rather than the household, analyzing the structure and size of houses only with school-age children present does not create a problem of representativeness, so long as the relevant population is kept in mind.

A further complication with using the mid-nineteenth-century manuscript census is that the unit of observation was the household, not the family. A household consisted of one or more people living at the same residence. Households included traditional families with or without extended family or other residents (such as live-in servants), one-person households, and boarding houses. Still, it is possible to identify traditional families residing in these city's enumerated households.

To better understand the prevalence of the traditional family, the sampled households were considered traditional if they appeared to be two-parent and nuclear, evidence of which is (1) an adult male is listed first on the census (the household head); (2) an adult female is listed second; (3) one or more minor children are then listed and their ages are consistent with the adult female being their mother or stepmother; (4) the adult male, adult female, and minor children all have the same last name; and (5) any non-nuclear family residents are likely to have been relatives (e.g., grandparents) or live-in domestics. It would have been preferable for the census to identify the relationship between members of each household. Given that it did not, the coding scheme is a reasonable approach to identifying traditional households.

Table 6.5 and Table 6.6 report statistics on the structure for households with white, black, and mixed-race heads in Baltimore and New Orleans in 1860. The tables reveal that in both Baltimore and New Orleans, single parenthood was common among parents in their twenties with school-age children. For white and black heads of households in their twenties, slightly more than one-half were part of a two-parent family; less than one-third of mixed-race heads in their twenties

Table 6.5 Baltimore Household Structure By Age and Color

Age Group	White	Black	Mixed-Race
Household head 20–29 years			
Traditional	57.5%	52.3%	30.6%
Single mother	12.4	20.0	28.6
Single father	30.1	27.7	40.8
Household head 30–39 years			
Traditional	81.0	72.0	72.0
Single mother	9.5	16.3	18.0
Single father	9.5	11.7	10.0
Household head 40–49 years			
Traditional	77.1	67.9	67.6
Single mother	14.1	19.3	22.1
Single father	8.8	12.8	10.3
Household head 50–59 years			
Traditional	73.0	56.0	61.0
Single mother	14.5	29.3	30.5
Single father	12.5	14.7	8.5

Notes: Traditional family inferred from household structure and recording convention of census marshals. Marshals tended to record traditional households as husband, wife, and children in descending order by age, followed by other household members, including grandparents, servants, and so on. Traditional households were identified as those that this pattern and where first-listed adult male and female shared the same surname. Sample includes only households with school-age children (6–16 years). *Source*: US Census Office, Eighth Census (1860), Baltimore population manuscripts.

lived in a traditional household. One notable feature is the prevalence of single fatherhood, especially among households in which the head was in his or her twenties. Maternal mortality was likely a contributory—if not the principal—source of single fatherhood, which appears to have been an equal-opportunity source of household disruption. Approximately 30 percent of white and black households were headed by a single father; lower rates at older ages are likely due to remarriage.[36]

Earlier studies of household structure attribute the relatively high proportion of single-parent households to markedly unbalanced sex ratios. Baltimore in 1860 had unequal sex ratios. For whites in their twenties, there were 925 men per 1,000 women; the number for African Americans was 798.[37] The relatively low rate of traditional marriage for household heads in their twenties is consistent with local sex ratios. The sex ratios for whites at older ages (1,042 for household heads in their thirties; forties, 1,062; and fifties, 1,017) and free African Americans (thirties, 827; forties, 902 and fifties, 826) account in great measure for the differential

Table 6.6 New Orleans Household Structure By Age and Color

Age Group	White	Black	Mixed-Race
Household head 20–29 years			
Traditional	22.2%	50.0%	18.4%
Single mother	16.7	50.0	44.7
Single father	61.1	0.0	36.9
Household head 30–39 years			
Traditional	72.4	45.0	52.5
Single mother	12.6	50.0	36.6
Single father	15.0	5.0	10.9
Household head 40–49 years			
Traditional	77.6	54.1	62.4
Single mother	9.1	40.1	22.8
Single father	13.3	5.8	14.8
Household head 50–59 years			
Traditional	76.7	26.7	75.7
Single mother	11.6	60.0	24.3
Single father	11.7	13.3	0.0

Notes: Traditional family inferred from household structure and recording convention of census marshals. Marshals tended to record traditional households as husband, wife, and children in descending order by age, followed by other household members, including grandparents, servants, and so on. Traditional households were identified as those that this pattern and where first-listed adult male and female shared the same surname. Sample includes only households with school-age children (6–16 years). *Source*: US Census Office, Eighth Census (1860), New Orleans population manuscripts.

experiences between whites and African Americans. Twenty-something white sex ratios favored "illegitimacy, delinquency, broken homes"—just not to the same extent as among black and mixed-race twenty-somethings.[38] At older ages, a sex ratio that favored white women encouraged traditional households, and about eight in ten white households were traditional, two-parent households. A sex ratio that favored free African-American men in the marriage market led to lower rates of traditional household formation. Still, about seven in ten African-American households in Baltimore were traditional, two-parent families.

New Orleans presents a seemingly different portrait of African-American family life. Although about 76 percent of households with school-age children and mixed-race household heads in their fifties were traditional households, in nearly every other group less than two-thirds were traditional, two-parent households. It would be easy enough to attribute the low rate of traditional households (or high rates of single parenthood), relative to Upper South and Mid-Atlantic places, to New Orleans's cosmopolitanism.

Within New Orleans's African-American community, perhaps, French sexual norms intersected with the Caribbean tendency toward miscegenation and created a society accepting of the quadroon ball, plaçage, and nonmarital race mixing. Such cultural factors undoubtedly influenced attitudes toward marriage and family, but attributing the city's low proportions of traditional families to an alternative cultural norm is simply too facile. Sex ratios were unbalanced in a way that encouraged white families and discouraged African-American families. Sex ratios favored white women in the marriage market (1,030 men per 1,000 women in their twenties; thirties, 1,290; forties, 1,610; and fifties, 1,320), whereas free African-American men were favored in that market (twenties, 613 per 1,000; thirties, 608; forties, 665; and fifties, 552). If mid-nineteenth-century urban black men were promiscuous it was not because slavery made them so; it was because they were in sufficiently short supply that they did not have to settle down to attract sexual partners. Free African Americans may have married or cohabited with slaves, and some did, but doing so would not have necessarily created a traditional, resident, two-parent household and increased the observed proportion of such families.

How scholars interpret the proportion of traditional households among African-American households seemingly depends as much on their priors and predilections as on the evidence. Hershberg, for example, finds that between 77 and 80 percent of Philadelphia's free African-American households were two-parent households, and considers these proportions evidence of black family decline and dysfunction.[39] Stevenson finds that 72 percent or more of free black households in Loudoun County, Virginia were male headed, and discusses the "very few men" in many households with whom black women could "share the burden of their financial, physical, and emotional responsibilities."[40] Gutman, on the other hand, finds that about 80 to 90 percent of African-American households were male-headed in such disparate places as rural Virginia (1865–1866) and Buffalo, New York (1855), and concludes that African American families were a functioning and vital institution. Although African-American men with skills "obviously had a better chance to build stable, two-parent households," the ubiquity of the two-parent structure across skill and income groups implies that the two-parent household "belonged" to nineteenth-century African Americans.[41] The mid-nineteenth-century African-American family took many and complex forms, but chaotic and casual, dysfunctional and disordered are not particularly useful notions.

Economic models of marriage markets posit that marriage rates vary positively with sex ratios and the supply of eligible men with bright earnings prospects. These models show that in equilibrium some women will remain childless, but small shocks to earning capacities or sex ratios can have profound effects on single parenthood.[42] Low marriage rates among young mothers in the mid-nineteenth century resulted from the convergence of three features. First, the imbalance in sex ratios meant that young men were scarce, so men of given characteristics could "marry up" more readily than they would have in an environment with more balanced sex ratios. Some women's preferences were such that they would rather remain single than pay the male scarcity premium.

Second, male mortality rates were higher at nearly all ages, so that some of the observed single mothers were widows. From a single man's perspective, a woman with another man's child presented a less desirable marriage partner.[43] Sex imbalances further reinforced the discount single mothers would have to offer in the marriage market to attract a mate. Again, there were women who preferred to raise children alone than offer such a discount. The result was single motherhood.

Third, when the gap between men's and women's earning potential narrows, women may substitute away from marriage. Establishing that (relative) income influences women's marriage choices is problematic, however, because marriage and occupational choice are jointly determined. Disentangling this effect is challenging and places more demands on the data than most early-nineteenth-century sources can meet. Some recent research overcomes this challenge and demonstrates that nineteenth-century white women responded as theory predicts, so it is not unreasonable to assume that African-American women responded in similar fashion.[44] Chapter 7 provides the details of African-American occupational opportunities, and it shows that the earnings gap between African-American men's and women's wages was narrower than for white men and women. Black and mixed-race women, therefore, were more positively disposed to single parenthood than white women.

On the question of family structure, Gutman's optimistic assessment appears warranted. School-age African-American children were less likely than white children to live in a traditional, two-parent household, but their experience was not dissimilar. Approximately two-thirds to three-quarters of school-age children lived in traditional households. The evidence is more consistent with economic models that emphasize the effect of unbalanced sex ratios on dating and marital outcomes than with persistent, systematic dysfunction in the African-American family. Traditional family structures were as much a part of the African-American as the white experience.

Color Matching and Household Size

Given that the agenda driving scholarly explorations into the nature of the black family was defined by Frazier's two-path thesis, the literature focuses on the extent of single motherhood, as well as its causes and consequences. Single motherhood was not uncommon, though far from the norm; one-fifth to one-third of all households with an African-American head was headed by a single mother. Single-mother households, regardless of the race of the mother, were smaller on average than two parent households. Single-mother households were, however, not smaller by one—the missing or absent husband. They tended to be missing other members of the typical two-parent household. Stevenson, for example, found that few single-mother households in Loudoun County, Virginia, had a second adult present. Two-parent households not only had two adult parents present; they often had other adult kin, many of whom were capable of contributing to the household. Single-mother households, on the other hand, had little domestic help other than older children. They rarely had another adult in the home who shared their burdens.

Household size is then a potentially informative metric by which to assess the success of families. Using the Baltimore and New Orleans household samples, it is possible to connect assortative matching with family size. The question of interest is whether color-assortative households were different in this one dimension from nonassortative households.

Table 6.7 provides matching matrices for the three races—white, black, mulatto—reported in the 1860 population census. Several notable features emerge from the larger Baltimore sample reported in Panel A. First, virtually no whites crossed the marital color line. Second, as noted earlier, there was a powerful impulse toward assortative mating on color among African Americans. Third, mixed-race households were larger on average than black households by about one-half person. Households with assortative matching on mixed-race were larger than households with at least one black resident parent, although the only statistically significant difference is that between mixed-mixed versus black-black households ($p=0.003$). Fewer generalizations can be drawn from the smaller New Orleans sample, the results of which appear in Panel B of Table 6.7. One feature stands out, however: namely, that the color-assortative households are larger than nonassortative households.

It is difficult to determine from the available evidence the causes of smaller black-black households. It may have been that black women married and started having children later; black children may have suffered from higher infant and child mortality; or black household life may have been more "fractured" than mixed-race households.[45] The census makes it difficult to sort out the relative weight of these factors, but they are likely influences.

Household resources surely influenced household size as well. Race-based occupational and wealth differences are explored in greater detail with more representative samples in later chapters, but evidence from the family structure sample is consistent with the hypothesis that resources influenced childbearing choices. Compared to black-black assortative households, mixed-mixed households were more likely to own real estate, and male heads of mixed-mixed households were more likely to work at skilled occupations. The average male head of a black-black household worked as a day labor or as a domestic servant; a typical head of a mixed-mixed household worked in construction or as a barber. Mixed-race

Table 6.7 Household Size By Assortative and Nonassortative Matches Baltimore and New Orleans in 1860

Panel A: Baltimore

Female color		Male color		
		White	Mixed	Black
	White	6.75 (2.29) [2,223]	3.00 (na) [1]	— [0]
	Mixed	— [0]	6.36 (2.20) [234]	6.16 (2.19) [95]
	Black	— [0]	5.71 (2.20) [24]	5.89 (2.10) [876]

Panel B: New Orleans

Female color		Male color		
		White	Mixed	Black
	White	6.29 (2.29) [248]	— [0]	— [0]
	Mixed	— [0]	6.80 (2.08) [146]	5.91 (2.43) [11]
	Black	— [0]	5.67 (1.33) [9]	6.38 (2.19) [26]

Notes: Statistics are for households with school-age children (6–16 years) resident in the household. Statistics are for traditional households with resident parent and/or stepparent. Table reports sample averages, with standard deviations in parentheses, and number of observations in brackets. *Sources:* US Census Office, Eighth Census (1860). Population manuscript schedules for Baltimore and New Orleans.

men were more likely to have a skill, earn higher incomes, and accumulate more wealth, which afforded them the opportunity to support larger households.[46]

In addition to more opportunities for assortative matching, African Americans may have preferred urban over rural life because it was possible to support larger families in cities. Nicholls reports 4.59 members in the average male-headed African-American household in Caroline County, Virginia in 1814; the average declined from 5.29 to 4.64 members in Lunenberg County between 1802 and 1820.[47] Stevenson reports similar averages (4.41 to 5.10) for male-headed, African-American households in Loudoun County between 1810 and 1860.[48] African-American families in Baltimore and New Orleans of all racial compositions were larger than African-American families in rural places.

Historians explain the African-American preference for urban places as attempts to escape rural racism or the drudgery of farm life, to the greater economic opportunities that were believed to exist even if they were not always realized, or to the release from customary obligations and expectations captured in the medieval German proverb *stadluft macht frei* (city air makes you free). The evidence presented here adds an extra dimension to these conjectures. While urban life presented its own challenges, the evidence suggests that it afforded African Americans brighter prospects for marriage and family, but the black-mixed divide is evident in cities as well.

Conclusion

In May 1759 an Amelia County, Virginia grand jury indicted Elizabeth Gallemore, a white woman, for cohabiting with Henry Jones's black slave and for having several mixed-race children.[49] Although Peter Fontaine's oft-quoted 1757 outburst that the country "swarms with mulatto bastards" was a taking to task of the many "base wretches" who took up with black women, he was no less concerned with cases like Elizabeth Gallemore's. Fontaine's principal concern, beyond the immorality of such interracial sexual unions, was that if in each generation the progeny of that original mixed-race bastard mated with a white person, the offspring would grow increasingly white. Eventually the original blackness would become undetectable, and three or four generations later the nearly white progeny might legally marry a white person.[50] Whiteness, Fomtaine feared, would become meaningless.

Observing the wave of manumissions a generation later, historian Michael Nicholls concludes that Fontaine's fears of secret amalgamation were unfounded. Color-blind manumission set in motion a process in which the "mulatto population was becoming more black."[51] Nicholls's conclusion of a blackening of Southside Virginia's African-American population is based on two premises: manumission was color-blind, and African Americans formed sexual unions randomly. Neither is true. Evidence presented in Chapter 5 of this volume shows that manumission was not color-blind. Mixed-race slaves were more likely to be manumitted and were manumitted at younger ages, so they would have been more likely to reproduce and capable of producing more offspring. Marriages were not formed randomly, either. Evidence presented in this chapter clearly demonstrates that mixed-race people were more likely to marry and reproduce with other mixed-race people. Moreover, assortative mixed-race families had larger families than assortative black or nonassortative black-mixed families. It seems unlikely that the Southside's African-American population was blackening. If anything, the light-skinned, mixed-race population was growing both absolutely and as a proportion of the African-American population. Marriage and the family played a crucial role in that process.

7

Work

Nineteenth-century Americans noticed color. They remarked on it. They saw subtle shades of it. They impressed upon their fellows how complexion complicated the world, yet made it inherently more interesting. Traveler and chronicler Charles Joseph Latrobe was "detained" in New Orleans for more than a month beginning in December 1832. In the rainy season the streets oozed mud up through the pavement and early winter temperatures near 80° F made his time there "penance." For Latrobe, unlike so many visitors to the city, the most remarkable thing about New Orleans was not the stuccoed Spanish-style buildings or the elaborate iron fretwork around their balconies or the constant coming and going of river traffic along the levees. Latrobe contended that there was nothing more remarkable than that which presented itself in front of the main cathedral (the area now known as Jackson Square). He described

> a cluster of mulatto women, sitting with kerchiefed [sic] heads and comfortable rabbit skin shawls folded around their persons, before the mats which display their various articles of traffic to the passenger—there a group of insurgent market-women tossing their empty baskets at one another, or pale-faced quadroon girls half veiled, followed by their duennas. On one side advances a negro, feathered from head to foot by the live turkies [sic] hung upon his person; on the other a string of mules, or a mulatto driving his dray in the primeval position of Greek charioteer. Then comes a party of half-a-dozen coloured people, clothed in the brightest hues imaginable, seated with knees and chins in contact, in a car drawn by a single old horse boring its way through the press, or a grey-haired negro going home with his christmas [sic] dinner, consisting of a fat hen and a string of onions, and grinning with delight from ear to ear.[1]

Color colored Latrobe's perceptions of the bustling port city.[2] To observe New Orleanians was to observe their colors as much as their activities.

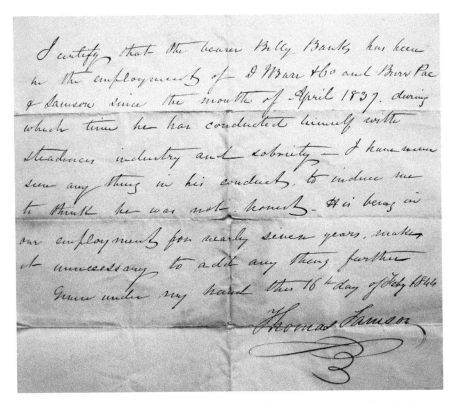

Figure 7.1 Affidavit in Support of Former Slave Billy Banks's Petition to Remain in Virginia. Courts looked to habits of sobriety, industriousness, and honesty in allowing exceptions to the rule that freed slaves emigrate within twelve months of manumission. It appears that Banks had remained without permission and believed that continuity of employment supported his request. Source: Free Negro and Slave Records, Albemarle County, Box 1 (1844), Library of Virginia.

So what were their activities? How did they earn their livelihoods? Being black (even only partly so) in America in the nineteenth century limited one's options so that many people of African descent toiled at menial tasks for little pay with little hope of advancement or improvement. The traditional telling of the plight of Americans of African descent might end right there.[3] But it turns out that color complicates the telling of their stories. It turns out that the labors of African Americans were heavily influenced by color.

Color and Urban Employment

Summarizing his discussion of occupations pursued by North Carolina's mid-nineteenth-century African Americans, John Hope Franklin wrote that they worked as "bakers, barbers, bartenders, blacksmiths, boatmen, butchers, cabinetmakers, carpenters, caulkers, cooks, coopers, distillers, engineers, drivers, hostlers, iron moulders, mariners, masons, millers, painters, plasterers, saddlers, seamstresses, shoemakers, spinners, tailors, tanners, wagoners, weavers, and wheelwrights."[4] Franklin's point, of course, was to recognize the breadth of black experience, but his list fails to provide much sense of the number of African-American carpenters, masons, or wheelwrights. Most analyses of the era's African-American occupational opportunities and choices remain hamstrung by a long-standing interpretation of free people as pitiful, poor, downtrodden masses—as slaves without masters. Looking back, Gary Nash portrays urban free African Americans as "excluded from the industrializing" sectors, who "toiled at service jobs that carried little status," and were commonly employed "at the bottom of the job hierarchy as common laborers."[5] Looking ahead, one contemporary African American observed that "drudgery is my prospective portion."[6]

Seth Rockman shows that drudgery, marginality, and poverty were the conditions for most urban working-class people, white or black.[7] Despite the prospective drudgery of many free African Americans, economic advance was within reach for a few. Martin Delany, in his call for self-help, recounted the achievements of several notable African Americans; Juliet Walker, too, highlights the entrepreneurial accomplishments of African-American men and women.[8] Even Ira Berlin, whose interpretations are more pessimistic than most, allowed that freedom afforded African Americans the opportunity to enjoy the fruits of their own labor.

In realizing whatever economic success they achieved African Americans overcame a number of obstacles, not the least of which was racism and colorism that limited the range of opportunities available to them. Even though some African Americans demonstrated enough industry to earn the respect of prominent whites (see Figure 7.1), an occupational color line operated in various degrees across antebellum southern cities; some work was white work and some was black. In Baltimore's shipyards, whites were ship carpenters and blacks were ship caulkers.[9] African Americans so dominated the profession that one traveler called barbering a black "birthright."[10] Kimberly Hanger contends that Spanish officials in colonial New Orleans attracted free African Americans because they were well suited for the "petty commercial and transportation jobs" eschewed by whites.[11] Black carpenters sawed "at the whipsaw and hewed out timber," work that white carpenters did not care to do.[12] What linked these tasks was their generally subordinate, servile, or semiskilled nature. Occupational segregation sometimes followed from employer discrimination, sometimes from white employees' refusal to work shoulder to shoulder with blacks or mixed-race peoples, and sometimes from customers' refusal to treat with African-American workers. In a workplace in which race and color enters into the decision calculus, there is a tendency toward job specialization and occupational segregation.[13]

When the color line failed to bar African Americans from certain jobs, white workers frustrated by the competition sought statutory bans. Every year one or another southern state legislature or city council received a petition or two asking for laws that might ban African Americans from one employment or another. Historian John Russell contends that one potentially useful measure of African-American inroads into contemporary labor markets is the list of occupations for which whites sought a ban.[14] Between 1776 and 1860, according to Russell, the Virginia legislature received petitions asking for the exclusion of blacks from 28 trades, most of which were semiskilled construction jobs (carpentry and plastering) or peddling (fishmongering and huckstering) or skilled trades (cabinetmaking and coopering). Despite the regular appearance of petitions praying for relief from workplace competition, few succeeded. Free African Americans were typically barred from trading with slaves, selling alcohol, vending without a license, operating a school, and river or harbor piloting.[15] They remained free to pursue most any other trade.

Historians remain divided over the effectiveness of the informal restrictions and formal prohibitions. Franklin contends that the antebellum era "was a period of unremitting effort on the part of whites to curtail or completely prevent the activities of black and mixed-race artisans."[16] Marina Wikramanayake portrays the period between 1830 and 1860 as "increasingly repressive."[17] On the other hand, Leonard Curry believes that the practical consequences of statutory prohibitions have been exaggerated.[18] State legislatures and city councils were reluctant to impose employment bans and reduce labor market competition. And when restrictions were enacted, they were selectively enforced. In 1857 Savannah, Georgia levied a discriminatory $6.25 license fee on African-American carters, hucksters and artisans. In 1860 only two black artisans paid the fee.[19] The most common and commonly enforced prohibitions were those than barred free people from selling liquor to slaves, yet whites regularly complained of black owned tippling shops tucked away in urban alleys and tenement basements.

A third point of scholarly disagreement concerns the consequences of immigration on African-American employment. More historians have given greater weight to the observations of such contemporaries as Frederick Douglass, who observed that "every hour sees us elbowed out of some employment to make room perhaps for some newly arrived immigrants," and less to Frederick Law Olmsted's observation that "poor blacks always manage to keep themselves more decent than poor whites."[20] The weight of historical interpretation, based mostly on anecdotal evidence, concludes that immigrant competition in the labor market reduced wages and left fewer remunerative employment opportunities for blacks. Ira Berlin ("influx of Irish and Germans . . . speeded up the exclusion of Negro freemen from many occupations"), Leon Litwack ("unskilled Irish labor continued to pour into the menial employments . . . and drive out Negro competitors"), Robert Reinders ("Europeans tended to replace free Negroes"), T. Stephen

Whitman ("free black workers themselves were replaced by European immigrants as the city's proletarian workers"), and Leo Hirsch ("the advent of foreigners was to drive the Negro from many of the occupations in which blacks had formerly been seen quite frequently") reiterate the pessimist's view.[21]

It turns out that the so-called immigrant-displacement interpretation is incomplete, if not incorrect. Evidence on African-American employment in Baltimore between 1815 and 1860 provides no strong evidence of systematic occupational decline. African-American representation in professional occupations, wholesale and retail selling, and the building trades, though modest, remained relatively constant. The proportion employed in skilled occupations declined from about 10 percent of African-American men reporting an occupation in 1825 to about 6.5 percent in 1860, while employment in semiskilled and service jobs expanded briskly.[22]

Economic theory offers guidance, but no simple answers concerning occupational segregation. Economic models of segregation—whether in occupation, residence, or education—posit the existence of stable and unstable equilibria and tipping points.[23] The logic that emerges from these mathematical models is that a job might be considered a black job dominated by black workers. But the entry of a sufficiently large number of white (or immigrant) workers with a preference for laboring beside other white (or immigrant) workers may lead to a tip, the job becomes white, and is subsequently dominated by white workers. Black workers exit the job, either by choice or exclusion, and find work in some other black job, or perhaps their migrating to new jobs causes one or more white jobs to tip the other way.

The data used here to study color-based differences in employment cannot and will not resolve whether employment opportunities improved or declined or tipped, because the 1860 census presents a single snapshot of an evolving employment environment. But it is important that such information as exists be interpreted in light of historiography and economic theory. The census's snapshot quality will not resolve the debate, but the census provides valuable employment information.

Information on urban occupations was taken from a sample of ten southern cities that range from bustling Baltimore to small-town Frederick, Maryland. Geographically, the sample spans the Old South and the New, the border states and the Deep South. The sample should capture both regional commonalities and local idiosyncrasies.[24] The dozens of occupations listed in the census are collapsed into the seven broad categories created by Otis Dudley Duncan and his colleagues in their study of mid-twentieth-century social status.[25] While it is probably inappropriate to apply Duncan's status values to nineteenth-century occupations, his classification scheme is useful in creating groups of occupations—Professionals/Managers, Sales/Clerical, Crafts, Operatives, Services, Labor, and No Occupation.

Table 7.1 reports the number of men per thousand by race and color employed in each of the seven broad occupational categories and includes 33 selected narrowly defined, commonly observed jobs within each category.[26] It is readily

Table 7.1 Male Employment Per 1,000 in Broad Occupational Categories and Narrow Jobs

CATEGORY/Job	Black men	Mixed-race men	White men
1. LABOR	320	167	235
a. Labor	271	141	216
b. Stevedore	10	5	1
c. Tobacco twister	17	4	0
2. SERVICE	149	175	31
a. Barber	17	47	2
b. Hostler	5	4	3
c. Porter	49	40	11
d. Steward	6	16	0
e. Waiter	57	45	1
3. OPERATIVE	306	193	125
a. Brickmaker	69	17	3
b. Carriage driver	30	28	16
c. Carter	96	49	36
d. Caulker	21	9	0
e. Sailor	42	32	11
f. Sawyer	19	1	2
4. CRAFT	133	313	269
a. Blacksmith	11	7	16
b. Bricklayer	8	38	5
c. Carpenter	25	103	43
d. Cooper	6	9	10
e. Machinist	0	1	10
f. Mason	5	16	12
g. Ship carpenter	1	3	7
h. Shoemaker	13	32	39
i. Tailor	3	22	30
j. Whitewasher	29	14	0
5. SALES/CLERICAL	8	6	22
a. Huckster/peddler	8	6	8
b. Salesman	0	0	3
c. Clerk	2	10	47

(Continued)

Table 7.1 Continued

CATEGORY/Job	Black men	Mixed-race men	White men
6. MANAGER / PROFESSIONAL	23	54	225
a. Merchant	5	9	65
b. Restaurant	0	1	5
c. Shopkeeper	5	18	75
d. Attorney	0	0	5
e. Clergy	4	5	5
f. Physician	0	0	7
g. Teacher	4	4	8

Notes: Narrow job titles do not include all jobs within a broad category; they are reported because they are representative of jobs within each category and substantial numbers of nineteenth-century whites and/or African Americans reported being employed in these jobs. The cities in the sample are Baton Rouge and New Orleans, Louisiana; Baltimore and Frederick, Maryland; Petersburg and Richmond, Virginia; Charleston, South Carolina; Louisville, Kentucky; Mobile, Alabama; and Nashville, Tennessee. *Source:* Author's calculations from the population manuscripts of the 1860 census.

apparent that on average, black, mixed-race, and white men labored at different tasks. African Americans were overrepresented as common laborers, operatives, and in service trades. Not surprisingly, they were underrepresented in sales and clerical work, as well as the professional and managerial ranks. Some worked at skilled trades and carved out places for themselves in the local economy. Men, like blacksmith Albert Cross, were so integral to the local economy that white men readily signed their petitions to remain in the state (see Figure 7.2). Still, occupational segregation was very real in the mid-nineteenth-century South.

How different were the occupational experiences of the three principal colors? One widely used measure of segregation is the *Index of Dissimilarity* (sometimes called the *Duncan Index*), which is based on racial representation across occupations.[27] The index takes on values between zero and one, where zero implies equal proportionate racial occupational representation and one implies perfect occupational segregation. Values are interpreted as the share of workers of each race who would need to change jobs to achieve proportionate racial representation across all occupations for those two races. Based on the ten-city 1860 sample, the black-mixed Index of Dissimilarity for men equals 0.277 based on 33 narrowly defined occupations and 0.266 based on seven broad categories. Thus about one-quarter of African-American men would have had to change jobs to achieve equal racial in employment for black and mixed-race men.

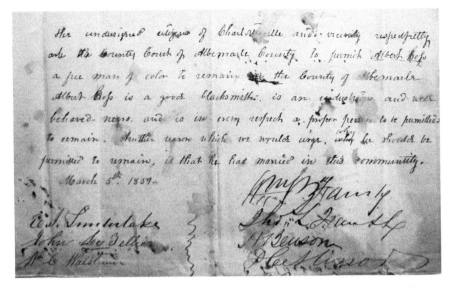

Figure 7.2 Affidavit in Support of Albert Cross's Petition to Remain in Virginia. Seven locally prominent white men supported Cross's application, in part because he was a skilled blacksmith. Source: Free Negro and Slave Records, Albemarle County, Box 1 (1859), Library of Virginia.

The color gap for black-mixed male employment was only slightly less pronounced than the racial gap. Based on the 33 narrow jobs, the black-white Index of Dissimilarity is 0.354; it is 0.397 for the seven broad occupational categories. Index values for mixed-white comparisons are similar; 0.293 when calculated using narrow job definitions and 0.292 using the broad categories. For African-American men, across-color (black-mixed) disparities were of approximately the same order of magnitude as the across-race (black-white) disparities.

While the Duncan Index is useful because it is easily interpretable—approximately one-quarter to one-third of men would have had to change occupations to achieve equal proportionate occupational representation—it is not immediately evident how that number compares to historical experience more generally. One obvious comparison is to the immigrant experience. Using the same seven-category calculation for immigrants and native-born whites observed in the ten-city urban sample, the Duncan Index is 0.299. So roughly a third of immigrant and native-born whites would have had to change occupations to achieve proportionate representation across jobs. The index value is consistent with what we know of the immigrant experience, especially that of the Irish, in southern cities.[28] Post-potato famine immigrants mostly found work as day laborers; few worked as clerks, shopkeepers, merchants, or attorneys.

An alternative approach to measuring the occupational complexion gap is through regression analysis, specifically multinomial logistic regression.

Multinomial regression is useful when a nominal outcome—occupational category—is not readily ordered or assigned a value, and is a generalization of a two-outcome logit regression. The odds of African-American occupational outcomes are specified as a linear combination of the predictor variables, with color as the predictor of principal interest. Regressions are specified with mixed-race as the excluded racial category so that the estimated coefficients on the black variable reflect the odds, relative to a mixed-race man, of a black man being employed in a particular occupation.

Table 7.2 reports the coefficients, or log odds, and standard errors of the relative likelihood of a black man reporting employment in one of seven occupational categories.[29] Because the regressions include only African Americans, the reference category is mixed-race, and the black coefficients capture the differential effect of color on employment by sector. The estimated coefficient -0.922 means that black is associated with a 0.922 decrease in the log odds of reporting employment in a service occupation versus common labor. The relative risk ratio, which is simply the exponent of the coefficient (i.e., $e^{0.922} = 0.398$), is interpreted as the odds (relative to a mixed-race man) that a black man reports employment in a service job.[30] Thus, compared to mixed-race men, black men are about 40 percent (0.40 times) as likely to report employment in a service task versus common labor. Other risk ratios are interpreted similarly, and reveal that black men were considerably less

Table 7.2 Estimated (Log) Odds of Black Employment By Occupational Category

Occupational category	Black men	Black women
Labor	Reference	Reference
Service	−0.922**	−0.609**
	(0.104)	(0.225)
Operative	−0.218*	−1.593**
	(0.098)	(0.261)
Craft	−0.534**	—
	(0.108)	
Sales/Clerical	−0.504	0.224
	(0.300)	(0.519)
Manager/	−0.989**	—
Professional	(0.190)	
Observations	5,184	1,929

Notes: Estimated coefficients from multinomial logistic regressions. The reported coefficients are those on the black dummy variable. Additional controls include age and its square, and dummy variables for each city. There are too few observations in some female occupational cells to estimate the model, so those categories are dropped. ** implies $p<0.01$; * implies $p<0.05$. *Sources*: Author's calculations from data in the 1860 census population for the ten-city sample.

likely than mixed-race men to report employment in any occupation other than common labor. Black men were about half as likely as mixed men to report skilled craft (0.58 times) or professional (0.37 times) employment. Black men were about 80 percent as likely as mixed men to report employment as an operative. It is hard to draw any conclusion other than black men were employed in less prestigious jobs than mixed-race men.

Index values and regression coefficients provide a readily interpreted measure of central tendencies, but it is informative to unpack these values by looking behind them. Although mixed-race men were more often found in skilled and semiskilled jobs, day labor was the most common employment for men of all races and colors, and Seth Rockman's and T. Stephen Whitman's depictions of the drudgery and insecurity of mid-nineteenth-century workers of all colors dashes any notion of the nobility of a simple workingman's life. Urban laborers scratched out a meager existence and suffered recurrent bouts of unemployment and hunger.[31]

Color, Self-Employment, and Entrepreneurship

Relative to whites, African Americans were overrepresented in service trades, which ran the gamut from lowly waiters in oyster houses to barbershop owners. Barbering, as Table 7.1 reveals, was a predominantly mixed-race occupation. The barbershop has garnered much attention, but contemporary black leaders were less enamored of barbering than subsequent generations of social historians. Whereas Lois and James Horton place the barbershop at the center of black urban culture, Martin Delany labeled the barbershop as the place where "great worth and talent . . . were permitted to expire."[32] Delany's criticism was born of frustration with the limits placed on black entrepreneurship, but seems unnecessarily critical of the men who pursued the trade. Some men realized their entrepreneurial potential as barbers. Frank Parrish, a mixed-race barber in Nashville, advertised his barbershop and bath house where in addition to providing haircuts, shaves, and warm baths, customers could purchase collars, fancy soaps, colognes, and the best cigars.[33] Of Baltimore's six-score barbers, a handful provided their customers with similarly posh surroundings. John A. Jones's shop at 46 East Baltimore Street, near the city's financial district, was variously described as barbershop, perfumery, and variety store.[34]

Although African-American-owned barbershops were less common in the Lower than the Upper South, they were not unheard of. A study of William Johnson's Natchez barbering business reveals why African Americans invested in the barbering trade.[35] In an era when day laborers earned 80¢ a day (when work was to be had) and skilled craftsmen about twice that, barbers charging 75¢ per haircut, 15¢ per shave, and $1 per tooth extraction could earn $25 or more each week. Juliet E. K. Walker found that William Johnson's average gross daily revenue was $3.67 in November 1830. While his gross revenue exceeded the daily wages of a skilled worker, it is impossible to determine from the reported evidence whether his profits, net of costs, exceeded skilled wages. One apparent advantage of barbering was the constancy of work; Johnson reported only one day in the month with no income. Moreover, the very nature of the business placed barbers in unusually favorable positions to learn of other entrepreneurial opportunities. As a place where bankers, merchants, and other white businessmen were at ease and engaged in leisurely discussions, black barbers were privy to all kinds of information. It was not uncommon for barbers to speculate in real estate and invest in other promising enterprises, and there are good reasons to suspect that they got market or investment tips from customers.[36]

Shop keeping was more common among mixed-race than black men. Eighteen of every thousand mixed-race men kept a shop compared to just five of one thousand black men. One not insignificant factor underlying the differential followed from the requirement that obtaining a shop keeper's license required the support of prominent white men. Mixed-race men were more likely to have developed connections with whites and were more likely to have the literacy and numeracy skills necessary to succeed. Figure 7.3 reproduces a document supporting William Lewis's petition for a shop signed by seven white men testifying to Lewis's honesty and industriousness.

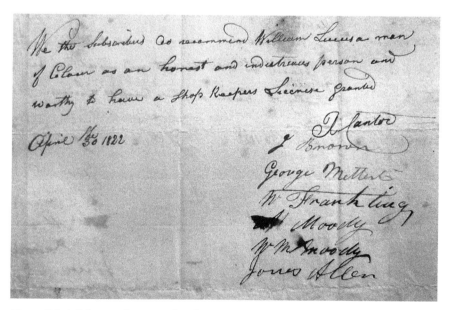

Figure 7.3 Affidavit in Support of William Lewis's Application for a Virginia Shopkeeper's License. Seven white men attested to Lewis's character. Shopkeeping was a relatively rare employment among free African Americans. Source: Free Negro and Slave Records, Henrico County, Box 2 (1822), Library of Virginia.

Other common African-American urban self-employment included carting, huckstering, and food service. Carting was vital in port cities and towns because carters moved goods between docks, warehouses, and retail shops. Street vendors of such goods as oysters, apples, milk, hay, fruits, and vegetables were collectively called hucksters and peddled goods, typically from horse-drawn carts. African-American restaurateurs operated modest "eating houses" or "cook shops," which served simple, hearty fare such as oyster stews, or grog shops and tippling houses, which served beer and liquor out of sight of the authorities.[37] What connects barbering, carting, huckstering, and dining is that their modest capital requirements provided opportunities for self-employment when race precluded or limited remunerative wage labor opportunities. Carting required a couple strong horses and a reliable cart, or about $100 in start-up capital. In the 1850s, carting generated a gross income of about $2 per day, double the daily wage of unskilled labor.[38] After maintaining the horses and the wagon the daily earnings of carters was probably about the same as laboring, but one advantage of carting over day labor was the independence and self-reliance afforded the self-employed carter. Huckstering, too, required little more than a horse, a cart, and access to victuals to vend.

One interesting feature of self-employment is its racial composition. Barbering was an overwhelmingly mixed-race occupation; nearly 62 percent of African-American barbers were identified as mixed-race in the 1860 census. Carting and huckstering were predominantly black occupations; four-fifths of African-American carters were blacks, as were seven in ten hucksters. Labor economists and sociologists attribute these patterns to labor market discrimination. Relatively low rates of self-employment in some occupations reflect customer discrimination.[39] Black service providers such as barbers, for example, attract prejudiced white customers only by offering a lower price than mixed-race barbers. The lower price compensates white customers for their distaste for being shaved by blacks. But if the distaste is powerful enough, the price differential will be so great as to make the trade unprofitable for blacks. If potential black and mixed-race barbers are of equal ability, the lower economic returns to black ability will dissuade blacks from entering the trade. Because self-employment is endogenous and depends on relative income opportunities in self-employment and wage employment, customer discrimination manifests itself in occupational sorting and in the observed ability of wage workers and the self-employed.

The alternative hypothesis, variously labeled "necessity" or "survivalist" entrepreneurship, holds that poor wage labor opportunities tend to push workers with little capital into self-employment in petty enterprises, like carting and huckstering.[40] Resource constraints limit the self-employment response, which will be reinforced by customer discrimination. Barbering appears to be an obvious case where racial prejudice would lead to customer discrimination. Not only did barbers come into physical contact with their customers, they held straight razors at their throats. Carting, huckstering, and other service trades appear less subject to the preferences of prejudiced clients.

George Borjas, Stephen Bronars, and Irwin Bernhardt develop theoretical and empirical models in which the probability of self-employment is determined by a prospective entrepreneur's age, literacy, marital status, residence, and economic resources.[41] Color is readily incorporated into these empirical models and estimation of a Borjas-Bronars-type model reveals that after controlling for age, land ownership, literacy, city of residence, and household status, black men were nearly 19 percent more likely than mixed-race men to be self-employed. When self-employment in the retail sector (grocers, dry goods, and so on who operated out of store fronts) is excluded so that only so-called petty trades, like carting and huckstering, are included in the self-employed category, black men were 45 percent more likely than mixed-race men to be self-employed.[42]

The greater likelihood of black self-employment can be conceptually decomposed into the part due to differences in the characteristics (age, literacy, and so on) of black and mixed-race men and the part due to differences in the mechanisms leading to self-employment. Coefficients from a regression that includes only mixed-race men can be used to predict the probability of black self-employment if the same mechanisms that determined self-employment for mixed-race men operated for black men.[43] The actual self-employment rate in petty trades for black men is 8.4 percent, while the predicted rate, based on mixed-race determinants, is 10.1 percent. When the black rates are compared to the mixed-race self-employment rate of just 4.7 percent, it appears that observed differences in black and mixed-race self-employment are primarily due to differences in black and mixed-race characteristics rather than the mechanism that selected blacks and mixed-race men into self-employment.

Black men's self-employment experiences, then, did not follow from discrimination in the labor market per se. Black male characteristics were more consistent with petty trade self-employment due to their different premarket experiences. Blacks were less likely than mixed-race men to be literate (60 versus 75 percent), less likely to own real estate (7 versus 17 percent), and resided in smaller households (1.29 versus 1.35 people).[44] Discrimination may have driven the divergent self-employment choices by black and mixed-race men, but labor market discrimination was not the driving force. Rather, the driving force was discrimination in other dimensions that manifested itself in less human capital and fewer familial resources, which made the returns to self-employment in petty trades attractive relative to the low wages to be earned in common laboring.

Women's Work

What of women's work? James McCune Smith, one of the first accredited African-American physicians who tended to children at New York City's Colored Orphan Asylum, described a common woman's employment:

> Saturday night! *Dunk!* goes the smoothing-iron, then a swift gliding sound as it passes smoothly over starched bosom and collar of one of the many dozen shirts that hang around the room on chairs, lines and every other thing capable of being hanged on.... In the corners, under the tables, and in all out-of-the-way places are stowed tubs of various sizes, some empty, some full of clothes soaking for next week's labor.... The washerwoman bends again to her task.... The iron flies as a weaver's shuttle, shirts appear and disappear with rapidity and at a quarter to twelve, the groaning table is cleared, and the poor washerwoman sinks upon her knees in prayer.[45]

Table 7.3 Female Employment Per 1000 in Broad Occupational Categories and Narrow Jobs

CATEGORY/Job	Black women	Mixed-race women	White women
1. LABOR	113	13	13
2. SERVICE	482	328	92
a. Boardinghouse	6	33	21
b. Cook	18	3	1
c. Domestic	34	22	14
d. Washer	415	249	50
3. OPERATIVE	43	121	100
a. Seamstress	38	118	93
4. CRAFT	4	8	45
a. Tailoress	1	1	27
5. SALES/CLERICAL	15	5	20
a. Huckster/peddler	15	5	20
6. MANAGER/PROFESSIONAL	11	1	9
a. Merchant	1	1	2
b. Retail	5	10	89

Notes: See Table 7.1. Sources: See Table 7.1.

Women's work differed from men's, although as Smith's portrayal suggests, African-American women were overrepresented in the service industry. Most made their living washing other people's clothes, cooking other people's meals, and cleaning other people's homes. Table 7.3 reports the number of women per thousand by race and color in each of seven broad occupational categories and 10 narrowly defined, commonly observed jobs within each category. Race- and color-based occupational segregation is apparent.

Within the broad service category, which was the sector in which most women worked, mixed-race women were more likely than black women to operate a boardinghouse or to work as a seamstress. Black women were much more likely to work as cooks, domestic servants, and washerwomen, despite Brenda Stevenson's assertion that even these low-paying jobs were "difficult to get on a permanent basis, particularly for dark-skinned women."[46] Black women, too, were more likely to work as common laborers, but they were also more likely to be self-employed peddlers and hucksters. When the *Index of Dissimilarity* is calculated using women's employment, the black-mixed index value is 0.198 based on 10 narrow job titles and 0.246 when based on seven broad categories. About one-fourth to one-fifth of African-American women would have had to change jobs to eliminate the observed patterns of occupational segregation. By way of comparison, index values for the black-mixed comparison are comparable to values for the mixed-white comparison: 0.194 for narrow jobs and 0.275 for broad categories. The extent of black-white occupational segregation was much greater, however. Based on narrow jobs, the black-white index value is 0.345 and the broad category value is 0.489. Between one-third and one-half of black and white women would have had to change jobs to eliminate the observed pattern of occupational segregation.

Multinomial logit regressions, like those estimated for male employments, reveal systematic race-based differences in employment probabilities for women as well. Because there are very few observations in many of the broad occupational categories (Craft, Clerical, and Professional), the results apply to a smaller set of occupations. But the results reported in Table 7.2 show that compared to being employed as a common laborer, black women were only about 60 percent as likely as mixed-race women to be employed in the service sector and only about 30 percent as likely to be a self-employed retailer. Black women were slightly more likely to be self-employed in the sales sector as peddlers and hucksters, but the estimate is not precisely estimated.

Unfortunately, the most common designation in the 1860 census manuscripts is simply "labor," and it is impossible to know exactly what tasks this category encompassed. Within the category, some specific tasks were sometimes listed and they included rag woman, factory work, cotton factory hand, and stemmer. The last was observed mostly in the tobacco mills of Petersburg and Richmond, Virginia. Stemmers cut out the thick vein running the length of the tobacco leaf before the leaf was processed into snuff, chew, or cigars. Petersburg's tobacco processing mills offered continuous, nearly year-round employment, but the work was repetitive and uninteresting, and cured tobacco leaves threw off dust that must have made breathing hard.

Only 2.9 percent of black women were self-employed, while 5.9 percent of mixed-race women were. Most self-employed women operated a boarding house or huckstered fruit, fish, and vegetables. If low-skilled but high productivity mixed-race women faced sufficiently low returns to their efforts in the wage-labor sector, they may have turned to petty trading where the returns were higher. Regressions estimate that black women were about 20 percent less likely than mixed-race women to be self-employed, but the effect is not statistically significant. And when mixed-race women's characteristics are substituted into a regression model estimated using only black women, the predicted probability of mixed-race, female self-employment is 5.3 percent, which is very close to the actual 5.9 percent value. It appears that as with the men, differences in the characteristics of black and mixed-race women (literacy, residence, and resources), rather than the mechanisms selecting them into self-employment, were responsible for the different experiences. Again, this does not suggest that African-American women did not battle prejudice and discrimination. It suggests instead that prejudice and discrimination manifested itself in other ways.

Color, Farm Ownership, and Rural Employment

Agricultural historians rely on the metaphor of the agricultural ladder, likening socioeconomic advance in rural communities to ascending to ever higher rungs on the land-tenure ladder.[47] Basic versions of the ladder hypothesis posit three rungs: agricultural laborers occupy the lowest rung, tenants occupy an intermediate rung, and owner-operators occupy the highest rung. Other versions posit longer ladders with more rungs: transient day laborers, for example, occupy a lower rung than laborers hired by the season; tenants can be separated into sharecroppers and cash renters; and owners may have a mortgage or lien on their farms, while farmers holding land free of encumbrance achieved the highest rung. The essential thesis, regardless of the number of steps, is that rural socioeconomic status is associated with a man's place on the ladder. Higher rungs imply higher status, greater independence, and higher material well-being.

Outright ownership was the preferred state for most rural folk, but many worked as farm laborers, and tenancy was common across the antebellum South.[48] For many men, tenancy provided access to land and a measure of economic independence to those unable to purchase their own land.[49] For others, tenancy served as an educational or apprentice-like learning opportunity. Owners provided land, capital, and supervision; tenants provided their labor and learned how to succeed as farmers.

In many parts of the Old South, tenancy provided opportunities for economic advancement exploited by rural, free African Americans. Contemporary reports in such disparate outlets as the *Baltimore American* and the journal of the Virginia House of Delegates remarked that in the absence of free African Americans, large tracts of the region's arable land would have gone untilled.

Antebellum censuses did not report land tenure, so an individual's place on the ladder must be inferred from information provided in the censuses.[50] The issue is the extent to which African Americans climbed above the bottom rungs of the agricultural ladder.[51] Using a standard approach to imputing a person's place on the ladder, Table 7.4 provides sample averages for different groups arrayed by occupation. In nearly all of the 26 sample counties, marshals separately identified "laborer" and "farm laborer." Max Grivno's study of pre-Civil War farmers and farm workers points toward an integrated rural labor market in that unskilled rural workers frequently moved between farm and nonfarm work as seasonal farm demand waxed and waned.[52]

Integrated markets suggest that rural laborers probably spent substantial time employed as farm laborers, and the categories are treated as equivalent. African-American men identified as laborers, and those identified as farm laborers were similar in most respects. They were approximately the same age, reported nearly equal value of personal property ownership, resided in households with just under five members, and the percentage black exceeded 80 percent in both groups. Mean values of their characteristics are reported in Row 1 of Table 7.4.

Donald Winters, Frederick Bode, and Donald Ginter argue that tenancy was relatively common in the antebellum South; county-level tenancy rates ranged between four and forty percent across Tennessee and Georgia.[53] Farm renting and tenancy were an integral part of rural life in the antebellum South, and while white tenancy is well documented, African-American tenancy is not. Row 2 in Table 7.4 reports information on tenants, which are defined, following Bogue, as individuals identified as farmers without real property in population manuscripts, but who appeared in the farm manuscripts. Farmers (Row 3) are those

Table 7.4 Characteristics of Rural African-American Men By Place on the Agricultural Ladder

	Proportion black	Age (yrs)	Number in household	Average farm value
1. Labor	0.84	42.2	4.8	—
2. Tenants	0.52	43.1	6.6	$1,708
3. Farmers	0.71	48.5	6.6	1,217

Sources: Author's calculations from population and agriculture manuscripts of the 1860 census, as reported in Bodenhorn, "The Complexion Gap," 53 (Table 2). Used by permission.

individuals identified as farmers in the population manuscripts and appeared with a real property in both the population and farm manuscripts. Certain features of the ladder are evident among African-American men: farmers were older than tenants, who were slightly older, on average, than laborers; farmers and tenants supported larger households than laborers; tenants worked farms of higher value, which probably reflects the credit constraints faced by prospective African-American landowners. Planters were willing to rent better pieces of property than blacks and mixed-race men could afford to purchase. Of particular interest is the disproportionate representation of mixed-race men as tenants.

To explore this observation further and to better understand whether blacks and mixed-race people followed alternate trajectories on the agricultural ladder, Table 7.5 reports unconditional rates of farm laboring, tenancy, and ownership per thousand rural adult male residents by color and quinquennial cohort.[54] For nearly every cohort after age 24, laboring rates for mixed-race men are well below the rates for black men, often by as much as 250 per 1000. Equally notable is the earlier movement up the ladder from laborer to tenant for mixed than black men.

Table 7.5 Farm Labor, Tenancy, and Ownership Rates By Race, Color, and Age Cohort (per 1,000 Men at Age and Color)

Age cohort	Farm labor		Tenants		Farmers	
	(mixed)	(black)	(mixed)	(black)	(mixed)	(black)
20–24	745	876	78	18	39	27
25–29	587	853	144	20	77	41
30–34	568	822	148	35	99	67
35–39	618	784	99	39	145	75
40–44	545	808	152	37	172	73
45–49	447	686	105	60	250	111
50–54	446	730	189	36	108	142
55–59	383	692	149	46	213	123
60–64	604	694	75	41	132	162
65–69	455	735	91	20	318	143
70–74	364	671	91	12	273	183
75–79	364	750	91	23	364	159

Notes: Farm labor includes men reporting "labor" and "farm labor" as occupation in census. Rows (by color) do not sum to 1,000 because men listed in the population census as farmers who do not appear in agricultural census are included in the denominator, but their representation is not reported here. *Source:* Author's calculations from population and agricultural manuscripts of the 1860 census, as reported in Bodenhorn, "The Complexion Gap," 54 (Table 3). Used by permission.

Tenancy rates for mixed-race men increased from about 78 per 1,000 for 20- to 24-year-old men to 148 per 1,000 at age 30 to 34. Black men were much less likely to advance into tenant status. At ages 20 to 24 only 18 per 1,000 black men were tenants; and the rate increased only to 35 per 1,000 for black men ages 30 to 34.

The color gap is apparent in ownership rates, too. Mixed-race men were more likely than black men to own their own farm at nearly every age. Ownership rates were low—less than 10 percent—for men in their twenties regardless of race. Mixed-race men in their thirties and forties were about twice as likely as blacks to own the land they farmed. Less easily summarized patterns emerge for men in their fifties and sixties, due largely to the small sample sizes in some cells. Nevertheless, the evidence is consistent with a mixed-race advantage in land ownership.

Some black and mixed-race men climbed the agricultural ladder. Most began at the bottom as farm laborers, and many remained there throughout their lives. But many made modest strides up the ladder. For mixed-race men, tenancy increased 1.4 times between the 20 to 24 and 45 to 49 cohorts. Among blacks in those same cohorts, tenancy doubled. It was in achieving the highest rung—ownership—that a definitive and economically meaningful color advantage appears. Ownership rates increased sixfold for mixed-race men between the 20 to 24 and the 45 to 49 cohorts; for blacks, ownership rates increased fourfold, which is a large effect, but only two-thirds the advance experienced by mixed-race men.

While evidence on land tenure taken from the 1860 census hints at life-cycle changes in land tenure, it is probably inappropriate to interpret the pattern as such. Too many confounding events occurred over the nineteenth century for a single cross-section to shed light on longitudinal changes. Opposition to the practice brought a rapid halt to the brief post-Revolution wave of manumissions. Chapter 5 shows that manumission continued up to the Civil War, but later manumissions occurred on a smaller scale and on different terms. Where Robert "Councillor" Carter III manumitted more than 400 slaves in the 1790s and established a tenancy system for those that remained on his property, later manumission was more selective and manumitted slaves were more likely to be sent off to fend for themselves in freedom. Changing manumission practices may in fact explain the relatively high ownership rates for black and mixed men alike in their late sixties and seventies. The nearly half-decade long recession between 1839 and 1843 also surely created obstacles for land ownership for men coming of age in that era.

Available evidence suggests that despite mixed-race advantages in moving up the ladder, they still lagged behind whites. Although Atack's and Winters's estimates are not directly comparable, their results imply that black and mixed-race men were much more likely to remain tenants at ages at which white men moved up into ownership. Atack estimates ownership rate for the 20 to 24 cohort of northern whites in 1860 at 691 per 1,000. Using his classification scheme, southern mixed-race men in the 20-24 cohort achieved ownership rates of 286 per 1000. The racial gap narrowed only slightly for older cohorts: 868 per 1000 for 45- to 49-year-old whites and 593 per 1,000 for mixed-race men. These figures once again underscore the stark reality that no matter the extent of mixed-race privileges relative to blacks, African Americans of all colors lagged far behind whites by any meaningful economic measure. Still, it should also not be forgotten that more than half of mixed-race men in their prime earning forties and fifties rose above the status of common laborer, and had some measure of economic independence either as tenants or owners. Rural free African Americans were not, as Ira Berlin contends, reduced to a state "barely distinguishable from slavery."[55] But neither did rural free African Americans, as Marina Wikramanayake asserts, maintain the "same economic standards as yeoman farmers who made up a majority" of the rural southern population.[56] African Americans as a rule occupied lower places on the agricultural ladder, but mixed-race men climbed higher than black men.

Concluding Remarks

In his popular travelogue, Englishman John Benwell noted that African Americans of all colors faced rather harsh discrimination. He observed that some kept small shops and restaurants that catered to other African Americans. A few men and women, despite the prejudices, rose above the "common level, and by probity of character and untiring energy . . . [became] men of substance."[57] Some in fact became quite successful by any standard. Julian A. Lacroix, who operated a large retail grocery on Victory Street in New Orleans, was estimated to be worth $250,000; his brother, François Lacroix, was a merchant tailor worth $200,000.[58] Bernard and Alvin Soulie, free light-skinned African-American men, worked as exchange brokers in New Orleans; "they are capitalists," wrote on white observer.[59] One A. Reggio, also of Louisiana, owned $70,000 in real estate and 100 slaves in 1860.

What connected the Lacroixes, the Soulies, and Reggio was their racial heritage. All were of mixed race, which was not unusual for successful, enterprising African-American men. Of the 14 retail grocers of African-American heritage identified in the 1860 census, 13 were of mixed race. Lacroix was one of them. Despite their differential abilities to climb the agricultural ladder or achieve success in relatively prestigious urban occupations, mixed-race men were never allowed to forget that they were part black. They were not black—just part black—but this was enough to separate them, no matter how successful they might be, from social equality. Economic success left some part-white men bitter or despondent. Benwell described one relatively successful mixed-race man as "always in a desponding mood, a tendency arising almost entirely from the insulting demeanor used toward him by the [white] citizens."[60] Success did not come easy and it did not open a racial escape hatch, even with fair skin, good hair, fine character, and modest wealth.

Discussions of early nineteenth-century African-American work typically take one of two paths. On one hand, tales of improbable success drive the narrative. On the other, tales of woe—the product of prejudice, poverty, and injustice—are the central theme. Both are true, but neither captures the fundamental reality. African Americans of all colors worked hard and earned little for their efforts, but so too did many whites. The difference is that those of (part) white heritage, on average, worked a little less hard and earned a little more. As urban historians Theodore Hershberg and Henry Williams note, the color "differential was not sufficient to suggest that occupational success was solely determined by skin color, but it was large enough to indicate that color did influence occupational achievement."[61]

8

Wealth

In 1800 Andrew Bryan, a black preacher of Savannah and founder of the first African-American church in the United States, wrote to John Rippon that "By a kind Providence I am well provided for as to worldly comforts (tho' I have very little given me as a minister), having a house and lot in this city, besides land on which several buildings stand, for which I receive a small rent, and a fifty-six acre-tract of land, with all necessary buildings, four mules in the country, and eight slaves."[1] Bryan then discussed the size of his flock (nearly 700) and the church's doings before turning to another matter of property. Bryan informed Rippon that Henry Francis, a mixed-race slave and long-time congregant who possessed "handsome ministerial gifts," had been lately purchased from the widow of Colonel Leroy Hammond and manumitted. Francis was scheduled to be ordained and given the task of teaching the ministry's youth to read and write.

Bryan's letter underscores two features of African-American life in the nineteenth-century South. First, African Americans owned property, often of substantial value. Bryan appeared to be at least as well off as many of his white neighbors; he owned a city house, a four-mule farm, and eight slaves. Bryan's holdings were atypical for a black man, but they reveal that African Americans could accumulate real, personal, and chattel property. Second, Bryan's relating Henry Francis's good fortune underscores that the most dear—if not the most expensive—property owned by free African Americans was freedom itself. Shawn Cole's analysis of more than 100,000 slave sales and self-purchases find that the average price of a slave was approximately $600 (constant 1800 dollars).[2] Given that per capita incomes for working people were about $200 circa 1800, self-purchase was monumentally expensive. A gift of freedom from "a few humane gentlemen" was, as Bryan notes, providential.

As Africans acculturated and adopted Anglo attitudes toward property, they learned its harder lessons as well. Ralph Waldo Emerson famously wrote that not to own land was bad; to own it was worse. "If a man owns land," Emerson opined, "the land owns him."[3] Although it was the source of constant consternation and unremitting effort, men and women went to great lengths to own land. Despite the legal and economic obstacles, free African Americans acquired property. They owned land. They owned buildings. They owned household goods. They owned farm equipment and livestock. They owned businesses. They owned slaves. They owned themselves. And though African Americans of all colors owned property, ownership favored the fair.

Rural Property Ownership, Real and Personal

Americans of African heritage initially acquired title to property in the first place they arrived in continental North America—on the western edge of the Delmarva Pennisula.[4] The most important property to which the early African Americans took title was to him or herself. Chapter 5 considers the economics of manumission, but it is a worthwhile reminder to consider the lengths to which enslaved peoples went to purchase themselves.

In May 1643, slave Francis Payne and slave owner Jane Eltonhead signed two agreements and recorded them with the Northampton County court.[5] In the first, Eltonhead assigned to Payne the entire crop he was then cultivating, provided he go about his work "quietly" and provided that he compensate her for the use of her land with 1,500 pounds of tobacco and six bushels of corn. The first agreement is striking in that it endowed a slave with the capacity to contract, which presupposes that he held a certain amount of "property-ness" in himself. The second agreement is even more noteworthy. In it Eltonhead agreed to grant Payne his freedom once he had purchased three indentured servants between 15 and 24 years of age, each with six or seven years to serve, and signed them over to Eltonhead. In effect, Payne contracted to exchange his lifelong bondage for the temporary bondage of three white servants. It took Payne longer to fulfill the contract than he anticipated, but he eventually satisfied the terms by assigning two servants and 1,650 pounds of tobacco. Interestingly, no one appeared to be "bothered that a black slave purchased [white] indentured servants to obtain his own liberty."[6] Other slaves obtained their freedom in various ways so that in 1668 nearly 30 percent of Northampton County's African Americans were free, many of whom were tithable householders.

Once they obtained title to themselves, former slaves began obtaining title to land. In the 1650s, the Johnson family took advantage of the Virginia colony's headright system and laid claim to several hundred acres in Accomack County on the Delmarva. Other African Americans became property owners by way of gifts and bequests of their former owners. It was not uncommon for the earliest manumitted slaves to be furnished with some real or chattel property when freed. Among the earliest mixed-race individuals to be so endowed were two mixed-race children freed with their mother by John Nicholls in 1697. The boy received 310 acres, the girl 200 acres, and both received various chattel. James Brewer argues that these and other economic activities of Virginia's earliest African Americans are not "of major historical significance," but they speak to two features of

African-American life: property ownership was a central concern, because it conveyed some measure of civic status and economic independence in a society preoccupied with status and independence; and the path to ownership differed systematically for blacks and those of mixed race.[7]

Any historical study that skips two centuries of experience invites criticism, but Luther Porter Jackson contends that it was not until the mid-nineteenth century that African-American property ownership "took on anything like appreciable proportions," so an analysis of property ownership that jumps ahead 150 years after Nicholls's bequest and makes use of mid-century sources will miss the details of its slow progress but capture the essentials of late-antebellum property ownership. What follows then is a mostly snapshot description of land ownership circa 1860.

Much of the extant history of nineteenth-century free African Americans centers on their exceptional accomplishments, and the history of property ownership is no different. Jackson appears most interested in discussing Virginians with several hundred acres, though by his own accounting most free African-American owners had less than 30.[8] Jackson's emphasis is understandable given the place and time in which he studied and wrote—Petersburg, Virginia in the 1930s and 1940s—because he wanted to challenge the then-dominant stereotype of African-American social dysfunction and economic failure. His studies portray early nineteenth-century African Americans as capable, acquisitive, responsible (non)citizens who made nontrivial contributions to the state fisc. Notable acquisitions of real and personal property were central to his narrative. Jackson acknowledged—but made little of the connection between—skin color (or racial heritage) and property ownership.

Schweninger, too, emphasizes the accomplishments of the wealthy few, and though he acknowledges color-based differences, de-emphasizes their significance.[9] Liberal attitudes toward free African Americans in Louisiana, for example, encouraged substantial accumulations of property, and Louisiana's experience is central to Schweninger's narrative. In the late antebellum era, 25 African Americans in Plaquemines Parish, for example, held title to at least $2,000 in real estate. Annette Dumford, a 52-year-old sugar planter, led the list with $50,000 in real and $60,000 in personal estate (mostly slaves). No fewer than eight African-American rice planters owned at least $5,000 in real estate in 1860. Only one was identified as black. Nearly every notable land owner in "free black" Louisiana was actually of mixed race.

Two important features of property ownership are missing from existing accounts: a depiction of the entire distribution of wealth, and the connection between color and property ownership. Table 8.1 offers some insight into the distribution of real and personal property by race and color. Using data from the Integrated Public Use Microdata Series (IPUMS), 1 percent sample of the 1860 census, the table includes information on the property-holding characteristics of rural, southern heads of households, both males and female. A substantial number

Table 8.1 Real and Personal Property Ownership in 1860: Male and female heads of households in the rural South

	Blacks	Mixed-race	Whites
Panel A: Male head of household			
Fraction owning real property	0.269	0.440	0.637
	(0.447)	(0.501)	(0.481)
Value of real property ($)	181.45	515.98	2478.71
(all households)	(767.94)	(1528.25)	(9748.10)
Value of real property ($)	675.39	1172.68	3891.62
(households reporting real property)	(1391.52)	(2154.72)	(11987.53)
Fraction reporting personal property	0.597	0.860	0.912
	(0.494)	(0.351)	(0.284)
Value of personal property ($)	125.93	312.50	3165.01
(all households)	(398.17)	(985.27)	(11325.88)
Value of personal property ($)	210.93	363.37	3471.39
(households reporting personal)	(499.91)	(1055.28)	(11816.55)
Number of observations	67	50	8822
Panel B: Female head of household			
Fraction owning real property	0.138	0.389	0.655
	(0.351)	(0.502)	(0.476)
Value of real property ($)	146.55	2894.00	2077.08
(all households)	(741.61)	(11758.65)	(4697.27)
Value of real property ($)	1062.50	7441.71	3172.99
(households reporting real property)	(1958.48)	(18768.86)	(5500.12)
Fraction owning personal property	0.621	0.667	0.879
	(0.494)	(0.485)	(0.327)
Value of personal property ($)	192.07	3885.00	3717.66
(all households)	(925.02)	(15272.56)	(10517.43)
Value of personal property ($)	309.44	5827.50	4230.17
(households reporting personal)	(1170.84)	(18658.24)	(11123.16)
Number of observations	29	18	553

Notes: Standard deviations in parentheses. Number of observations equals the number of households in which head is between 25 and 64 years old, in the labor force, and not residing in group quarters or an institution. Head of household is considered to be in the labor force if IPUMS reports a nonzero value of the Duncan SEI Index. *Source:* Author's calculations from data in Ruggles et al., *Integrated Public Use Microdata Series* (1860 US Census).

of African-American households were headed by single mothers, so understanding household wealth requires knowing about those households as well; between one-third and one-quarter of rural African-American households were headed by single women in the labor force.

William Collins and Robert Margo analyze the evolution of African-American home ownership in the post-Civil War United States and find that the African-American home ownership rate among male householders increased from about 8 percent in 1870 to nearly 25 percent in 1910.[10] The 1870 value results from the emancipated slaves' low incomes and lack of inherited wealth, so that few had the financial wherewithal to purchase land in the half-decade after the war. A generation or so of freedom did not bring equality, but it brought post-war African-American ownership rates to about the same level observed among free black householders before the war, though comparisons between ante- and postbellum populations need to be drawn cautiously. The ownership rate for free mixed-race men was nearly 20 percentage points higher. (Information on white households will not be discussed in detail, but is offered for comparison.) Linear probability regressions also imply that black home ownership rates, after controlling for age, literacy, and state of residence, lagged mixed-race rates by 10 to 15 percentage points. Fewer black than mixed-race householders owned real property. (See Appendix 8.1 for details.)

It is not surprising then that the dollar value of real estate owned by black householders was notably lower than the value owned by mixed-race householders. Any analysis of property values reported in the census must confront the fact that values are self-reported and may reflect the owner's subjective valuation more than market prices. In his studies Jackson allowed for a "certain amount of over-valuation," and comparative data he collected for Petersburg, Virginia reveal a substantial difference between transaction prices and values reported in the 1860 census.[11] An analysis of the 180 African-American holdings he reports shows that the average 1860 census value ($487.48) exceeds the inflation-adjusted purchase price ($198.70) by a wide margin. It is possible that owners made additional investments in their properties after purchasing them, but there is no way to determine whether this explains the valuation gap. A second analysis comparing the average reported value in the 1860 census ($7,923.53) and the tax commissioner's assessment ($7,439.88) of the property value for 127 Petersburg properties owned by black, mixed-race, and white householders reveals a greater correspondence in valuations. Either African Americans persistently overvalued their property holdings, or the values reported in the 1860 census reflect the most recent assessed value for tax purposes rather than earlier transaction prices. Owners would have been aware of the assessed value of their properties– their annual taxes were tied directly to the assessments—so the latter appears to be the more plausible interpretation.

Using the unconditional means reported in the upper panel of Table 8.1, it is readily seen that the value of male black-owned real estate ($181) amounted to only 35.1 percent of the value of mixed-race-owned real estate ($515) when all African Americans, including those who owned no real estate, are included in the calculation. If the sample is restricted to those who reported a positive value of real estate, the value of black property ($675) rises to 57.5 percent of mixed-race property ($1,173). Comparing sample means may not be informative because blacks and mixed-race households may not have been similar in other regards, so some lurking variables may account for any apparent systematic difference. Log wealth regressions controlling for other factors—namely age, literacy, and state of residence—reveal that the value of black male householder-owned real estate ownership was just 30 to 35 percent of the value of male mixed-race ownership. The values for females are comparable, but neither sample is large enough to generate statistically precise estimates of the black-mixed differential.

As previously mentioned, Jackson disputes the contention that mixed-race people were more likely to own property. The "color factor," as he labels it, is less evident to him than he had expected to see in the data. But Jackson bases his conclusion on the observation that more blacks than mixed-race people owned property in the counties he samples. In counting the absolute numbers of owners, however, Jackson is not measuring an ownership rate. There were far more blacks than mixed-race people in antebellum Virginia, so absolute values are not informative; a lower black ownership *rate* is fully consistent with a larger absolute *number* of black owners. Representative samples of rural places reveal a decided mixed-race advantage in both ownership rates and the average dollar value of properties owned. A representative sample of urban places, discussed below, also reveals a mixed-race advantage.

African-American realty ownership can be discussed from two perspectives. A gloomy case would focus on the low home and farm ownership rate—one-fifth of black households and one-third of mixed-race households—among the rural South's African Americans. Moreover, the gloomy case would deepen, given that even those black households that owned property held small parcels of apparently low-value, low-productivity land. A more hopeful case would focus on the fact that in the shadow of slavery with all its negative social, political, and economic ramifications for African Americans, one-fifth of black and one-third of mixed-race householders owned the land they tilled. Black ownership rates lagged behind, but were not insubstantial. Thus Jackson is justified in his assessment that African-American achievement deserves recognition, though he is less justified in discounting the role of color in that achievement.

Personal Property

Each panel of Table 8.1 also provides statistics on the ownership of personal property using the IPUMS sample of the 1860 census manuscripts. Approximately two-thirds to four-fifths of African-American households owned personal property. What was included in the enumerations of personal property? Marshals were instructed to "include the value of all the [nonreal] property, possessions, or wealth of each individual . . . consist of what it may; the value of bonds, mortgages, notes, slaves, live stock, plate, jewels, or furniture; in fine, the value of whatever constitutes the personal wealth of individuals."[12] It appears, however, that census marshals failed to return values in the personal property cell below an idiosyncratic censoring point. In the 25-county rural sample of nearly 3,000 African-American households described in Appendix 8.2, there were few returns below $10 and fewer still below $5.[13] In all likelihood, blank cells in the personal property column of the population manuscripts reflect marshals failing to report small values rather than the absence of wealth of any sort.

Table 8.2 uses the 25-county sample of African-American households to study the distribution of wealth. This sample, which is much larger than the IPUMS sample of free African Americans—nearly 3,000 households, compared to 164 in the IPUMS—affords an opportunity to split the sample by race, color, and sex. The upper panel provides unconditional (raw) means, medians, and other points of the wealth distribution. Without controlling for any confounding factors, mixed-race households, both male- or female-headed, owned more personal property than black households at every point in the wealth distribution.

Table 8.2 Personal Property By Color and Sex of Household Heads in 1860: Unconditional and conditional estimates

	Black Men	Mixed-Race Men	Black Women	Mixed-Race Women
Unconditional estimates				
Mean	$145	$203	$67	$164
Median	50	75	25	50
75th percentile	150	200	50	100
95th percentile	500	650	200	650
Conditional estimates				
Mean	$115	$121	$73	$90
Median	172	184	na	na
75th percentile	293	320	181	259
90th percentile	708	856	443	555

Notes: Conditional estimates derived from ordinary least squares (OLS) and quantile regressions with controls for occupation, age, and state of residence. The reported values are predicted values for 40-year-old Maryland farmers. na = not available; the conditional median could not be estimated for female-headed households because it falls below the censoring point. *Source*: Calculated from regressions reported in Bodenhorn, "Complexion Gap," Tables 5 and 6. Used by permission. The data were drawn from a stratified random sample of 25 southern counties included in the 1860 manuscript population census. See Appendix 8.2 for county selection criteria and list of included counties.

The lower panel reports the dollar value of personal wealth at different points in the distribution estimated from regressions that control for age, occupation, and state of residence. The conditional estimates are for 40-year-old farm owners. When comparing like with like, color-based wealth differentials remain but are much less pronounced. Mean and median personal wealth differences were trivial for male-headed households and relatively modest for female-headed households. When we consider points further out in the wealth distribution, the color-based wealth gap widens. The black-mixed personal wealth ratio for men at the median is 0.92; at the 95th percentile it is 0.83. The class of relatively well-to-do southern African Americans was dominated by light-skinned, mixed-race men and women.

So what constituted rural property? How were its components distributed? The manuscript population census does not offer much insight, but the agricultural census does. A smaller sample of farmers identified in the 25-county sample was linked to the 1860 manuscript agricultural census. One feature of the agriculture census is its documentation of farm acreage, the value of implements, various types of livestock, and crop yields. Table 8.3 provides some insight into the distribution and nature of rural personal property ownership. The table reports holdings at several points in the wealth distribution. Black farm owners at the 10th percentile, for example, owned just 20 acres of land; mixed-race farm owner-operators at the 10th percentile worked just 25 acres. It was this group—those in the bottom 10 percent of land holdings by acreage—that John Hope Franklin characterized as holding small, possibly uneconomically small, parcels. Still, Franklin writes, land owners of even the smallest parcels were land owners, and many such men and women "steadily rose in economic independence" through land ownership.[14]

Table 8.3 Percentiles of Selected Farm Assets in 1860 Census By Color

Percentile	Farm acres		Horses		Oxen		Cattle		Swine	
	Black	Mixed	Black	Mixed	Black	Mixed	Black	Mixed	Black	Mixed
10th	20	25	0	0	0	0	0	0	1	4
25th	40	40	0	0	0	1	1	2	4	6.5
50th	72.5	66.5	1	0	1	3	3	4	7	12
75th	120	132	2	2	2	2	5	6.5	11	18.5
90th	180	210	3	3	2	2	7	10	18	26
Mean	103.6	109.9	1.6	1.2	0.9	1.0	4.0	4.7	9.2	13.7
(std dev)	(131.7)	(167.0)	(1.2)	(1.3)	(1.2)	(1.2)	(5.0)	(4.1)	(10.6)	(11.1)

Notes: Farm operators matched from 1860 manuscript agriculture census to manuscript population census from the 25-county sample described in Appendix 8.2. *Sources:* US Census Bureau, Eighth Census (1860). Population and agriculture manuscripts.

Three other features stand out. First, and not surprisingly, rural personal wealth was tied up in livestock. Southern farmers owned or aspired to a horse or two, a yoke of oxen, a half-dozen cows, and hogs—lots and lots of hogs. The second notable feature of property ownership among African-American farm owner-operators is the modest differences between black and mixed-race farms in the bottom half of the wealth distribution. Differences across colors are modest up to the median (50th percentile) of the wealth distribution. A modest mixed-race advantage appears in the upper end of the wealth distribution. At the 75th or 90th percentile, mixed-race farms were larger when measured by acreage, cattle, and hogs. A third feature is that within-color inequality is similar for blacks and mixed-race households. Standard measures of inequality are the ratios of the 10th to the 90th, or 25th to 75th, percentiles. The 25-to-75 land ratio for blacks (0.33) and mixed-race (0.30) are approximately the same, as are the 10-to-90 ratios (0.11). Similarly, the 25-to-75 ratio for hogs is also about the same (0.35) for each race. The data set is not large enough to break it into meaningful subsamples to determine whether controlling for other factors, such as age, might reduce within-group inequalities. But it is important to recall that inequality within the African-American community was not driven wholly by color. Within-color inequality was potentially as great as across-color inequality.

Information from other sources is consistent with the finding that rural wealth was tied up in livestock and crops. Farm tenancy, as Chapter 7 makes clear, was a common form of land tenure among rural African Americans. While tenants did not hold title to land, they held title to their moveable property, which served as collateral for credit. Thus, Anderson Tate—28 years old, black, married to the mixed-race Julia and with a son—of Cople Parish, Westmoreland County, Virginia was in debt to the merchant firm Atwell & Hutt. As collateral Tate registered a debt lien in the county deed book and offered eleven hogs, two cows, one mare, a cart, and one-half of the wheat growing in his fields as collateral.[15] His neighbor Campbell Tate—30 years old, black, married to mixed-race Mary and with four children ages one to six—owed his provisioning merchant $61 and offered a yoke of oxen, other livestock, and his crop of wheat and corn as collateral. Debtors offered what collateral they could; for free African Americans it was most often livestock and crops in the field.

After poring through the deed books of 43 Virginia county courts, Jackson concluded that African-American families rarely obtained more than 500 acres through their own efforts.[16] Large holdings were invariably the gifts or bequests of white benefactors. But to focus on ownership by way of gift or bequest diminishes black and mixed-race people's pursuit of property, which inhered owners with a measure of economic independence and social, if not civic, standing. Despite the long-standing belief that the mixed-race resource advantage resulted from white fathers deeding property to mixed-race offspring, the historical record suggests otherwise.[17] Legal restrictions and social prescriptions militated against such deeds and bequests. Parental endowments are enormously consequential in shaping the recipients' opportunities, but neither black nor mixed-race men nor women could reasonably anticipate intergenerational bequests.[18] Increasing rates of property ownership points to a vibrant, improving African-American community in the late antebellum era, but one in which light color brought greater rewards.

Urban Property, Real and Personal

Jackson claims that the proportional gains in African-Virginian property ownership realized by rural residents between 1830 and 1860 were dwarfed by urban gains. In 1830, 157 African Virginians owned urban lots with an assessed value of nearly $75,000 ($67,000 in constant 1860 dollars); in 1860, 683 owners owned urban lots with a reported value of more than $460,000. Jackson considers this 6.4 percent annual average growth rate in the value of African Virginian-owned property remarkable, mostly because very little of it was obtained through inheritance and even less from white benefactors. Skilled craftsmen, like Fredericksburg blacksmith Thomas Carey, accumulated property over their lifetimes. In 1809, he owned two houses; he bought two more in 1813, another in 1820, and by 1824 he owned nine properties. Carey the blacksmith was also Carey the landlord; his property tax was based on assessed annual rental value of $1,050.[19] It was not just that skilled craftsmen like Carey acquired property, but that they accumulated more of it.

If people with skills were more likely to acquire property and mixed-race people were more skilled on average, then it is reasonable to expect that mixed-race householders were more likely to own property and to own more valuable property. Statistics reported in Tables 8.4 and 8.5 are consistent with this conjecture. Table 8.4 is constructed from the IPUMS 1 percent sample of the 1860 census and includes heads of households living in southern, urban places. Table 8.5 is constructed from an oversample of African Americans appearing in the 1860 census and includes more than 9,000 urban, southern householders rather than the 121 African-American householders in the IPUMS sample. The samples agree on the fraction of households with a gainfully employed household head between 25 and 64 years that report owning property—about 8 percent for black-headed households and 20 percent mixed-race-headed households—but diverge somewhat in the value of property owned. A case can be made for using the IPUMS (Table 8.4) because it is a random sample, but the 10-city sample of African Americans (Table 8.5) is large enough to draw statistical inferences about the association between household characteristics and property ownership. (Statistics for whites are offered for comparative purposes, but are not discussed.) That the two

Table 8.4 Real and Personal Property Ownership in 1860: Male and female heads of households in the urban South (IPUMS sample)

	Blacks	Mixed-Race	Whites
Panel A: Male head of household			
Fraction owning real property	.113	0.375	0.282
	(0.321)	(0.492)	(0.450)
Value of real property ($) (all households)	70.45	1012.50	2232.79
	(220.55)	(2407.75)	(10453.19)
Value of real property ($) (households reporting real property)	620.00	2700.00	7912.31
	(311.45)	(3371.54)	(18516.07)
Fraction reporting personal property	0.591	0.718	0.739
	(0.497)	(0.457)	(0.439)
Value of personal property ($)	58.95	949.06	2597.41
(all households)	(125.08)	(4395.19)	(17236.41)
Value of personal property ($) (households reporting personal)	99.77	1320.44	3511.32
	(150.59)	(5167.96)	(19962.76)
Number of observations	44	32	1460
Panel B: Female head of household			
Fraction owning real property	0	0.150	0.228
		(0.366)	(0.421)
Value of real property ($) (all households)	0	50.00	345.83
		(131.79)	(1238.49)
Value of real property ($) (households reporting real property)	0	333.33	1518.65
		(152.75)	(2260.53)
Fraction owning personal property	0.360	0.550	0.613
	(0.489)	(0.510)	(0.489)
Value of personal property ($)	60.32	31.25	398.56
(all households)	(199.20)	(38.90)	(1422.39)
Value of personal property ($)	167.56	56.82	649.27

Table 8.4 Continued

	Blacks	Mixed-Race	Whites
(households reporting personal)	(314.36)	(35.73)	(1775.19)
Number of observations	25	20	101

Notes: Standard deviations in parentheses. Number of observations equals the number of households in which head is between 25 and 64 years old, in the labor force, and not residing in group quarters or an institution. Head of household is considered to be in the labor force if IPUMS reports a nonzero value of the Duncan SEI Index. *Source:* Author's calculations from data in Ruggles et al., *Integrated Public Use Microdata Series* (1860 US Census).

samples agree on the fraction of households reporting any wealth offers reassurance that the 10-city sample captures the urban South experience.

Controlling for mixed-race, age, literacy, and city of residence, households headed by black males were about 6 to 9 percentage points less likely than mixed-race households to own real estate, compared to the 12 to 15 percentage-point differences in the raw averages.[20] Including similar controls in a log wealth regression implies that households headed by black males, on average, owned 25 to 42 percent as much real estate wealth as mixed-race householders, which is consistent with the 22 percent ratio derived from the raw averages reported in Table 8.5. Black female-headed households were 5 to 7 percentage points less likely than mixed-race female householders to own property, and the property they owned was worth about 35 to 46 percent of the value of that owned by mixed-race females.

Because the conditional mean is not necessarily the best characterization of wealth holding, Table 8.6 provides alternative estimates of personal and real wealth held by urban, southern African-American households taken from the 10-city sample. Using coefficients estimated from quantile regressions, the table provides estimates of wealth holding by black and mixed-race households across the upper tail of the wealth distribution.[21] The reported values are for literate, 40-year-old, Baltimore householders, but are representative of black-mixed differences elsewhere in the South. At the estimated median (50th percentile) of the wealth distribution a mixed-race household owned $42 in personal wealth; the median black household owned just $4. Comparisons of the male mixed-race predicted mean ($178) and median ($42) values of personal property reveal the highly skewed nature of wealth holdings.[22]

The table also shows that the black-mixed wealth gap persists across the entire distribution, for all types of property, and for both sexes. Consider male householders' personal property. At the 60th percentile of personal property (those households whose wealth holdings placed them above the lowest 60 percent of households), blacks owned 63 percent of the value of property owned

Table 8.5 Real and Personal Property Ownership in 1860: Male and female heads of households in the urban South 10-city sample

	Blacks	Mixed-Race	Whites
Panel A: Male head of household			
Fraction owning real property	0.085	0.223	0.238
	(0.279)	(0.417)	(0.426)
Value of real property ($)	100.38	553.07	1988.33
(all households)	(597.63)	(2245.09)	(11794.49)
Value of real property ($)	1179.74	2472.87	8331.10
(households reporting real property)	(1712.82)	(4221.52)	(23027.62)
Fraction reporting personal property	0.554	0.532	0.674
	(0.497)	(0.499)	(0.468)
Value of personal property ($)	116.52	295.70	2112.01
(all households)	(679.26)	(1572.65)	(11629.10)
Value of personal property ($)	210.02	555.29	3130.68
(households reporting personal)	(901.23)	(2121.90)	(14045.91)
Number of observations	3185	1784	6792
Panel B: Female head of household			
Fraction owning real property	0.054	0.108	0.128
	(0.226)	(0.311)	(0.333)
Value of real property ($)	46.50	208.28	872.89
(all households)	(249.83)	(947.48)	(8277.41)
Value of real property ($)	860.94	1921.73	6864.09
(households reporting real property)	(678.73)	(2246.22)	(22455.71)
Fraction owning personal property	0.467	0.406	0.632
	(0.499)	(0.491)	(0.483)

(*Continued*)

Table 8.5 Continued

	Blacks	Mixed-Race	Whites
Value of personal property ($) (all households)	51.86 (272.30)	153.91 (529.51)	705.80 (3954.94)
Value of personal property ($) (households reporting personal)	111.12 (390.44)	379.02 (778.66)	1116.80 (4931.26)
Number of observations	1185	692	519

Notes: Standard deviations in parentheses. Number of observations equals the number of households in which head is between 25 and 64 years old, in the labor force, and not residing in group quarters or an institution. Head of household is considered to be in the labor force if the household head reported an occupation. *Source:* Author's calculations from data in Ruggles et al., *Integrated Public Use Microdata Series* (1860 US Census).

Table 8.6 Distribution of Real and Personal Wealth Held by African-American Households in 1860

Percentile	Male-Headed Households				Female-Headed Households			
	Personal Property		Real Property		Personal Property		Real Property	
	Black	Mixed	Black	Mixed	Black	Mixed	Black	Mixed
0.975	$611	$955	$480	$1,183	$198	$338	$118	$336
0.95	503	697	81	821	161	256	4	21
0.90	362	500	4	59	110			
0.85	192	249						
0.80	127	172			47	62		
0.75	93	131			40	50		
0.70	72	100			31	38		
0.65	56	77			27	32		
0.60	43	68						
0.55	33	61						
0.50	4	42						

Notes: Property values calculated from coefficients estimated using quantile regressions. See Appendix 8.1 for details. *Sources:* Author's calculations from 10-city sample drawn from Census Bureau, Eighth Census (1860), population manuscripts.

by mixed-race households. At the 70th, 80th, and 90th percentiles blacks owned about 72 percent of mixed personal property, but the ratio declined to 64 percent for the wealthiest 2½ percent of households. Among female-headed households, the black-mixed ratio declines as we move up the distribution—from 82 percent at the 70th percentile to 58 percent at the 97.5th percentile.

Few African-American households reported real estate ownership, because urban land ownership was limited only to the most well-to-do African-American households (those in the top 5 to 10 percent of the overall wealth distribution). It is also not surprising that the color-based wealth gap is apparent for both real and personal property. Regardless of how the data are parsed and regardless of the statistical technique used, urban black householders were less likely than mixed-race householders to own property, and owned less when they did own it.

Where a hopeful case could be made for rural land ownership, the mid-nineteenth-century urban experience is less hopeful. Although Baltimore's African-American real estate owners lived in two-story brick row houses characteristic of urban working-class families, only a small fraction owned their own home.[23] Most free families rented and occupied crowded, sometimes dilapidated wooden structures lining the city's many alleys. No significant African-American land-owning class emerged in late-antebellum southern cities. Urban home-ownership rates lagged far behind any modern metric. The realities of urban life in nineteenth-century America were such that most families rented. Clearly something other than property ownership drew free African Americans to cities. Previous chapters have explored marriage markets and employment opportunities as urban features that might attract African Americans from the hinterlands. The difficulty of owning property may not have offered inducements to urban living, but the potential for investments in other forms of wealth, namely, human capital, may have lured them in.

Human Capital

Adam Smith, in the *Wealth of Nations*, famously wrote that: "Those talents . . . of a workman may be considered in the same light as a machine . . . though it costs a certain expence [*sic*], [it] repays that expence with a profit."[24] The idea that people make forward-looking investments in themselves—in human capital—may not have been original to Smith, but it was thereafter integral to economic analysis. How important is human capital? In 1973 about 52 percent of per capita wealth in the United States was human capital; in 1992 the share was about 66 percent in low net-wealth, preretirement-age American households.[25] Human capital represented an even larger share of household wealth in the mid-nineteenth century—approximately 90 percent for urban Virginia's African-American households.[26]

Given the relatively low saving rate among modern Americans, it is not surprising that human capital accounts for the lion's share of individual and household wealth for all but the richest.[27] Wages—rather than interest, dividends, entrepreneurial returns, rental property incomes, and capital gains—are the source of most household's incomes. Because wages are highly correlated with prior human capital investments, households have strong incentives to invest in the human capital of their members. Altruistic parents, in particular, will invest in their children's human capital so that their children can lead productive, prosperous, and rewarding adult lives. In the nineteenth century parents need not have been purely altruistic in their investments in their children. The old-age security hypothesis holds that parents view children as a retirement fund, so that investment in children's earnings capacity is fully consistent with self-interested parents. Regardless of the parents' motivations, their children's earnings and consumption possibilities were heavily dependent on wage income—and, therefore, their human capital. Nineteenth-century African-American parents should have taken a keen interest their children's acquisition of marketable skills.

In the nineteenth century parents invested in their children's human capital in three principal ways: children could work in the family business and learn occupational skills under the tutelage of an already trained parent; children not wanting to follow in their parent's footsteps could be apprenticed to a master artisan to gather certain occupation-specific skills; or children could be sent to school to gather certain generalized skills, such as literacy and numeracy. It is not unreasonable to think that most nonorphaned children were exposed to a combination of all three forms, gaining some combination of generalized and job-specific human capital.

Nineteenth-century African Americans took advantage of the apprenticeship system to provide their children with the skills necessary to learn a trade. Christopher Phillips contends that free African-American parents "felt keenly that the greatest tool for their progenies' advancement was a skill with which they could carve out a better life for themselves."[28] In Maryland, for example, African-American parents who voluntarily bound their boys into an apprenticeship typically placed boys when they were about 12 years old.[29] More than half (56 percent), not surprisingly, were apprenticed to learn the "art and mystery" of farming. About one-fourth (22 percent) were apprenticed into service trades (barbers, cooks, waiters); another 9 percent were bound into semiskilled trades (brick maker, cigar maker, ship caulker). Just less than 10 percent were apprenticed to a skilled craftsman (coopers, shoemakers). Unfortunately, the Maryland records do not clearly distinguish between black and mixed-race youth, so it is impossible to determine whether there was differential placement into trades by color.

One alternative to apprenticeship was schooling. In comparing the two, Claudia Goldin argues that specialized skill training (apprenticeship) is cost-effective for individuals who expect to spend most of their working lives in the same place engaged in the same occupation.[30] Alternatively, formal schooling is initially more costly than apprenticeship, but it better enables people to change occupations over their lifetimes because it provides skills that are more flexible and transferable across places and occupations. Apprenticeship and school need not be, and were not, mutually exclusive. Some states required masters to provide apprentices with schooling, and the Maryland apprentice records reveal that masters regularly contracted to provide their young charges with both skill training and basic literacy.

Because there were no state-supported schools open to black and mixed-race children, the requirement to educate African-American apprentices sometimes proved burdensome to masters. Maryland and Missouri amended their laws allowing masters to offer apprentices a cash payment at the end of their indenture in lieu of education.[31] Only four of the nearly 120 African-American parents who apprenticed their sons in six Maryland counties chose the cash option, so there must have been educational opportunities for African-American children, even though the state did not provide for or support African-American education.

What the state failed to provide, philanthropy and private enterprise did. In the late eighteenth century Quakers and Methodists took a special interest in African-American education, offering both religious and academic instruction.[32] But educating African Americans grew increasingly unpopular, so by mid-century Quakers and Methodists had largely abandoned their educational mission.[33] Other religious and philanthropic groups stepped in, however. As Daniel Walker Howe notes, reading was central to Protestantism, even African-American Protestantism, and congregations across the South offered some instruction to African Americans.[34] Even some Catholics took up the cause of African-American education. In Baltimore, the Oblate Sisters of Providence Convent opened the St. Francis Academy for African-American girls; in St. Louis the Sisters of the Sacred Heart operated free day schools.[35] Although Sunday schools had a strong religious component, the earliest incarnations aimed mostly at providing poor children with basic literacy. Only after the wide adoption of regular weekday education did Sunday schools concentrate on religious instruction.

Profit-oriented African-American schools also operated across the United States, including the South. Thomas Bonneau's school in Charleston, South Carolina, which operated between 1803 and 1829, attracted students from as far away as Augusta, Georgia. Bonneau had so many students that he hired several assistants.[36] In September 1850, the *Nashville Union* reported that "Until yesterday we were not aware that there were several schools for free negroes in the city, and all of them in flourishing condition."[37] Any number of private schools came and went in New Orleans in the pre-Civil War era, and for-profit schools were in demand in rural parishes as well. In St. Landry Parish, Grimble Bell offered primary and secondary instruction, and typically enrolled about 125 students.[38] And in October 1854 the New Bern, North Carolina *Atlantic* claimed as "notorious fact" that schools were available for free African Americans.[39]

African-American education, as the reports from Nashville's and New Bern's newspapers makes clear, did not go unnoticed, and reactionary forces responded negatively. Many whites had long expressed concerns with the education of free African Americans, but the clamor to suppress or prohibit it did not gain real political traction until after Nat Turner's insurrection. Enough whites across the South became convinced that educated African Americans posed a threat to slavery and security that legislatures banned it. Virginia's and Georgia's 1831 prohibitions led the way; Alabama (1832), South Carolina (1834), and North Carolina (1835) soon followed.[40] Statutory bans were discussed in Maryland, Kentucky, and Tennessee, but no laws were passed. Statutory prohibitions meant that known schools were shuttered, but education was not so easily squelched. Schools operated clandestinely. In St. Louis, for instance, girls were taught to read under the guise of sewing classes; boys rowed out to classes conducted on an old steamboat in the Mississippi River anchored just outside Missouri's territorial waters.[41]

Despite the many efforts to educate African-American youth, when law and public sentiment was hostile to it, those who persisted were probably a select group whose selected nature responded to changes in public sentiment. To mitigate selection bias in an analysis of education, this study uses data drawn from 1860 population manuscripts of Baltimore, Maryland and New Orleans, Louisiana, two cities with sizeable African-American communities and no prohibitions on African-American education. Both cities had ample educational facilities. In fact, when Professor Ethan Allen Andrews arrived in Baltimore in 1835 on a fact-finding mission for the American Union for the Relief and Improvement of the Colored People, he found the city's African Americans well provided with educational opportunities.[42] The African Methodist Church, the Methodist Bethel Church, and the Episcopalians each operated a school; free women previously educated by the Oblate Sisters ran a handful of schools, too.

One shortcoming of the 1860 census is that enumerators asked only whether an individual had received any instruction during the past year at a public school, private academy, or with a tutor. The nature of the question precludes knowing which children attended regularly, which attended occasionally, and which attended just a few times. Economic historians have not come to any consensus on how best to interpret the responses, so prudence counsels that positive responses in the census may be reasonably interpreted as occasional attendance.[43] Treating each positive response equally likely overestimates *regular* attendance. At the same time, treating each negative response equally probably underestimates *any* school attendance. Youth whose educations were limited to Sunday schools were not recorded as having attended school, when they may have received some academic instruction. Taking negative responses at face value also fails to account for the possibility of home schooling. Frederick Douglass, lest we forget, received a combination of home schooling and irregular lessons from white schoolboys who shared their lesson books with him. The data, though imperfect, may still shed light on differential school participation and human capital investment by black and mixed-race families. The results are instructive, so long as neither black nor mixed-race families systematically under- or overreported enrollment.

Data was collected on all African-American youth appearing in the two city's manuscript censuses between the ages of 6 and 16. Maris Vinovskis reports a general resistance among contemporaries to sending children less than nine years old to school, and little attendance prior to age six.[44] The prime school-age years at mid-century were between nine and twelve, and, she argues, attendance dropped off rapidly thereafter. Table 8.7 reports the proportion of youth by age, sex, and color reported by their parents as having enrolled in school at some point during the previous year. Three features are immediately apparent. First, enrollment patterns are broadly consistent with Vinovskis's dating, though attendance among six- to eight-year-olds is too high to be consistent with a general resistance to early schooling. Second, enrollment rates for girls are not much different from that for boys. And, third, there were marked differences, especially at younger and older ages, in enrollment rates for blacks and mixed-race youth. Enrollment rates never approach the near universal rates Vinovskis uncovers for white children elsewhere in the United States, but approximately one-half of 11-year-old African-American boys and girls reported being enrolled. Moreover, mixed-race enrollment rates for boys, at least, do not drop off as precipitously after age 12 as for black youth. Whether this implies that mixed-race youth were more likely to enroll at all ages

Table 8.7 School Enrollment Rates for Black and Mixed-Race Youth

Age (years)	Black		Mixed-Race	
	Boys	Girls	Boys	Girls
6	0.19	0.13	0.15	0.24
7	0.23	0.22	0.26	0.41
8	0.28	0.31	0.45	0.32
9	0.37	0.33	0.42	0.38
10	0.38	0.32	0.39	0.37
11	0.44	0.36	0.50	0.49
12	0.32	0.27	0.53	0.44
13	0.42	0.21	0.39	0.43
14	0.15	0.16	0.28	0.30
15	0.05	0.06	0.12	0.21
16	0.01	0.02	0.13	0.05

Notes: Each column reports the fraction of youth by age, color, and sex that reported being enrolled in school in Baltimore and New Orleans in 1860. Further details can be found in Appendix 8.2 and Bodenhorn, "Single Parenthood and Childhood Outcomes." *Source*: Census Bureau, Eighth Census (1860), population manuscripts for Baltimore and New Orleans.

or whether they received cumulatively more schooling is impossible to determine absent longitudinal data.

Regression analysis further supports conclusions drawn from the raw means. After controlling for parental resources, family size and structure, and potential availability of schools, estimates from linear probability models imply that black children between the ages of six and eight were between 4 and 5 percentage points less likely than mixed-race children to report being enrolled. Given that less than one-fourth of black children reported being enrolled, a 4 percentage point reduction is meaningful. There were, however, no meaningful differences in reported enrollment rates for children between nine and 13 years. But black children 14 through 16 years were 6 percentage points less likely than mixed-race children to report being enrolled. Unless there was systematically differential attendance or learning for a reported enrollment rate, it is difficult to draw any other conclusion than that mixed-race boys and girls received more education than black boys and girls.

Black-mixed differences in school enrollments in Baltimore and New Orleans are consistent with scattered bits of evidence in other studies. James and Lois Horton argue that mixed-race men and women were generally better equipped than blacks to exploit their freedom. Mixed-race adults were more likely to be literate, and literacy in adulthood was most likely realized through schooling in youth.[45] Moreover, it was not uncommon for white opposition to arise around the education of any African American of "not very light complexion."[46] Whites feared educated African Americans. Most were not favorably disposed to providing education to African Americans, and many discouraged others from doing so. To the extent schooling was accepted, it was more acceptable if only light-skinned children participated.

The school enrollment results, too, are consistent with the human capital measures reported in the opening to this section and in Appendix 8.3. Human capital—wealth in the form of one's productive capacity—constituted a modestly larger fraction of a household's total wealth for mixed-race households than for black households. The mixed-race human capital advantage was not the result of purposeful mixed-race portfolio allocations away from other assets toward human capital. Mixed-race households had—in absolute dollar values—nearly as much real estate wealth, more consumer durable wealth, more slave wealth, and more valuable livestock than blacks. The mixed-race human capital advantage resulted from holding more remunerative occupations, on average, than blacks. Access to more rewarding jobs followed from more and better training and education.

The results raise questions of motivation. Why did light-skinned, mixed-race families differentially invest in their children's education, whether through more skilled craft training or more schooling? Prejudice, racism, and discrimination against any but the lightest complected African Americans surely entered into the equation. Winthrop Jordan and the Hortons emphasize this factor.[47] And in speaking of later generations of postbellum African Americans—though he would probably have drawn the same conclusion about the antebellum era—E. Franklin Frazier derogates the academic achievements of light-skinned, mixed-race individuals as little more than investments in the perpetuation of existing class distinctions.[48] For Frazier, mixed-race families "placed an exaggerated importance upon academic[s]" because it raised them above not only the less-educated black masses, but above the mass of poor southern whites with inferior educations. Education provided mixed-race men and women a cultural superiority without much economic payoff. African-American schools, Frazier asserted, were the tools of puritans used to inculcate respectability, and mixed-race families bought in.[49]

It is hard to read Lawrence Otis Graham's *Our Kind of People* and not come away thinking that Frazier was not far from the mark. And, like discrimination, education as a vehicle of cultural separation may have entered into the decision calculus of many mid-nineteenth-century mixed-race families. Cultural and social factors mattered, but economics can account for a large fraction of observed differences in education as well.[50]

Still a large fraction of African-American children and youth received little or no education even when schools were available. Were African-American parents unaware of the benefits of schooling? Or did they believe that the expected payoff did not justify the initial investment? Labor economists posit that labor market discrimination inhibits human capital investments. At any time, a young person can choose between school attendance, compensated market work, and leisure. The higher the anticipated reward for increased school attendance and accomplishment, the greater the effort at school. But labor market discrimination against the labor services provided by black adults reduces the incentive to invest in skills in youth that will only much later enhance the worker's capabilities (and income). Thus, youth who anticipate being discriminated against tomorrow will expend less effort in learning and obtaining skills today. In the alternative these youth will either work, or consume leisure when the marginal value of leisure exceeds the marginal value of current or future income foregone.[51] Interestingly, mid-nineteenth-century black school-age youth (14–16 years) did not work at noticeably higher rates than mixed-race youth, which implies that they consumed a lot of leisure or did lots of chores around the home. Given the difficulties the working poor faced in scratching out a living in nineteenth-century Baltimore, leisure (unemployment) was costly to one's health and well-being.

Nineteenth-century whites often spoke disparagingly of illiterate and shiftless blacks. Ironically, it was the prejudices whites held and the discriminatory acts they engaged in that convinced at least some black youth to aspire to less than they might have under an alternative racial regime. Statistical discrimination took its toll then, as it does now, by setting in motion a vicious circle. Discrimination made skill acquisition uneconomic, and blacks' lack of skills only further reinforced existing racial prejudices.

Conclusion

It is evident that mixed-race African Americans held more wealth than blacks. Before extolling the accomplishments of the well-to-do, mid-century mulatto as many contemporaries and some historians do, it is important to place those accomplishments in perspective. The importance of the statistical findings reported above transcends the obvious: namely, that African Americans acquired property and that acquisition was influenced by color. Perhaps the true importance of the findings lies in a greater appreciation of American values, most notably a respect for property and a respect for the right to acquire and control one's own property even when the person doing the acquiring was not of the favored or privileged class.

Two generations of scholars coming from very different perspectives recognize this.[52] Free African Americans were ceded the common-law right to acquire property with few limitations. Rights to property were in fact one of the few rights exercised by black and mixed-race people that went relatively untrammeled. In 1838 the Virginia state supreme court protected the right unequivocally: free people of all races were entitled to acquire and enjoy property, and they retained the right to seek redress for trespass and other injuries. Although the earliest Virginians of African heritage had no prior familiarity with common-law traditions, they quickly learned to how to use it to their advantage. In 1651 Francis Payne, a black man, sued Joseph Stowe for failure to pay for a heifer Payne had sold him on credit. The court found in Payne's favor. Two decades later, Payne sued a respected white Northampton, Virginia planter who, according to Payne's testimony and that of a supporting witness, had stolen and slaughtered one of Payne's hogs. The case was continued to the next session, and nothing is known about its ultimate resolution. "The most significant aspect of the entire exchange," according to T. H. Breen and Stephen Innes, "was Payne's expectation that he could receive a fair trial."[53] There is no indication that he did not. White Americans did not universally appreciate free African Americans in their midst, but few disavowed their right to property.

The right to property was critical to the modest economic advances realized by early nineteenth-century African Americans. Although it is possible to document occupational choices, little is known about African-American incomes. Information about wealth, on the other hand, is reasonably abundant. Ultimately, wealth may be a more appropriate yardstick by which to measure well-being; wealth provides households with the capacity to support themselves in the event that the breadwinner becomes temporarily unemployed or incapacitated, and it enhances a family's capacity to take advantage of opportunities. Wealth offers security and opportunity. Thomas Shapiro contends that "Americans survive on their incomes while assets feed dreams of a better life."[54] It is hard to defend the idea that white society protected African-American property because property offered hope. It is not hard to defend the idea that nineteenth-century whites defended black property because African-American property owners "tended to be industrious, law abiding, and respected members of society."[55] Jefferson championed a republic of yeoman farmers because he believed ownership made good citizens. Whites were not willing to cede them citizenship, but ownership might encourage free African Americans to exert, persevere, and accomplish. Ownership would make them productive and valuable—if not valued—participants in the American experiment.

9

Height, Health, and Mortality

In the previous chapter I argued that even self-interested parents had incentives to invest in their children's human capital. The old-age security hypothesis holds that in the absence of good alternative investments, parents rely on their children for support in old age and retirement. One implication is that a substantial share of African-American wealth was tied up in earning capacities, developed through training and education. In fact, about nine-tenths of mid-nineteenth-century African-American wealth was human capital.

Although formal education, apprenticeship, and informal training provide marketable skills that enhance a person's capacity to earn a living, the most basic form of human capital is health. Sickly people tend to receive lower wages than healthy people; the dead are paid even less. The development economist and demographer T. Paul Schultz contends that economists should be cognizant of what he labels "health human capital," and Nobel-laureate Amartya Sen and others characterize private and social investments in health and health infrastructure as both developmental and human rights goals.[1] Society has an abiding interest in investments in health infrastructure because alleviating squalid living conditions among the poor has large spillover effects.[2] Infectious disease outbreaks originating in ghettoes rarely respect political and social boundaries. The wealthy serve their own interests and improve their own health in improving the health of the poor. Politicians face seemingly counterintuitive incentives. What appears to be coordinated charity directed at assisting discriminated against groups is in fact self-interested investments that generate large private and social benefits through the mitigation of infectious externalities.

The issue for the economic historian is how best to measure investments in health human capital. Unfortunately, no household budget surveys were conducted in the mid-nineteenth century, so there is no good way to reconstruct how much families spent on food, clothing, shelter, medical care, and so on. Plantation records have been used to reconstruct plantation expenditures on slave diets, clothes, shelter, and health care, but not without controversy. Absent reliable measures of inputs, economic historians have turned to the observable outputs of investments in health, namely height and mortality. The connection between health and mortality is obvious; sick, poorly nourished, ill-housed people tend not to live particularly long lives. The connection between height and health is less obvious. Subsequent sections of this chapter provide a brief synopsis of the health-height connection, but suffice it to say for now that human biologists agree that healthier groups of people are taller on average than genetically comparable but less healthy groups.

This chapter provides evidence of color-based differences in average heights. A large sample of free black and mixed-race men and women drawn from archival records shows that after controlling for other factors, mixed-race men and women were approximately one-half inch taller than blacks. One-half inch may not appear to be a notable difference, but human biology reveals that one-centimeter differences are sometimes telling. Half-inches are large indeed. Despite notable differences in height, which points toward color-based differences in biological well-being, there is little evidence of color-based differences in early-age mortality, at least within legal status (free or slave). Mortality rates among free African Americans were lower than for slaves, especially for the young and the elderly, but there is little evidence of systematic differences in mortality within status across color. Where white society, it seems, acted on their color prejudices to the advantage of the light complected, the reaper was color-blind.

Height and History

The study of how humans grow—anthropometry—has engaged scientists for centuries, and careful, scientific studies date to the early nineteenth century.[3] One of the earliest US physicians to produce a systematic study of human growth was the Harvard physiologist Henry Pickering Bowditch, who recorded the heights of two dozen children over 25 years and in 1872 published a brief abstract of his observations. Bowditch reported that growth is most rapid early in life; up to age 12 boys are taller than girls; between 12 and 13 years of age, girls grow faster than boys and by age 14 are taller; around age 14, boys start growing faster than girls; girls stop growing around age 16, boys around age 19; and adult men are taller than women.[4] Bowditch's initial foray into anthropometry was valuable not for its findings, which are now and were then well known, but because it laid the foundation for a rigorous, large-scale study of the heights and weights of Gilded-Age Boston schoolchildren. By the time his study was complete nearly 14,000 boys and 11,000 girls between 5 and 18 years had been measured (without shoes) and weighed (in indoor clothes). The birthplaces of the children's parents were recorded, as were the parents' occupations. Bowditch was so meticulous that his initial review of the raw data uncovered 40 suspect observations and those children were remeasured. The result was "a classic of the international growth literature."[5]

Figure 9.1 show two views of the growth of nineteenth-century white Boston children constructed from Bowditch's 1872 data. Figure 9.1 plots the height of two representative children, Annie (a girl) and Ned (a boy), between ages 3 and 20; Figure 9.2 plots annual incremental increases in height from one age to the next, called *velocity*, expressed in inches per year for Annie and Ned. If we consider human growth from conception to maturity as a type of travel, the curves traced in Figure 9.1 are graphical height odometers. They trace the distances traveled by Annie and Ned over their journeys up to each age. As with any odometer, the reported values trace out previous stages of the journey. Figure 9.2 presents graphical height speedometers. The lines record the speed at which Annie and Ned passed through each checkpoint (presumably birthdays) on their respective journeys and represents the incremental rate at which each child grew over the past year.

One shortcoming of height curves, like Figure 9.1, is that the scale masks important biological events that the velocity curve makes apparent. Velocity of growth gradually declines from birth until around age 11 or 12 for girls or age 13 or 14 for boys, when there is a marked acceleration called the *adolescent growth spurt*. After approximately three years of accelerated growth during adolescence velocity declines rapidly, and ceases altogether around age 15 or 16 for girls and 17 or 18 for healthy boys. Each person's growth path is unique, but normal children raised in reasonably salubrious environments will exhibit a path not unlike Annie's or Ned's. The adolescent growth spurt may occur earlier or later, depending on the individual, and some but not all children experience a brief mid-growth spurt around age 7.[6]

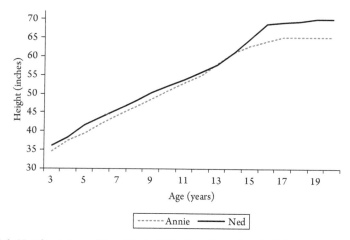

Figure 9.1 Height-at-Age of Two Typical Children from Bowditch's 1872 Study.
Source: Tanner, History of the Study, 186–187.

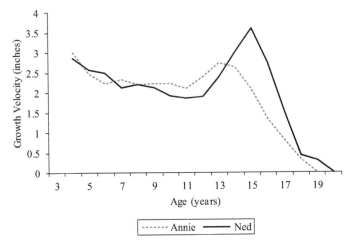

Figure 9.2 Height Growth Velocity of Two Typical Children from Bowditch's 1872 Study. Source: Tanner, History of the Study, 186–187.

Since Bowditch's time, human biologists around the world have conducted thousands of studies of variable scientific reliability. Careful and reliable studies reveal the diversity of the human biological experience, many of which are familiar. Compared to mid-twentieth-century adult male Londoners (68.8 inches), for example, urban Norwegians (70.6 inches) were tall, and rural Poles (65.0 inches) were short.[7] When Scandinavians passed Americans in average height in the late twentieth century it was considered newsworthy.[8]

In the past 30 years, economic historians have combed archives from around the world and gathered and reported a great deal of information on the heights of historical populations.[9] Scholars have documented the heights of soldiers, slaves, students, prisoners, passport holders, legislators, and other individuals who were measured and weighed since the seventeenth century.[10] Like Bowditch, modern anthropometric historians collect and analyze height data to better understand temporal and spatial differences in physiological well-being. They then connect observed differences in physiological well-being to economic well-being. In drawing the connection, anthropometric historians rely on the contention by modern human biologists that a "child's growth rate reflects, better than any other single index, his state of health and nutrition" and that average heights at each age "reflect accurately the state of a nation's public health and the average nutritional status of its citizens, when appropriate allowance is made for differences, if any, in genetic potential."[11] Combining this fundamental insight with the historical fact that a large fraction of household budgets was spent on food and health, anthropometric historians use height as a measure of economic well-being when standard measures, such as per capita income or consumption, are unavailable.

Although height-at-age is a valuable index of well-being, it is important not to claim more than the evidence provides. While it is well known that a child's environment influences his or her growth path, and thus height, there is less agreement about which factors matter more or how different factors interact. If we take two genetically similar groups and observe that one group is consistently taller than the other (on average), it is not unreasonable to conclude that the taller group was raised in a more salutary environment. It may be unreasonable, however, to attribute observed differences to specific factors, no matter how well measured. The list of potential influences is long, and if the historical anthropometrician takes this fact seriously, it is apparent that any monocausal explanation is almost certainly misleading if not just plain wrong. With that caveat in mind let us now turn to the evidence, which reveals that mixed-race people were consistently taller than blacks. This suggests some measure of (relative) material advantage among mixed-race people, which is consistent with—but not completely explained by—the evidence presented in previous chapters.

Growth and Stature

Casual observation of human heights masks the most fundamental insight of human biology: systematic variations in human heights across societies are correlated with certain characteristics of those societies. Casual observers note the presence of (relatively) short and tall people in all places at all times, and attribute differences to the idiosyncracies of genetic variation. Thomas Jefferson (6' 2½"), for example, towered over James Madison (5' 4") even though they were near contemporaries, born and raised in relative affluence in the Virginia Piedmont. Human biology has little to say about these sorts of individual differences in stature, other than that Jefferson's genetic potential height probably exceeded Madison's. Human biology has much to say about systematic differences in heights between large, well-defined groups. Modern American whites, for instance, are about two inches taller than mid-nineteenth-century American whites. Genetic changes over the past 150 years explain no more than tiny fraction of that increase. Rather, environmental factors—notably improvements in nutrition, reductions in the incidence and severity of chronic and acute infections, and changes in work effort during childhood, as well as the complex interactions among these factors—likely explain most of the observed temporal differences in US heights.[12]

While certain details of the process remain unexplained, two centuries of medical research into human growth have generated consensus on the basics. The size and shape a child attains as he or she matures is the result of continuous interactions between genes and environment during the whole period of growth, and the interactions are complex, nonadditive, and synergistic. Environmental circumstances during two periods are critical to growth: birth to five years, and adolescence.[13] Severe nutritional or infectious insults during these critical periods may push a person onto a permanently lower growth path, but the detrimental long-term growth effects of deprivation in early childhood appear to be more readily overcome if nutrition and health improves later. Children who suffer only brief periods of nutritional deprivation or severe infection usually experience a period of accelerated growth, labeled "catch-up growth," after the privation or infection is abated.[14] If conditions improve less than fully, children may enter the adolescent growth spurt later and grow more slowly for a longer time.

Neither pronounced nor severe privation nor infection is necessary to generate observable differences in mean heights between groups within a population. Moderate but persistent deprivation may retard growth. Numerous studies reveal that children of the well-to-do are taller than the children of manual laborers. Bowditch found this in his study of 1870s Boston schoolchildren; Charles Roberts, as part of a Parliamentary commission, found it for 1870s British children; it has been found dozens of times since in developed and developing countries.[15] It is this observation that affords historical anthopometricians opportunities to consider the comparative nutritional well-being (broadly defined) of different groups.

An obvious concern that arises in a study of the heights of blacks and mixed-race peoples is that race mixing may yield some systematic genetically based height advantage—an effect sometimes labeled *hybrid vigor*—that may be mistaken for unobserved environmental factors. Existing evidence is more consistent with environmental influences than hybrid vigor, however. Studies of mixed-race people were conducted in 1960s Jamaica, Mozambique, and South Africa.[16] The Jamaican study included only relatively privileged children attending the same private school and found no notable differences in heights between racial groups. The environmental effect was more obvious in the South African study, which found that mixed-race people—mixes of white, blacks, Indian, and Malay—were the shortest, but they were also the most nutritionally deprived group. Hybrid vigor is not the principal cause of racial differences in height.

A second, less obvious concern in comparing the heights of mixed-race and black Americans is that there may have been differential dynamic height-based selection into the sample among mixed-race and blacks. That is, although Maryland and Virginia laws mandated universal registration, not everyone subject to the law registered. If blacks and mixed-race people selected differently into the sample in a way that a higher proportion of tall mixed-race people registered than tall blacks, the resulting statistics will point to a mixed-race height (and health) advantage where none existed. Howard Bodenhorn, Timothy Guinnane, and Thomas Mroz find evidence of height-based selection for all African Americans into the sample, but there is no available statistical test to determine whether blacks and mixed-race people differentially selected in.[17] Thus, the results should be interpreted cautiously and with this caveat in mind.

Finally, it is important to note that there is no optimal body size or shape or growth pattern. Africans are more skeletally mature at birth, and Japanese girls enter puberty earlier than Europeans. Shorter people may be able to exert the same amount of effort as taller ones, and do so by more efficiently converting calories into work effort.[18] Armed with these insights, a study of the growth patterns and terminal heights of blacks and mixed-race African Americans provide some further evidence of the different treatment of black and mixed-race Americans in the nineteenth century.

Color and Childhood Growth in the Nineteenth-Century Chesapeake

Anthropometric information on African-American children living in late eighteenth and early nineteenth-century Maryland and Virginia was gathered from ledgers maintained by county court clerks. In the 1790s, both states passed laws requiring free African Americans to register with the county court. For a small fee (25¢ in Virginia), clerks provided registrants with their freedom papers and recorded a copy of the registration in the official county court records. Most registrations provided reasonably detailed description of the registrant—his or her name, along with any known aliases, age, sex, height, and color (dark yellow or light mulatto, among many others), any identifying scars or other notable physical attributes, and whether the registrant was born free or manumitted. Less commonly, registrations included information about the registrant's county of birth or prior residence, his or her mother's name, or the name of a manumitted slave's previous owner. The registers provide a wealth of information on individuals unavailable in other sources and represent a valuable resource for examining the connection between color and height. Details about the samples and their collection are provided in Appendices 5.1 and 9.1.

Figures 9.3, 9.4, and 9.5 reproduce three representative registrations from Virginia. Figure 9.3 reveals that 33-year old George Somerhill of Richmond, Virginia was dark complected and five feet, eight inches tall. Jordin Lookado (Figure 9.4) of Albemarle County, Virginia was of yellow color and five foot six inches. And 42-year old Morman Morgan (Figure 9.5) was dark complected and six feet tall.

Due to the small number of observations at some ages and the presence of outliers at others that excessively influence raw averages, the height-at-age profiles represented in Figures 9.6 (boys) and 9.7 (girls) are derived from height-at-age estimated using the Preece-Baines method (see Appendix 9.1 for details). From these smoothed height curves, centiles of modern stature are calculated and presented in the diagrams. Centiles provide a useful benchmark for comparison in

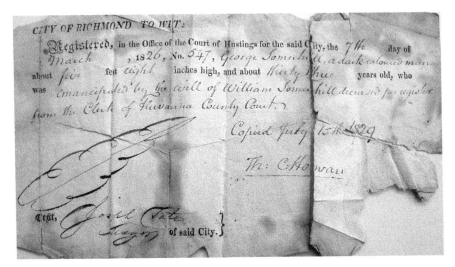

Figure 9.3 Registration of George Somerhill in Richmond Hustings Court (1826, copied 1829) Surrendered to Albemarle County Court After Relocating. Source: Free Negro and Slave Records, Albemarle County, Box 1, Library of Virginia.

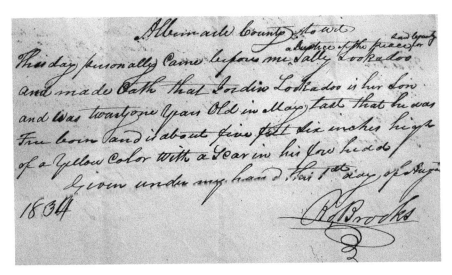

Figure 9.4 Registration of Jordin Lookadoo in Albemarle County Court. Source: Free Negro and Slave Records, Albemarle County, Box 1 (1834), Library of Virginia.

that the fiftieth centile is that attained by an average late-twentieth-century child at each age. If the average African-American child growing up in Maryland or Virginia in the nineteenth century had been as tall as the average American child in the late-twentieth century United States, the figures would display straight lines at the fiftieth centile. That is, the average nineteenth-century child would

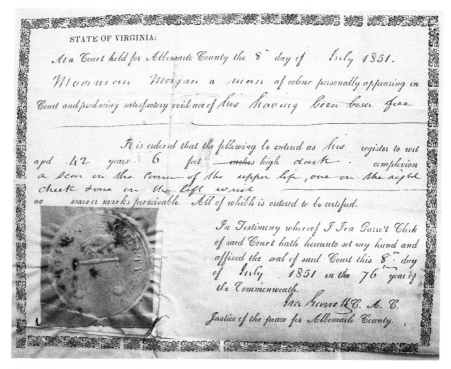

Figure 9.5 Registration of Sarah Yates in Augusta County Court (1846) Surrendered to Albemarle County Court After Relocating. Source: Free Negro and Slave Records, Albemarle County, Box 1, Library of Virginia.

have been taller than the shortest 49.5 percent of modern children and shorter than the tallest 49.5 percent of modern children. Centiles facilitate comparisons across groups by offering a common, well-defined standard of comparison.

Several notable features are evident in Figures 9.6 and 9.7. First, nineteenth-century African-American children were short by modern standards before age five. Average heights for four- and five-year-olds were between the fifth and tenth centiles of modern stature and would, at 1.5 standard deviations below the modern median, present as stunted to a modern observer.[19] Second, relative to modern standards, the heights of nineteenth-century African Americans recover up to age eight or nine and approach or exceed the 30th centile of modern stature. Richard Steckel found a comparable if less pronounced recovery among young slaves sold in the interregional slave trade and attributed it to the better nutrition provided to slaves as they started contributing to plantation production.[20]

Economists and economic historians model youth nutrition and height as one outcome of a complex household dynamic optimization problem. Caregivers may care about a child's height, mostly because it provides signals about contemporary health and future productivity. If caregivers observe lagging growth or incipient

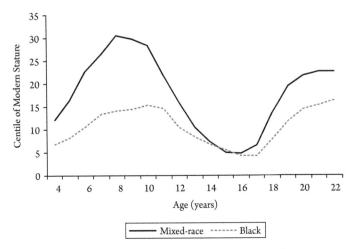

Figure 9.6 Centiles of Modern Stature—Nineteenth-Century African-American Boys.
Source: Author's calculations from Maryland and Virginia register sample; see Komlos, "Toward an Anthropometric History," and Appendix 5.1 for detailed descriptions of the data.

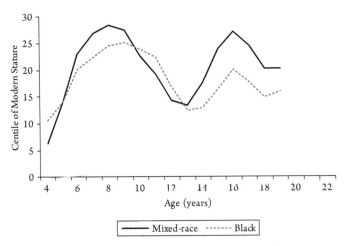

Figure 9.7 Centiles of Modern stature—Nineteenth-Century African-American Girls.
Source: Author's calculations from Maryland and Virginia register sample; see Komlos, "Toward an Anthropometric History," and Appendix 5.1 for detailed descriptions of the data.

stunting in a child, they may reallocate health or nutritional resources to that child until he or she demonstrates some catch-up growth.[21] Anecdotal evidence from the nineteenth century is consistent with these models. On his Georgia sea island plantation, Charles Manigault expected his slaves to provide their own fish and shellfish for protein. Pork was provided to adults only during harvest, when there was little free time for fishing. No pork was allocated to children, unless a particular child appeared "drooping."[22] Otherwise, slave children lived on whatever corn, fish, molasses, and unmarketable rice was left after their parents had satisfied their appetites.

It seems likely that slave children were subordinate claimants on food, after their parents and older working siblings were fed, which is consistent with poor nutrition as a contributory factor to the small stature of enslaved children of both races. It is notable, however, that recently manumitted children do not exhibit the pathological stunting noted by Steckel, which suggests that they and their families held privileged positions on Upper South farms and plantations up to the moment of manumission. Recently manumitted, 10-year-old black boys attained the 16th centile of modern stature compared to the 2nd centile for 10-year-old boys entering the interregional slave trade.[23] It is possible that neither sample reveals much about the population mean of slave children, because slave owners may have selected on height for manumission (positively) and sale (negatively). Moreover, height and disposition (sale or manumission) may have been endogenous or simultaneously determined. However, mean height among free-born, 10-year-old black boys reached the 15th centile of modern stature, which is close to the height of manumitted children.

A third notable feature of Figures 9.6 and 9.7 is that nineteenth-century African-American child heights decline relative to modern standards beginning around age 10 for boys and age 8 for girls. These relative height declines are consistent with the relatively later age at which nineteenth-century African Americans experienced their adolescent growth spurt. Moderately deprived children, or those growing in less salubrious environments, will experience their growth spurt later than well-fed, healthy children. Estimates of age at takeoff and age at peak height velocity derived from the coefficients of the Preece-Baines growth model (see Appendix 9.1 for details), reported in Table 9.1, show that age at takeoff was 12 years for free-born, mixed-race boys and 10.9 years for free-born, black boys. Age at peak height velocity (or the age at which a child is growing fastest during adolescence) occurred at 15.6 years for free-born, mixed-race and 14.6 years for free-born black boys. Both age at takeoff and age at peak height velocity among nineteenth-century African-American boys occur about one and a half to two and a half years later than for modern American boys (takeoff at 9.4 years; peak velocity at 13.4 years). The later entry into adolescence in the nineteenth century explains the observed decline from about the 25th to the 10th centile during adolescence, as well as the recovery to approximately the 20th centile at maturity and is consistent with J. M. Tanner's observation that over the last two centuries, there has been a tendency for youth to mature earlier and grow larger.[24]

Table 9.1 compares age at takeoff and age at peak height velocity for nineteenth-century African-American children in the greater Chesapeake region to select historical and modern populations. The estimated ages reveal that adolescence in fact arrived relatively late for nineteenth-century African-American children—generally about one to two years later than the comparison groups—but

Table 9.1 Age at Takeoff and Age at Peak Velocity Select Groups

Country/ Region	Group	Date	Obs	Age at Takeoff (yrs)	Age at Peak Velocity (yrs)
Boys					
Va-Md	Free-born mixed-race	1790–1865	1080	12.0	15.6
Va-Md	Free-born black	1790–1865	3723	10.9	14.6
France	National	ca. 1953	48	10.0	13.9
Guatemala	Well-to-do	ca. 1979	78	10.0	13.6
Jamaica	Private school	ca. 1973	20	10.4	14.2
India	Middle class	ca. 1952	303	10.5	14.3
United States	National	1979	na	9.4	13.4
Girls					
Va-Md	Free-born mixed-race	1790–1865	927	9.7	12.2
Va-Md	Free-born black	1790–1865	3074	8.7	10.4
France	National	ca. 1953	43	8.2	11.6
Guatemala	Well-to-do	ca. 1979	85	8.9	12.0
Jamaica	Private school	ca. 1973	20	8.5	11.6
India	Middle class	ca. 1952	260	9.3	12.4
United States	National	1979	na	7.8	11.1

Notes: Dates with ca. are longitudinal studies that followed children through maturity beginning at reported date. Age at takeoff and age at peak velocity estimated from Preece-Baines Model 1 coefficients. *Sources:* Va-Md: author's calculations; France: Ledford and Cole, "Mathematical Models"; Guatemala: Bogin et al., "Longitudinal Analysis"; Jamaica: Singhal et al., "Delayed Adolescent Growth"; India: Hauspie et al., "Longitudinal Study"; United States: Ward et al., "Simple Method."

persisted for about the same three to four year period. Diet and disease are likely culprits.[25] The nutritional case is compelling, not least because although antebellum planters may not have understood the causal pathways, they understood the association between nutrition and growth. In 1860, Gabriel Manigault considered taking in a 15-year-old slave boy as a house servant, but expressed concern with the boy's diminutive stature. Manigault wrote that "I am sorry to say that [the boy] is not well grown for his age. He ought to soon take a start though . . . the good food that he is likely to have as a house servant ought to accelerate his growth."[26] The nearly complete lack of planters' and parents' understanding of disease pathways was of great consequence as well, and cannot be discounted as a contributory factor for the late onset of the adolescent growth spurt among nineteenth-century youth.[27]

Despite their relatively small stature and late spurt, relative to the modern US population, Figure 9.8 points to a relatively salubrious Chesapeake-area environment for African-American children. Measured 10-year-old nineteenth-century African Americans compare favorably to mid-nineteenth century Europeans and mid-twentieth century Indians. Chesapeake blacks were approximately the same height as relatively privileged Jamaicans and Ghanians in the 1960s.[28] Modern American children are taller than nineteenth-century African Americans but until very recently, Americans, including free black and mixed-race peoples, were among the tallest people on Earth. To the extent that the Chesapeake samples are representative of the region's African-American population, it appears they were tall and seemingly healthy.[29]

The fourth notable feature of Figures 9.6 and 9.7 is that mixed-race boys were consistently taller at every age than black boys; mixed-race girls were taller at most, but not all, ages than black girls. By 22 years free-born mixed-race men attained the 23rd centile, while free-born black men attained the 16th; the differences are similar between mixed-race and black women. Table 9.2 shows that mixed-race men and women were about one-half inch taller than their black counterparts, regardless of slave or free status. The nineteenth-century pattern appears in modern contexts as well. In her study of race and height in South Africa and Brazil—two societies with sizeable mixed-race populations—Sarah Burghard

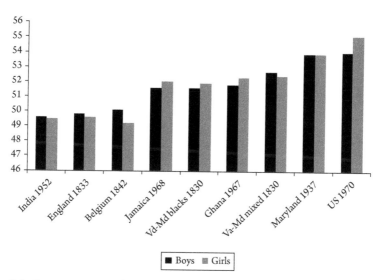

Figure 9.8 Comparative Heights of 10-Year-Old African-American Boys and Girls.
Sources: India (1952): Hauspie et al., "Longitudinal Study"; England (1833) and Belgium (1842): Bowditch, *Growth of Children*; Jamaica (1968), Ghana (1867), and the United States (1970): Eveleth and Tanner, *Worldwide Variation*; Maryland (1937): Wolff, "Study of Height"; and Virginia-Maryland (1830): author's calculations from Maryland and Virginia register sample; see Komlos, "Toward an Anthropometric History," and Appendix 5.1 for descriptions of the data.

Table 9.2 Black and Mixed-Race Heights and Select Comparison Groups

Country	Group	Year(s) Measured	Male Heights (inches)
United States	Va-Md free-born mixed-race	1792–1865	67.9
United States	Va-Md free-born black	1792–1865	67.3
United States	Va-Md manumitted mixed-race	1792–1865	67.5
United States	Va-Md manumitted black	1792–1865	67.0
United States	New England farmers[a]	1860s	68.6
United States	New England urban laborers[a]	1860s	67.8
United States	Yale University students[b]	ca. 1890	67.9
United States	Amherst College students (22yrs)[c]	1861–1885	67.6
United States	Amherst College students[b]	ca. 1890	67.9
United States	University of Wisconsin students[b]	ca. 1890	68.0
United States	West Point cadets (21 yrs)[d]	1880s	67.8
England	Convicts[e]	1812–1857	65.4
England	Military recruits[e]	1812–1817	66.7
England	Convicts, rural-born[f]	1770–1815	66.0
England	Convicts, urban-born[f]	1770–1815	65.4
Ireland	English East India Co. army recruits[g]		65.6
Ireland	Convicts, rural-born[f]	1770–1815	66.1
Ireland	Convicts, urban-born[f]	1770–1815	65.8

Notes: Before concluding that African Americans were as tall as privileged whites, it must be recalled that nineteenth-century African Americans entering the sample may not have been a random draw from the underlying height distribution. Bodenhorn, Guinnane, and Mroz, "Caveat Lector," report evidence of selection into the sample. Still, average heights suggests that at least some African Americans matured in a disease and nutritional environment not unlike that experienced by relatively privileged whites. *Sources:* [a] Margo and Steckel, "Heights of Native-Born"; [b] Seaver, *Anthropometry*; [c] Hitchcock, "Anthropometric Statistics"; [d] Komlos, "Height and Weight of West Point Cadets"; [e] Johnson and Nicholas, "Male and Female Living Standards"; [f] Nicholas and Steckel, "Heights and Living Standards," [g] Mokyr and Ó Gráda, "Heights of the British and the Irish."

finds that mixed-race children were about twice as likely as white children to be stunted (more than two standard deviations below mean white height), but black children were more than three times as likely to be stunted. Burghard cannot tease out causal effects, but household resources, which are correlated with environmental contamination, nutritional adequacy, and illness, are important determinants of child height. Even if nutritionally deprived children continue to grow past the age at which healthy youth grow, mixed-race people will be taller than blacks on average.

Table 9.2 provides some evidence on the comparative heights of black and mixed-race African Americans. Whether considering raw averages or estimates from ordinary least squares (OLS) or nonlinear least squares Preece-Baines estimates, mixed-race male and female terminal heights were about one-half inch greater than black terminal heights (see Appendix 9.1 for details), a result that appears for both free-born and manumitted people.

Just as African-American child and youth heights compare favorably to contemporary and modern standards, suggesting that Maryland and Virginia children were raised under reasonably salutary conditions (by historical standards, at least), African-American adults compare favorably to contemporary US and European whites. Terminal adult male heights between 67 and 68 inches are less than the 68.6 inches reported for New England farmers, but they are approximately the same as heights attained by New England urban laborers and students at some of America's elite colleges and universities. Twenty-one and 22-year-old students at Amherst College, Yale University, the University of Wisconsin, and the US Army Academy measured between the 1860s and the 1880s were no taller than Chesapeake region African Americans of the previous generation. Given that nineteenth-century university students were drawn from the well-to-do and tend to be among the tallest persons in most countries, the available evidence on the heights of African Americans suggest that the nineteenth-century Chesapeake was amenable to human health and growth for at least some segments of the African-American population.[30]

It is not the purpose of this chapter to explain the source of mixed-race people's height advantage over blacks. The historical record simply does not provide the necessary evidence to unravel the myriad factors responsible for differential growth between people of different races and statuses. Some combination of access to food, health care, differences in work effort during growth, and differential selection into the sample may account for the differences. Any number of alternative plausible explanations can be constructed that account for these features, but all explanations remain speculative absent supporting evidence. The purpose of this chapter then is simply to provide one more piece of evidence consistent with the overall thesis of this study. The height evidence is consistent with the hypothesis that the antebellum South was not a two-race society riven by the one-drop rule. Antebellum Southerners recognized, acted on, and even embraced

the ambiguities of color. There was no sharply drawn color line. Mixed-race people benefitted from advantageous treatment relative to that received by blacks.

Color and Mortality

In June 1852 Margaret Douglass of Norfolk, Virginia, opened a school for free
African-American children. Douglass tells us that for several months the children's
lessons followed an ordinary routine until one student—a studious, "humble and
obedient," 14-year-old black girl—fell seriously ill. The student was slender with
a delicate constitution, and Mrs. Douglass frequently thought that her studiousness would eventually injure her health. Studiousness was not the girl's problem;
she suffered from tuberculosis. Visiting the student's home, Douglass found that
the girl and her mother lived in a "miserable apology for a human habitation," consisting of two rooms furnished only with some broken chairs and a bed supported
by some boards. A hollow cough revealed that the mother, too, was afflicted with
tuberculosis and unable to provide for her dying daughter. "Here is a scene of suf-
fering," wrote Mrs. Douglass, "and no one to administer to the wants of the dying
or the living."[31]

With no resources and no one to administer to mother's or daughter's needs,
Mrs. Douglass took charge of the funeral arrangements. Six of the girl's classmates,
dressed in white, served as pall bearers; the other students followed in proces-
sion. Funeral processions reminded everyone of the inevitability of death and the
universality of loss.[32] Though destitute and anonymous to nearly all of Norfolk's
white residents—her brief biography does not even reveal her name—the solem-
nity and dignity afforded the young girl's death illuminated the fact that even for
those who lived among the shadows, there was love and loss.

Margaret Douglass attributed the girl's early demise to the family's destitu-
tion. Earlier discussions have documented less remunerative employment, lower
wealth, and shorter stature of blacks relative to mixed-race and whites. Low-paying
jobs and low wealth are typically correlated with poor overall health. Poverty
reduces nutrition and medical care, one consequence of which is greater early-age
mortality. The evidence points toward a general level of black and mixed-race
health in youth, adolescence, and adulthood consistent with the relatively tall
stature of African Americans at mid-century. Not surprisingly, southern African
Americans—disproportionately among the urban poor—died higher rates than
whites, but the differences are less pronounced than might be expected.[33]

Urban African-American early mortality at mid-century was likely driven by
several common contemporary causes. In his *Medical Annals of Baltimore*, Dr. John
E Quinan reports smallpox outbreaks in 1846, 1847, and 1863. The last outbreak
was credited with 263 deaths. In 1849 and 1854, cholera outbreaks appeared in
certain neighborhoods. In the 1849 incident, 155 reported cases resulted in 86

deaths, all blamed on a "fouled sewer."[34] In 1853 and 1857 measles and scarlet fever epidemics appeared. Yellow fever outbreaks appeared in the Fells Point neighborhood in 1853 and 1854, resulting in 18 cases and 18 deaths in the former year and 40 cases and 20 deaths in the latter. Baltimore, a city of more than 200,000 inhabitants in 1860, was served by 325 physicians, who risked their own well-being ministering to the sick. One of the notable medical events of 1860 recounted by Quinan was that Dr. Charles Frick contracted diptheria from a "poor negress whom he was treating."[35]

The physical separation afforded by rural residence provided limited protection against communicable disease. In his study of mostly rural counties, Joseph Ferrie finds that early death was commonly attributed to consumption, cholera, typhoid, and other gastrointestinal and respiratory infections.[36] Kenneth Kiple and Virginia Kiple also contend that the typical southern diet of fatty pork and corn left most southern African Americans undernourished. Undernourishment, which creates its own health problems, also leaves the weakened individual more susceptible to infections and less able to recover from them.[37] Other scholars emphasize alternative infections, namely malaria and hookworm, as important causes of short stature and early mortality.[38] Malaria was surely endemic in the antebellum era, but it is not clear its health effects were as severe as sometimes claimed, nor is it clear that the well-documented incidence of hookworm and pellagra in parts of the postbellum South were common before the war.[39] Any attempt to untangle the relative incidence of disease and the principal causes of antebellum early mortality are plagued by poor evidence. Researchers are well served treating the accuracy and validity of the causes of death provided in the antebellum censuses skeptically. The discussion that follows, therefore, simply compares all-cause mortality by race, color, and sex.

Because the 1860 population census does not report the details of color by age and sex—it reports free and slave African Americans by the age groups listed in Table 9.3 and Table 9.4 (under 1, 1-4 years, etc.), and it reports the total number of black and mixed-race people by status (slave and free)—calculating differential mortality by age, color, and sex requires estimates of the black and mixed-race populations at each age. The simplest way to construct such estimates are to use the proportion black or mixed-race across all ages by status and multiply that fraction by the African-American population within each age group. Thus, an estimate of the free black male population under 1 year of age in Baltimore is calculated by multiplying the fraction black among males of all ages in Baltimore by the number of African Americans under 1 year in Baltimore. The same procedure is followed for each of the 25 counties and 5 cities included in the mortality sample.[40] County and city estimates are then aggregated and used to calculate mortality rates by age, sex, color, and status.

The 1860 mortality census asked the head of each interviewed household to list any deaths occurring in that household in the previous year. When a death

Table 9.3 Male Mortality Rates By Race, Color, Age, and Status: Boys and Men

Age	White	Free Mixed	Free Black	Slave Mixed	Slave Black
Under 1	.072	.089	.074	.116	.116
1–4 yrs	.022	.030	.021	.029	.027
5–9 yrs	.006	.007	.006	.006	.006
10–14 yrs	.003	.004	.003	.003	.005
15–19 yrs	.003	.005	.006	.003	.006
20–29 yrs	.005	.008	.006	.005	.006
30–39 yrs	.007	.012	.005	.011	.007
40–49 yrs	.009	.007	.005	.012	.010
50–59 yrs	.011	.012	.015	.013	.017
60–69 yrs	.022	.010	.018	.011	.027
70–79 yrs	.054	.031	.027	.038	.063

Notes: Published volumes of the 1860 population census do not report black and mixed-race by age group. It reports status (free or slave) by age in one table by state and the total number of blacks and mixed-race people by status and state in another. The number of black and mixed-race for each age group is estimated by using the total free or slave population at age and multiplying those values by the proportion black and mixed in the total populations. Mortality rates are calculated as [number died by age, color and sex / (number died by age color and sex + estimated number surviving by age, color and sex)]. Data from the 25-county sample discussed in Appendix 8.2 (except that Chesterfield County, Virginia is substituted for Caroline County, Maryland), plus the cities of Baltimore, Louisville, Nashville, Petersburg, and Richmond. Sources: US Census Office, Eighth Census (1860), *Population of the United States*; census of mortality manuscripts.

was reported information on the deceased was collected, including the decedent's name, age at death, sex, color, occupation (if any), cause of death, number of days sick prior to death, and nativity. There are obvious shortcomings with the mortality census—imperfect recall, inaccurate reporting of ages or causes of death, or underreporting deaths in households that dissolved following one or more members' deaths. Unless any of the shortcomings is systematically correlated with color, the evidence should provide reasonable approximations of mortality rates across groups. One positive feature of the mortality census is that it identifies color (black and mixed-race), which makes it useful in investigating differential mortality, if any, across color groups.

Tables 9.3 and 9.4 report basic mortality estimates by race and color. White mortality rates at all ages are consistent with (if somewhat higher than) the rates reported in Ferrie's study of the 1850 and 1860 censuses. Ferrie reports predicted mortality rates of 0.048 for white female infants under 1 year and 0.065 for white male infants.[41] The slightly higher rates found here (0.059 for white female and

Table 9.4 Female Mortality Rates By Race, Color, Age and Status: Girls
and Women

Age	White	Free Mixed	Free Black	Slave Mixed	Slave Black
Under 1	.059	.066	.070	.100	.108
1–4 yrs	.020	.015	.016	.026	.024
5–9 yrs	.006	.005	.004	.007	.006
10–14 yrs	.002	.002	.003	.007	.005
15–19 yrs	.004	.005	.006	.005	.008
20–29 yrs	.005	.004	.006	.003	.008
30–39 yrs	.006	.005	.008	.011	.008
40–49 yrs	.006	.010	.008	.008	.010
50–59 yrs	.009	.018	.012	.012	.016
60–69 yrs	.018	.013	.010	.009	.026
70–79 yrs	.037	.018	.032	.019	.039

Notes: Published volumes of the 1860 population census do not report black and mixed-race by age group. It reports status (free or slave) by age in one table by state and the total number of blacks and mixed-race people by status and state in another. The number of black and mixed-race for each age group is estimated by using the total free or slave population at age and multiplying those values by the proportion black and mixed in the total populations. Mortality rates are calculated as: [number died by age, color and sex / (number died by age color and sex + estimated number surviving by age, color and sex)]. Data from the 25-county sample discussed in Appendix 8.2 (except that Chesterfield County, Virginia is substituted for Caroline County, Maryland), plus the cities of Baltimore, Louisville, Nashville, Petersburg, and Richmond. *Sources:* US Census Office, Eighth Census (1860), *Population of the United States;* census of mortality manuscripts.

0.072 for white male infants) may follow from the inclusion of more large urban places than in Ferrie's study. Nineteenth-century cities were notoriously dirty places with higher infection rates than their hinterlands, so the slightly higher rates at all ages is consistent with a higher urban disease load.

Tables 9.3 and 9.4 reveal several features of mid-nineteenth-century mortality. First, age-specific mortality follows a traditional U-shape. Very high infant mortality gives way to substantially lower youth mortality. Mortality rates levels off at about 0.003 to 0.006 (0.3 to 0.6 percent) for people between about 5 and 30 years. Mortality creeps upward until age 70, after which it increases to about 3 to 6 percent per year. Modern mortality rates by age show a similar U-shape, but at notably lower levels. Infant mortality rates in 2007 ranged from.005 for white females to.013 for black males. Modern rates do not reach nineteenth-century levels until about age 75, when modern rates range between 0.016 and 0.036 (1.6 to 3.6 percent), which are only slightly below mid-nineteenth-century rates for free African Americans.

The second notable feature of nineteenth-century mortality rates is the gap between whites and slaves for infants and children. The male slave infant mortality rate was 60 percent higher than the white male rate. For female slave children (1–4 years), the rate was 23 to 32 percent higher. Rates generally converge until about age 30, after which the slave mortality rate increases relative to whites and free African Americans.

Finally, there is little evidence of a systematic black-mixed-race mortality gap, except among older slaves. One of the more remarkable features of death at mid-century is that for individuals in the prime of their lives, it was an equal-opportunity visitor. Mortality rates for black and mixed-race African Americans, both free and slave, from their early teens through their twenties, were more alike—mostly between 0.003 and 0.006 (0.3 to 0.6 percent)—than different. Differential mortality by color appears only systematically among elderly slaves.

Using micro data, Ferrie finds that family property ownership is the only socioeconomic factor significantly correlated with lower early-age mortality among whites. From earlier chapters we know that mixed-race families were more likely than blacks to own property and to report more when they owned property. But because property was less dispersed among African Americans and plots, when owned, were smaller and less productive than among whites, property ownership may have provided less insulation from nutritional deprivation and disease than for whites. The conclusion to draw from mid-nineteenth-century mortality censuses is not that of Thomas Hobbes in *Leviathan*: life at mid-century was not "solitary, poore, nasty, brutish, and short." It was precarious, however. The primitive state of contemporary medicine could do little to abate the prevalence of deadly infectious disease.

Conclusions

A dedicated group of economic historians contend that historical height and mortality data provide better, or at least a more balanced, depictions of human well-being than do traditional measures such as wages, income or wealth. Their contention is based on two premises. First, historical data underlying traditional measures of well-being are relatively sparse, and not particularly reliable or representative. Height and mortality data, alternatively, are more widely available and tend to be of better quality. It is not unusual for heights researchers to compile tens of thousands of observations measured to the quarter-inch or even the eighth-inch. Second, height provides what some label a "fine-scale" indicator of human well-being in that it can be viewed as an indicator not just of income but of work load, disease load, and other factors influencing well-being during the critical growth years. Height provides a more comprehensive measure of well-being than income, an argument not unlike that offered in favor of the United Nations' Human Development Index (HDI) over per capita gross domestic product.

As with any scholarly enterprise, it is best not claim more than theory and observation can reveal. In the case at hand, the data reveal a mixed-race height advantage. Mixed-race men and women, both free-born and manumitted slaves, were about a half-inch taller on average than black men and women. Everything we know about the connection between heights and traditional measures of economic well-being points toward a mixed-race nutritional and health advantage. In this the height data is consistent with what is now known about a general mixed-race advantage, conventionally measured. Mixed-race people were, on average, wealthier and worked at more remunerative occupations. The evidence also points to the curious result that economic advantages did not translate into a mortality advantage. Age-specific mortality did not differ dramatically by color, a result that points more toward the primitive state of mid-nineteenth-century health care than the absence of favorable treatment. Infectious disease did not draw social distinctions, which is why contemporary Southerners of all races and colors dreaded the summer sickly season. Those that could afford to do so took up residence in the up-country. In effect, they quarantined themselves. Few African Americans, light or dark, could afford such a luxury.

Epilogue

In 2013 a television advertisement for Cheerios breakfast cereal generated so many and such negative, nearly vitriolic comments that General Mills shut down the comments section on its YouTube website. What forced General Mills' hand? An otherwise innocuous television commercial set in a bright, sunlit middle-class kitchen featured a white mother, a black father, and a daughter who appeared to be their mixed-race child. Crossing the color line within a household, even a fictional one, was more than some could countenance, thus the controversy. One commentator argued that the advertisement struck a nerve because it placed a traditional American product in an untraditional family setting.[1]

Some dismissed the dust-up, attributing it to the ranting of a few racists free to post anonymously to an Internet site. But the Cheerios controversy appeared just one day after a white Virginia man was visited by the police on suspicion of kidnapping three young mixed-race girls. It turned out that the girls were the man's daughters and the police had been alerted by a Walmart security guard who was told by a customer that the "children didn't fit."[2] Comments posted to the online version of the story reveal that this Virginia family's experience was not unique. Some members of the Walmart shopping public, at least, are so unfamiliar with racially mixed marriages and mixed-race children that seeing a white father with mixed-race children leads some to suspect wrongdoing rather than paternal care.

It was not always thus. Not even in Virginia. In 1780 Thomas Wright, a white man residing in Bedford County, Virginia, had a mixed-race son, Robert, by Sylvia, a "very black" slave woman with whom he had been cohabiting for more than a year. In 1791 Thomas fell out with his white relatives for reasons unrelated to his cohabiting with a slave woman, and in 1805 Robert inherited nearly the entirety of Thomas's estate—his land, slaves, livestock, and equipment. Through his inheritance and his father's position, the mixed-race Robert was so well accepted by and integrated into the local white elite that his marriage in 1806 to Mary Godsey, a white woman, barely raised an eyebrow. Their neighbors ignored Robert and Mary's open violation of the state's prohibition on mixed marriage. It was only after Mary abandoned the marriage in 1815, and Wright took up with Polly Davidson, another white woman, before being granted a divorce, that public opinion changed. Polly moved into Wright's family home, and although her relatives were "pleased at her living with him," Wright's neighbors were not.[3] It is probably not coincidental that Robert's race changed from white to mulatto in the county tax assessor's book after Mary's leaving and Polly's taking up residence. Robert's white neighbors were willing to overlook his having cross the marriage color line until he chose to openly cohabitate without having secured a divorce. So long as the mixed-race Robert Wright kept up appearances and behaved as "an honest, upright man, and good citizen," his neighbors were willing to accept the social fiction—if not the legal fiction—of Robert's whiteness. His penchant for gambling, drinking, and frolicking were forgivable; his cohabiting with one white woman while still married to another was not. Wright's bad behavior altered his social standing and his race.

Several recent studies cast doubt on the notion that mixed-race individuals inhabited a racial middle ground or that race was negotiable and heavily influenced by color in the first half to two-thirds of the twentieth century. In a longitudinal study that links death registration records of African-American men with census enumeration in 1920, which distinguished between black and mixed-race peoples, Mark Hill finds only modest color difference. Further, he finds that the mixed-race advantage nearly disappears after controlling for early life family characteristics.[4] Roy Mill and Luke Stein exploit differences in sibling colors recorded in the 1910 and 1940 censuses to investigate the mulatto advantage.[5] They find that within-family differences in several outcomes, including education and earnings, are less pronounced for brothers than differences observed in the general population, though their estimates still reveal that black siblings were less likely to be literate, were less likely to attend school, and have lower weekly earnings. The results of these carefully crafted papers are consistent with Bruce Sacerdote's conclusion that the post-Civil War convergence in education and occupation for the children and grandchildren of former slaves and the children and grandchildren of pre-Civil War free blacks was the consequence racist institutions under which "whites began treating free black and former slaves with the same contempt."[6] Sacerdote does not control for the color of pre-Civil War free persons and slaves, but we know that slaves were on average blacker than free people, so the convergence by ancestral status is probably correlated with convergence by ancestral color. Jim Crow left little space for a light-skinned intermediate group, though the antipathies generated by discussions of the "talented tenth" suggest that color still mattered within the black community. Because it didn't matter as much outside a few elite African-American communities, whites just forgot.

Thus, the findings of these studies are not at odds with the conclusions drawn here. From the early eighteenth through the middle of the nineteenth century, mixed-race Americans inhabited a racial middle ground. That middle ground narrowed in the decades following emancipation and finally disappeared in the early decades of the twentieth century. Hochschild et al. and others document efforts

190 THE COLOR FACTOR

by census officials to further refine the mixed-race categories and obtain reliable counts of mulattoes, quadroons, and octoroons.[7] Because racial assignments were based on subjective evaluations of color and other physical features, rather than verifiable evidence, the census considered its efforts a failure. Ultimately, census officials followed social practice and abandoned any effort to distinguish between African Americans of different racial backgrounds. Color lost its social significance, and government officials lost interest in documenting it.

But race-mixing and color is recently resurgent. Figure E.1 plots the relative appearance of the word "mulatto" in American English literature between 1800 and 2008. Between 1800 and 1865, the word appeared at a rate of 2.03 times per million published words. The word most often appeared in state laws, revised codes, and court cases, though mixed-race people and race mixing were subjects not unknown to contemporary fiction and essays. Between 1865 and 1940 the word appeared at a rate of 1.25 times per million published words, but peak usage occurred in 1918 with the publication of Edward Byron Reuter's *Mulatto in the United States* and the US Census Bureau's *Negro Population in the United States, 1790–1915*. Between 1940 and 2008, "mulatto" made up about 1.35 of each million published words, and usage persists at that rate despite the word's fall from favor in many circles.[8]

Despite the relative constancy in the usage of the word "mulatto" during the past century, the increased usage of the word "miscegenation" points to a growing interest in race-mixing and its social, psychological, and economic consequences.[9]

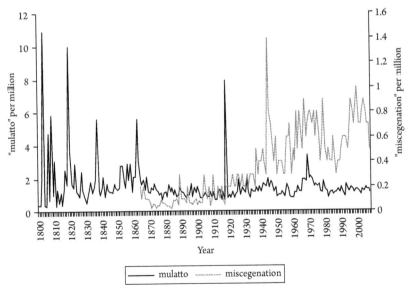

Figure E.1 Relative Use of "Mulatto" and "Miscegenation" in American English, 1800–2012. Source: [https://books.google.com/ngrams].

Modern interest in race mixing is wide ranging; it appears in historical studies, the social sciences, memoirs, and fiction; it also addresses many of the issues explored here—sex, marriage, work, income, and wealth.

One reason for the increasing relative usage of the term "miscegenation" is the increasing prevalence of marriages across races and ethnicities. In February 2012 the *Wall Street Journal* reported that about 15 percent of newlyweds married outside their own ethnic or racial group, which was more than double the share of interracial or interethnic marriages in 1980.[10] Of the 275,000 mixed marriages recorded in 2010, 43 percent were white-Hispanic, 14 percent were white-Asian, and 12 percent were white-black. Although the numbers are climbing, the white-black intermarriage rate remains small—the 2010 numbers imply that approximately 1.8 percent of all new marriages cross the white-black divide—so that the existing stock of white-black marriages represents no more than 1.0 percent of the total. Still, this small fraction represents something of a sea change in America. Roland Fryer found that between 1880 and 1920, the white man-black woman intermarriage rate was less than 0.05 percent (yes!— approximately one-twentieth of one percent) of the existing *stock* of marriages involving white men; the white woman-black man marriage rate was only marginally higher.[11] The white-black interracial marriage rate remained below 0.2 percent of marriages until the Supreme Court of the United States struck down interracial marriage bans in 1967.[12] Between 1970 and 2000, interracial marriages more than doubled from approximately 0.2 percent to about 0.5 percent of all marriages involving one white partner.

Not every interracial adult relationship ends in marriage, but adult interracial relationships, regardless of the specific legal form they take, produce mixed-race children, and social scientists have grown increasingly interested in the lives of mixed-race people. Interest in the growing incidence of race mixing and an emergent, self-identified mixed-race group led the US Census Bureau to allow individuals to choose more than one race on the 2000 decennial census, and in 2001 the bureau reported that 2.4 percent of Americans identified with more than one race.[13] A small but growing fraction of the US population considers themselves to be of mixed race. Most tend to be young. So while Gullickson finds a declining significance of race for cohorts of men and women born in the mid- to late twentieth century, the early twenty-first century may mark the reemergence of the salience of color.[14]

Census snapshot surveys, which are typically completed by older household members comfortable with monoracial designations, may not fully capture how a young person views him or herself or how racial identities change with one's color and circumstances. Compared to the traditional view that race is static, fixed, dichotomous, and determined at birth (i.e., exogenous), the possibility that race is dynamic, fluid, multidimensional, and changeable (i.e., endogenous) opens up exciting and entirely new theoretical opportunities and empirical approaches for social scientists. Recognizing that racial self-identification is most likely to be endogenous among light-skinned, mixed-race youth, sociologists David Harris and Jeremiah Joseph Sim use the 1994 to 1995 wave of the National Longitudinal Study of Adolescent Health to identify fluidity in racial identification among mixed-race youth.[15] Only 59.5 percent of youth who identified themselves as a mix of white and black ancestries at school answered the same way when interviewed a second time at home. Another 20.8 percent who self-identified as black at school self-identified as a white-black mix at home. When asked at home to provide a "best single race" classification, white-black youth overwhelmingly label themselves black (74.5 percent) rather than white (17.1 percent).[16] When asked to self-identify in front of their parents, the one-drop rule remains the default way of thinking about race mixing. But we are left to speculate about how much longer. When away from their parents race is fluid, color- and context-dependent, and endogenous to a host of factors among mixed-race youth.

Although younger mixed-race Americans are less willing than their parents to be defined by the so-called one-drop rule (that any black ancestry, no matter how many generations removed, makes a person legally, socially, and economically black), the rule continues to shape how most Americans think about race. One source of the persistence of the one-drop rule is bureaucratic path dependence. Use of the "one-drop rule" keeps categorization and recordkeeping simple. Job applicants check the appropriate box and employers report to the government, hopeful that their practices can withstand an affirmative action inquiry. But employers attuned to the blunt instrument of race may not be attuned to the sharper blade of color.

Imagine, then, some people's confusion when one African-American employee initiated a racial discrimination suit charging that another African-American employee discriminated against her because of color. Tracy Walker, a light-skinned woman, worked as a clerk in the Atlanta office of the Internal Revenue Service.[17] In 1985 Walker's supervisor was replaced by Ruby Lewis, a dark-skinned African-American woman. Walker enjoyed a cordial working relationship with her previous supervisor, but her interactions with Lewis were strained and unpleasant from the outset. Walker met with the office's equal opportunity officer, claiming that her new supervisor discriminated against her because of her light complexion. Two weeks later Walker was discharged on Lewis's recommendation. A federal court concluded that Walker's Title VII claim was not barred because both parties were of the same race. The court ruled that race and color were distinct factors, and that color-based discrimination was as actionable as race-based discrimination.

Tracy Walker's complaint put colorism on the federal court docket, just as the cases of racial determination discussed in Chapter 3 put color on trial in the eighteenth and nineteenth centuries. Like those cases, Walker's case shows that race is not now and was not then black and white. Now people need to be aware not just of race per se but of intraracial phenotypic variation—gradations of color—and the contentious interpersonal interactions that they sometimes create. Color bias within (and without) the African-American community is of long standing and is a type of open secret. Writing in 1962, St. Clair Drake and Horace Cayton observed that some whites professed "shock" when they learned of these biases, and found color distinctions made among blacks "disconcerting."[18] One measure of how attuned anyone is to black cultural norms might be how sensitive they are to the many manifestations of colorism. Comedian Chris Rock's documentary film *Good Hair*, which took viewers on a tour of the market for relaxed or straightened hair among African-American women, was alternatively provocative, comedic, and eye-opening for those unfamiliar with the culture of black hair. The forms it takes, as nineteenth-century whites were aware, are due in part to the extent of the African-American person's racial (part white) heritage. The greater the share white ancestry, the straighter the hair. The straighter the hair, the more desirable the person.

Humanists and social scientists are starting to recognize the complexity of color and are increasingly attuned to its ramifications. Accounts of mixed-race lives expose the difficulties of being dark-complected with African features in an African-American culture that values light complexions and white features. Lawrence Otis Graham provides a history of the conflict between dark- and light-skinned African Americans, showing that the modern "color complex" dates back to slavery and remains a powerful and often divisive force within the African-American community.[19] Marita Golden's memoir recounts her own struggles as a dark woman in a light woman's world, and contends that the emotional health, self-esteem, and pride of African Americans of all complexions are casualties of complexion biases within the African-American community. It is, to her, nothing less than an ongoing war within the community. Golden's assessment is unmistakably clear: she considers the undervaluation of dark-skinned men and women a "three-hundred-year-long human rights violation committed against people of African descent in America."[20] Graham's exposé of color prejudices within the black upper class uses more measured terms, but his conclusions are not dissimilar.[21] The light-skinned elite distance themselves—literally and figuratively—from the dark-skinned masses.

Although casual discussions of colorism are common within the African-American community, it is an under- but not unstudied phenomenon. Academic and scientific explorations of colorism date to the mid-nineteenth century, but the topic entered mainstream academic discourse for a brief period in the 1920s with the publication of a series of studies by the sociologist Edward Reuter.[22] Reuter noted that virtually all eminent African Americans were partly to mostly white and recommended moving beyond the one-drop rule of racial classification, though his proffered classification scheme—white, black, mulatto—was little more than a reversion to nineteenth-century categorizations;

his interpretations, while not couched in the overt racism of the earlier era, were not far removed from those of Josiah Nott and other early American race theorists discussed in Chapter 4. Reuter's many critics were harsh. He was taken to task for labeling as mulatto any African American thought to have had one or more white progenitors, regardless of how many or how far removed. His definition lacked scientific precision, and given the historical extent of race mixing, it would have excluded few people. Reuter was censured, too, because his work supported the notion of black intellectual inferiority. Mixed-race people were eminent due in part to their white heritage, and his call for a tripartite racial system grounded in color-based eminence raised hackles.[23] Kelly Miller labeled a two-caste system "undemocratic and un-Christian enough," adding that an intermediate class of mixed-race people based on the intersection of eminence and racial mixture represented an "inexcusable compounding of iniquity."[24]

Scholarly interest in mixed-race people reemerged in the 1940s with the publication of Everett V. Stonequist's *Marginal Man* (1937), E. Franklin Frazier's *The Negro Family in the United States* (1939), Luther Porter Jackson's *Free Negro Labor and Property Holding in Virginia* (1942), and John Hope Franklin's *Free Negro in North Carolina* (1943), among others. Stonequist's and Frazier's studies were the more controversial. Stonequist extended sociologist Robert Park's notion of the mixed-race American as a frustrated, conflicted marginal man.[25] Crossing between discordant white and black cultures, mixed-race people were prone to being swallowed up by the "distracting incertitude" of their uncertain place.[26] The marginal man's social maladjustment manifested itself along the continuum from malaise to madness. Frazier, as is well known, investigated the black family. A small fraction of African-American families, mostly privileged and light-skinned, adopted the two-parent structure; many blacks lived in matrifocal households. Chapter 7 shows that the single-parent African-American family of the twentieth century was unlike the predominatly two-parent, free African-American family of the nineteenth.

With the publication of Winthrop Jordan's *White over Black* (1968) and the long-delayed publication of James Hugo Johnston's *Race Relations and Miscegenation in the South* (1970), post-Civil Rights scholarly explorations of mixed-race people took hard-edged looks at interracial sex then and now. Johnston's book chronicled the consequences of the complex sexual lives of whites and blacks in antebellum Virginia, and was the inspiration for my own investigation of interracial sex on the plantation offered in Chapter 5. Influenced by Robert Parks's sociological perspectives, Johnston portrays the social place of the mixed-race offspring from illicit relationships as peculiar and precarious. Jordan's was the more ambitious, more provocative study of the colonial American white man's conceptualization of blackness and how those ideas coalesced around slavery and miscegenation. Jordan's controversial central theme is that the white man's professed abhorrence of the African's libidinousness was in fact a projection of his own fears, desires, and sexual guilt. White males sexually exploited black women—so that "white over black" takes on both literal and metaphorical meanings—and then excused their own failures on the African's heightened sexuality and low morals. Racism, in Jordan's telling, sprang from illicit sex. Thus in her review of the 2012 republication of Jordan's volume, Annette Gordon-Reed contends that the book retains its power because "the phenomenon of interracial mixture is a continuing story for black Americans."[27] The history of sex reveals itself in black America through skin color, hair texture, and facial features that is without parallel in white America.

Modern social science studies of race, mixed-race, and color date to the 1960s. In the mid-1960s Howard Freeman and his colleagues, for example, interviewed 250 married African-American women living in the Boston area to investigate the extent whether light skin earned an economic reward. To avoid the Reuter error—namely, consciously or unconsciously attributing lighter skin or other mixed-race characteristics to people of higher social status—interviewers were provided with a color chart divided into five shades: white, yellow, light brown, dark brown, and ebony black. Interviewers rated the skin color by comparing the cards to the back of each subject's hand. "It is difficult," they wrote, "to reach any other conclusion than that skin color is at least a concomitant, if not a determinant, of social status."[28]

Other studies followed. In 1971 Richard Udry and his colleagues reported that color-based mate selection among African Americans persisted, but that the impulse was selectively weakened by the civil rights and black power movements.[29] Chapter 6 shows that the impulse toward homogamous or color-assortative mating among African Americans dates well back into the nineteenth century, if not earlier. Udry and his colleagues also reported that the status advantage of light-skinned women remained, but younger dark-skinned men were equally and perhaps more upwardly mobile than light-skinned men—which, if correct, represents something of a change from the mid-nineteenth century when the light-skinned, male job-market advantage was substantially more pronounced than that for light-skinned women (see Chapter 7). Using a 1968 survey of 2,800 African Americans in 15 US cities, Ozzie Edwards reported that light-skinned men were twice as likely as dark men to have attended college, nearly twice as likely to work in a white-collar occupation, and less likely to live in a low-income census tract.[30] Light-skinned African Americans were less likely to have experienced job discrimination or impolite treatment in public places.

Interest in issues surrounding race mixing has been on the rise since the early to mid-1980s, when the experiences of mixed-race were explored across several disciplines. Judith Berzon's *Neither White Nor Black* (1978) explores literary treatments of mixed-race people. Historian Joel Williamson's *New People* (1980) traces the history of mixed-race people from the early days of slavery into the twentieth century. Sociologist Virginia Dominguez's *White by Definition* (1986) investigates the strange career of race in Louisiana, a place with a long history of tolerance for race mixing. These studies provide the foundation for several subsequent book-length studies, including James Davis's *Who is Black?* (2001) and Werner Sollors's *Neither Black Nor White Yet Both* (1997), among many others.

Sociological studies from the 1990s and 2000s find little dissipation in the power of color over people's lives. Verna Keith and Cedric Herring find that light-skinned blacks complete more years of school, work in higher status occupations, and enjoy higher incomes. Despite fundamental socioeconomic differences, there are notably few differences across color in political affiliation, "confidence in American institutions, satisfaction with . . . one's personal life, anomie," or political participation.[31] Mark Hill, as previously mentioned, finds that mixed-race males were more likely than blacks to find employment in higher-status and white-collar occupations.[32] Aaron Gullickson, however, argues that the power of color dissipated in the mid- to late twentieth century.[33] The lack of consensus in the sociological literature opens the door for new studies and lively debate.

It is only in the 2000s that economists have taken an interest in colorism, and their studies extend findings in the sociological literature. Using the National Survey of Black Americans and the Multi-City Study of Urban Inequality, Arthur Goldsmith, Darrick Hamilton, William Darity, and Joni Hersch find that the racial wage gap widens in darker skin tones.[34] The darkest African Americans earn 11 to 20 percent less than whites and light-skinned African Americans earn about 4 to 14 percent less, controlling for other factors. Hersch finds that darker skinned immigrants also earn less than lighter skinned immigrants, though the effects are less pronounced for immigrants than native-born blacks.[35]

Color not only affects earnings; it has wider ramifications. Dark-skinned African Americans complete fewer years of school. Using racial self-identification in the 2000 US census, Robert Fairlie finds that mixed-race individuals' mean reported years of education (13.0 years) lies midway between mean reported years for whites (13.6 years) and blacks (12.4 years), a not-unexpected result except that parents of mixed-race children tend to have more years of education than parents of white or black children.[36] Linda Datcher Loury's research suggests that skin tone differences in educational achievement within the mixed-race group may explain, in part, the lower average years of education observed for mixed-race people. Loury finds that relative to light-skinned African Americans, dark-skinned individuals between 25 and 35 years of age in 1979 completed about 0.80 fewer years of school.[37] Dark-skinned individual between 36 and 70 years old completed about 1.4 fewer years of school. Even after the Civil Rights and Black Power movements, skin tones remain a powerful force in determining educational outcomes.

My own research with Chris Ruebeck and Susan Averett, as well as parallel research by Roland Fryer and his coauthors, find that mixed-race youth are less happy and less likely to develop close personal attachments at school than monoracial youth.[38] Our theoretical models recognize that mixed-race children face conflicting familial and peer pressures to conform to competing racial norms and behaviors, which include speech patterns, clothing styles, and musical genres, as well as curricular and extracurricular activities. Consistent with the models, both studies find that mixed-race youth behaviors are more variable and riskier than either black or white behaviors. Absent a well-defined mixed-race norm, mixed-race youth selectively choose behaviors depending on the salience of racial identification at the moment. At times mixed-race youth select stereotypical white behaviors, at other times they choose stereotypical black behaviors, and at yet other times they adopt neither. Freyer and his coauthors relate this back to Park and Stonequist's hypotheses that mixed-race people are sociologically "disorganized" and that disorganization manifests itself in higher rates of anti-social behaviors, including delinquency and crime.[39] Their observation is consistent with Gyimah-Brempong and Price's finding that among African Americans, dark-skinned men are more likely than light-skinned men to be incarcerated and are incarcerated at younger ages.[40]

As my research on this topic has progressed I have grown increasingly skeptical of the marginal man hypothesis, though I readily acknowledge that a society comfortable with two races separated by a bright line cannot provide a particularly welcoming environment for individuals who span the divide. My discomfiture with the marginal-man construct may follow from the political baggage attached to the (post-) modern overuse (abuse?) of *marginality* as a descriptive device, or it may follow from a better appreciation of a history in which mixed-race people were not marginalized, at least in the modern sense of the term. Mixed-race men and women were privileged in the mid-nineteenth century. Unloved perhaps, misunderstood almost surely, but cast off as unimportant or relegated to social insignificance definitely not.

APPENDICES

Appendix 2.1 Statistical Analysis of Racial Determination Cases

Ariela Gross provides a table of 69 trials of racial determination in the South between 1808 and 1896, most of which occurred prior to the Civil War.[1] Her table enumerates the state and year in which each trial took place; the sex of the person in question; the outcome (white or not white) at trial; whether the trial court decision was affirmed, reversed, or remanded; and the types of evidence introduced at trial. The types of evidence, including the person's physical appearance, discussion of ancestry, physical inspection in court, a documentary record, public reputation, rights of whiteness previously exercised, social performance, and scientific evidence, are the principal concern here. To determine which, if any, type of evidence was associated with the likelihood of finding the individual white, probit and ordinary least squares (OLS) (linear probability) regressions were estimated from the information included in Gross's appendix table. The results are reported in Appendix Table A2.1.1.

The estimated equations take the following general form:

$$\mathbf{Pr}\left(\mathbf{White} = 0/1\right)_{itc} = \alpha + \beta \mathbf{X}_{itc} + \gamma_t + \delta_c + \varepsilon_{itc}$$

where i indexes the individual, t the time period, and c the case type. X is a vector of evidence types presented at trial (looks, ancestry, documents, etc.). γ_t represents year fixed effects; δ_c represents case type fixed effects; and ε_{itc} is the error term.

Regression analysis shows that the only statistically significant determinant of a finding of whiteness at trial is whether the petitioner was male. Jurors were about one-half less likely to find a male than a female petitioner white. Moreover, the magnitude of the coefficient estimate points to it legal importance. Nineteenth-century jurors considered men less deserving of the benefits

Table A2.1.1 Determinants of Race in Trials of Racial Determination

Variable	Mean	Probit	OLS	OLS	OLS
Male	0.696	−0.506	−0.468	−0.338	−0.129
		(0.157)**	(0.170)**	(0.378)	(0.716)
Looks	0.899	0.015	−0.012	−0.509	−0.214
		(0.124)	(0.140)	(0.526)	(1.772)
Ancestry	0.725	−0.091	−0.050	−0.334	−0.252
		(0.139)	(0.127)	(0.186)	(0.334)
Rights	0.261	−0.132	−0.077	0.028	0.076
		(0.134)	(0.104)	(0.236)	(0.429)
Inspection	0.319	0.226	0.162	−0.009	0.078
		(0.200)	(0.180)	(0.225)	(0.334)
Science	0.159	0.220	0.151	0.329	0.186
		(0.124)	(0.125)	(0.233)	(0.395)
Performance	0.464	0.042	0.023	0.076	0.037
		(0.134)	(0.103)	(0.214)	(0.471)
Reputation	0.667	0.089	0.066	−0.104	−0.045
		(0.197)	(0.145)	(0.373)	(0.685)
Documents	0.217	0.266	0.172	−0.076	−0.034
		(0.160)	(0.155)	(0.240)	(0.472)
Constant			0.675	1.929	0.910
			(0.198)**	(0.815)*	(2.283)
Year Fixed Effects		No	No	Yes	Yes
Case Type FE		No	No	No	Yes
R-square		0.23	0.28	0.77	0.79

Notes: Dependent variable =1 if trial court determined the petitioner was white; zero otherwise (mean = 0.449). All regressions have 69 observations. Robust standard errors clustered on state in which trial occurred reported in parentheses. ** implies $p<0.01$; * implies $p<0.05$. Probit specification reports marginal effects rather than estimated coefficients. Source: Author's calculation from information reported in Gross, "Litigating Whiteness," 186–188.

of whiteness, holding all else constant. This is consistent with historical accounts. One of the abolitionists' favorite cudgels in their battles with slavery's defenders was the tale of the white slave, especially the virtuous, white female slave powerless against the tyrannical forces of slave owner and overseers who rarely relented to pleas to be released from a life of immoral, if not illegal, bound servitude.[2] As immoral as was black slavery, white slavery—and with it the prospect of the economic and sexual exploitation of a defenseless white woman—was even more so.

The smaller and less significant coefficients on male in the specifications with year and trial type fixed effects may be the result of attenuation bias that can emerge when the fixed effects absorb most of the variation in the dependent variable.[3] Neither of the types of evidence emphasized by critical race theorists as fundamental in trials of racial determination—performance and reputation—is statistically significant. But neither are any of the other types of evidence presented at these trials, which might be the result of a small sample, or poorly defined variables, or a host of other statistical problems. Ancestry approaches statistical significance (i.e., $p<0.10$) in two specifications. But the largest coefficients are on documents, physical appearance, and science or medical evidence. This very preliminary statistical investigation suggests that juries responded more to what they saw in front of them than to stories about racial performance and reputation in making their determinations. An obvious contribution to the literature would be to move beyond studies that rely on a small number of cases of racial determination that found their way into the appellate courts. A better understanding of the law of race on the ground is likely to be found closer to the ground, in county courts, and in records of justices of the peace who first heard such cases and chose (or not) to allow them to move forward.

Appendix 2.2 Economic Approach to Freedom Suits

Consider, following Paul Rubin, the choice of settlement between a single slave (plaintiff) petitioning for freedom and a single slave owner (defendant) who wishes to retain rights to the slave.[4] Settlement in this instance might be manumission through self-purchase, if the slave had accumulated some resources. It might be a contract for *in futuro* manumission in return for a promise by the slave to be obedient and work hard for a term. It might any number of alternative contractual arrangements reached between slaves and slave owners. Litigation was costly, but many light-complected slaves had few options other than litigation. Self-purchase required a large cash accumulation and several states banned manumission.

Represent the plaintiff slave by P and defendant slave owner as D. Let X_p represent the plaintiff's recovery if she prevails in her freedom suit. Nominally, we can think of X_p as her market wages less the maintenance previously paid by the slave owner plus her subjective value of freedom. Let X_D represent the amount lost by the defendant (lost value of marginal product less maintenance costs) if his slave prevails in her freedom suit. Additionally, ρ_p is the slave's estimate of her probability of winning her freedom suit; ρ_D is the slave owner's estimate of the *probability that his slave will prevail.* C_p and C_D are the costs of litigation. Although the state paid the slave's attorney's fees if a court-appointed investigator determined that the case had enough merit to proceed to trial, the slave faced potential costs in terms of lost goodwill with her owner, which might manifest in itself in loss of privileges, a more grueling work regime, sale away from familiar surroundings, or whipping.[5] The defendant slave owner's costs include attorney fees and any other related costs. Recall, from earlier discussions, that one slave owner was arrested and spent time in jail when he attempted to retrieve a woman he claimed as his slave; another faced a belligerent mob when he attempted to assert his rights.[6]

Define V_P as the expected gain to the plaintiff slave of winning her freedom suit and V_D as the expected loss to the defendant slave owner of losing at trial, where:

$$V_P = \rho_P X_P - C_P \tag{1}$$

$$V_D = \rho_D X_D + C_D \tag{2}$$

If the state-appointed counsel deems the slave's petition meritorious so that the trial will commence, V_P represents the minimum amount the slave would accept to settle out of court (promises of future manumission, perhaps, or other concessions by the slave owner). The slave owner would be willing to settle for any amount less than V_D (note that the litigation costs are added to the defendant's expected losses from losing at trial).

The slave and the slave owner settle out of court if $V_D > V_P$ because there is some amount M that satisfies the inequality $V_D \geq M \geq V_D$, or that when the slave-owner's expected loss exceeds the slave's expected gain, settlement is possible, even likely.

No settlement occurs if $V_D < V_P$, which can be rewritten as:

$$\rho_P X_P - C_P > \rho_D X_D + C_D \tag{3}$$

For the sake of argument, assume that slave and slave owner assign the same probability to the slave winning at trial, such that $\rho_P = \rho_D = \rho$. We can then rewrite equation (3) as:

$$\rho \left(X_P - X_D \right) > C_P + C_D \tag{4}$$

Several implications for the nineteenth-century experience follow from equation (4):

1. An increase in the slave's value of freedom (X_P), holding constant the slave owner's valuation of the slave, the more likely the slave was to petition for freedom than to pursue out-of-court settlement. From a social perspective, the greater the inefficiency of holding a particular slave in bondage, the greater the likelihood a freedom suit was filed. To the extent that the law seeks to eliminate inefficiencies, the more likely jurors were to find for the plaintiffs in these cases. If mixed-race or light-complected people faced better employment prospects or would have gained more out of slavery than black or dark-complected

slaves, then mixed-race, light-complected slaves were more likely to initiate freedom suits.

2. Similarly, if the slave's value to the slave owner increased, holding constant the slave's subjective value of freedom, settlement became less likely and freedom suits more likely. The more profitable the slave was to the slave owner's operation, the less likely that slave owner was to manumit the slave or reach some other accommodation.

3. The lower the cost to the slave of filing a petition for freedom (due, perhaps, to lesser retribution by slave owner in the event the suit failed), the less likely was settlement and the more likely litigation. Similarly, the lower the cost to the slave owner of defending a freedom suit, the less likely was settlement and the more likely was litigation.

4. For given costs and payoffs, an increase in the probability that a slave would prevail at trial, the greater the likelihood that slaves would pursue freedom suits.

There are avenues for more sophisticated analyses in future research. Interactions between slave and slave owner, and the choice to settle or litigate, might be more fruitfully modeled in a game-theoretic approach as a repeated game. It remains for others to pursue these lines of inquiry.

Appendix 3.1 Statistical Analysis of Black and Mulatto Age Structure, and Physical and Mental Disabilities

The data come from the Integrated Public Use Microdata Series (IPUMS) sample of the 1860 slave census, which includes a representative random sample of 195,270 black and mulatto slaves. Slaves classified as Indian are excluded.[7] The sample is a 1-in-20 sample. Each page of the slave census manuscripts contain 80 lines, with each line given over to an individual slave. If a slave holding unit was selected, all slaves living on that unit (farm/plantation/city household) were included. Because this is a flat sample, sampling weights are not required for statistical analysis.

Compared to the population census of 1860, the slave census is spartan. Marshals recorded the name of the slave owner and then listed the resident slaves, without names, by sex and age. Many marshals recorded the information by age from oldest to youngest, so it is impossible to infer anything about family structure from the order in which slaves are recorded. In addition to sex and age the census listed disabilities, including deaf, dumb, blind, insane, or idiotic. Slave holders were also asked to provide information about the number of manumitted or runaway slaves in the prior year. Table A3.1.1 reports and Figures A2.1.1 and A2.1.2 present the five-year interval age distribution of slaves by sex and race.

Table A3.1.1 Slave Sex and Color Distribution by Age

Age (years)	Male Black	Male Mulatto	Female Black	Female Mulatto
years ≤ 5	17,094	2,465	17,345	2,514
6 < years ≤ 10	13,200	1,743	12,784	1,786
11 < years ≤ 15	11,235	1,471	10.591	1,507
16 < years ≤ 20	10,453	1,209	10,755	1,455
21 < years ≤ 25	9,075	1,006	8,217	1,068
26 < years ≤ 30	7,138	705	6,902	847
31 < years ≤ 35	4,690	419	4,535	533
36 < years ≤ 40	4,433	441	4,626	491
41 < years ≤ 45	2,810	226	2,732	284
46 < years ≤ 50	2,855	213	2,813	231
51 < years ≤ 55	1,349	97	1,216	83
56 < years ≤ 60	1,742	103	1,588	104
61 < years ≤ 65	746	46	673	58
66 < years ≤ 70	588	27	596	43
71 < years ≤ 75	250	14	235	15
years > 75	360	8	376	24

Source: Menard et al., *Public Use Microdata ... Slave Population,* 2004.

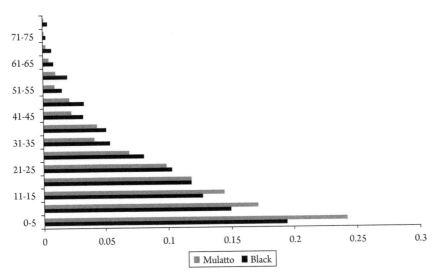

Figure A2.1.1 Age Distributions of Black and Mulatto Slave Males in 1860.
Source: Menard et al., *Public Use Microdata ... Slave Sample,* 2004.

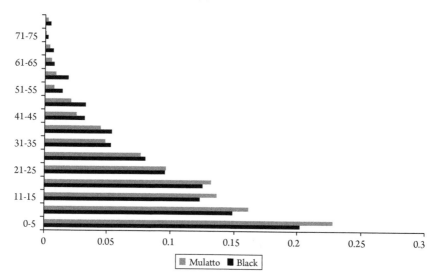

Figure A2.1.2 Age Distributions of Black and Mulatto Slave Females in 1860.
Source: Menard et al., *Public Use Microdata . . . Slave Sample*, 2004.

Some early nineteenth-century scientists and anthropologists argued that mixed-race slaves were less hardy and healthy than either of their constituent races—white or black—and were therefore shorter-lived. The age distributions show, in fact, that the proportion of mixed-race slaves was considerably lower than the proportion of blacks at older ages. A test of sample proportions for females over 50, for example, show that the mixed proportion (2.96 percent) was statistically significantly lower than the black proportion (5.45 percent). The Z-statistic is 11.32, with a p-value < 0.001. For females over 60, the mixed proportion (1.27 percent) was statistically lower than the black proportion (2.19 percent) (Z-statistic = 6.57; p value < 0.001). The same was true for males over 50—mixed (2.89 percent); blacks (5.72) (Z-statistic = 11.80)—and males over 60—mixed (0.93 percent); blacks (2.21 percent) (Z-statistic = 8.53).

Table A3.1.2 provides a sample life table by race and sex generated from the same data. Life tables report the mean number of additional years remaining until death for individuals who survived to each age. Thus the value 16.0 for e^{20} for black males implies that a typical black male slave aged 20 years in 1860 could expect to live for an additional 16.0 years, for a total life span of 36.0 years.

A life table constructed from a single cross section or snapshot is of course inaccurate, because the construction of a true life table requires observing cohorts longitudinally. This table is constructed from the 1860 census using standard, modern techniques not because it offers an accurate portrayal of life expectancy, but because nineteenth-century conclusions were based on this sort of information.

Table A3.1.2 Life Expectancy By Race and Sex in 1860

	Black males	*Mulatto males*	*Black females*	*Mulatto females*
e^0	21.1	17.5	20.9	18.3
e^{10}	18.2	15.1	18.3	15.7
e^{20}	16.0	13.5	16.1	13.6
e^{30}	14.1	12.0	14.0	11.8
e^{40}	11.8	10.0	11.6	10.4
e^{50}	9.6	7.7	9.7	9.3

Note: The value reported in each cell (e^x) is interpreted as the additional years of life expectancy at age x. Thus, the value of $e^0 = 21.1$ for black males is interpreted to mean that, at birth, black males might expect to live an additional 21.1 years. *Source*: Author's calculations from data in Menard et al., *Public Use Microdata . . . Slave Population*, 2004.

Not only did contemporary observers posit that mixed-race men and women were shorter-lived than blacks, transcription errors incorporated into the published 1840 census volume interpreted as high rates of insanity among mixes led many nineteenth-century writers to conclude that they were more susceptible to madness and other physical and mental disorders.[8] The IPUMS sample of the 1860 slave census provides quality data with which to conduct statistical tests of these nineteenth-century hypotheses.

Estimated regression equations, reported in Table A3.1.3, take the following general form:

$$\Pr(\text{disability} = 0/1)_{\text{isco}} = \alpha + \beta M_{\text{isco}} + \gamma_s + \delta_c + \zeta_o + \varepsilon_{\text{isco}}$$

where the dependent variable represents a outcome for a slave i living in state s city c (if resident in an urban place) and belonging to owner o. M is a dummy variable equal to 1 if the slave was identified as mulatto in the census manuscript. γ_s is a series of state fixed effects; δ_c equals 1 if the slave resided in an urban place; ζ_o is an owner fixed effect; and $\varepsilon_{\text{isco}}$ is the error term.

The regressions are estimated using simple linear probability (OLS) methods. The dependent variables are blind, deaf, blind+deaf (for physical disability), idiotic, insane, idiotic+insane (for mental disability), and blind+deaf+idiotic+insane (any disability). The independent variable of principal interest is the mulatto indicator variable.

The results are generally inconsistent with the physical or mental inferiority of mixed-race slaves. In most cases, the mulatto coefficient is very small and statistically insignificant. In the three cases in which it is significant—blind, blind+deaf, and idiotic—it goes against the hypothesis. That is, mixed-race slaves were, if anything, less susceptible to the physical and mental disabilities severe enough to be recorded in the census.

Table A3.1.3 Determinants of Slave Mental and Physical Disabilities

	Blind	Deaf	Blind+ Deaf	Idiotic	Insane	Idiotic+ Insane	Disabled	Age>50
Mulatto	−0.00025	0.00001	−0.0003	−0.0003	0.0001	−0.0001	−0.0004	−0.27
	(0.0001)**	(0.00002)	(0.0001)*	(0.0001)*	(0.0001)	(0.0001)	(0.0002)	(0.01)**
Controls								
Sex	Y	Y	Y	Y	Y	Y	Y	Y
State	Y	Y	Y	Y	Y	Y	Y	Y
City	Y	Y	Y	Y	Y	Y	Y	Y
Owner	Y	Y	Y	Y	Y	Y	Y	Y
F-stat	1.21	0.60	1.69**	1.43*	0.33	1.76**	3.42**	99.19**
R-square	0.000	0.0003	0.0002	0.0005	0.0003	0.0005	0.0004	0.006
Cases	81	32	113	96	22	118	230	

Notes: Linear probability (OLS) coefficient estimates. Number of observations = 195,270. ** implies $p<0.01$; * implies $p<0.05$.
Source: Author's calculations from Menard et al., *Public Use Microdata... Slave Sample,* 2004.

Appendix 4.1 Amalgamation and Slavery

The data come from the IPUMS sample of the 1850 and 1860 slave censuses, which include representative random samples of 195,270 (1860) black and mulatto slaves. Slaves classified as Indian are excluded.[9] Both samples are 1-in-20 samples. Each page of the slave census manuscripts contain 80 lines, with each line given over to an individual slave. If a slave holding unit was selected, all slaves living on that unit (farm/plantation/city household) were included. Because this is a flat sample, sampling weights are not required for statistical analysis.

The unit of observation in the IPUMS sample is the individual slave, but we are interested in slave holding as the relevant unit. Only one observation per slave-holding unit was retained. After dropping slave holdings with unreported or likely erroneous values for the number of houses per holding, the 1850 sample includes 17,132 observations and the 1860 sample 14,033 plantation-level observations. Summary statistics are reported in Table A4.1.1.

The dependent variable of interest (the presence of a mixed-race child two years of age or younger) is a binary indicator variable (0/1). The independent variable of principal interest is the size of the slave holding, but several other variables are available in the data set. The estimated equations take the following general form:

$$\mathbf{Pr}\left(\mathbf{MixedRace} \leq \mathbf{2\ years} = \mathbf{0/1}\right)_{ijkl} = \alpha_{ijkl} + \beta X_{ijkl} + \gamma_j + \delta_k + \zeta_l + \varepsilon_{ijkl}$$

where X_{ijkl} includes plantation level variables including number of slaves, number of houses, and slaves per house; γ_j is a vector of plantation-type (owner-operated, overseer-operated, etc.) fixed effects; δ_k is a vector of county fixed effects; ζ_l is a vector of state fixed effects; and ε_{ijkl} is the mean zero error term. The equation is estimated using linear probability (OLS) and nonlinear (probit) methods.

The approach follows Steckel's with two exceptions discussed in the chapter. First, Steckel codes a slaveholding as having a mixed-race child whenever a child 10 years or less is observed. Ten years seems too long a period given the changes that could occur on a plantation over that period. Several overseers may have come and gone; neighbors could have moved in or out; slaves may have been bought or sold. The approach here codes a plantation with a mixed-race child (= 1) only when a child two years or younger is observed; otherwise, the plantation is coded with a zero. Second, Steckel imposed a linear term on the number of slaves on the plantation (size), but the incidence of race mixing may not have changed linearly in plantation size. Absent a strong prior on the appropriate functional form, several alternative specifications are estimated. Basic regressions include the number of slaves. A second regression includes the number of

Table A4.1.1 Summary Statistics for 1850 and 1860 Slave Censuses, Mixed-Race Children on Plantation

	1850 census	*1860 census*
Mixed-race child on unit	0.066	0.113
	(0.249)	(0.316)
Number of slaves	8.58	11.83
	(13.86)	(18.97)
ln(slaves)	1.484	1.838
	(1.116)	(1.103)
1–5 slaves	0.58	0.44
	(0.493)	(0.497)
6–15 slaves	0.278	0.344
	(0.448)	(0.475)
16–50 slaves	0.122	0.173
	(0.327)	(0.378)
>50 slaves	0.019	0.033
	(0.136)	(0.180)
Urban residence	0.087	0.042
	(0.281)	(0.201)
Observations	17,132	14,207

Note: Standard deviations in parentheses. *Source*: Menard et al., *Public Use Microdata . . . Slave Population,* 2004.

slaves and its square. A third includes the natural log of the number of slaves. Including the log eases interpretation in that the coefficient is interpreted as the change in the likelihood of observing a mixed-race child on a plantation. Finally, following the plantation productivity literature, separate dummy variables are included for plantations with 6 to 15 slaves, 15 to 50 slaves, and more than 50 slaves.[10]

In addition to the number of slaves on the plantation, the 1850 census includes controls for urban residence, as well as county and plantation-type fixed effects. Plantation types include owner-managed and overseer-managed plantations, in addition to those administered by a trustee or executor. The 1860 regressions, additionally, include controls for the number of slave houses on the slave-holding unit and slaves per house. These are included because they may have influenced race mixing on the slaveholding. Less crowded slave quarters afforded more privacy, which may have facilitated race mixing.

The results of linear probability regressions reported in Tables A4.1.2 (1850) and A3.1.3 (1860) are consistent across specifications in that they show that the

Table A4.1.2 Correlates of Observing a Mixed-Race Child on a Plantation in 1850

	1	*2*	*3*	*4*
Slaves	0.003	0.005		
	(0.0003)**	(0.0004)**		
Slaves squared		-0.00002		
		(3.9e-6)**		
ln(slaves)			0.049	
			(0.002)**	
1–5 slaves				reference
6–15 slaves				0.056
				(0.005)**
16–50 slaves				0.117
				(0.008)**
51+ slaves				0.236
				(0.024)**
Urban residence	0.009	0.013	0.017	0.013
	(0.007)	(0.008)**	(0.008)**	(0.008)**
Constant	0.018	0.007	-0.024	0.012
	(0.012)	(0.012)	(0.012)	(0.012)
Plantation type FE	Y	Y	Y	Y
County FE	Y	Y	Y	Y
R-square	0.05	0.05	0.06	0.05

Notes: Number of observations = 17,132 in all regressions; ** implies p<0.01 *Source*: Author's calculations from Menard et al., *Public Use Microdata. . . Slave Population*, 2004.

probability of observing a mixed-race child on a slaveholding increases in the number of slaves. Estimated coefficients in regressions (2) in each table, which includes the number of slaves and its square, imply that the probability of a mixed-race child is maximized on plantations with 250 slaves (1850 sample) or 341 slaves (1860 sample).[11] The text discusses the results of regressions (4), which divides slaveholding units into size classes found to be relevant in the plantation productivity literature. One advantage of this specification is that the coefficients have a straight forward interpretation: the probability of observing a mixed-race child on plantations with 6 to 15 slaves is about 5 to 6 percentage points higher than on a reference group plantation (1-5 slaves). Probabilities increase in slaveholding, so that the differential probability increases to 15 to 24 percentage points on the largest slaveholding units.

Table A4.1.3 Correlates of Observing a Mixed-Race Child on a Plantation in 1860

	1	2	3	4
Slaves	0.001	0.003		
	(0.0007)	(0.0007)**		
Slaves squared		−8.77e-6		
		(1.7e−6)**		
ln(slaves)			0.051	
			(0.005)**	
1–5 slaves				reference
6–15 slaves				0.047
				(0.008)**
16–50 slaves				0.085
				(0.013)**
51+ slaves				0.148
				(0.034)**
Urban residence	0.003	0.006	0.010	0.007
	(0.014)	(0.013)	(0.014)	(0.014)
Slaves houses	0.003	0.001	0.0008	0.003
	(0.003)	(0.003)	(0.001)	(0.002)
Slaves per house	0.019	0.015	0.007	0.013
	(0.002)**	(0.002)**	(0.002)**	(0.002)**
Constant	0.007	0.008	-0.016	0.007
	(0.042)	(0.042)	(0.042)	(0.042)
Plantation type FE	Y	Y	Y	Y
County FE	Y	Y	Y	Y
R-square	0.06	0.06	0.06	0.06

Notes: Number of observations = 14,207 in all regressions; ** implies $p<0.01$ *Source*: Author's calculations from Menard et al., *Public Use Microdata... Slave Population*, 2004.

Appendix 5.1 Virginia Register Sample

Beginning in 1793 Virginia law required every free African American

> who resides in any county in this Commonwealth, shall be registered and numbered in a book, to be kept for that purpose, by the clerk of the court of the said county, which register shall specify the age, name, colour and

stature of such free negro or mulatto, together with any apparent mark or scar, on his or her face, head or hands.[12]

With the payment of a 25-cent fee, registrants received a hand-written copy with an official seal that served as the person's freedom papers. The registrants were legally obligated to renew their papers every three years, or when their current papers were lost or destroyed.

Registers of free-born persons sometimes identified the mother and identified her race. Thus white mothers of free-born, mixed-race people appear in some registers. Registers of manumitted slaves included the name of former owners, and sometimes the date the deed or will was recorded, and, less often, the actual date of manumission. Table A5.1.1 provides the basic information on the sample: counties, the years in which registrants were recorded; the number of registrants; the number of manumissions with sufficient information to determine the precise date of manumission; and the number of marriages between registrants (described in greater detail in Appendix 6.1).

Given the details about the physical attributes of free African Americans, the registers provide a valuable resource in any study of early nineteenth-century mixed-race people and of differences in color and complexion. An attractive feature of the registers is that they provide detailed information on race and complexion. Unlike the 1850 and 1860 censuses (discussed in Appendix 6.2), which report African Americans as "black" or "mulatto," the Virginia registers include 45 separate race/color combinations. Some individuals were reported as "black" or "negro" or "mulatto," but many were described in much greater detail, with designations such as "copper," "chestnut," "tawny," or "olive," among many others.

One point of concern with the registration data is that only a fraction of those legally required to register actually did so. In Campbell County, for example, the court clerk's ledger provides information on 331 African-American registrants between 1801 and 1850. The 1850 census enumerated 846 free African Americans residing in that county in that year. Clearly, many people legally required to register did not. There are many reasons why an individual might not register. Young children are underrepresented in the registers, for example, but people in their late teens and early twenties are overrepresented. It is likely that youth registered when they sought employment away from home. Virginia law required any free person employed outside the home to have registered and to carry his or her papers.[13] If apprehended without having registered, the person was to be committed to jail and then hired out for a sufficient period to reimburse the county for the costs of apprehension and imprisonment. Other people might not register because they could not conveniently get to the county courthouse. Still others may not have wanted to pay the 25-cent registration fee, especially if the local magistrates were lax in their enforcement of the employment law.

Table A5.1.1 Virginia Register Sample

County	Dates	Registrations	Manumissions	Marriages
Alleghany	1855–1856	38	0	1
Amherst	1822–1864	390	2	10
Arlington	1797–1861	2,131	121	30
Augusta	1810–1864	740	48	17
Bedford	1808–1860	780	18	5
Botetourt	1802–1836	100	0	0
Brunswick	1803–1849	550	14	8
Campbell	1801–1850	331	8	7
Charles City	1823–1864	718	0	9
Chesterfield	1804–1854	1,624	0	11
Cumberland	1821–1860	31	0	0
Essex	1843–1861	189	13	0
Fairfax	1822–1861	880	53	0
Fauquier	1817–1865	839	67	4
Fluvanna	1851–1862	158	1	4
Henrico	1845–1865	1,450	17	20
Lancaster	1804–1852	314	0	0
Loudon	1844–1861	1,137	48	7
Louisa	1816–1865	681	110	4
Lynchburg (City)	1851–1858	481	4	4
Middlesex	1800–1862	273	0	2
Montgomery	1823–1863	136	62	2
Nelson	1853–1865	43	0	0
Norfolk	1850–1862	716	4	10
Northampton	1853–1861	293	3	7
Northumberland	1843–1852	348	0	6
Orange	1838–1850	92	0	0
Petersburg (City)	1850–1865	1,260	112	19
Pittsylvania	1807–1864	624	136	18
Princess Anne	1845–1862	151	0	0
Powhatan	1845–1865	399	41	0
Roanoke	1838–1865	124	0	0
Rockingham	1804–1856	540	0	0
Surry	1794–1862	1,320	46	0
Westmoreland	1828–1849	544	0	0
Totals		20,425	928	205

Notes: See Appendix 5.2 for a description and analysis of the manumission data, and Chapter 6 and Appendix 6.1 for a description and analysis of the marriage data. *Sources*: See References §1.7 "Virginia Free Black Registers."

The failure of so many free African Americans to register raises concerns about selection bias: was there some observable or unobservable characteristic—race, color, height, intelligence—among free people that led some to register and others not? This is a problem that plagues many historical anthropometric studies. If the likelihood of registering and appearing in the sample differ across individuals in ways that are correlated with one of the characteristics of interest, the sample distribution of those characteristics are unlikely to be an unbiased measure of the true distribution of characteristics in the population.[14]

The choice by African Americans to register with the county court may have been correlated with one of the observable characteristics: namely, complexion or height if the likelihood of registering was a correlated with employment outside the home and the attractiveness of market employment was correlated with complexion or height. If market employment opportunities changed over time, due perhaps to recession, and employment opportunities at all times depended on height, then observed changes in sample heights might be due, not to changes in heights in the population but to changes in selection into the sample created by economic, political, or social changes.

Bodenhorn, Guinnane, and Mroz develop a diagnostic test of selection on height. A simple OLS regression with height (measured in inches) as the dependent variable includes two types of variables. The first is "cohort conditions," and the second is "current conditions." A proxy for cohort conditions can be year of birth. Under the historical height interpretation of the standard of living, year of birth dummy variables capture the individual's experience as a child and youth. Every person born in 1820 and raised in a particular place faced comparable economic factors and similar biological conditions (chronic and acute disease environments—malaria or cholera—as well as similar harvests, and so on). As a proxy for current conditions Bodenhorn, Guinnane, and Mroz use the year during which the individual registered, though current conditions might be controlled for by measures such as gross domestic product, average wages, unemployment, or other relevant measures of economic activity correlated with employment prospects and, hence, an individual's probability of registering.

The argument for a simple dummy variable for year of registration is straightforward. Consider, for example, two representative groups of men born in 1820 in the same town, who then reside there until they register. One group registers with the county court in 1842; the other in 1845. Because the members of each group should have achieved terminal adult height by the time he registered, there is no *environmental* reason why one group should, on average, be taller than the other. It is possible, however, that social or economic conditions in 1842 differed from those in 1845. If market employment was more attractive for taller African Americans in the later year, then we will observe an increase in average heights between 1842 and

1845 because more tall people are drawn into market employment when, in fact, the heights of population have not changed.

If there is no selection, the current conditions variable should have no explanatory power in a regression of registrant heights on birth years, registration year, and other correlates. If the current condition variable affects the conditional mean height of registrants, there is reason to be concerned about selection bias. I do not report the full battery of tests here; they are reported and discussed in detail in Bodenhorn, Guinnane, and Mroz. The interested reader is referred to their article for an analysis of dynamic selection.[15]

The point of concern in this study is less the evolution of African-American heights over time (though Komlos and Bodenhorn focus on this) than with cross-sectional differences in heights between black and mixed-race peoples.[16] If blacks and mixed-race people opt into the sample under the same dynamic selection process, there are few concerns in drawing cross-sectional inferences about height. If, however, blacks and mixed-race people were differentially drawn into the sample at different points in time and the selection process by color differed in some way correlated with height, then even cross-sectional inferences are problematic. While Bodenhorn, Guinnane, and Mroz have developed a simple test for dynamic selection in the time series, any potential cross-sectional selection is less readily accounted for. All interpretations of the results must take this into account and great care must be exercised in drawing inferences about differences in heights between blacks and mixed-race people in the Chesapeake region in the first half of the nineteenth century.

Appendix 5.2 Manumission Analysis from Virginia Register Sample

Age at manumission was determined from information contained in the Virginia Register Sample, described in greater detail in Appendix 5.1. The typical registration contained information on the name of the registrant, including any known aliases. Most registers recorded the free person's age. Some registers included an explicit acknowledgment of the registrant's sex (i.e., Sally, the daughter of Sarah), but sex is typically inferred from given names. When the name was ambiguous, no sex was recorded and the observation was dropped in the formal statistical analyses. Most registers included a statement of the registrants' heights, usually to the nearest inch. Measurements to the half- and quarter-inch were common, and a not insignificant number of observations recorded height to the nearest eighth-inch. Registers also recorded race (black or mulatto) and complexion (light and dark, among others). The law also instructed court clerks to record identifying scars or marks that would be readily visible on the registrants hands, arms, or face. Some clerks recorded additional notable details, including hair color, length or texture, missing teeth, tattoos, and so on.

Although approximately 22 percent of the 18,000 registrants included in the sample were manumitted at some time in their life, it was possible to determine the definitive year of manumission for only 898 registrants. To provide a concrete example, consider the following registrations from Petersburg, Virginia's Hustings Court:

> 1850 August 19. No. 5224. Polly a free woman of colour is hereby duly registered in obedience to an order of the Husting Court of the town of Petersburg made the 16th instant, and she is of the following description, to wit: five feet seven inches high, about seventy two years of a black complexion, has a large scar on her left arm extending from the wrist to the elbow, the little finger of the left hand crooked and was emancipated by the last will & testament of Elizabeth Gilliam, dec'd, admitted to record in the County Court of Sussex County 1 December 1796. Jno Mann, DC

and

> 1850 September 20. No. 5314 Charlotte a free woman of colour is hereby duly registered in obedience to an order of the Hustings Court of the town of Petersburg made the 19th instant, and she is of the following description, to wit: five feet three inches high, about 64 years old, of a light complexion, has a scar on her right arm near the elbow and one on her breast, and was emancipated by Jethro Charles per deed dated 20th August 1850 and recorded in the Clerks' office of the said court Sept 13th 1850. Jno Mann, DC

Polly's registration is useful in studying the connection between complexion and height as described in Appendix 5.1, because her register provides details on age, height, complexion, place of registration, and place of prior residence. It is not useful in studying age at manumission, because her register provides no clue about when she was released from slavery. We know she was born in 1778 and that her owner recorded a deed of manumission in 1796 when she was 18 years old. What cannot be determined from her register is whether it was a delayed manumission or part of a term slavery contract. In all likelihood Polly was given her freedom in 1796 (when she reached her age of majority), but she is not included in the manumission sample because it is impossible to assign a definitive date (or age) at manumission.

Charlotte, on the other hand, is included in the manumission sample. The variables used in the analysis are included: sex (determined from the word "her" in the description), complexion (light), height, current age, the sex of the owner who freed her, and manumission document (deed). Most importantly, however, the register narrows the range of manumission dates to a 24-day period between August 20, when the deed was dated, and September 13, when the deed was officially recorded in the court clerk's office. Her freedom papers were approved by the Hustings Court the following week. By law, Charlotte was neither legally free nor registered until the deed and registration had been approved by the court.

Restricting the data set to registrations in which it is possible to narrow the date of manumission to a single date or a narrow interval is necessary to mitigate the errors-in-variables problem and obtain meaningful results, but it means that several notable manumissions are excluded. Robert Carter III, for instance, liberated 480 slaves over a 10-year period. Some of Carter's former slaves were found in the registers, but could not be used because many of his slaves shared common names making it virtually impossible to assign a date of manumission to the individual. Similarly, several dozen of George Washington's former slaves are included in register sample, but they suffer from the same problem as the Carter manumissions.

Two related approaches are used to estimate the effects of observable variables on the nature of manumission. The economic model of manumission developed in Chapter 5 generates a variable of interest, namely the proportion of a slave's productive life spent in bondage (t^* / T). One advantage of this specification is that is easily interpretable; a disadvantage lay in translating the terms of the theoretical model into an empirical strategy. It requires some knowledge of each slave's expected productive lifetime, which is unobservable. Although the slave-specific expectation is unobservable and dependent on a host of factors—health, nutrition, work load, and so on—it is not unreasonable to proxy for that unobservable with the life expectancy at particular ages for slaves more generally. Jack Eblen published life tables for male and female slaves and reports life expectancy at 10-year intervals (namely, $e_0, e_{10} \ldots, e_{70}$ which are interpreted as the additional expected years of life at age 0, age 10 and so on).[17]

To create the t^*/T variable, the ratio is calculated for each age-sex group. For young adults between 20 and 29 years, for example, the ratio is calculated using Eblen's estimate of e_{20}; for adults between 30 and 39 years, the ratio is calculated using Eblen's estimate of e_{30}, and so on. Life expectancy did not differ markedly by sex—at birth a slave's life expectancy was 35 years—nor did it change much over the first half of the nineteenth century.

OLS regressions of the following general form were estimated:

$$(t^*/T)_{ict} = X_{i'} \beta + \gamma_c + \gamma_t + u_i$$

where X is a vector of slave-specific characteristics (discussed below). γ_c captures region fixed effects; and γ_t captures time fixed effects; and, u_i is the error term.

An alternative approach is to assume a uniform period of productivity and estimate an empirical model based on the age (t^*) at which a slave transitions from slavery to freedom, which is directly observable. Imposing this restriction comes at some cost, but it allows us to interpret the age at manumission, in the language of duration statistics, as the end of a "spell" spent in bondage. Adopting this approach also allows for the use of the familiar Weibull proportional hazards statistical technique. A hazard approach is particularly useful in a study of manumission because it estimates the conditional probability that we observe a transition from slavery to freedom at time t*, conditional on being in bondage up to t^*.

The length of time spent in slavery can be statistically modeled as:

$$\mathbf{h(t) = h(0)} \exp \left(\mathbf{X}_{i'} \, \beta + \gamma_c + \gamma_t \right)$$

where $h(0) = pt^{p-1} \exp(\beta_0)$ is the baseline hazard in which p is a shape parameter, t is time, and $\exp(\beta_0)$ is a scale parameter.[18] The exponential specification implies that $\delta \ln h(t)/\delta x = \beta$. The estimated coefficients are the analog of the partial derivative interpretation of the β vector in ordinary least squares. The β's can be interpreted as the constant proportional effect of x on the conditional probability of observing the transition from slavery to freedom. Instead of coefficient, it is common to report hazard ratios $(\exp(\beta))$; values greater than one imply a greater hazard (earlier freedom) and values less than one imply a lesser hazard (later freedom).

Table A5.2.1 presents summary statistics of the variables included in the regressions. Sample statistics are reported both for the entire sample and for a restricted sample of slaves who transition to freedom as adults (18 years for women and 21 years for men). Child and youth manumissions may have been driven by a different calculus than that explicated in the economic model. It seems unlikely that a young child could had saved enough or built up a sufficient stock of goodwill to induce a slave owner to free him or her. His or her parent may have, but the manumitted child had not. Ultimately, the basic results are qualitatively invariant to the inclusion of children.

The independent variables included in the regressions are largely self-explanatory. Unlike some other New World manumission regimes, men were slightly overrepresented in Virginia. The average age for the full sample is consistent with other studies. Average age for the adult-only sample is, by necessity, greater than for the full sample. The adult-only sample may be more appropriate for drawing inferences about the economics of manumission, however, because the manumission of children was more likely to be purely gratuitous and driven, at least in part, by noneconomic factors.[19] About one-fourth of manumitted slaves were mixed race. Mixed-race slaves were overrepresented among those manumitted, which is consistent with previous studies.

Stephen Whitman speculated that the female slave owners' manumission practices may have differed from those of male slave owners.[20] Whitman hypothesized that female slave owners were more likely to manumit male slaves because male slaves were more likely to challenge a female slave owner's authority. Female

Table A5.2.1 Summary Statistics for Manumission Sample

Variable	Definition	Adult sample (n=514)	Full sample (n=863)
Age (t*)	Age at manumission (years)	37.17	26.07
		(13.19)	(17.25)
t* / T	Proportion of life in slavery	0.59	0.44
		(0.15)	(0.23)
Slave female	Manumitted slave female	0.46	0.45
Mixed race	Manumitted slave mulatto	0.24	0.26
Owner female	Manumitting owner female	0.20	0.20
Group	Manumitted as part of group	0.61	0.75
Family	Manumitted with family members	0.49	0.67
Deed	Manumitted by deed	0.50	0.45
Court order	Manumitted by court order	0.04	0.03
Will	Manumitted by will	0.46	0.52
1796–1806	Liberal manumission period	0.04	0.03
1807–1815	Manumitted slaves forced to emigrate	0.02	0.01
1816–1819	Emigration waiver from county court	0.02	0.02
1820–1831	Waiver for "merit" only	0.22	0.23
1831–1862	Waiver for "merit," post Nat Turner	0.70	0.71
Urban	Manumitted in urban place	0.13	0.13
Tidewater	Manumitted in eastern county	0.09	0.08
Mountain	Manumitted in western county	0.11	0.11
Piedmont	Manumitted in central Virginia	0.80	0.81

Notes: Mixed-race category includes those described as mulatto, bright mulatto, dark mulatto, and nearly white. Urban places include Lynchburg, Petersburg, and Norfolk. Tidewater region includes Norfolk, Northampton, Surry, and Essex counties. Mountain region includes Montgomery and Augusta counties. Piedmont includes Petersburg and Lynchburg cities, and Amherst, Arlington, Bedford, Brunswick, Campbell, Fairfax, Fauquier, Fluvanna, Henrico, Louisa, Loudon, Pittsylvania, and Powhatan counties. *Sources*: See Appendix A5.1 and References §1.7.

slave owners might have responded by hiring a male overseer, but doing so introduced additional complexities into the principal-agent problem and the added cost of supervision would have delayed manumission, making male slaves even harder to manage. A simpler and less expensive path would have been to selectively manumit unruly adult male slaves, but doing so would create perverse incentives. Rewarding unruly behavior with earlier manumission would only have encouraged unruly behavior. It is not possible to sort out Whitman's conjecture because the data do not reveal anything about a slave's behavior. Statements of good conduct in manumission papers would not prove particularly useful in any case. Courts were charged with approving manumissions and few would have consented had the document contained "good riddance" rather than "good behavior" statements.

The regressions also include an indicator variable equal to 1 if the slave was manumitted as part of a group (zero otherwise) and an indicator variable equal to 1 if the slave was manumitted with other members of his or her family (zero otherwise). The majority of manumissions were group manumission (meaning that two or more slaves were manumitted by the same slave owner at approximately the same time). The most common family manumission was an adult mother with minor children, though the simultaneous manumission of husbands and wives or siblings was also observed in the data.

The regressions also include indicator variables for four time periods, which correspond to different legal manumission regimes. Luther Porter Jackson divided the years between 1782 and 1865 into four periods, based on revisions in Virginia manumission law. A post-Revolutionary period of liberal manumission with no restrictions reigned between 1782 and 1806. The law was amended in 1807, so that newly manumitted slaves were required to emigrate within 12 months or face possible seizure and sale back into slavery. A waiver of the emigration requirement might be obtained from the Virginia legislature, but the procedure was costly and the legislators were loath to grant waivers. In 1816, the right to grant waivers was transferred from the state legislature to county courts, which were more open to petitions from local slave owners than was the legislature. In 1820, the law was further amended so that the court-issued waiver had to be based on a demonstrably meritorious act. I further divide the post-1820 regime at 1831 to capture any possible consequences of Nat Turner's insurrection. Negative sentiments toward manumission increased after the insurrection and may have reduced the number of manumissions after that event.

Table A5.2.2 reports estimated coefficients from OLS regressions (t^*/T) and Weibull proportional hazard regressions on (t^*). One concern with using OLS on survival-type data is that the time to an event is unlikely to be normally distributed, so that the residuals from a parametric OLS regression of time to failure on one or more independent variables will not be normally distributed. Non-normality is a violation of one of the fundamental assumptions of OLS regression, and while OLS is reasonably robust to non-normality, it is not robust to asymmetric residuals. In the present case, the dependent variable in the OLS specification is the percentage of time spent in slavery rather than time itself. A check of the normal probability plot of the residuals from the reported regressions shows that they lie close to the 45-degree line, so the normality assumption is unlikely to have been violated.

Table A5.2.2 Determinants of Time Spent in Slavery by Race

Variable	OLS: dependent variable = t^*/T		Weibull hazard: dependent variable=t^*	
	Adults only	Full sample	Adults only	Full sample
Mixed race	−0.087	−0.083	2.181	1.441
	(0.014)**	(0.018)**	(0.253)**	(0.135)**
Slave male	0.018	0.001	1.016	1.072
	(0.014)	(0.012)	(0.104)	(0.069)
Owner female	−0.072	−0.037	1.790	1.272
	(0.024)*	(0.023)	(0.320)**	(0.126)**
Slave male*	0.090	−0.004	0.486	0.878
female owner	(0.032)**	(0.026)	(0.118)**	(0.105)
Group	−0.028	−0.081	1.149	1.331
(0.019)	(0.024)**	(0.161)	(0.115)**	
Family	0.028	−0.155	0.743	1.158
(0.021)	(0.026)**	(0.098)*	(0.153)**	
Court order	−0.053	−0.140	1.301	1.575
(0.030)	(0.040)**	(0.453)	(0.236)**	
Deed	0.034	−0.001	0.825	1.026
(0.017)*	(0.017)	(0.094)	(0.091)	
1807–1815	0.027	0.017	0.839	0.947
(0.040)	(0.054)	(0.219)	(0.160)	
1816–1819	−0.067	−0.165	1.266	1.753
(0.053)	(0.052)**	(0.449)	(0.385)**	
1820–1831	0.069	0.007	0.469	0.877
(0.035)**	(0.035)	(0.089)**	(0.106)	
1832–1862	0.076	0.026	0.498	0.874
(0.029)**	(0.032)	(0.077)**	(0.103)	
Urban	0.037	−0.023	0.850	1.082
(0.018)*	(0.020)	(0.109)	(0.088)	
Tidewater	0.050	0.025	0.643	0.878
(0.029)	(0.037)	(0.111)**	(0.152)	
Mountain	0.045	0.010	0.818	0.946
(0.018)*	(0.021)	(0.110)	(0.098)	
Constant	0.516	0.618		
	(0.034)**	(0.039)**		
F / Wald statistic	9.63**	23.22**	152.7**	235.6**
R-square	0.13	0.21		
ln(p)			1.178	0.426
			(0.033)**	(0.068)**

Notes: Robust standard errors corrected for clustering on group manumission. * p < 0.05 ** p < 0.01.
Sources: Author's calculations from data described in Appendix 5.1.

The estimated coefficients from the OLS regressions imply that the average manumitted adult slave, contingent on being manumitted, spent about 51 percent of his or her adult life in bondage. With a slave life expectancy of about 51 years for both sexes, the estimates imply manumission at about age 35, which is close to the sample average. The estimated constant on the full sample (including children) implies that eventually manumitted slaves spent about 32 years in slavery, which estimates is higher than the unconditional sample average of 26 years.

The estimate that Virginia slaves, on average, attained their freedom in their early thirties is consistent with other studies of Virginia. The average age at manumission reported by Babcock is 33 years, though Wolf reports an average of 26 years.[21] The estimates are also consistent with the economic approach to manumission. Slave owners who had a slave from birth broke even, in the sense that their expropriation of the difference between the slave's marginal product and his or her consumption during the slave's productive years just compensated the slave owner for the costs of raising, feeding, clothing and housing the slave up to that point.[22]

Table A5.2.3 Determinants of Time Spent in Slavery Within Race by Color

	OLS: dependent variable = t^*/T		Weibull hazard: dependent variable=t^*	
	Full sample	Full sample	Full sample	Full sample
	black only	mixed only	black only	mixed only
Light black	-0.007		1.119	
	(0.032)		(0.193)	
Dark black	0.092		0.641	
	(0.025)**		(0.088)**	
Light mixed		-0.084		1.660
		(0.033)*		(0.297)**
Dark mixed		0.034		0.932
		(0.037)		(0.141)
Added controls		Same as in Table A5.2.2		
Observations	641	222	641	222
F / Wald stat	24.9**	10.22**	303.7**	123.3**
R-square	0.25	0.24		

Notes: Light black category includes light negro, bright negro, light brown, and very bright negro. Dark black includes dark, dark negro, dark drown, dark copper, black, and very black. Excluded category—medium black—includes negro, brown, and copper. Light mixed includes bright mulatto, light mulatto, and nearly white. Dark mixed includes dark mulatto. Freed slaves classified as yellow were excluded because the term was applied to both blacks and mulattoes, often without qualification. * $p < 0.05$; ** $p < 0.01$. *Sources:* Author's calculation from data described in Appendix 5.1.

Mixed-race slaves spent about 8 percent less of their life enslaved than blacks. The Weibull hazard estimates imply that for slaves of all ages, the risk of manumission for mixed-race slaves at age t, conditional on not having been manumitted prior to time t, was about 1.4 times the risk of a black being manumitted. Once slaves reached adulthood, the mixed-race hazard was twice that of blacks. In short, mixed-race people were differentially more likely than blacks to be manumitted and were manumitted at earlier ages when they were manumitted.

Table A5.2.3 reports regression results when the sample is divided into black and mixed race subsamples. The OLS results imply that dark-skinned black slaves served about nine percent more of their lives enslaves, compared to blacks of medium color. Similarly, among mixed-race slaves, the lightest skinned slaves spent about eight percent less of their lives enslaved. The Weibull estimates are consistent with the OLS results; dark blacks were at a lower hazard of realizing freedom, while light mixed-race people were at a greater hazard.

Appendix 5.3   Economics of Runaways, and Analysis of Runaway Advertisements

The Economics of Running

Understanding the economics of slave runaways demands that the act be considered from the perspective of the slave and the slave owner, and how those points of view interacted with color. Let's start with the prospective runaway slave's calculus.

One way to approach this is with a Roy-type model of occupational choice. Suppose each slave's utility depends on his or her compensation (or wage plus in-kind payments) in slavery and in freedom. Each slave also has a parameter that describes his or her (dis)taste for slavery, which implies that faced with two otherwise comparable slaves in comparable circumstances, one will run while the other will not.

Further, assume that compensation in slavery and in freedom is a function of color. This assumption may follow from either of two sources. One is that slaveholders or employers, based on their prejudices, may reward color itself. The other is that slaveholders or employers believe that color reveals something about productivity. Light-skinned slaves and free people, for example, may be more literate or more skilled on average than dark-skinned slaves and free people, so that employers are willing to offer them more compensation per hour.

If slaveholders compensate slaves as a function of their color, M, and any other productive slave-based characteristics captured by the variable π_s, then the following function can be used to express a slave's log compensation:

$$\ln(c_s) = \alpha_s + \beta_s M + \gamma_s \pi_s$$

The extent of the slave's tolerance for slavery is captured by preference parameter τ_s (which may be negative), and if the individual slave's utility is additive in compensation and his or her taste for slavery, the slave's utility function is:

$$U(s)=\ln(c_s)+ \tau_s = \alpha_s + \beta_s M + \gamma_s \pi_s + \tau_s$$

Should the slave run away and find employment while on the run, he or she will be compensated according to the following log-compensation function:

$$\ln(c_r)= \alpha_r +\beta_r M+ \gamma_r \pi_s +\delta_r \pi_r$$

where the subscript r represents "on the run." Note that the color and other slave characteristics (π_s) might be valued by both slaveholders and employers (say, the ability to pick cotton), but another set of productive characteristics (π_r) are valued only in freedom (say, the ability to read and write). Individual preferences for freedom are denoted by τ_r, and the punishment cost of being caught and returning is P, so that the expected utility of running is:

$$U(r)=\ln(c_r)+\tau_r =\alpha_r +\beta_r M+\gamma_r \pi_s +\delta_r \pi_r +\tau_r -P$$

A utility maximizing slave will run if and only if $U(s) < U(r)$, which can be written as:

$$(\alpha_s -\alpha_r)<(\beta_r -\beta_s)M + (\gamma_r -\gamma_s)\pi_s + (\tau_r -\tau_s)+\delta_r \pi_r -P$$

The last equation shows that the decision to run is based on a comparison between the difference between autonomous compensation in and out of slavery, $(\alpha_s - \alpha_r)$ and the differences in the returns to characteristics in slavery and in running net of punishment costs (the right-hand side of the inequality). More fundamentally, the last equation illustrates that differences between slavery and running are what drive the choice to run. If the returns to slave activity (e.g., picking cotton) are higher with running, the slave will run, all else being equal. If the taste for running is higher than the taste for staying, all else being equal, the slave will run. But most importantly for present purposes, is that the higher the returns to color in running relative to staying (e.g., $\beta_r - \beta_s$), the more likely slaves of favored colors are to run. If the characteristics are distributed according to some known distributions and certain features such as color and productivity are correlated, it is possible to generate a model of selection into running.[23]

This is a static, one-period model in which the slave, at a point in time, chooses to run or not. The model can be extended to a dynamic context in which potential runaways maximize over a time-series of expected values. A dynamic model, the derivation of which is beyond the scope of the present case, would also incorporate the selection process into running away, which may be conditioned on color or some other characteristic. Under certain conditions, a slave that chooses not to run today might choose to run tomorrow or next week or next year. Some slaves will run today, some will delay running until some future time, and others will never run.

Economics of Runaway Advertising

Slave owner rationality implies that the reward offered equals the product of the increased likelihood that the slave is captured and returned *as a consequence of the reward* and the slave's value to the owner, which is approximated using market prices. Mathematically, this can be written as *reward = Δp × market price*. Of course, Δp is not observed, but it can be inferred from the available information. Rearranging the reward equation, it can be written as $\Delta p = reward / market price$. If different slave types have different probabilities of successfully running away ($q=1-p$), an economically rational slave owner offers reward ratios that equalize the change in probability across slave types.

Information on runaway slaves was collected from advertisements reproduced by Daniel Meaders and Freddie Parker, of which the following is representative:

$25 REWARD

Ran Away from the Subscriber, on the 14th May last, negro JOHN, his wife CINDERILLA, and their child FRANK, about two years old—John is about 30 years old, 5 feet 7 or 8 inches high, dark complexion, thin visage, and high cheek bones. Cinderilla is a likely negro, about 20 years old, tall, well made, and dark complexion. John belongs to the heirs of Danl. Redmond, but is hired to me for the present year. Cinderilla and her child were purchased by me in January last, at the sale of Bell & Joyner's property in Edgecombe county—said negroes are supposed to lurking in the neighborhood between Tarborough and Teat's bridge. A reward of $25, will be given for the apprehension of the above negroes, if delivered to me or secured in any jail so that I can get them again; or, ten dollars for either of the grown negroes, and five dollars for the child. ROBT. JELKS. Halifax County, July, 1829. (Tarboro) Free Press, 17 July 1829.
(Reprinted in Parker, *Stealing a Little Freedom.*)

All relevant information included in and concerning the advertisement was coded for statistical analysis. Separate observations were created for each advertised slave—John, Cinderilla, and Frank. For each slave his or her age, race (black or mixed), complexion (dark or light), height, and age were coded when reported. Some advertisements reported whether the runaway slave was literate or worked at a skilled or semiskilled occupation. This information was also coded.

The reward offered for the slave was coded in current dollars. When slaves ran in groups, advertisements like the one reproduced above usually stated the reward for the return of all of the slaves, as well as separate rewards for the return of any of the individuals. The reward price coded in the data was the separate price, when available. If a total reward was offered but individuals rewards were not, the coded reward is the total reward divided by the total number of advertised runaways. (There were relatively few such cases.) If the slave ran away as part of a group, that information was also coded in the data. Finally, the data included the year the advertisement appeared as well as the county of publication.

Advertisements provided information on rewards, as well as information about the runaway slave's age, sex, race and skills, the summary statistics are reported in Table A5.3.1. This information can be used to approximate the market price, which makes it possible to generate estimates of the reward ratio (*reward / market price*). The price of prime-age black male slaves sold in New Orleans was taken

Table A5.3.1 Summary Statistics for Virginia and North Carolina Runaways 1800–1840

Variable	Definition	Mean (std dev)
Mixed race	Runaway was advertised as mulatto, light mulatto, or dark mulatto	0.148
Literate	Slave advertised as capable of reading and/or writing	0.032
Occupation	Slave advertised with specific occupation listed	0.138
Female	Slave female	0.144
Multiple	Slave ran with one or more fellow slaves	0.233
Reward	Dollar amount of reward in advertisement ($)	23.22 (19.22)
Real reward	Reward amount adjusted for inflation ($)	30.19 (25.72)
Reward ratio	Reward value / average slave price adjusted for sex and age	0.042 (0.034)
Age	Reported age (years)	27.1 (8.44)
Height	Height, in inches (males > 21 years)	68.2 (2.98)

Notes: For descriptions of data and use, see text of Appendix 5.3. *Sources:* North Carolina runaway advertisements: Virginia runaway advertisements: Inflation adjustments: EH.net "How Much Is That?" calculator using consumer price index adjustment available at http://eh.net/howmuchisthat/; Slave prices for reward ratio: Carter et al., *Historical Statistics*, series Bb209-218.

from the *Historical Statistics of the United States*, Series Bb209-214, for the same year that the advertisement appeared.[24] These prices were then adjusted by average prices by age and sex (Series Bb215-216). A 15-year-old male slave in the Old South, for example, sold for an average of 64.4 percent of the price of a prime-age (18–30-year-old) male slave in the New South. Skilled slaves sold on average for 33 percent more than field hands, so the denominator was increased by this amount of the runaway was advertised as having a skill. Finally, mixed-race males sold on average for 12.9 percent more than black males, and mixed-race females sold for 9.7 percent more.[25] The denominator was adjusted by this factor if the runaway was advertised as mulatto.

The average estimated reward ratio (Δp = reward / market price) across all slaves was 0.042, which is close to the ratio of 0.05 estimated by Franklin and Schweninger from their five-state sample of runaway slaves generated without the same adjustments to the denominator as those described above. They conclude that "owners generally offered extremely modest rewards," probably because owners relied on an increasingly sophisticated and efficient system of runaway recovery that mitigated the need to offer large rewards to induce recovery efforts.[26]

Franklin and Schweninger are probably correct that slave owners could rely on an efficient system of runaway recovery. The rewards were not so modest as they suggest, however. Inflation-adjusted rewards varied from a pittance (2¢) to a tidy sum ($274), and averaged just over $30. While $30 appears modest, recall that the average unskilled worker in the South Atlantic region earned about 75¢ per day between 1820 and 1840, and might expect to work about 180 to 200 days per year.[27] While recovering a runaway slave could be risky if the runaway put up a fight, a $30 reward represented 20 percent of an unskilled laborer's annual earnings. For skilled workers (artisans), it represented about 10 percent of annual earnings. Rewards of this magnitude seem sufficient to induce effort among the working classes.

From an economic perspective, the rewards may have been inefficiently large in that they induced excessive effort, and too many people searched and duplicated each other's costly recovery efforts.[28] It should also be noted as well that Franklin and Schweninger do not appear to recognize that rewards were offered to induce incremental effort that increased the marginal probability of recovery. The implied marginal effect on the probability of recovery at the mean reward was about 4 percent. Given that so few runaways were successful, meaning that the probability p, was relatively large (but unknown to us), the marginal effects appear to be substantial. Slave owners went to great expense to have their chattel property returned. Slaves were valuable, of course, but capture, recovery, and punishment of runaways acted as a deterrent to others who contemplated running.

To investigate slave owner rationality, regressions of the following form were estimated:

$$\Delta p_{jt} = (reward \ / \ market \ price) = X_{jt} \cdot \beta + \alpha_j + \gamma_t + \delta_{jt} + \varepsilon_{jt}$$

where X_{jt} includes personal characteristics of the runaway slave: sex, race, skilled and whether he or she ran away alone or as part of a group. α_j is a set of 10-year (21–30 years; 31–40 years, etc.) age fixed effects. γ_t are year fixed effects. δ_{jt} are county fixed effects. ε_{jt} is the error term. The parameters were estimated using ordinary least squares corrected for heteroskedasticity.

Recall in this instance that efficiency criteria suggest that none of the slave's personal characteristics will be economically meaningful. The estimated constant, reported in Table A5.3.2 implies an average incremental effect of 4 to 5 percent. But as expected, the remaining coefficient estimates are all small in magnitude and statistically insignificant. Adjustments made to the market price for age, sex,

Table A5.3.2 Determinants of Rewards for Runaway Slaves

Variable	Full sample			Males only		
	(F1)	(F2)	(F3)	(M1)	(M2)	(M3)
Mixed race	-0.0005	-0.0004	-0.0023	-0.0010	-0.0007	-0.0027
	(0.0018)	(0.0018)	(0.0018)	(0.002)	(0.002)	(0.002)
Female	0.0023	0.0023	-0.0000	—	—	—
	(0.0022)	(0.0021)	(0.0020)			
Multiple	-0.0029	-0.0027	-0.0022	-0.0034	-0.0035	-0.0037
	(0.0014)*	(0.0014)	(0.0015)	(0.0014)	(0.0015)	(0.0016)
Occupation	0.0008	-0.0004	-0.0004	0.0004	-0.0008	-0.0010
	(0.0020)	(0.0020)	(0.0020)	(0.0021)	(0.0021)	(0.0021)
Literate	0.0062	0.0061	0.0082	0.0063	0.0068	0.0088
	(0.0035)	(0.0036)	(0.0037)*	(0.0036)	(0.0036)	(0.0039)*
Constant	0.0370	0.0455	0.0498	0.0360	0.0524	0.0548
	(0.0045)**	(0.0086)**	(0.101)**	(0.0047)**	(0.0111)**	(0.0118)**
Age Fes	Y	Y	Y	Y	Y	Y
Year Fes	N	Y	Y	N	Y	Y
County Fes	N	N	Y	N	N	Y
Obs	2476	2476	2476	2119	2119	2119
R-square	0.06	0.10	0.24	0.07	0.11	0.26
F-stat	6.26**	3.79**	—	6.31**	3.79**	—

Note: Dependent variable = reward ratio (reward/market price). See text for description and meaning of the reward ratio. Robust standard errors in parentheses. * implies $p < 0.05$; ** implies $p < 0.01$.
Sources: See Table A5.3.1.

skills, and race, while imprecise appear to capture the subjective valuations places on slaves by their owners. Given differences in relative market prices across slave types—sex, age, race, and so on—slave owners were efficiently adjusting reward values to equalize the likelihood of return across types.

Appendix 6.1   The Economics of Assortative Mating on Race and Complexion

If the family is the basic economic unit, individuals maximize their well-being by taking spouses offering the most attractive combination of cultural and economic resources. Becker argues that within the context of the traditional family, assortative mating leads women to seek men with high earning potentials while men seek women with other resources, such as homemaking or child rearing abilities.[29] As the gender gap narrowed in the twentieth century, however, the nature of family exchange has changed so that both men and women seek partners with economic prestige or potential. Each spouse's human and social capital generates economic opportunities for the other.[30] As sex roles evolved, partners became more economically similar. In other words, the closing of the gender gap has produced economic homogamy.

As compelling as Becker's economic choice model is to rational choice social scientists, it surely does not capture the totality of the marriage decision. Marriage partner selection is also about combining and sharing cultural resources.[31] Cultural resources include a variety of values and behaviors such as political attitudes, appreciation for the arts, religious devotion, styles of speech and dress, and child-rearing philosophies. Cultural resources determine how people react to one another and how well they jointly produce relational goods, such as affection and happiness. It is likely that the joint production of relational goods is more efficient the larger the number of shared cultural resources, or the greater the degree of cultural homogamy. There is of course no reason why cultural resources and economic prestige cannot be highly correlated, but there is also no particular reason why they would. Kalmijn, in fact, finds that high economic prestige individuals (doctors and lawyers) are more likely to marry individuals with high cultural status and moderate economic prestige (teachers and professors).[32] Cultural homogamy is stronger than economic homogamy, though the latter remains a powerful impulse. Some research suggests that education, hence economic, homogamy is on the increase and of increasing economic importance to household outcomes. Greenwood, Guner, Kocharkov, and Santos contend that increases in educational homogamy are partly responsible for increasing income inequality since the 1960s.[33]

Given the difficulty of determining the relative importance of cultural and economic homogamy, the model of homogamy presented here collapses them into a single metric that Burdett and Coles label "pizazz." They develop a matching model, like those used in labor economics, to study the microeconomics of the marriage market. The matching framework is appropriate because it assumes (1) that singles have difficulty contacting each other; (2) each single's objective is to form a long-term relationship; and (3) singles compete, doing the best he or she can given the constraints they face. The model yields predictions consistent with positive assortative mating, or homogamy, which implies a positive correlation between partners' traits—education, intelligence, height, attractiveness, family background, wealth, religion, and so forth.[34]

Although searching for an attractive marriage partner is a complex undertaking, Burdett and Coles reduce it to potential partners' evaluations of each other's "pizazz," which they assume can be characterized by a real number. The flow of utility to the male partner from marriage equals the female's pizazz value. Similarly, the female's flow of utility from marriage equals the male's pizazz value. Males and females meet randomly, but when they do they instantly recognize the other's pizazz score and either propose or continue searching. The obvious advantage of having high pizazz is that it enables the individual to attract someone else of high pizazz. The selection process generates an equilibrium in which singles partition themselves into classes according to their pizazz levels. Men in a high-pizazz class will only propose to women in the same or higher pizazz class and always reject a woman from a lower class. Women do the same. In equilibrium, marriage occurs between men and women from the same class. Belding develops a generalized version of the Burdett and Coles model, which is adapted to the issue at hand—complexion homogamy within the African-American community.[35] In what follows, it is assumed that a person's pizazz is a function of his or her complexion.

Suppose that individuals of complexion c only marry another with complexion $C^1 \geq C^1_{lightest}(c) - f[G(c)]$, where $C^1_{lightest}(c)$ represents the lightest complexion individual willing to marry a suitor with complexion c, and $f[G(c)] \geq 0$ is the selectivity function describing the distribution of complexions $G(c)$ among those willing to marry an individual with complexion c. This description of each individual's preferences in conjunction with assuming that each individual maximizes his or her utility, where utility is a function of a partner's complexion, yields complexion homogamy contingent on the following additional assumptions:

(1) all individuals, both male and female, employ a single uniform complexion metric to evaluate potential mates;
(2) the complexions of any two individuals can be compared and comparisons are transitive, that is, if $c(a1) \geq c(a2)$ and $c(a2) \geq c(a3) \Rightarrow c(a1) \geq c(a3)$;[36]
(3) individuals are always willing to marry the lightest complected individual willing to marry them;

(4) all males will propose to the lightest complected available female (that is, the woman represented by the complexion $c^f_{lightest}$), and all females will propose to the lightest complected available male (that is, the man with the complexion $c^m_{lightest}$);

(5) if an individual is willing to marry another of a given complexion, he or she is also willing to marry all lighter-complected individuals. Let $Ua^m_2 = U(c(a^f_2))$ represent the utility derived by male a^m_2, which is a function of the complexion of female a^f_2 and such a marriage is a viable match between a male (from the male's viewpoint) of complexion group 2 and a female of complexion group 2. If $c(a^f_1) \geq c(a^f_2)$, then a match (M) between male a^m_2 and a female satisfying $c(a^f_1)$ ($M(a^m_2, a^f_1)$) is also possible because $Ua^m_2 = U(c(a^f_1)) \geq U(c(a^f_2))$;

(6) acceptance of a suitor is nondecreasing in lighter complexions. That is, let the match $M(a^m_1, a^f_3)$ be a viable match as defined in assumption (5) and let $c(a^m_1)$ > $c(a^m_2)$, then $M(a^m_2, a^f_3)$ is also possible. In other words, individuals are always willing to marry another from a lighter complexion group, even if it not the lightest group.

Following Belding, the proof of complexion homogamy is as follows: All males propose to the lightest complected female (she who satisfies $c^f_{lightest}$). This female, in turn, proposes to the lightest complected male (he who satisfies $c^m_{lightest}$), as well as all other males who satisfy the condition $C' \geq C^m_{lightest}(c) - f[G(c^f_{lightest})]$, where $f[.]$ represents the selectivity function of the lightest complected female.

Because the lightest complected female proposes to all males satisfying $C' \geq C^m_{lightest}(c) - f[G(c^f_{lightest})]$, all other women are willing to propose to any male satisfying the lightest complected woman's selectivity criterion.[37] This group of men is in the same position as the lightest complected male. Call this set C^m_1. Every member of C^m_1 is willing to marry the lightest complected female as well as any available woman satisfying $C'' \geq C^f_{lightest} - f[G(c^m_{lightest})]$, where $f[.]$ is the selectivity function of the lightest complected male. Call the set of women satisfying this criterion C^f_1. All women in this set will follow the same rule as the lightest complected female, which is to propose only to those men in set C^m_1. Thus, the women in set C^f_1 will propose only to those men in C^m_1, and vice versa. The lightest complected men and women pair off, implying complexion homogamy among the very light complected. Complexion homogamy will not be restricted to just the lightest, however. The pattern established by the most desirable marriage partners filters down to darker complected people as well.

To form the next lightest complexion group, remove those members of C^m_1 and C^f_1 and repeat the process beginning with the female just excluded from the group C^f_1, or that woman described by $C^f_{lightest} - f[G(c^m_{lightest})] - \delta_f$, where δ_f is some infinitesimally small value.[38] Similarly, begin with the male just excluded from the group C^m_1, or that man described by $C^m_{lightest}(c) - f[G(c^f_{lightest})] - \delta_m$. All remaining males propose to the lightest complected remaining female and this female, in turn, proposes to all remaining men satisfying her selectivity function. If she is willing to propose to these men, all darker women are as well. These men are then in the same position as the lightest complected remaining male. Call this set C_2^m. The equivalent set of women, C_2^f, will form in parallel fashion. The process continues until sets of the darkest complected men and women, C_n^m and C_n^f (where n represents the ultimate number of sets), form. The result (complexion homogamy) is demonstrated in Figure 6.1 (in the main text).

Belding's generalization of Burdett and Coles's proof holds so long as the two basic mechanisms underlying homogamy are (1) that all individuals decide whether to marry another based on the other's complexion relative to the complexion of the lightest individual willing to marry them; and (2) that there is a known upper boundary to complexion.[39] Further, Belding shows that the outcome is not dependent on individuals having a well defined $f[G(c)]$ function. Complexion homogamy emerges even if we adopt the simplest formulation, namely that $f[G(c)] = \varepsilon$, where ε is a positive constant. For simplicity Figure 5.1 is drawn with this assumption because it simplifies the notation in the diagram without loss of generality. The outcome is not dependent on this particular specification of the selectivity function. Homogamy also emerges if men and women have different selectivity functions.[40]

Appendix 6.2   Assortative Marriage and Urban Residence

Using marriages identified in the Virginia Register Sample (see Appendix 5.1 for a description of the sample), the following considers some basic correlates of assortative marriage. Variations on the following specification are estimated:

$$\text{Assortative marriage}_{it}\,(=1\text{ if yes}) = \alpha + \beta\,\text{Urban}_i + \delta\,X_{it} + \gamma_t + \varepsilon_{it}$$

where the dependent variable =1 if the marriage was complexion assortative (black-black, mixed-mixed) and 0 otherwise. The coefficient of interest is that on the *Urban* variable, which equals 1 if the couple is observed in Lynchburg, Norfolk, Petersburg, or Richmond, and zero otherwise. It is important to note the coefficient cannot be interpreted as a causal effect because it is unknown whether the couple married elsewhere and then moved to a city or whether the couple married in the city. The choice of marriage partner and location were jointly determined and are both endogenous. Absent a instrumental variable for urban residence, the estimated coefficient is evidence of correlation alone.

The vector X includes other observable features believed to influence the choice of marriage partner, including the absolute age differential between the husband and wife, each partner's status at birth (slave or free-born), and each partners height expressed as a Z-statistic of modern height standards.[41] That is, the height variable is expressed as Z = (height—modern mean height)/(modern std dev of height). Finally, γ_t represents a series of decade (1820s-1860s) fixed effects to account for systematic differences across time.

Table A6.2.1 provides summary statistics for the sample. Nearly half of all marriages were race/complexion assortative; about 25 percent of registrants lived in a city or town; the typical marriage was observed in 1845; husbands were about 6 years older than wives; and mean heights by sex are consistent with those observed in the larger Virginia-Maryland height samples analyzed in detail in Chapter 9. In short, the subsample appears to be representative of free African Americans in the Upper South who registered prior to Emancipation. (See the discussion in Appendix 5.1 about the representativeness of the sample of the population of African Americans.)

Table A6.2.2 reports the estimated linear probability coefficients from the equation discussed above. The estimated constants imply that between one-half and two-thirds of all marriages were assortative. Urban residents were about 20 to 25 percent less likely to be partnered with someone of like complexion than rural residents, holding all else constant. The urban coefficient suggests either of two possibilities. First, urban residents may have been less color-conscious than rural

Table A6.2.1 Summary Statistics for Virginia Register Sample Marriages

Variable	Mean	Std Dev
Assortative marriage (0/1)	0.46	0.50
Urban (0/1)	0.25	0.44
Male age (years)	38.90	11.94
Female age (years)	33.94	10.69
Age difference (years)	6.41	5.85
Male height (inches)	67.71	2.49
Male height Z-score	-0.74	0.98
Female height (inches)	62.92	2.62
Female height Z-score	-0.66	1.14
Year	1844	13.3
Decade pre-1820	0.06	0.23
Decade 1820	0.11	0.31
Decade 1830	0.16	0.37
Decade 1840	0.13	0.34
Decade 1850	0.49	0.50
Decade 1860	0.06	0.24

Notes: 208 observations. *Sources:* See Appendix 5.1 for details and References §1.7 for details and description.

Table A6.2.2 Determinants of Assortative Marriages in Virginia

Variable	1	2	3
Urban	-0.233	-0.256	-0.225
	(0.074)**	(0.084)**	(0.096)*
Male free-born			-0.032
			(0.114)
Female free-born			-0.042
			(0.119)
Age difference			-0.004
			(0.007)
Male height Z-score			-0.024
			(0.038)
Female height Z-score			0.013
			(0.031)
Decade fixed effects	No	Yes	Yes
Constant	0.516	0.583	0.645
	(0.040)**	(0.145)**	(0.154)**
R-square	0.042	0.047	0.056
F-stat	9.98**	1.84	1.09

Notes: 208 observations. ** implies $p<0.01$; * implies $p < 0.05$. *Source:* Author's calculations from Virginia Register Sample, see Appendix 5.1 and References §1.7 for details and description of the sample.

residents, but this may represent a type of color-consciousness selection effect in that less color conscious people were more likely to locate in cities. Second, the larger urban dating pools allowed potential mates more opportunities to match on characteristics other than color. Other sources are needed to sort out the causal effect, because the Virginia Register Sample does not provide enough information to distinguish between them.

Appendix 6.3 Assortative Marriages and Economic Well-Being

Using married couples identified in the school sample discussed in Chapter 6 and more fully in Chapter 8, the following considers the extent to which assortative marriages had greater economic resources. Specifically, it investigates the extent to which households with assortative marriage partners were more likely to own real estate and whether they worked at more skilled (and presumably more remunerative) occupations. Ordinary least squares equations of the following form are estimated:

$$\text{Outcome}_{ij} = \alpha + \beta_1 \text{ww}_{ij} + \beta_2 \text{mm}_{ij} + \beta_3 \text{mb}_{ij} + \beta_4 \text{bm}_{ij} + \delta_1 \text{Age}_{ij} + \delta_2 \text{Age}_{ij}^2 + \gamma_j + \varepsilon_{ij}$$

where i indexes couples and j the city/ward of residence. The coefficients of interest are the β's, which estimate the effect of different types of marriages on economic outcomes. The variable ww equals one if the marriage is white-white(male listed first); mm equals one if marriage is mixed-mixed; mb equals one if marriage is mixed-black; and bm equals one if marriage is black-mixed. The excluded category is black-black. Age variables are included to capture any cohort effects on wealth accumulation or occupational training. The square of age is included because cross-sectional studies tend to find an inverted U-shape of wealth in age.

Table A6.3.1 reports the summary statistics and regression results for three variants on the above equation. Dependent variables include real estate ownership (0/1); skilled occupation (0/1) and socioeconomic index (0≤ SEI ≤ 100).

Table A6.3.1 Assortative Marriage Correlates of Wealth and Occupation

	Mean (Std dev)	Real estate (0/1) mean=0.174	Skill occupation (0/1) mean=0.372	Socioeconomic Index mean=20.39
White-white	0.634 (0.481)	0.141 (0.012)**	0.342 (0.016)**	10.604 (0.537)**
Mixed-mixed	0.097 (0.297)	0.090 (0.021)**	0.150 (0.026)**	3.183 (0.750)**
Mixed-black	0.008 (0.091)	0.027 (0.050)	0.088 (0.076)	-2.098 (1.371)
Black-mixed	0.027 (0.162)	-0.006 (0.025)	0.035 (0.040)	1.213 (1.225)
Age	41.04 (8.64)	0.011 (0.005)*	0.008 (0.006)	0.233 (0.242)
Age square	1758.91 (757.48)	-0.000 (0.000)	-0.000 (0.000)	-0.000 (0.003)
Constant		-0.270 (0.103)**	-0.139 (0.135)	0.382 (5.063)
Ward fixed effects		Yes	Yes	Yes
R-square		0.10	0.12	0.11
F-stat		24.4**	31.4**	24.7**
Obs		3898	3898	3819

Notes: ** implies p≤ 0.01. *Sources:* Author's calculations from data found in US Census Bureau, Eighth Census (1860) population manuscripts of Baltimore and New York.

Households with white-white traditional families and school-age children were about 14 percent more likely to own real estate, 34 percent more likely to work at a skilled occupation, and worked at jobs 10 points higher in the socioeconomic scale than households with black-black marriages and school-age children. This is a not unexpected result. Whiles were known to be better off than African Americans. The interesting result is that households composed of mixed-mixed marriage and with school-age children were 9 percent more likely to own real estate, 15 percent more likely to work at a skilled occupation, and worked at jobs more than 3 points higher on the socioeconomic index than households populated with black-black marriages and school-age children.

The estimated effects are not causal. In fact, it is likely that mixed-race men with more wealth and better prospects prior to marriage were more attractive to more desirable women. The results reported in Appendix 6.2 suggest that race or complexion was not the only feature on which couples matched, but it was an important feature. The results of this section can be seen as supporting evidence that mixed-race men working in more skilled occupations were more attractive partners to mixed-race women, who themselves may have brought more assets to a marriage than black women. Evidence reported in Chapters 7 and 8 shows that mixed-race men and women—not just married men with school-age children—worked at better jobs and had more wealth than black men and black women. But it is interesting to note that marriage behaviors reinforced the wealth and occupational effects, something that Greenwood et al. posit as a factor contributing to increasing inequality since the 1960s.[42]

Appendix 7.1 African-American Self-Employment

An econometric model of the self-employment choice concerns the behavior of well informed workers who choose between self-employment and wage labor.[43] The approach assumes that workers know their potential earnings in each sector, as well as their personal valuation of nonpecuniary features of self-employment and wage labor. Self-employment is chosen if $[Y_{si} / Y_{wi}] > C_i$, where Y_{si} and Y_{wi} are potential earnings in self-employment (s) and wage labor (w) and C_i represents a reservation value of the nonincome features of self-employment relative to wage labor. C_i is less than one if independence and self-direction are highly valued, or if individual circumstances reduce the risks of self-employment. High net worth individuals, for instance, may have C_i values less than one if their net worth provides insurance against low ex post realizations in self-employment. C_i is greater than one if the individual has a low tolerance for risk, or for a given tolerance, self-employment is risky.

A reduced-form self-employment—wage-labor choice results from a three equation system defined by:

$$\ln Y_{si} = \alpha_s X_i + \varepsilon_{si} \qquad (6.1.1)$$

$$\ln Y_{wi} = \alpha_w X_i + \varepsilon_{wi} \qquad (6.1.2)$$

$$\ln C_i = \gamma R_i + \varepsilon_{ci} \qquad (6.1.3)$$

The first two equations are the potential earnings for all individuals who face the choice between self-employment and wage labor regardless of their actual choices. Choice of sector depends on observable human capital characteristics, family characteristics, and location (which may be endogenously chosen) captured in vector X, plus the effects of unobservable characteristics and measurement error. Equation 3 captures the reservation value determined by nonpecuniary features of the choice.

Self-employment is chosen if:

$$X_i(\alpha_s - \alpha_w) - \gamma R_i > \varepsilon_{wi} - \varepsilon_{si} + \varepsilon_{ci} \qquad (6.1.4)$$

which can be rewritten as:

$$\beta X_i > \varepsilon_{0i} \qquad (6.1.5)$$

which further yields a reduced-form indicator estimator of the form:

$$I = 1 \text{ if } \beta X_i > \varepsilon_{0i} \qquad (6.1.6)$$

0 otherwise.

Equation 6.1.6 is estimated by logit regression, where the indicator variable equals one if the person is self-employed. The sample is restricted to heads of households. Because the choice between self-employment and wage labor is only interesting in the case of relatively low-skilled workers—nineteenth-century skilled crafts workers, retail and wholesale merchants, and professionals were self-employed nearly by definition—the self employment choice is relevant only for those individuals self-employed in service (washerwomen), operative (carters), and sales (huckster) trades. Entering into retail, wholesale, craft work, or the professions was not an available option for most low-skilled workers.

In addition to a black indicator variable, the explanatory variables included in the estimation include a quadratic in age, literacy, natural log of household size, and city fixed effects. Literacy is likely to increase the benefits of self-employment. Basic literacy and numeracy would reduce the likelihood being taken advantage of in transactions. The effects of age and household size are ambiguous. Larger households and more dependents, for instance, may have made self-employment a risky option, given the other members' dependence on the head of household's earnings. Alternatively, larger households may have meant more potential income earners, which may have smoothed current income and reduced the perceived downside risks to self-employment.

Bernhardt contends that a measure of household wealth should also be included in the estimation. Wealth may be endogenous in that those who expect to be self-employed may save more prior to embarking on self-employment. While this endogeneity may be at work, a large component of wealth comes from gifts or inheritance, which may have played an important role in the choices made by manumitted slaves, so that some nontrivial component of wealth is arguably exogenous. No obvious instrumental variable presented itself in the census to control for wealth, so the regressions include a dummy variable for real estate ownership (regardless of amount) to capture wealth. No causal interpretation can be offered between wealth and the self-employment choice, but it is important for the regressions to control for a wealth effect.

Also, like Bernhardt, the regressions do not control for occupation or industry. Self-employment occurs when an individual observes and acts on an apparent market disequilibrium. If a person with a propensity to self-employment invests in search for profitable self-employment opportunities, he or she may pursue self-employment wherever exploitable opportunities appear. Thus, the choice between self-employment and wage labor is made prior to or jointly with the choice of industry or occupation. That is, a man employed as a wage laborer in the late 1850s may have been open to the possibility of self-employment as either a huckster or a carter. If the potential profitable opportunities in carting appeared to be higher than in huckstering, the man can be expected to become a carter. His choice to become self-employed was conditional on his choice to become a carter. A more complicated model is needed to explain the self-employment and industry choice. The econometric model estimated here can be viewed as a reduced-form equation of that larger, more complex model.

The estimated equation takes the general form:

$$\text{Self}_{isc} = \beta X_{isc} + \gamma \text{Color}_i + \delta_c + \varepsilon_{isc} \qquad (6.1.7)$$

where i indexes individuals, s indexes sex, and c indexes city. The dependent variable equals one if the individual is self-employed in the service, operative, or laboring sector. X_{isc} is a vector of individual controls, including age and its square, literacy (0/1), whether the individual reports owning real estate (0/1), and the natural log of the household size. δ_c is a vector of city fixed effects. Color (0/1) is a vector of dummy variables (black or mixed) that equal one if the census identifies the individual as either black or mixed race. In regressions that include all household heads (by sex), the reference category is white; in regressions that include only African-American households, the reference category is mixed race. The regressions are estimated with robust standard errors.

Summary statistics are provided in Table A7.1.1. Black men outnumbered mixed-race men about 7 to 3; black women outnumbered mixed-race women about 6 to 4. The average age of household heads was between 38 and 41 years (the sample was restricted to household heads between 20 and 65 years). About two-thirds of African-American male and female heads were literate and about 10 percent reported owning some real estate. Male heads of households resided in houses with about 4.3 inhabitants (or, ln(household size) = 1.45), and female heads resided in houses with approximately 3.3 residents. Female-headed households, it seems, were missing an adult male.

The regressions reported in Table A7.1.2 imply that self-employment is not readily explained by observable characteristics. Among men the choice was influenced by literacy, real estate ownership, and household size, all of which are reasonable influences. Literate men were about 25 percent more likely than nonliterate men to enter into self-employment. Men who reported real estate

Table A7.1.1 Summary Statistics for Self-Employment Sample

	African American	All	African American	All
	Men	*Men*	*Women*	*Women*
Black	0.703	0.375	0.591	0.446
	(0.457)	(0.484)	(0.492)	(0.497)
Mixed race	0.297	0.159	0.409	0.308
	(0.457)	(0.365)	(0.492)	(0.462)
White	—	0.466	—	0.246
		(0.499)		(0.431)
Age	38.99	38.58	40.41	41.13
	(10.35)	(10.16)	(11.53)	(11.48)
Literate	0.626	0.732	0.692	0.736
(0.484)	(0.443)	(0.462)	(0.441)
Real estate	0.096	0.120	0.100	0.118
owner	(0.294)	(0.325)	(0.300)	(0.323)
ln(household size)	1.414	1.479	1.190	1.233
	(0.532)	(0.506)	(0.631)	(0.618)
Observations	4,208	7,885	2,918	3,869

Notes: The sample includes all African-American household heads and an equal number of randomly selected white household heads. The ten cities include Baltimore and Frederick, Maryland; Baton Rouge and New Orleans, Louisiana; Charleston, South Carolina; Louisville, Kentucky; Mobile, Alabama; Nashville, Tennessee; Petersburg and Richmond, Virginia. *Sources:* Author's calculations from 10-city southern sample; US Census Bureau, Eighth Census (1860), population manuscripts.

Table A7.1.2 Determinants of Self-EmploymentLogistic Regression Coefficients (Log Odds)

	African American	All	African American	All
	Men	Men	Women	Women
Black	0.389	0.140	1.313	−0.242
	(0.128)	(0.080)	(0.496)**	(0.308)
Mixed race	—	−0.196	—	−1.389
		(0.112)		(0.462)**
Age	0.053	0.026	−0.128	0.018
(0.035)	(0.026)	(0.088)	(0.078)	
Age squared	−0.0006	−0.003	0.002	-0.0003
(0.0004)	(0.003)	(0.0010	(0.0009)	
Literate (0/1)	0.220	0.277	0.743	0.512
(0.109)*	(0.088)**	(0.424)	(0.348)	
Real estate (0/1)	0.213	0.432	1.242	0.714
(0.187)	(0.110)**	(0.527)*	(0.411)	
ln(household size)	0.191	0.179	−0.322	−0.187
(0.094)*	(0.073)**	(0.252)	(0.223)	
Constant	−3.664	−2.858	−2.901	−3.571
(0.714)**	(0.520)**	(1.843)	(1.511)*	
City fixed effects	Y	Y	Y	Y
Observations	4,208	7,885	2,918	3,869
log likelihood	−1472.82	−2831.68	−178.42	−305.99
Wald χ^2	72.3**	121.1**	32.2**	45.9**
Pseudo R^2	0.03	0.03	0.10	0.08
Black = Mixed F-test	—	8.03**	—	5.69*

Notes: * implies $p<0.05$; ** implies $p<0.01$. *Sources:* See Table A7.1.1.

ownership were 20 to 50 percent more likely than men without real estate to enter into self-employment. Men from larger households, too, were more likely to be self-employed. Human capital and familial resources influenced the choice to exit the wage-labor sector for self-employment.

While the coefficients on race are not statistically significant, the difference between black and mixed-race men is. Black men were about 15 percent more likely than white men to be self-employed; mixed-race men were about 18 percent less likely, and the test statistic rejects the null hypothesis of coefficient equality (p<0.01). Color-based differences are also apparent for women. The coefficient on black in the African-American sample implies that black women were nearly three times more likely than mixed-race, female heads of households to be self-employed. Coefficients from the all women sample imply a significant difference between black and mixed-race women, with mixed-race women less likely to be self-employed.

Different racial propensities toward self-employment point to discrimination in the wage labor market. Black men and women with enough human capital and familial resources to make self-employment a viable alternative were more likely than mixed-race men and woman similarly situated to enter into self-employment. Although the hypothesis cannot be tested, the Borjas-Bronars model predicts that the self-employment choice is attractive when the potential earnings in self-employment exceed the potential earnings in wage labor sufficiently to compensate for the risks of self-employment. The observed patterns of black and mixed-race self-employment, notwithstanding the visibility of mixed-race entrepreneurs in a handful of notable occupations, suggest that blacks were less well compensated for similar work performed by similarly qualified individuals. Self-employment offered a limited escape hatch for men and women of all races, but was a relatively more attractive option for black men, who may have suffered more discrimination than other race-sex groups.

Appendix 8.1   Regression Analysis of Real Estate Ownership by Race and Color

To study property ownership among southern free African Americans a large, regionally representative sample was drawn from the population manuscripts of the 1860 United States census. Twenty-five counties were selected using the procedure described in Appendix 8.2. Ten cities were selected in less formal fashion, but were chosen based on a close reading of historical sources and studies. Joel Williamson notes that the border states formed what he labeled a "mulatto belt," which contained a high proportion of mixed-race to black free people.[44] Cities representing this belt include Baltimore and Frederick, Maryland and Richmond and Petersburg, Virginia. Historians also refer to Lower South cities known for their vibrant free African-American communities. Cities representing these areas include New Orleans and Baton Rouge, Louisiana; Mobile, Alabama; and Charleston, South Carolina. There were also sizeable African-American communities in the southwestern states. Nashville, Tennessee and Louisville, Kentucky represent these areas. These urban places vary dramatically in size, racial composition, age of settlement, and treatment of African Americans.

Information was collected on every household headed by a black or mixed-race adult. An equal number of randomly selected white households were also drawn from the same cities. For Nashville, for example, 142 African-American households with usable data were identified. A "skip sample" of randomly selected households was created and if the resulting household was headed by a white adult, the same information was collected as for the African-American households.[45] The skip procedure yielded 180 white households in Nashville. Across all 10 cities, the sample process yielded 18,179 households. Details by race, color, and sex are provided in Table A8.1.1.

The empirical strategy is to estimate parsimonious log wealth functions of the following form:

$$\ln(\omega_{ij}) = \beta_0 + \beta_1 \mathbf{Black}_{ij} + \beta_2 \mathbf{Mixed}_{ij} + \beta_3 \mathbf{Literate}_{ij} + \Sigma_k \beta_k \left(\mathbf{Age}_{ij}\right)^k + \Sigma_j \gamma_j + \varepsilon_{ij}$$

Table A8.1.1 Summary Statistics for 10-City Sample

Variable	Male householders			Female householders		
	Black	*Mixed*	*White*	*Black*	*Mixed*	*White*
Age	41.00	40.08	39.68	43.01	41.22	44.91
	(12.15)	(11.50)	(11.38)	(13.90)	(13.78)	(13.14)
Literate	0.607	0.787	0.917	0.626	0.764	0.881
Baltimore, MD	0.723	0.322	0.498	0.462	0.175	0.520
Baton Rouge, LA	0.001	0.016	0.009	0.003	0.017	0.013
Charleston, SC	0.022	0.095	0.079	0.069	0.181	0.086
Frederick, MD	0.025	0.033	0.024	0.019	0.023	0.031
Louisville, KY	0.036	0.038	0.041	0.042	0.030	0.029
Mobile, AL	0.004	0.044	0.024	0.008	0.038	0.024
Nashville, TN	0.011	0.013	0.020	0.016	0.027	0.022
New Orleans, LA	0.063	0.360	0.178	0.118	0.359	0.149
Petersburg, VA	0.090	0.034	0.076	0.186	0.064	0.076
Richmond, VA	0.026	0.049	0.051	0.076	0.087	0.049
Observations	3,671	2,099	7,617	1,976	1,453	1,343

Notes: Sample includes only heads of households. *Sources:* Author's calculations from 10-city sample. See text for description of dataset.

where ω_{ij} represents real (or personal) wealth of individual i residing in city j. The coefficients of principal interest are those on the black and mixed coefficients. Additional controls include an indicator variable (0/1) for literacy, a third-degree polynomial in age, and either nine city or 68 ward fixed effects (γ_j) ε_{ij} is a mean zero error term. The regressions were estimated with Huber-White robust standard errors (when applicable).

Several issues arise when using the common log wealth specification with a limited set of controls. First, most data sources (the 1860 manuscript censuses included) do not measure all the relevant characteristics, such as ability, motivation, and inheritance, that influence wealth accumulation. Without measures or reasonable proxies, the resulting estimates may generate misleading estimates of discrimination.[46] The predicted black-mixed wealth gap, for instance, cannot be attributed to discriminatory practices. Premarket discrimination may have discouraged some people from investing in education or entering into certain occupations that would have generated greater wealth. Measured discrimination is likely to be underestimated to the extent that premarket discrimination is not taken into account. On the other hand, educational and occupational differences by color may also reflect systematic color-based differences in tastes.

Second, a third-order polynomial in age is used because the standard quadratic specification may lead to biased estimates of the true age-wealth profile. Quadratic specifications tend to overstate wealth at early ages by substantial amounts, overstate wealth at middle age to a modest extent, and understate wealth in late life.[47] Quadratic specifications tend to understate wealth growth early and overstate wealth decline in retirement. A third-order polynomial is a more flexible specification. In practical terms, moreover, the first three terms tend to be significant at 5 percent or better; fourth- and fifth-degree terms only rarely approached a p-value of 0.10.

Third, even if all the relevant control variables were included, the log-linear specification imposes the constraint that a unit change in an independent variable leads to a constant percentage change in the dependent variable. This may be reasonable as a first approximation around the central tendency of the data, but wealth is known to be right-skewed and relationships that hold at around the mean may not provide good estimates of relationships at other points in the distribution. Timothy Conley and David Galenson, therefore, recommend using quantile regression techniques to estimate the relationships between wealth and the control variables at several points in the distribution.[48]

Ordinary least squares (OLS) techniques will not provide unbiased estimates because the error term is correlated with the independent variables. The bias will not necessarily disappear in large sample sizes, so estimates may be inconsistent as well. OLS estimates are also sensitive to the values imputed for missing (blank) entries, the most common imputations being $1 or $0.01 (the latter is used in the regressions reported below). Finally, it is not clear that the conditional mean of

Table A8.1.2 Correlates of Real WealthMale African-American Householders in Urban South

	Male householders		Female householders	
	Black	Mixed-race	Black	Mixed-race
Estimation Procedure	*Dependent variable = ln (wealth)*			
OLS	-1.441	-0.495	-1.327	-0.703
	(0.083)*	(0.119)*‡	(0.149)*	(0.181)*‡
OLS	-1.258	-0.427	-1.269	-0.595
	(0.091)*	(0.121)*‡	(0.162)*	(0.189)*‡
Tobit	-8.585	-1.529	-10.386	-4.121
	(0.568)*	(0.544)*‡	(1.139)*	(1.073)*‡
Tobit	-7.301	-0.969	-9.424	-3.003
	(0.583)*	(0.542)‡	(1.172)*	(1.077)*‡
Quantile (90th)	-4.187	-1.425	-2.632	-1.741
	(0.495)*	(0.189)*‡	(0.866)*	(0.492)*
Quantile (90th)	-2.322	-1.245	-1.781	-1.349
	(0.290)*	(0.134)*‡	(0.479)*	(0.401)*
	Dependent variable = Real (0/1)			
OLS	-0.105	-0.025	-0.102	-0.049
	(0.007)	(0.010)*‡	(0.012)*	(0.015)*‡
OLS	-0.090	-0.019	-0.096	-0.039
	(0.008)	(0.010)‡	(0.013)*	(0.015)*‡
Probit	-0.112	-0.019	-0.096	-0.037
	(0.007)*	(0.008)*‡	(0.010)*	(0.010)*‡
Probit	-0.091	-0.011	-0.092	-0.029
	(0.007)ᵛ	(0.008)‡	(0.011)*	(0.010)*‡

Notes: N=13,387 for all regressions. Excluded racial category is white. * implies p-value <0.01 for coefficient; ‡ implies that test of black=mixed coefficient rejects the null of equality at p<0.01. Test statistics for coefficient equality all exceed 10.00; most exceed 20. Probit regression report marginal effects. All regressions include a third-degree polynomial in age, literacy (0/1) dummy variable and either city or ward fixed effects. *Sources*: Author's calculations from 10-city southern sample. See text for description.

the wealth distribution is an informative statistic given that wealth is subject to extreme values.

In a previous study of personal wealth holdings for households included in the (now lost) rural 25-county sample, I used quantile methods because it was apparent from the data that there was idiosyncratic, census-marshal specific censoring. Only a handful of marshals returned values less than $5; a few more apparently censored around $10; still others around $20. With censoring, even quantile regressions are constrained to estimating relationships above the censoring point. For personal wealth it is likely that blank entries represented a censored entry, because "it would have been virtually impossible for anyone to have had no personal wealth under the definition provided in the instructions to enumerators."[49] Blank cells are very nearly prima facie evidence of censoring.

When considering personal wealth, attributing blank cells to censoring is reasonable and justifiable. In the case of real wealth, however, it seems less likely that marshals censored, at least to a meaningful extent. In the 10-city urban sample, values as low as $30 were reported, but $100 appears to be a common least reported amount across counties. The IPUMS sample, restricted to household heads in the South, returns real estate values less than $10. Even if these are erroneous entries, there are dozens of returns reporting real estate values less $50. Small values do not guarantee that no censoring occurred, but it is likely to be less consistent than censoring of personal property. That censoring is more common in personal property reports is evident in instances in which households report positive real estate values and blank personal property cells. Is it is hard to imagine that home owners owned no furniture or other household belongings.[50]

The takeaway from the literature is that there is no best technique to deal with nonreporting households, though three principal alternatives have emerged in the literature. Whether one prefers Tobit estimators that account for censoring, OLS for its ease of interpretation and its estimation of the conditional mean, or quantile regression that characterizes points other than the mean depends on the researcher's objective.[51] Regression coefficients, using all three procedures, are reported in Table A8.1.2. The results are discussed at length in Chapter 8.

Appendix 8.2 Selection of 25-County Rural Sample

The IPUMS provides a 1-percent random sample of US households in the 1860 census, which for the rural South includes just 173 households headed by a black adult and 99 households headed by a mixed-race adult. To provide a larger but still representative sample of African-American households in the rural South, I followed the county selection procedure outlined in Alice Hanson Jones's *Wealth of a Nation to Be.*

The procedure begins by ordering all southern rural counties by their free African-American populations in 1860 from most to least populous. Primarily urban counties (e.g., Baltimore, Maryland; Henrico (Richmond), Virginia; New Orleans, Louisiana) were dropped from this selection to ensure a focus on the rural South. Once the counties were ordered by population from Gibson County, Tennessee (93 free African Americans) to Frederick County, Maryland (4,957 free

African Americans). The free African-American population was then rounded to the nearest 100 and the cumulative population in rounded hundreds was assigned to each county, and a range of values surrounding the cumulative total for each county is then calculated. Table A8.2.1 clarifies the approach. Once the rounded cumulative totals were calculated, a random number generator provided a "start" value (=57) and a skip value (=64) was calculated to yield a sample of 25 counties. For a county to be included in the final sample, its cumulative rounded population value had to fall in the range defined by the series (57 + n×64), where

Table A8.2.1 Rural County Selection Procedure

Rank	State	County	Free Af-Am population	Rounded population	Cumulative population	Selection value
1	MD	Frederick	4957	50	1553–1602	1593
2	MD	Anne Arundel	4864	49	1504–1552	1529
3	MD	Dorchester	4684	47	1457–1503	1465
4	MD	Harford	3644	36	1375–1410	1401
5	VA	Accomack	3418	34	1305–1338	1337
6	MD	Kent	3411	34	1271–1304	1273
7	MD	Talbot	2964	30	1207–1236	1209
8	MD	Caroline	2786	28	1122–1149	1145
9	NC	Halifax	2452	25	1072–1096	1081
10	VA	Southampton	1794	18	1017–1034	1017
11	NC	Robeson	1462	15	953–967	953
12	NC	Craven	1332	13	884–896	889
13	MD	Prince George's	1198	12	822–833	825
14	VA	Campbell	1029	10	757–766	761
15	VA	Fauquier	821	8	692–699	697
16	VA	Goochland	703	7	633–639	633
17	VA	Northampton	659	7	565–571	569
18	LA	Baton Rouge-East	532	5	501–505	505
19	KY	Franklin	459	5	441–445	441
20	NC	Edgecomb	389	4	376–379	377
21	VA	Stafford	319	3	313–315	313
22	VA	Warren	284	3	247–249	249
23	VA	Northumberland	222	2	185–186	185
24	TN	Claiborne	176	2	121–122	121
25	KY	Bath	141	1	57	57

Source: US Census Bureau, Eighth Census (1860) *Census of Population*.

n=0, 1, 2, 3, . . ., 25. The county with the cumulative rounded value of 57 is Bath County, Kentucky; the county with the cumulative rounded value of 121 (57+64) is Claiborne County, Tennessee; the county with the cumulative rounded value of 185 (57+64+64) is Northumberland County, Virginia. The selection process yields the 25 counties included in Table A8.2.1.

Stratifying the counties in this way means that the most populous counties are more likely to be included. Smaller counties are less likely to be included. But every county was at risk for inclusion in the sample, depending on the randomly selected start value. The procedure yielded 2,794 rural African-American households. More details about the sample can be found in Bodenhorn, "Complexion Gap."

Appendix 8.3   Capitalized Wages and Human Capital

An economy's aggregate capital stock can be divided into four compo-nents: (1) machines and tools, (2) buildings and structures, (3) improvements to land, and (4) the productive capacities of workers, or what Adam Smith labeled the "acquired and useful abilities of all the inhabitants of members of the soci-ety."[52] Household studies tend to substitute machines and tools with financial capital—stocks and bonds—which are negotiable instruments that provide their owners with a (residual) claim on the produce of the machines and tools used by the firms owned by households. Thus research into the portfolios of modern households focuses on financial assets, real estate, proprietary business wealth, and human capital.[53]

Human capital is measured as "capitalized wages," which is defined as the pres-ent value of expected future income flows over the remainder of an individual's working life. For low-wealth, preretirement households ($10,000 to $100,000 in net worth), capitalized wages represent 66.2 percent of household wealth. For mid-wealth ($100,000 to $1 million) preretirement households, capitalized wages represent 48.2 percent of household wealth, but just 21.1 percent for high-wealth (more than $1 million net worth) preretirement households. Only the very wealthy rely primarily on nonwage sources of income to fund present and future consump-tion, so a complete description household wealth must account for human capital.

This appendix provides a preliminary study of differences in urban house-hold wealth by race, mixed race, and color in mid-nineteenth-century Virginia. Virginia's tax records provide a useful source for the study because Virginia taxed both personal and real property.[54] Taxes were imposed on a host of personal prop-erty, including slaves, animals, various household goods, monies invested in busi-nesses and rental properties, corporate share holdings, and land and buildings. For some taxable property the tax records list the number of taxable units (e.g., slaves 16 years or older, and slaves 12 to 16 years).[55] For some taxable property, values were added as well. The personal property tax sheets include both the number and value of horses, hogs, cattle, carriages, clocks, watches, and pianos. In yet other instances—namely gold, furniture, money invested in businesses, and corporate shares—marshals recorded only estimated values.

The personal property tax records were matched to the land tax records by taxpayer's name and location. Not every individual was matched, because not every owner of personal property was a land owner. When a personal property holder did not appear in the land tax book, it is assumed that the individual rented rather than owned his or her residence. Although real and personal property were recorded in separate ledgers they were enumerated at the same time, so it seems unlikely that tax commissioners would systematically fail to enumerate real property holdings of personal property owners.

Land tax records included less information than the personal property ledgers. In 1860 the city land tax records included the name of the owner, the number of lots owned, the value of buildings, the aggregate value of land and buildings, and the amount of tax due. The combined value of land and buildings is used in the wealth calculations. Although it is beyond the purpose of this study, it might be of interest to derive the imputed value of land separate from the structures on it.

Finally, the property and land tax records were matched to the 1860 census manuscripts. Using the individual's name, the names of neighbors, and locations, it was possible to match an unusually large 61.1 percent (1379 / 2256) of taxpayer cases to the census manuscripts. The census manuscripts were then used to identify the race and age of the taxpayer.

Using the matched cases, it is possible to determine the mean and median characteristics of householders in three Virginia cities. The sample is not representative of African Americans outside urban Virginia. The results cannot be extended to the South generally or even to the Upper South, given differences in the condition of African Americans in Maryland, Virginia, and North Carolina. Despite their limited applicability, the linked records do shed light on property ownership, its distribution, and its composition. The remainder of this appendix describes how the values for each of the principal wealth categories were constructed.

Value of Animals, Durables, and Real Estate

The value of animals (horses, cattle, and hogs) were taken directly from the personal property tax records. Virginia law excluded the first $100 of animals from state tax, so any reported value is the value in excess of $100. No adjustment is made to the reported amounts because little is known about the distribution of ownership below $100.

As with animals, the tax ledgers report not just the number of units but the total value of such household durables as clocks, watches, pianos, household and kitchen furniture, and carriages. The ledgers also record the value of gold and silver plate an jewelry.

Tax commissioners kept a separate ledger for recording the details of taxable real estate. Land owned by religious and fraternal groups, burial grounds, and schools and land owned by railroads were exempt. Ledgers include information on the name of the owner, the nature of the title (e.g., fee simple, life estate), the estimated or assessed value of any structures on a lot, the combined value of land and structures, the number of city lots constituting the land holding, and the amount of tax due. In the wealth calculations to follow, the combined value of land and structures is used as a measure of real estate wealth. Using the value recorded in the land tax records underestimates real estate wealth among the wealthy elite, who owned urban properties, as well as farms and plantations, or perhaps real estate in cities other than those investigated here.

Value of Slaves

Calculating the value of slaves owned is complicated because the tax records do not provide an assessed value. Rather, the ledgers report the number of slaves 16 years and older and the number of slaves between 12 and 16 years. Generating an estimate requires several assumptions. First, the distribution of slaves by age and sex can be determined from the 1860 census of population, which reports slaves by age categories (10–14, 15–19, 20–29, . . . 90–99) and sex. Second, from Alfred Conrad and Joseph Meyer's classic study, we know that the price of a prime field hand circa 1859/1860 was about $1,650. Third, price relatives by age and sex reported in Historical Statistics (Series) are used to estimate average slave prices by age category and sex. These values are then multiplied by the proportion of slaves in each sex/age category and the values summed to generate a population weighted average price of slaves in the three Virginia cities—Fredericksburg, Petersburg, and Richmond.[56] The results imply that the average price of slaves 12 to 15 years is $850, and the average for slaves 16 years and older is $710. The smaller value for older slaves follows from the rapid decline in price relatives beyond 30 years and the relatively large proportions of slave in those age categories.

Value of Business and Financial Assets

The value of proprietary business assets is reported in the tax ledgers as "capital invested" and included investments (other than real estate) invested in manufacturing or other unlicensed trade or business other than agriculture. The licensed trades included taverns and inns, so they are not included. The value of financial assets is taken from the tax ledgers, which included an amount of securities (stocks and bonds) of solvent companies. To the extent that tax records under-enumerate household wealth, this category seems most subject to misrepresentation by taxpayers. The reported values are used in the analysis, recognizing that they are likely establish a lower bound measure.

Value of Capitalized Wages (Human Capital)

Unlike the value of other assets, which were mostly taken from the tax ledgers themselves, an estimate of capitalized wages (human capital) is derived from the mean characteristics of the sample and information from outside sources. Several facts are necessary to generate estimates of the value of human capital: age, remaining working life, a discount rate, a representative occupation, and the average wage within that occupation. Each is discussed in turn.

Age and Remaining Working Life From the subsample of taxpayers linked to the 1860 census manuscripts, we know that the average age of mixed-race male householders in the sample is 36 years; for black and white male householders it is 38 years. For white males alive circa 1860, the best available estimates imply that life expectancy at age 35 was about 30 years.[57] Given the grueling nature of working-class jobs, I assume that at age 35, men might expect an additional 20 years of productive employment.[58] Altering the number of working years by modest amounts, either up or down, does not substantially change the results reported below.

Discount Rate Forensic economists who calculate the value of lost earnings in tort suits have not reached consensus on the appropriate basis for a discount factor. Some apply the risk-free rate on US Treasury obligations; others use returns on corporate bonds, large-cap stocks, or the return on a broad portfolio that includes a mix of each asset class.[59] For the mid-nineteenth century, 6 percent is a reasonable discount rate. Dividends on bank stock and bank lending rates varied around 6 percent over most of the period. Commercial paper rates were somewhat lower, but considerably more variable.[60] In the late 1850s, Virginia 6 percent state bonds traded at about $95, or a current yield of about 6.3 percent.[61] A 6 percent discount rate is reasonable.

Occupations and Wages Because African-American wealth was primarily earning capacity, the choice of wages is critical. Three alternative measures are used. First, the IPUMS 1860 sample of the manuscript census reports a socioeconomic index (SEI) score for each occupation. Restricting IPUMS to the South, the average black male SEI score is 10, the average mixed-race male SEI score is 15, and the average white male SEI score is 28. An SEI of 10 is consistent with an average occupation of domestic servant or an unskilled mill hand. An SEI of 15 is consistent with a blacksmith, and an SEI of 28 is consistent with a stone mason or a railroad conductor. Using the log wage regressions reported in Robert Margo and Georgia Villaflor's study of wages paid by the army for civilian workers implies that in the 1850s, common laborers were paid about $1.09 per day at southern forts. Blacksmiths were paid $1.58 per day. These values are used to generate one estimate of capitalized wages, assuming that workers were employed about 250 days per year. Corporate reports submitted to the Virginia legislature show that conductors on the Winchester and Potomac Railroad were paid $400 per year. Estimates of capitalized wages derived from these derivations appear in Table A8.3.1 as the Margo-Villaflor values.

A second estimate of capitalized wages is derived from information provided in the Virginia tax ledgers. The ledgers report incomes for selected individuals, because Virginia's tax code imposed an income tax on individuals paid a regular salary rather than daily or weekly wages. Using the subsample of the Virginia tax ledgers matched to the 1860 census, it is possible to identify incomes for blacks ($200/year), mixed-race ($400/year) and whites ($500/year). Estimates of capitalized wages derived from these values appear in Table A8.3.1 as the Virginia Tax Legder values.

A third estimate of capitalized wages was derived from information reported to the Virginia legislature from railroad reports on traffic, investment, revenues, and expenses in 1851. The Virginia Central Railroad reported that it paid 68 "colored" hands for road repair a total of $5,296.[62] The average repair worker (presumably unskilled) received an annual wage of $78. This value is used as an estimate of black wages. It is consistent with the IPUMS average of unskilled common labor for black males. The railroad also reported that it paid 28 "colored" workers employed in its machine shop a total of $6,202. The average skilled shop worker received an annual payment of $220. This value is used as an estimate of mixed-race wages; it is consistent with smithing as the average mixed-race employment. And the railroad paid its conductors $480 per year. This value is used as the average white wage. An advantage of these estimates is that they come from a single employer and industry. If repair work, shop work, and more skilled work were closely related to the railroad's routine operations, it reduces the need to estimate days worked per year. Estimates of capitalized wages derived from the Virginia Central records appear in Table A8.3.1 as the Virginia Central values.

Table A8.3.1 provides estimates of average household wealth by race and color. Approximately 90 percent of African-American wealth was human capital (capitalized wages). Black households held slightly more real estate, though the difference is neither statistically significant nor economically meaningful. Using the Virginia Central Railroad wages as the basis for comparison, black households held a considerably larger share of their wealth in real estate than mixed-race households. Eight percent of black household wealth was in real estate, compared to 3 percent among mixed-race households. Consumer durables—furniture, watches, and clocks—represented only 1 percent of household wealth for both blacks and mixed-race householders. Slaves represented 2 percent for both. Given that the records are for urban household and that Virginia's tax code excluded the first $100 in animals from taxation, livestock represented a trivial share of household wealth. Neither blacks nor mixed-race people had notable amounts invested in businesses or financial securities.

African-American wealth was almost entirely made up their human capital. Approximately 90 percent of African-American wealth was capitalized wages.

Table A9.1.1 Summary Statistics of the Virginia-Maryland Free African-American Adult Sample

	Free-born	*Manumitted*	*Free-born*	*Manumitted*
	Males	*Males*	*Females*	*Females*
Mixed race	0.21	0.13	0.21	0.14
Height	67.38	67.09	62.64	62.48
Coastal region	0.61	0.60	0.67	0.71
Mountain region	0.06	0.06	0.04	0.04
Piedmont region	0.33	0.34	0.29	0.25
Urban	0.11	0.03	0.13	0.04
Birth year	1817	1800	1818	1803
Registration year	1845	1832	1844	1834
Virginia	0.63	0.27	0.60	0.22

Notes: Adult sample includes males 22 to 45 years and females 19 to 45 years, or those likely to have reached terminal adult height and prior to the onset of old-age shrinkage. *Sources:* See References §1.3 and §1.7.

compared to 21 percent in the Virginia-Maryland sample. The sample proportions for free-born men and women are close to the population proportions. The table illuminates one notable difference between Virginia and Maryland, namely, that term slavery was much more common in Maryland than Virginia, which is evident in the much higher proportion of Virginia observations in the free-born samples and the higher proportion of Maryland observations in the manumitted sample.

Table A9.1.2 reports the basic OLS regression results with height in inches as the dependent variable. Estimated coefficients are consistent with the separate Komlos and Bodenhorn studies notably that free blacks living on or near the Atlantic Ocean or Chesapeake Bay were shorter than African Americans living in the Piedmont or the Blue Ridge Mountain. Urban registrants, too, were shorter than rural registrants. The coefficient of principal interest is of course the coefficient on mixed-race, which is consistent with taller average stature of mixed-race men and women after controlling for location of registration and birth cohort. Mixed-race men were an estimated 0.3 to 0.4 inches taller than black men, and mixed-race women were an estimated 0.2 to 0.4 inches taller than black women.

Estimates of height-at-age for each of the subgroups were also generated using Preece-Baines Model I. The Preece-Baines growth model is a family of logistic curves that conform to the human growth pattern. Although the model was

Table A9.1.2 Correlates of Adult Height By Sex and Status

	Free-born Males	Manumitted Males	Free-born Females	Manumitted Females
Mixed race	0.43	0.30	0.24	0.36
	(0.11)	(0.13)	(0.11)	(0.12)
Coastal region	−0.51	−0.30	−0.27	−0.32
	(0.16)	(0.22)	(0.13)	(0.16)
Mountain region	0.40	0.67	0.60	0.26
	(0.17)	(0.33)	(0.22)	(0.27)
Urban residence	−0.76	−0.65	−0.36	−0.30
	(0.14)	(0.35)	(0.13)	(0.11)
Born 1750s	−1.28	0.07	0.45	0.18
	(0.28)	(0.23)	(1.87)	(0.86)
Born 1760s	0.51	−0.61	−0.81	−0.04
	(0.59)	(0.32)	(0.76)	(0.34)
Born 1770s	0.45	−0.48	−0.36	0.42
	(0.29)	(0.18)	(0.40)	(0.09)
Born 1780s	−0.05	−0.19	−0.31	0.07
	(0.24)	(0.23)	(0.24)	(0.13)
Born 1790s	−0.00	−0.24	−0.02	0.22
	(0.16)	(0.15)	(0.12)	(0.12)
Born 1800s	0.18	−0.16	−0.09	0.12
	(0.12)	(0.14)	(0.15)	(0.15)
Born 1810s	reference groups			
Born 1820s	0.27	0.37	−0.12	−0.19
	(0.13)	(0.17)	(0.14)	(0.12)
Born 1830s	−0.08	−0.07	−0.57	−0.55
	(0.16)	(0.22)	(0.16)	(0.17)
Born 1840s	0.11	1.02	−0.49	−1.25
	(0.48)	(0.78)	(0.30)	(0.34)
Constant	67.56	67.32	62.98	62.62
	(0.18)	(0.27)	(0.16)	(0.17)
Observations	5,715	4,211	7,098	4,517
R-square	0.03	0.02	0.02	0.02
F-statistic	17.84	6.73	12.60	39.80

Notes: For males, constant refers to black man between 22 and 45 years of age registered in the rural Piedmont and born in the 1810s. For females, constant refers to a black woman between 19 and 45 years, registered in the rural Piedmont region and born in the 1810s. Robust standard errors, clustered on county of registration in parentheses. *Sources*: See Table A9.1.1.

developed and most often used for the analysis of longitudinal records from individual subjects, it can be applied to cross-sectional data.[64]

The Preece-Baines model is written as:

$$h_t = h_1 - \left[2(h_1 - h_\theta)\right] / \left\{\exp\left[s_0(t - \theta)\right] + \exp\left[s_1(t - \theta)\right]\right\}$$

where h_t is observed height at age t. The five estimated parameters are h_1, the terminal height; θ a time constant related to age at peak velocity; h_θ, height at age θ; and s_0 and s_1, which are age scale factors. The Preece-Baines equation has several advantages over alternative specifications: only five parameters are estimated, compared to six or seven parameters in other approaches; terminal height does not have to be observed but rather is estimated from the model; the equation adequately captures child growth between ages two and adulthood, especially the adolescent growth spurt; the equation nearly always converges using nonlinear least squares; and the resulting estimates are robust to a reasonable range of initial parameter values.[65] The disadvantages of the Preece-Baines model is that is does not adequately model growth prior to age two, which is not an issue in the present case because only children ages four or older are included in the estimation; and it generates premature age-at-takeoff estimates (actual takeoff occurs about 18 to 24 months later than the Preece-Baines model predicts), while its estimate of age-at-peak-velocity tends to be accurate.[66]

Table A9.1.3 reports the estimated parameter values for the principal race-sex groups. The estimates are plausible and well behaved for the groups for which there are about 1,000 or more observations. Estimates of terminal heights (h_1) are generally consistent with observed (out-of-sample) terminal adult heights—67 inches for males and 63 inches for females. Estimates of age at takeoff and age at peak velocity, derived from the estimated coefficients, are also consistent with estimated values for children growing in less than optimal circumstances (see discussion in Chapter 9).

Because height-at-age derived from the Preece-Baines coefficient estimates are smoothed and not subject to reversals (as are the actual observed values and the OLS estimates), they are used to construct centiles of modern stature. The estimated centiles, reported in the final columns of Table A9.1.4 through A9.1.11, delineate, at each age, where the average nineteenth-century African-American child of each sex and race would lie in the distribution of modern US heights. If early to mid-nineteenth-century African-American children matured at the same rate as children in the late 1970s United States, the estimated centiles would equal 50, or the mean height of the 1970s population. The estimated centiles, however, reveal that nineteenth-century African-American children were short by modern standards. The estimated terminal height of free-born, mixed-race males, for example, show that average member of that group achieved just the twenty-second centile of modern stature. That is, 78 percent of US adult males circa 1979 were taller than the average mid-nineteenth-century free-born, mixed-race male that registered in Virginia or Maryland.

Table A9.1.3 Preece-Baines Model 1 Parameter Estimates

	Obs	h_1	h_θ	Θ	s_0	s_1
Free-born, mixed-race						
Boys	1,080	67.72	63.91	16.17	0.11	1.04
		(0.12)	(0.29)	(0.23)	(0.006)	(0.16)
Girls	927	62.60	59.12	13.09	0.14	1.03
		(0.12)	(0.45)	(0.31)	(0.01)	(0.18)
Free-born, black						
Boys	3,723	67.12	62.69	15.64	0.10	0.81
		(0.08)	(0.29)	(0.20)	(0.006)	(0.07)
Girls	3,074	62.22	57.85	12.44	0.12	0.75
		(0.08)	(0.59)	(0.36)	(0.01)	(0.08)
Manumitted, mixed-race						
Boys	186	69.93	47.91	7.84	-0.004	0.23
		(2.60)	(43.49)	(17.51)	(0.26)	(0.22)
Girls	184	62.76	60.34	12.95	0.19	2.65
		(0.22)	(0.45)	(0.42)	(0.02)	(2.04)
Manumitted, black						
Boys	781	66.93	61.30	14.35	0.09	0.66
		(0.18)	(0.87)	(0.52)	(0.01)	(0.12)
Girls	647	62.86	56.31	11.29	0.09	0.51
		(0.29)	(3.87)	(2.12)	(0.05)	(0.15)

Notes: See text for discussion of Preece-Baines model. Sources: Author's calculations from combined Virginia-Maryland register sample. See References §1.3 and §1.7 for details.

Table A9.1.4 Heights of Free-Born, Mixed-Race Males

Age	Obs	Average	Std Dev	OLS	PB-I	Centile
4±	9	39.6	3.36	39.7	38.3	12.1
5±	6	41.0	1.74	40.8	41.4	16.4
6±	6	41.6	1.71	41.6	44.2	22.7
7±	11	46.6	5.50	46.6	46.6	26.4
8±	7	49.0	2.78	48.6	48.9	30.5
9±	13	50.2	2.57	50.3	50.9	29.8
10±	22	52.8	3.42	53.0	52.7	28.4
11±	10	55.3	2.80	55.5	54.3	21.8
12±	23	56.0	2.86	56.2	55.9	16.1
13±	18	57.2	4.70	57.5	57.4	10.6
14±	26	59.3	3.45	59.6	59.2	7.4
15±	28	61.4	3.01	61.6	61.2	5.1
16±	30	63.5	3.45	63.7	63.5	4.8
17±	40	65.1	3.72	65.4	65.5	6.6

(Continued)

Table A9.1.4 Continued

Age	Obs	Average	Std Dev	OLS	PB-I	Centile
18±	59	67.0	2.66	67.2	66.8	13.6
19±	73	67.8	2.84	68.2	67.4	19.5
20±	113	67.4	2.74	67.8	67.6	21.8
21±	355	67.7	2.50	68.0	67.7	22.7
22±	231	67.7	2.64	68.0	67.7	22.7
22–45	1178	67.9	2.66	—	—	—
22–70	1271	67.9	2.66	—	—	—

Notes: OLS estimates from regressions that control for decade of birth, region of registration, and urban-rural registration. PB-I estimates refer to estimates derived from a nonlinear least squares estimation of Preece-Baines model I. Centiles calculated from modern standards useful for historical comparisons reported in Steckel, "Percentiles," and heights generated from Preece-Baines estimation. *Sources*: Author's calculations from combined Maryland and Virginia register sample. See References §1.3 and §1.7 for details. Maryland sample described in Komlos, *Height of Free African Americans*. Virginia sample described in Appendix 5.1.

Table A9.1.5 Heights of Free-Born, Black Males

Age	Obs	Average	Std Dev	OLS	PB-I	Centile
4±	12	37.2	3.97	36.7	37.7	6.8
5±	16	40.2	3.05	39.7	40.6	8.2
6±	17	43.9	4.68	43.4	43.2	10.6
7±	20	46.3	1.98	45.7	45.6	13.4
8±	28	47.1	2.80	46.6	47.7	14.2
9±	29	49.9	2.68	49.5	49.7	14.5
10±	33	51.8	4.03	51.5	51.6	15.4
11±	33	52.5	3.51	52.3	53.3	14.7
12±	55	56.0	3.51	55.7	55.1	10.6
13±	67	56.1	3.16	55.9	57.0	8.5
14±	79	59.3	3.63	59.2	59.1	6.9
15±	82	61.7	3.59	61.5	61.3	5.5
16±	102	63.3	4.13	63.1	63.4	4.4
17±	135	64.9	2.80	64.8	65.0	4.4
18±	188	66.0	2.75	65.9	66.0	7.9
19±	202	66.4	2.77	66.3	66.6	11.9
20±	313	66.9	2.73	66.7	66.9	14.5
21±	1367	67.1	2.77	66.8	67.0	15.4
22±	945	67.0	2.75	66.8	67.1	16.4
22–45	4537	67.3	2.77	—	—	—
22–70	4843	67.2	2.77	—	—	—

Notes and sources: See Table A9.1.4.

Table A9.1.6 Heights of Slave-Born, Mixed-Race Males

Age	Obs	Average	Std Dev	OLS	PB-I	Centile
4±	1	40.0	—	39.5	39.2	24.5
5±	5	41.0	1.58	40.6	41.2	14.0
6±	0	—	—	—	—	—
7±	6	46.1	3.72	45.5	45.8	15.6
8±	1	42.0	—	41.7	48.3	21.5
9±	3	52.8	1.25	52.0	50.7	26.8
10±	4	54.3	2.90	53.4	53.1	34.1
11±	7	55.4	3.72	55.2	55.4	35.6
12±	3	58.0	3.43	57.7	57.6	33.4
13±	5	56.3	4.49	55.8	59.5	26.4
14±	8	60.5	3.59	60.5	61.2	19.2
15±	3	65.8	1.61	65.5	62.7	12.1
16±	11	65.2	3.19	65.1	64.0	6.7
17±	6	64.8	2.99	64.6	65.0	4.4
18±	6	66.0	3.00	65.7	65.9	7.4
19±	14	66.7	2.93	66.3	66.7	12.7
20±	13	67.3	4.33	67.2	67.3	18.4
21±	50	67.2	2.77	67.3	67.8	23.9
22±	40	68.8	2.85	68.6	68.2	29.1
22–45	554	67.5	2.72	—	—	—
22–70	648	67.4	2.71	—	—	—

Notes and sources: See Table A9.1.4.

Table A9.1.7 Heights of Slave-Born, Black Males

Age	Obs	Average	Std Dev	OLS	PB-I	Centile
4±	12	38.7	3.64	38.2	39.0	21.2
5±	3	44.8	2.25	45.3	41.4	16.4
6±	10	42.5	2.21	42.4	43.6	14.7
7±	9	45.3	3.20	45.0	45.7	14.5
8±	13	49.9	2.46	49.7	47.7	14.2
9±	15	48.3	6.14	47.9	49.7	14.5
10±	13	51.7	3.12	52.0	51.7	16.4
11±	18	54.2	2.98	54.0	53.8	16.9
12±	22	55.3	3.30	55.1	56.0	16.9
13±	10	59.4	2.63	59.2	58.3	16.1

(*Continued*)

Table A9.1.7 Continued

Age	Obs	Average	Std Dev	OLS	PB-I	Centile
14±	20	60.5	3.36	60.4	60.5	14.2
15±	14	63.1	4.88	63.4	62.6	11.5
16±	20	64.0	2.48	64.1	64.2	7.6
17±	32	64.5	3.46	64.6	65.3	5.5
18±	30	66.8	3.05	67.0	66.0	7.9
19±	37	66.9	2.66	67.2	66.4	10.6
20±	71	66.3	3.09	66.5	66.7	12.7
21±	238	66.8	2.85	67.1	66.8	13.6
22±	194	66.8	2.46	67.2	66.9	14.5
22–45	3657	67.0	2.63	—	—	—
22–70	4251	67.0	2.66	—	—	—

Notes and Sources: See Table A9.1.4.

Table A9.1.8 Heights of Free-Born, Mixed-Race Females

Age	Obs	Average	Std Dev	OLS	PB-I	Centile
4±	5	36.7	0.67	33.9	37.3	6.3
5±	9	41.4	4.45	38.7	40.7	14.0
6±	8	42.9	3.08	40.6	43.6	23.0
7±	16	46.2	4.17	43.6	46.1	26.8
8±	8	48.3	3.83	45.6	48.4	28.4
9±	21	50.8	3.52	48.0	50.5	27.4
10±	18	52.4	3.74	49.7	52.4	22.7
11+	16	54.2	4.02	51.6	54.5	19.2
12±	31	56.5	3.60	53.7	56.7	14.2
13±	30	59.2	3.00	56.4	58.9	13.4
14±	51	60.8	2.13	58.2	60.7	17.4
15±	63	61.6	2.40	58.9	61.8	23.9
16±	94	62.3	2.30	59.6	62.3	27.1
17±	114	62.3	2.61	59.7	62.5	24.5
18±	177	62.6	2.36	59.9	62.6	20.3
19±	146	62.7	2.53	60.0	62.6	20.3
20±	120	62.6	2.25	60.0	62.6	20.3
20–45	1318	63.0	2.64	—	—	—
20–70	1422	63.0	2.62	—	—	—

Notes and Sources: See Table A9.1.4.

Table A9.1.9 Heights of Free-Born, Black Females

Age	Obs	Average	Std Dev	OLS	PB-I	Centile
4±	22	37.2	2.53	37.9	37.8	10.6
5±	19	41.5	2.39	42.3	40.7	14.0
6±	22	42.6	3.07	43.3	43.4	20.1
7±	36	46.9	4.19	47.7	45.8	22.4
8±	21	48.0	4.08	48.8	48.1	24.5
9±	31	49.8	2.41	50.6	50.3	25.1
10±	30	51.9	4.16	52.7	52.5	23.9
11±	47	54.4	3.41	55.1	54.8	22.4
12±	78	57.1	3.33	57.9	57.0	16.9
13±	94	59.3	3.42	60.2	58.8	12.5
14±	135	60.4	2.92	61.2	60.2	12.9
15±	170	60.8	2.50	61.6	61.1	16.4
16±	321	61.6	2.59	62.3	61.7	20.1
17±	413	61.8	2.38	62.6	61.9	17.6
18±	585	62.0	2.38	62.8	62.1	14.9
19±	509	62.4	2.54	63.1	62.2	15.9
20±	541	62.2	2.57	62.9	62.2	15.9
22–45	5125	62.6	2.50	—	—	—
22–70	5474	62.6	2.49	—	—	—

Notes and Sources: See Table A9.1.4.

Table A9.1.10 Heights of Slave-Born, Mixed-Race Females

Age	Obs	Average	Std Dev	OLS	PB-I	Centile
4±	4	33.9	3.97	35.2	35.5	0.5
5±	7	41.8	2.60	43.2	40.3	9.9
6±	5	44.9	2.46	45.9	44.2	32.6
7±	3	46.2	3.62	47.0	47.5	50.0
8±	4	49.1	2.17	50.0	50.2	56.4
9±	3	51.0	4.77	52.6	52.4	54.4
10±	3	54.3	2.25	55.4	54.2	45.6
11±	3	57.7	2.52	58.9	55.8	33.7
12±	8	57.4	3.39	59.2	57.5	21.8
13±	4	60.5	2.94	61.2	60.5	30.2

(Continued)

Table A9.1.10 Continued

Age	Obs	Average	Std Dev	OLS	PB-I	Centile
14±	7	62.5	2.17	63.5	62.5	39.7
15±	11	63.4	3.30	64.1	62.7	35.2
16±	14	61.8	2.30	62.7	62.8	33.7
17±	15	63.7	2.18	64.6	62.8	28.4
18±	31	63.0	2.39	63.8	62.8	23.0
19±	29	62.3	2.43	63.2	62.8	23.0
20±	33	62.8	2.42	63.5	62.8	23.0
22–45	612	62.9	2.33	—	—	—
22–70	707	62.9	2.36	—	—	—

Notes and Sources: see Table A9.1.4.

Table A9.1.11 Heights of Slave-Born, Black Females

Age	Obs	Average	Std Dev	OLS	PB-I	Centile
4±	7	38.8	2.68	39.2	39.1	30.5
5±	15	41.7	2.43	42.3	41.6	27.8
6±	5	44.9	2.75	45.0	44.0	29.1
7±	14	46.5	3.37	47.1	46.5	33.0
8±	9	48.8	2.06	49.3	48.9	35.9
9±	15	50.8	4.13	51.4	51.3	38.2
10±	12	53.1	2.89	53.1	53.6	37.5
11±	7	57.1	2.58	57.3	55.7	32.6
12±	13	58.7	4.35	59.0	57.6	23.0
13±	16	58.8	4.67	59.0	59.2	15.9
14±	25	59.8	2.76	60.1	60.4	14.5
15±	28	61.5	2.13	61.7	61.2	17.4
16±	64	61.6	2.86	61.6	61.8	21.2
17±	91	62.2	2.36	62.3	62.2	20.9
18±	118	62.7	2.61	62.9	62.5	19.2
19±	81	62.5	2.56	62.6	62.6	20.3
20±	127	62.7	2.75	62.7	62.7	21.8
22–45	3795	62.4	2.41	—	—	—
22–70	4321	62.4	2.42	—	—	—

Notes and Sources: see Table A9.1.4.

NOTES

Chapter 1

1. *Ex parte John Scott Bailey*, Free Negro and Slave Records, Henrico County, Box 2 (1852), Library of Virginia.
2. *Ex parte Braxton Smith*, Free Negro and Slave Records, Henrico County, Box 2 (1853), Library of Virginia.
3. See Elliott, "Telling the Difference," Gross, "Litigating Whiteness," and Chapter 2 in this volume for the details of cases of racial determination across the South.
4. Berlin, *Slaves without Masters*, is the classic study.
5. Bureau of the Census, Seventh Census (1850), City of Richmond, Henrico County population manuscripts, 293–294.
6. Hochschild, Weaver, and Burch, "Destablizing the American Racial Order," 152.
7. Hochschild and Powell, "Racial Reorganization"; Walker, *In Search*, 290.
8. See, for example, Russell, Wilson, and Hall, *Color Complex*, for a discussion of colorism in its modern context.
9. "Hustings Court Registry of Free Negroes and Mulattoes" (Petersburg City, Virginia), Register 5296 (August 31, 1850).
10. *Register of Free Negroes and Mulattoes* (Henrico County, Virginia), Registers 1412–1413 (March 12, 1851).
11. The contributor to the nineteenth-century *Encyclopædia Perthensis*, 709, defined "mulatto" thus: "yellow-blackish colour, with black, short, frizzy hair."
12. Meaders, *Advertisements for Runaway Slaves*.
13. "Hustings Court Registry of Free Negroes and Mulattoes" (Petersburg City, Virginia), Register 5665 (December 29, 1851).
14. Ibrahim et al., *Fauquier County, Virginia Register*, various registers, #140–238.
15. In Brazil, there is a belief that money "whitens," in that richer people tend to be described as less dark than people with lower incomes and similar phenotypes. An intriguing but difficult to implement study would be to assess whether straight hair, narrow noses, or thin lips would have a similar whitening effect. There is little evidence that money whitened in the nineteenth-century Chesapeake region. See note 24 below.
16. Parra et al., "Color and Genomic Ancestry, 177–178."
17. Parra et al., "Color and Genomic Ancestry," 177.
18. Telles, "Racial Ambiguity," 12; and Parra et al., "Color and Genomic Ancestry," 177.
19. Harris, "Racial Identity in Brazil," 25–26; Telles, "Racial Ambiguity," 12.
20. Harris, "Racial Identity in Brazil," 22.

21. Parra et al., "Color and Genomic Ancestry"; Suarez-Kurtz et al., "Self-Reported Skin Color"; and Pimenta et al., "Color and Genomic Ancestry."

22. Parra et al., "Color and Genomic Ancestry," 180.

23. Pimenta et al., "Color and Genomic Ancestry," 11. Suarez-Kurtz, "Self-Reported Skin Color," 770, draw a similar conclusion.

24. Appendix 5.1 provides a description of the Virginia county court sources.

25. The baseline linear probability regressions, in which the binary dependent variable equals one if the individuals was categorized as black in the census, include county fixed effects and dummy variables that control for the individuals sex (female=1) and the census (1850=1). The standard errors are clustered on the census marshal to control for idiosyncratic classification across marshals. The constant term (0.63) is consistent with the overall proportion of free African Americans reported as black in the 1860 census (0.64), but slightly greater than the proportion in the slave South (0.59). US Census Office, 8th Census, *Population*, xi–xii.

26. In statistical parlance, the coefficients on occupation categories (construction, craft, farming, service, or professional employment) are small in absolute value and are neither individually or jointly significant.

27. Templeton, "Human Races." In their review of the genomic literature on race, Hochschild, Weaver, and Burch, *Creating a New Racial Order*, 87–93, argue that the social scientist's "social construct" theory is premised mostly on the fact that within-race genomic variation is greater than across-race variation, which suggests that people are more alike than not. The reality is that conventionally defined races—white, black, Asian, and Amerindian—have scientific usefulness. A genomic marker map of Asia is notably different than one of Europe. Hochschild et al., *Creating*, 92, conclude by stating "a genomic scientist's insistence that racial boundaries are irreducibly blurred is not the same thing as social scientists' insistence that race is a purely social construction." Notable differences in genomic markers between West Africans and Portuguese can be seen in Parra et al., "Color and Genomic Ancestry," Figure 2, 179. Box-and-whisker plots reveal no genetic marker overlap on an index of African ancestry.

28. Hochschild, Weaver, and Burch, *Creating a New Racial Order*, 10.

29. Nott and Gliddon, *Types of Mankind*, 450, 459. Charles Darwin's 1871 review of the literature reveals that contemporary scientific opinion ranged from as few as two to as many as sixty-three distinct races. See Hochschild, Weaver, and Burch, *Creating a New Racial Order*, 4.

30. Van Evrie, *Negroes and Negro "Slavery,"* 77.

31. Knox, *Races of Men*. It is not hard to find nineteenth-century drawings and lithographs that show the Irish with monkey-like faces. See, for example, the illustration titled "How the Street-Cleaning Authorities in New York Guard Against Summer Epidemics," in *Frank Leslie's Illustrated Newspaper* (August 2, 1879), reprinted in Anbinder, *Five Points*, 84.

32. Wilentz, *Rise of American Democracy*, 448–450, 479.

33. Curry, *Free Black in Urban America*, provides maps of several US cities, locating African-American residences.

34. Hartley, *The Go-Between*, 1.

35. Goodman, "Comment," 808. On the contrary view, see sources in footnote 21 and the discussion in footnote 27. See also Wade, *Troublesome Inheritance*; Murray, "Diversity of Life"; and Wade, "Race Has a Biological Basis."

36. Sollors, *Neither Black Nor White Yet Both*, 124.

37. Stephenson, *Race Distinctions in American Law*, 18. Stephenson was writing in the early twentieth century, by which time the one-drop rule was becoming the standard approach to racial classification. At that time, X would have been considered a mulatto by common usage, but would have been treated as socially, politically, and legally black. A century earlier, X would have been considered a mulatto and *not* socially—or, in some circumstances, legally—black. See Chapter 2 for a discussion of the law of race in the early nineteenth-century United States.

38. Stephenson, *Race Distinctions in American Law*, 19.

39. Jefferson to Francis C. Gray, *Writings of Thomas Jefferson: Correspondence*, VI, 436.
40. Jefferson to Francis C. Gray, *Writing of Thomas Jefferson: Correspondence*, VI, 437.
41. For a modern exploration of this phenomenon, see Chris Rock's documentary film *Good Hair* (2009). He discusses the importance of good hair with several prominent African Americans and shows the lengths to which African Americans go to straighten and otherwise alter their hair.
42. Stanton, *Leopard's Spots*, 150–151. See Browne, *Classification of Mankind*, for the nomenclature.
43. Sollors, *Neither Black Nor White Yet Both*, 119.
44. Mumford, "After Hugh," 287; Sollors, *Neither Black Nor White Yet Both*, 127–128.
45. Joseph, *Transcending Blackness*, 9–10.
46. Reuter, *Mulatto in the United States*. For criticisms of Reuter's research see Woodson, "Review of *The Mulatto in the United States*," 175 and Miller, "Review of *The Mulatto in the United States*," 219.
47. Cipolla, *Between Two Cultures*, 13.
48. Degler, *Neither Black Nor White*, 102.
49. Sollors, *Neither Black Nor White Yet Both*, 15.

Chapter 2

1. Baker, *Following the Color Line*, 151.
2. Stephenson, *Race Distinctions in American Law*, 19.
3. Davis, *Who Is Black*, 5.
4. *Plessy v. Ferguson*, 541.
5. In some accounts of this case, Ms. Phipps's first name is spelled "Susie." It is spelled "Suzy" in the court records, and I follow the spelling as it appears in the record.
6. A common-law writ, a mandamus ("command" in Latin) is a court-ordered writ requiring a government official to perform duties he or she either neglects or refuses to do. *Jane Doe v. State of Louisiana*, 371.
7. To see this, consider Jefferson's racial calculus if at each generation Suzy's forebear marries a white. At the first generation—Suzy's great-great-great grandparents—the cross between a black slave and a white would yield a mulatto ($M = \frac{1}{2}W + \frac{1}{2}B$), so that Suzy's great-great grandparent was a quadroon ($Q = \frac{3}{4}W + \frac{1}{4}B$), her great grandparent was an octoroon ($O = \frac{7}{8}W + \frac{1}{8}B$), her grandparent a meamelouc ($ME = 15/16W + 1/16B$), and her parent was a quarteron ($QU = 31/32W + 1/32B$). By nineteenth-century designation, Suzy then was sang-mele or one-sixty-fourth part black. See Table 1.1 and text for details of nomenclature and calculation.
8. *Jane Doe v. State of Louisiana*, 373.
9. Domínguez, *White By Definition*, 3.
10. See *Korematsu v. United States; Bolling v. Sharpe; McLaughlin v. Florida; Anderson v. Martin*; and Domínguez, *White by Definition*, 4–5.
11. *Plessy v. Ferguson*, 549.
12. Carbado and Moran, "Introduction," 14.
13. Jordan, "American Chiaroscuro"; Jordan, *White over Black*; Jordan, *White Man's Burden*.
14. Wright, "Who's Black," 521.
15. James, *New and Enlarged Military Dictionary*, unpaginated; Jordan, "American Chiaroscuro," 192; *New Encyclopedia*, vol. 15, 709.
16. Stewart, *Account of Jamaica*, 296; *New Encyclopedia*, vol. 15, 709.
17. Higginbotham, *Shades of Freedom*, 38.
18. Williamson, *New People*, 13. Given the presumption that at one-eighth black it was difficult to distinguish blackness, Williamson's quote may overstate the case. Nevertheless, after 1785 the law recognized as white some people previously considered mulatto.
19. Johnston, *Race Relations*, 192–194.

20. Higginbotham, *Shades of Freedom*, 36.
21. Williamson, *New People*. For the proliferation of the region's black laws in the eighteenth and nineteenth centuries see Guild, *Black Laws of Virginia* and Snethen, *Black Code of the District of Columbia*.
22. Gillmer, "Suing for Freedom," 594; *Anderson v. Millikin*, 9 Ohio 568. Although South Carolina never adopted a statutory definition, the precedent established in *State v. Cantey* (20 S.C. Law 614 (1835)) held that a man of one-sixteenth black ancestry could be considered white at law so long as the "person has been received and treated as white." The court held that to treat such people as black would be "cruel and mischievous." In practice, the decision created a fuzzy boundary between white and black, and one that was open to local interpretation.
23. Berlin, *Slaves without Masters*, 161–162.
24. In 1910 the statutory classification for a person of color was defined as having descended from a Negro to the third generation (one-eighth) in Florida, Georgia, Indiana, Kentucky, Maryland, Mississippi, North Carolina, South Carolina, Tennessee, and Texas. Michigan, Nebraska, Oregon, and Virginia had a second-generation (one-fourth) rule. Alabama had a fifth-generation (one-thirty-second) rule, which Virginia would later adopt. Still later Louisiana adopted a one-thirty-second rule and Virginia the any-known-ancestry (or one-drop) rule. See Stephenson, *Race Distinctions*, 16–19.
25. Berlin, *Slaves without Masters*, 99.
26. Gross, *What Blood Won't Tell*, 25–30; *Gregory v. Baugh*, 25 Va. 611.
27. A statistical analysis of the 69 most widely discussed cases presented in Appendix 2.1 suggests that performance was not determinative in the typical case, but this is not inconsistent with the hypothesis that performance mattered in some high-profile cases.
28. Gross, "Litigating Whiteness," 186–187. Helen Catterall, *Judicial Cases concerning American Slavery*, collects all kinds of appellate-level cases involving African Americans, including freedom suits.
29. See, for example, Hickman, "Devil and the One-Drop Rule," 1185, in which she dismisses the traditional explanation for including separate *mulatto* and *black* categories in mid-nineteenth-century censuses; namely, that mulattoes were held in higher esteem than blacks. She attributes the separate census counts as part of a white agenda to discredit existing notions of mulatto superiority.
30. *Gobu v. Gobu*, 1 N.C. 188 (1802).
31. See, for example, *Rawlings v. Boston*, 3 H. & McH. (Md.) 139 (1793); *Hudgins v. Wrights*, 11 Va. 134 (1806); *Hook v. Nanny Pagee*, 16 Va. 379 (1811); *Gregory v. Baugh* 25 Va. 611 (1827); *Adelle v. Beauregard*, 1. Mart. 183 (1810); *Vaughan v. Phebe*, 8 Tenn. 5 (1827); *Miller v. Denman*, 16 Tenn. 233 (1835); *Gentry v. McMinnis*, 33 Ky. 302 (1835), Johnson, "Slave Trader," 13–38.
32. *Hook v. Nanny Pagee*, 16 Va. 379 (1811).
33. Gross, "Litigating Whiteness"; Gross, *What Blood Won't Tell*; and Johnson, "Slave Trader." Stephan Talty, *Mulatto America*, 7, also argues that white slaves might "unnerve an entire town."
34. See Appendix 2.1.
35. *Miller v. Denman*, 16 Tenn. 233 (1835).
36. Quoted in Gross, *What Blood Won't Tell*, 1.
37. DeCuir and Dixson, "'So When it Comes Out,'" 26.
38. Of 15,372 inhabitants in Jefferson Parish in 1860, 5120 were slaves and 287 were free colored. See mapserver. lib.virginia.edu/php/county.php.
39. DeCuir and Dixson, "'So When It Comes Out,'" offer an approachable account of critical race theory and its application to education studies. Carbado and Gulati, in "Law and Economics," attempt a reconciliation of critical race theory and the economics of law.
40. Sharfstein, "Secret History," 1473.
41. In 1958, John Calhoun ("Who Is a Negro?") considered it "ludicrous" that a person with one-sixteenth black ancestry might legally change races by moving from Prince Georges County, Maryland to Prince George County, Virginia.

42. See, for example, Harris, "Whiteness as Property."
43. Rubin, "Why is the Common Law Efficient?" Bodenhorn and Ruebeck, "Endogeneity of Race," offer a simple game-theoretic model consistent with critical race theory's hypothesis that race is determined by circumstances; Ruebeck, Averett, and Bodenhorn, "Acting White or Acting Black," and Fryer et al., "Plight of Mixed Race Adolescents," offer models and empirical investigations into the racial choices of mixed-race people based on the traditional maximizing rational choice approach.
44. Berlin, *Slaves without Masters*, 33–34; but see also Grinberg, "Freedom Suits," who believes that freedom suits became less rather than more common as the antebellum era progressed. She might be correct, but the decline might be the result of more settlements and fewer cases once the law was well established.
45. Coase, "Problem of Social Cost."
46. Chapter 4 provides a detailed analysis of manumission as do Bodenhorn, "Manumission in Nineteenth-Century Virginia" and Cole, "Capitalism and Freedom." Critical race theorists are not alone in their inconsistent assessment of slave agency. Many modern studies recognize slave agency in filing freedom suits, but emphasize their victimization in other areas of their lives. Walter Johnson, for example, inheres the white, female slave with agency in her pursuit of freedom, but strips her of it in matters of sex and sexual exploitation. If white planters were ambivalent about an all-but white slave serving at hard field labor, they were probably at least as ambivalent about white all-but slaves as unwilling sexual partners. See Johnson, "Slave Trader," who discusses how white planters projected their sexual fantasies on white slaves.
47. Higginbotham and Kopytoff, "Racial Purity," 1984.
48. Sharfstein, "Secret History of Race," 1498–1499.
49. Degler, *Neither Black Nor White*, 225. After reviewing several of the same cases discussed above, Degler concludes that American carved out very little space for mulattoes and then only grudgingly (pp. 239–245). I think Degler's conclusion fails to appreciate many of the subtleties of nineteenth-century American race relations. Chapters 4 through 10 in this volume make, I believe, a compelling case for nineteenth-century American mulatto exceptionalism.
50. That the statutes explicitly included mulattoes suggests that people accepted legal and social differences between whites and blacks and mulattoes. A black code that did not explicitly include mulattoes was presumed to exclude them because mulattoes were not inherently the same as blacks.
51. Virginia Acts 1832, Ch. 80, §1, p. 51; quoted also in Higginbotham and Kopytoff, "Racial Purity."
52. *Code of Virginia*, Ch. CVII, 465–468.
53. Patrick Henry delivered his famous "give me liberty, or give me death" speech in St. John's Church. Burton, *Annals of Henrico Parish*, 225–260.
54. *State v. Kimber* (1859 Ohio. Misc. LEXIS 58).

Chapter 3

1. Quoted in Gross, *What Color Won't Tell*, 50.
2. Gross, "Beyond Black and White," 650.
3. Child, "The Quadroons," 117, 133.
4. Brown, *Clotel*, 63.
5. Zanger, "Tragic Octoroon," 63, lists 17 accounts of the tragic mulatto tale. There are countless lesser ones and many others, such as Cooper's account of Cora in *Last of the Mohicans*, that do not technically qualify as a tragedy because the heroine's death is not directly attributable to the surprise discovery of her part-African ancestry. See Cooper, *Last of the Mohicans*, II: 92 for Colonel Munro's revelation of Cora's ancestry to Major Duncan Heyward.
6. See Joseph, *Transcending Blackness*, Chapters 1 and 2 for a discussion of modern tragic mulattas.

7. Zanger, "Tragic Octoroon," 64.

8. Guillory, "Some Enchanted Evening."

9. Sollors, *Neither White Nor Black Yet Both*, 240.

10. For the authoritative account of the Jefferson-Hemings saga see Gordon-Reed, *Hemingses of Monticello*. Despite Gordon-Reed's monumental effort, the extent of the Jefferson-Hemings relationship remains unclear.

11. Reid, "Oçeola," 33.

12. Reid, "Oçeola," 34.

13. Stowe, *Uncle Tom's Cabin*, 112.

14. Stowe, *Uncle Tom's Cabin*, 184–186.

15. Frederickson, *Black Image in the White Mind*.

16. Sollors, *Neither White Nor Black Yet Both*, 240.

17. Walt Whitman, *Franklin Evans*, quoted in Sollors, *Neither Black Nor White Yet Both*, 204.

18. Reid, "Oçeola," 425.

19. Bernard, *Travels through North America*, II, 62.

20. Guillory, "Some Enchanted Evening," 5–6; Sullivan, *Rambles and Scrambles*, 223; Tasistro, *Random Shots*, II, 20; Lachance, "Formation of a Three-Caste Society."

21. Stedman, *Narrative of Joanna*, 5–6; Price and Price, *Narrative Account*.

22. Jefferson, *Notes on the State of Virginia*, 230–231.

23. Jefferson, *Works*, V, 277; Jefferson, *Works*, IV, 98.

24. Martineau, *Society in America*, I, 150, 262, 155, 268.

25. Kemble, *Journal of a Residence*, 98, 194, 199; see also Olmsted, *Cotton Kingdom*, I, 140.

26. Sullivan, *Rambles and Scrambles*, 201, 362.

27. Sullivan, *Rambles and Scrambles*, 357; Olmsted, *Cotton Kingdom*, I, 302; Kemble, *Journal of a Residence*, 98.

28. Olmsted, *Cotton Kingdom*, I, 40, 142; Wright, *Views of Society*, 461.

29. Dain, *Hideous Monster of the Mind*, 7.

30. Stocking, *Race, Culture, and Evolution*, 45.

31. Horsman, *Josiah Nott of Mobile*, 104–105.

32. Quoted in Sellers, *Neither Black Nor White Yet Both*, 38–39.

33. A *farrago*, of course, is a confused mixture.

34. Brackenridge, *Adventures of Captain Farrago*, 140–141.

35. Lawrence, *Lectures on Physiology*, 225–226.

36. Lawrence, *Lectures on Physiology*, 241–242. This definition of species persists: *Webster's New World Dictionary* (1976) defines species as "the fundamental biological classification, comprising a subdivision of a genus and consisting of a number of plants or animals all of which have a high degree of similarity, can generally interbreed only among themselves, and show persistent differences from members of allied species."

37. Lawrence, *Lectures on Physiology*, 245.

38. Lawrence, *Lectures on Physiology*, 250.

39. Stanton, *Leopard's Spots*, 46.

40. Horsman, *Josiah Nott of Mobile*, 210–220.

41. Nott's life and career and theories have been studied by many scholars. The definitive account is Horsman's *Josiah Nott of Mobile*. Useful accounts appear in Stanton, *Leopard's Spots*, Frederickson's *Black Image in the White Mind*, Smedley's *Race in North America*, and Toplin's "Between Black and White."

42. Nott, "Mulatto A Hybrid," 253–254.

43. Nott, "Mulatto A Hybrid," 255.

44. Horsman, *Josiah Nott of Mobile*, 156–167.

45. Stocking, *Race, Culture, and Evolution*, 49.

46. Stocking, *Race, Culture, and Evolution*, 48.

47. Nott, "Mulatto A Hybrid," 255.

48. Barrow, Sandilands, and Hill, "Recent Accounts," 159–161. Salmond, *Bligh*, finds that the early reports of success of the Pitcairn colony were overstated, but Nott had no basis other than his skepticism to reject recent accounts.

49. As Irmscher, *Louis Agassiz*, 232 notes, the most striking feature of the photos to modern eyes is the slaves' fundamental humanity despite their captivity and degrading treatment.

50. Gould, *Mismeasure of Man*, 82–104 shows that Morton's measurements and statistical analyses were flawed, but attributes it to honest error rather than deliberate mispresentation.

51. Irmscher, *Louis Agassiz*, 239.

52. Campbell, "Negro-Mania," 522.

53. See Tenzer, *Forgotten Cause*, Chapter 3, for a discussion of Wilson, Kneeland, Kennedy, and others who accepted and repeated Nott's conclusions.

54. Irmscher, *Louis Agassiz*, 227–229.

55. See Berzon, *Neither White Nor Black*, 24–25.

56. Quoted in Tenzer, *Forgotten Cause*, Chapter 3.

57. Anonymous, "Black and Mulatto Population," 588.

58. Nott, "Geographical Distribution of Animals and Races of Men," quoted in Stanton, *Leopard's Spots*, 160.

59. Averages reported in Stanton, *Leopard's Spots*, 51; see Morton, *Crania Ægyptiaca*, 17 for his presentation of raw data and his conclusion that at least some Egyptians were mixed-race people.

60. For a recent reinterpretation of Morton's data and conclusions see Lehrer, "When We See What We Want," C12.

61. Irmscher, *Louis Agassiz*, 259–260.

62. Toplin, "Between Black and White," 197–198.

63. Quoted in Irmscher, *Louis Agassiz*, 247.

64. Gatewood, *Aristocrats of Color*, 154.

65. Quoted in Irmscher, *Louis Agassiz*, 252.

66. Croly and Wakeman, *Miscegenation*.

67. Howells, *An Imperative Duty*, 5 (quoted in Berzon, *Neither Black nor White*, 110).

68. See Hamermesh and Biddle, "Beauty and the Labor Market," for an early study of the connection between attractiveness and labor market outcomes.

Chapter 4

1. Johnston, *Race Relations*, 254–255.

2. Rothman, "James Callender and Social Knowledge," 96–108.

3. See Gordon-Reed, "Logic and Experience," and *Hemingses*, as well as essays in Lewis and Onuf (eds), *Sally Hemings & Thomas Jefferson*. In her interpretation of Jefferson's life, Gordon-Reed does not cast Jefferson as a hypocritical racist. She presents him as a complicated man—simultaneously a political revolutionary and legal conservative, an advocate of liberty and owner of slaves, a race-relations optimist and a racial pragmatist—subject to sexual impulses and the constraints of his own and his contemporary's opinions. Contradictory beliefs and acts are not necessarily hypocrisy.

4. McFeely, *Frederick Douglass*, 5–8.

5. McFeely, *Frederick Douglass*, 21–23.

6. McFeely, *Frederick Douglass*, 29.

7. Despite the privileges bestowed on him at Wye House, Douglass wrote: "I had been treated as a *pig* on the plantation; in this new [Baltimore] house, I was treated as a *child*." Douglass, *My Bondage and My Freedom*, 142.

8. Winthrop Jordan, "Foreword," in Johnston, *Race Relations*, vi.

9. Although *miscegenation* is more commonly used, the term was not coined until 1863 in a pamphlet titled *Miscegenation: The Theory of the Blending of the Races Applied to the American White Man and Negro*, designed to unseat Abraham Lincoln in the presidential race. Revealed as a

hoax, the pamphlet written by proslavery men David Croly and George Wakeman claimed to reveal that the secret agenda underlying Lincoln's war of emancipation was race mixing and interracial marriage. This was a long-standing contention used by proslavery advocates to undermine abolitionism. The American Colonization Society, for example, was compelled to state that it found amalgamation repugnant (see "Amalgamation of Races"). The term *miscegenation* did not gain widespread usage until well after the Civil War. Antebellum Americans were far more likely to use *amalgamation*—which means a mixture or blend—to signify race mixing, and I employ the latter term here. See Young, *Colonial Desire*, 144–146, and Hollinger, "Amalgamation and Hypodescent."

10. Guild, *Black Laws*, 21. One anonymous reader suggested that the language used may indicate that the black in question was not a woman, so that the "abuse" was homo- rather than heterosexual intercourse. There is no way to determine this from the source, but it was not uncommon for contemporaries to use the word *negress* when discussing female blacks. No other historian, to my knowledge, has advanced the homosexual interpretation.

11. Guild, *Black Laws*, 24–31.

12. Johnston, *Race Relations*, 166; Snethen, *Black Code of the District of Columbia*, 11.

13. Chamberlayne, *Vestry Book*, 36.

14. Fogel and Engerman, "Philanthropy at Bargain Prices," 390.

15. Posner, *Sex and Reason*, 209; see also 184–185.

16. Maryland's 1661 law prohibiting interracial marriage required any English woman who subsequently married a slave to serve the slave's master during her husband's life and declared any children from the marriage slaves. Any children of then-existing marriages were to serve until age 30. Woodson, "Beginnings," 339–340.

17. Stampp, *Peculiar Institution*, 22; Johnston, *Race Relations*, 186; Kinney, *Amalgamation!*, 4.

18. Stampp, *Peculiar Institution*, 22. Stampp's assertion is consistent with studies in evolutionary psychology, which show that people are more likely to attribute traits to others based on age and sex than on race (see Ridley, "Basic Human Nature," C4). Moreover, America's sharp racial divide was not yet fully formed in the seventeenth century (see Jordan, *White Over Black*), so that race mixing was more likely in the seventeenth than the nineteenth century.

19. Morgan, "Interracial Sex in the Chesapeake," 60; Gillmer, "Suing for Freedom," 557 estimates that between one-quarter and one-third of mixed-race children were born to white women in the colonial era. Heinegg, *Free African Americans*, finds that a small fraction of mixed-race families originated from white men and black women; most were the legacy of relationships between black men and white women.

20. Russell, *Free Negro in Virginia*, 125.

21. Woodson, "Beginnings," 347.

22. "Account of the Number of Souls in the Province of Maryland," 261.

23. Woodson, "Beginnings," 350.

24. American Anti-Slavery Society, *Legion of Liberty!*, unpaginated.

25. Blassingame, *Slave Testimony*, 221.

26. Blassingame, *Slave Testimony*, 400–401.

27. Morgan, "Interracial Sex in the Chesapeake," 63.

28. Stampp, *Peculiar Institution*, 353.

29. Kemble, *Journal of a Residence*, 209, 229, relates three such instances from her experience on a Georgia rice island: one mixed-race slave child's white father was a local bricklayer; another was the daughter of a slave and an overseer; the third was the product of a slave and a neighboring planter's son. Kemble was troubled by interracial relationships, but locals accepted them as rather matter-of-fact occurrences.

30. Dusinberre, *Them Dark Days*, 111–112.

31. Genovese, *Roll Jordan Roll*, 415, 422.

32. Stampp, *Peculiar Institution*, 355.

33. Stampp, *Peculiar Institution*, 355.

34. McLaurin, *Celia, A Slave*.

35. Morgan, "Interracial Sex in the Chesapeake," 75.
36. Jones, "Rape in Black and White," 93.
37. Hickman, "Devil and the One Drop Rule," 1177; Jones, "Rape in Black and White," 95.
38. Posner, *Sex and Reason*, 30.
39. Fogel and Engerman, *Time on the Cross*; Gutman and Sutch, "Victorians All?"; and Steckel, "Miscegenation."
40. My discussion follows Francis, "Economics of Sexuality."
41. "There is no dispute." See Becker and Stigler, "De Gustibus Non Est Disputandum."
42. Posner, *Sex and Reason*, 113.
43. Quoted in Guillory, *Some Enchanted Evening*, 80.
44. Olmsted, *Cotton Kingdom*, I, 307–308; Johnston, *Race Relations*, 237–238; Rothman, "James Callender and Social Knowledge," 96.
45. Blassingame, *Slave Community*, 156.
46. Martineau, *Society in America*, I, 260.
47. Stampp, *Peculiar Institution*, 359.
48. Quoted in Genovese, *Roll Jordan Roll*, 421.
49. Quoted in Jones, "Rape in Black and White," 98.
50. Rothman, *Notorious in the Neighborhood*, 127, relates several stories of mob justice. In 1856, for example, approximately 20 men broke into the house of Jordina Mayo, a black woman who lived in Richmond, Virginia's riverfront district. They were looking for John McRoberts, a white man known to have taken up with Jordina. McRoberts was dragged from Jordina's residence, bound with a rope, and thrown into the canal. When the pulled him out, nearly drowned, they painted him black, so he would match the color of his "paramour." Both Jordina and John were told to stop cohabiting and to leave. It appears, however, that the mob was concerned with more than interracial sex. Jordina was of notoriously bad character, ran a "disorderly house," and the police had rousted her on several occasions, but without the desired effect. The mob exploited Jordina and John's interracial relationship to bring about an extralegal resolution to recurring issue with Jordina's behavior. After this incident, Richmond's Mayor's court sentenced Jordina Mayo to ten lashes and John McRoberts to a jail term. The message was clear: interracial sex might be tolerated and bad behavior might be overlooked up to a point, but bad behavior and interracial sex would not go unpunished.
51. Billings, "Law of Servants and Slaves," 55.
52. Stampp, *Peculiar Institution*, 350.
53. Russell, *Free Negro in Virginia*, 127.
54. Jones, "Sex in Black and White,"
55. White, *Ar'n't I a Woman*, 86; Clover, "This Horably Wicked Action."
56. Wallenstein, *Tell the Court*, 47.
57. Johnston, *Race Relations*, 221–222.
58. Kinney, *Amalgamation!*, 9.
59. Block, *Rape and Sexual Power*, 242–243.
60. Economists discuss two alternative income effects. If consumption rises with income, the good is labeled "normal"; if consumption falls with income, it is labeled "inferior." Neither term has a normative connotation. Pizza, for example, is delicious, but higher income people tend to consume less pizza than lower income people, so pizza is considered an inferior good.
61. Rothman, *Notorious in the Neighborhood*, ch. 3.
62. Fogel and Engerman, in *Time on the Cross*, 133, estimate that white men fathered about one to two percent of children on plantations. Gutman and Sutch, "Victorians All," 148–153, generate an estimate in the range of four to eight percent. Using the WPA slave narratives, Thelma Jennings, "Us Colored Women," 66, found that about one in eight slave women (63 of 514 interviewees) mentioned interracial sex; of those 63, 22 claim to have been involved, 9 claimed to have been the children of white masters, and 36 noted that masters engaged in sex with slaves. Jennings's finding that 9 of 514 (1.75 percent) former female slaves claim to

have been the child of a white master is consistent with the Fogel and Engerman estimate. The 4.3 percent (22 of 514) estimate seems low for the extent of interracial mixing, but most of the slaves interviewed by the WPA would not have been sexually mature at emancipation. Catherine Clinton, "Caught in the Web," estimates that forcible rape may have occurred on about one in five southern plantations. Sex, along the spectrum from consensual intimacy to rape, occurred on plantations, but not at the same rate, which suggests that white men had different preferences and/or faced different costs.

63. Steckel, "Miscegenation," used the presence of a mixed-race child 10 years or younger. A lot could change on a plantation in 33 months, a lot more could change in 129 months, so a briefer window seems preferable.

64. Fogel and Engerman, *Time on the Cross*.

65. The results are not inconsistent with the hypothesis that larger plantations simply afforded more opportunities for nonconsensual sex with slave women. Dusinberre, *Them Dark Days*, 248–250 offers this argument. He contends that overseers were wanton sexual carousers on the larger plantations; more females made for more forcible sex and more mixed-race children. But the regressions underlying Figure 4.1 and reported in Appendix 4.1 control for plantation administration types and the coefficients on overseer managed plantations are universally negative, though they are small in magnitude (typically -0.02 to -0.03, or a 2 to 3 percent lower probability of observing a mixed-race child on these plantations) and not significantly different from the comparison group owner-managed plantations.

66. Quoted in Genovese, *Roll Jordan Roll*, 413.

67. Johnston, *Race Relations*, 217.

68. Jacobs, *Incidents in the Life of a Slave Girl*.

69. See Lachance, "Formation of a Three-Caste Society," for a discussion of Louisiana slave owners providing bequests to slaves.

70. Douglass, *Life and Times*, 37.

71. Benwell, *Englishman's Travels in America*, 117–118.

72. Dusinberre, *Them Dark Days*, 113–114.

73. Dusinberre, *Them Dark Days*, 114–115.

74. Benwell, *An Englishman's Travels*, 118.

75. Kemble, *Journal of a Residence*, 194.

76. Kemble, *Journal of a Residence*, 240.

77. Quoted in Johnston, *Race Relations*, 299.

78. Frazier, *Black Bourgeoisie*, 113, 136–137.

79. Jordan, *White Over Black*, 169.

80. Genovese, *Roll Jordan Roll*, 328; see Gillmer, "Suing for Freedom," 594 for a more recent statement.

81. Olson, "Occupational Structure," 159–160.

82. Kotlikoff, "Quantitative Description."

83. Margo, "Civilian Occupations," 178 (table 9.5).

84. Toplin, "Between Black and White," 192.

85. Olmsted, *Journey in the Seaboard States*, 421, 426–429.

86. Toplin, "Between Black and White," 188.

87. Kotlikoff, "Structure of Slave Prices," 501 (table II).

88. Kotlikoff, "Quantitative Description," 43.

89. Calomiris and Pritchett, "Preserving Slave Families for Profit."

90. Cole, "Capitalism and Freedom," 1022 (table 5).

91. Kotlikoff, "Quantitative Description."

92. Dusinberre, *Them Dark Days*, 156.

93. Sullivan, *Rambles and Scrambles*, 223, 360.

94. Sullivan, *Rambles and Scrambles*, 200–201.

95. Quoted in Talty, *Mulatto America*, 7.

96. Bennett, "Miscegenation in America," 95.

97. Kotlikoff, "Quantitative Description."
98. Dusinberre, *Them Dark Days*, 191.
99. Dusinberre, *Them Dark Days*, 178–210, especially 195–201.

Chapter 5

1. Quoted in McFeely, *Frederick Douglass*, 54.
2. US Census Office, 8th Census, *Population*, xii.
3. Quoted in Turtle, "Slave Manumission in Virginia," 65.
4. Jefferson to John Holmes (April 22, 1820) on the Missouri question. In Ford (ed.), *Works of Thomas Jefferson*, vol. 12, 159.
5. Quoted in Finkelman, "Jefferson and Slavery," 192.
6. Jackson, "Manumission in Certain Virginia Cities," for example, notes that nearly every petition to remain that came before the Petersburg, Virginia Hustings Court was granted.
7. *M'Cutchen et al v. Marshall et al.* (33 US 220 at 238).
8. *Fisher's Negroes v. Dabbs et al.* (14 Tenn. 119 at 126).
9. Patton, "Progress of Emancipation," 75.
10. Klebaner, "American Manumission Laws," emphasizes this explanation.
11. In his autobiography, former slave William Green wrote: "Having a great many relations who were almost all free, and I being a slave, made me very unhappy, and every day I became more and more determined to be free or die in the attempt." (Quoted in Condon, "Significance of Group Manumission," 84.)
12. Jefferson, *Notes on Virginia*, 209–210.
13. Brana-Shute and Sparks, *Paths to Freedom*, vii.
14. Caroll, "Religious Influences," contends that manumission in early Maryland was driven largely by religious beliefs, especially among Quakers, Nicholites and Methodists whose congregants turned against slavery in the mid-eighteenth century.
15. Wolf, "Manumission and the Two-Race System," 309.
16. Whitman, *Price of Freedom*; and Wolf, *Race and Liberty* and "Manumission and the Two-Race System."
17. In *Bryan v. Wadsworth* (18 N.C. 384) the Supreme Court of North Carolina declared that even after a slave's performance of some extraordinarily meritorious act, the legislature could not manumit a slave without the owner's consent.
18. West, *Family or Freedom*, contends that we gain a deeper understanding of slave societies by investigating whether the state allowed, and, if so, when it allowed people to voluntarily seek to enslave themselves. In 1856 Virginia passed a law that facilitated voluntary African-American enslavement. She reports that between 1856 and 1865 35 people were legally re-enslaved. This is an average of 3.5 persons per year. With a free African-American population of 58,000, her re-enslavement estimates imply that 0.006 percent of free blacks per year were granted re-enslavement. Not every request was granted. William Ewing expressed a not uncommon attitude, even among Southerners, when he wrote: "I do not think... that a man had a right to dispose of his freedom by his own voluntary act.... Liberty is that thing with which he is endowed by his Creator, and being so endowed, he cannot, by his own act, dispose of it" (quoted in West, *Family or Freedom*, 43). Slavery was an involuntary condition, which was an idea Southerners were comfortable with.
19. Brana-Shute, "Sex and Gender," 179.
20. Patterson, "Three Notes to Freedom," 17–18; Whitman, *Price of Freedom*; Phillips, *Freedom's Port*; Wolf, *Race and Liberty*; Budros, "Social Shocks."
21. Wolf, "Manumission and the Two-Race System," 322.
22. Quoted in Wolf, "Manumission and the Two-Race System," 324.
23. Turtle, "Slave Manumission in Virginia," 42, 59. Olwell, "Becoming Free," found a similar, if less pronounced, wave of manumissions in post-Revolutionary South Carolina. Between

1775 and 1785, about 25 manumissions were recorded each year of that decade, compared with an average of five per year between 1737 and 1774.

24. Philips, *Freedom's Port*, 36–37. Counter to traditional interpretations, Irwin, "Explaining," shows that slavery and grain production were compatible and that the economics of slavery in cotton and tobacco, such as economies of scale, applied to grain production.

25. Acemoglu and Wolitzky, "Economics of Labor Coercion."

26. Goldin, *Urban Slavery*.

27. Quoted in Dalzell, *The Good Rich*, 40–41.

28. Findlay, "Slavery, Incentives and Manumission," was the first to derive a formal economic model. Lewis, "Transition from Slavery," extended it. The discussion here follows Lewis' formulation.

29. Lewis, "Transition from Slavery," notes that if slaves can borrow, slave owners are willing to sell at the market price and the slaves' marginal product in freedom is at least as great as his marginal product in slavery, slaves would purchase their freedom early in life. While slave borrowing was rare, it was not unheard of. Around 1800 Pompey Branch, a slave in Isle of Wight County, Virginia, contracted with his owner for his freedom. The price they agreed on exceeded Pompey's savings, but he borrowed money from two white men. Through his "industry and economy" in freedom, he repaid them. Johnston, *Race Relations*, 6.

30. Fogel and Engerman, *Time on the Cross*, and Fogel and Engerman, "Explaining."

31. Jackson, "Manumission in Certain Virginia Cities"; Matison, "Manumission by Purchase"; Cole, "Capitalism and Freedom."

32. Matison, "Manumission by Purchase," 158; Jackson, "Manumission in Certain Virginia Cities," 309.

33. Of 1,182 manumissions by will and deed recorded in Anne Arundel County, Maryland between 1790 and 1820, only one invokes the immorality of slavery as the purpose of the manumission. Only 15 mention religious motivations and just five invoke natural rights arguments. See Condon, *Family Strategies*, 58, 76.

34. Morris, *Southern Slavery*.

35. *Waddill v. Martin*, 3 Iredell Eq. 562 (N.C. 1845).

36. Wolf, "Manumission in Two-Race," 311; Russell, *Free Negro in Virginia*, 174; Condon, "Slave Owner's Family," 341; and Condon, *Family Strategies*, 81; Whitman, "Diverse Good Causes," 346; Babcock, "Manumission in Virginia."

37. Camerer and Kunreuther, "Decision Processes," 565–592.

38. See also Tversky and Kahneman, "Framing of Decision," 453–458, for a description of the framing effect, which may have influenced slave beliefs and behaviors.

39. Condon, *Family Strategies*, 117–118; Cole, "Capitalism and Freedom," 1015.

40. *Southampton County Deed Book 16* (1818–1820), 137; Southampton County Deeds, Microfilm #7, Library of Virginia. http://libguides.usu.edu/virginia-manumissions.

41. *Southampton County Deed Book 7* (1787–1793), 339; Southampton County Deeds, Microfilm #3, Library of Virginia. http://libguides.usu.edu/virginia-manumissions.

42. *Southampton County Deed Book 11* (1805–1809), 137; Southampton County Deeds Microfilm #5, Library of Virginia. http://libguides.usu.edu/virginia-manumissions.

43. Female mortality was lower than male mortality before age 20 and after age 40 (the child-bearing years); it was approximately the same during the child-bearing years. The time-in-slavery estimates reflect differences in life expectancy. Life expectancy at age by sex is taken from Eblen, "New Estimates of the Vital Rates."

44. Goldin, *Urban Slavery*, argues that the declining fraction of slaves residing in urban areas in the late antebellum era was driven by rising profitability of slave employment in cotton production. To the extent that the market was efficient, the competition for labor across sectors would have left the slaves with the highest urban productivity in cities.

45. These mean age at manumission are greater than the overall mean because this analysis includes only adult (defined as 20 years or older) eventually manumitted slaves.

46. Brana-Shute, "Sex and Gender," 184.
47. Kotlikoff and Rupert, "Manumission," 180 report that free blacks represented a substantial proportion of manumitters.
48. Quoted in Campbell, "How Free is Free," 143.
49. Johnson, "Manumission in Colonial Buenos Aries," 266.
50. Martin, *Mind of Frederick Douglass*, 15.
51. One Maryland slave owner became so frustrated at one of his slave's repeated running that in exchange for not running, the owner would pay his slave $6 for each month of good service, allow the slave to hire his own time, and be freed after three years. Moreover, the owner offered his slave a buyout option. The slave could have his freedom at any time in exchange for $175 (Franklin and Schweninger, *Runaway Slaves*, 106–107).
52. Quoted in Whitman, "Diverse Good Causes," 343.
53. Franklin and Schweninger, *Runaway Slaves*, 35.
54. Hyperbolic discounting is the tendency of people to act more impulsively as the end of a waiting period approaches. When offered a larger reward in exchange for waiting a given period, people act less impulsively as the reward is farther in the future. But, as the anticipated event nears, people increasingly avoid the wait. Hyperbolic discounting, in more technical terms, means that people's discount rates are not constant over the relevant window. Discount rates decline (people are more patient) as the promised award occurs farther in the future. The classical economic approach to discounting posits that future rewards can be compared to current rewards by multiplying the future reward by $1/(1+k)^t$ where k is the constant discount rate and t is time. Hyperbolic discounting, on the other hand, assumes a present-future comparison based on $1/(1+kt)^\beta$, which is just the mathematical formula for a hyperbola.
55. Condon, *Family Strategies*, 149.
56. Olmsted, *Journey in the Back Country*, 476. There are many excellent studies of runaways; the authoritative study is Franklin and Schweninger, *Runaway Slaves*.
57. Franklin and Schweninger, *Runaway Slaves*, 282.
58. Dittmar and Naidu, "Contested Property," argue that the extent of running is generally underestimated. Specifically, they cite the 1850 and 1860 censuses, which report only 1011 and 803 currently AWOL slaves out of a population of 3.2 and 3.9 million slaves. Yet their extensive search of runaway advertisements, which covers between one-third and one-half of the slave-holding South, generates only about 160 advertised runaways, on average, per year between 1840 and 1860. Multiplying by three to extend the coverage to the whole of the slave-holding South and assuming that one-half of all runaways are advertised yields a runaway value (=960) consistent with census reports. Of course, we do not know what fraction of runaways was actually advertised. If the fraction was notably less than one-half then Dittmar and Naidu are correct in their assertion that running was more widespread than believed.
59. Bodenhorn, Guinnane, and Mroz, "Problems of Sample-Selection Bias."
60. Dittmar and Naidu, "Contested Property."
61. Grivno, *Gleanings of Freedom*, 115–151.
62. *Perry & Van Hoyten v. Beardslee & Wife*, 10 Mo. 568 (1847). Beardslee sued the steamboat's agents who, in hiring David, became the slave's bailees and were legally liable for the loss suffered due to his escape. The trial court found for the Beardslees, but the Missouri supreme court reversed and remanded because the trial court had given the jury contradictory and inaccurate instructions concerning the existing law on liability.
63. Franklin and Schweninger, *Runaway Slaves*, 119.
64. Mullin, *Flight and Rebellion*, 106.
65. *Perry & Van Houten v. Beardslee & Wife*, 10 Mo. 570 (1847).
66. Carbado and Weise, *Long Walk to Freedom*, offers twelve first-person slave accounts.
67. Blassingame, *Slave Testimony*, 217–219.
68. Franklin and Schweninger, *Runaway Slaves*, Chapter 11.

69. Franklin and Schweninger, "Quest for Freedom," 28. The five states are Virginia, North Carolina, South Carolina, Tennessee, and Louisiana.
70. Bodenhorn, "Troublesome Caste," Table 2, 983; Margo and Steckel, "Heights of American Slaves," Table 1, 518. Based on the Margo and Steckel (Table 2, 520), the height of advertised Virginia slaves exceeded the "manifest sample" heights by 1 to 1.5 inches. For a discussion of potential selection in the interstate slave trade sample, see Pritchett, "Interregional Slave Trade." For a discussion of selection problems in the height literature more generally, see Bodenhorn, Guinnane, and Mroz, "Problems of Sample-Selection Bias."
71. Bogger, *Free Blacks in Norfolk*.
72. Dusinberre, *Them Dark Days*, 255–258.
73. James, *Digest of the Laws of South-Carolina*, ¶ XXVI–XXX. See also Henry, *Police Control of the Slave*.
74. Shavell, *Foundations*, 40–41.
75. James, *Digest of the Laws of South-Carolina*, ¶ XXVI states that failure to turn a recovered slave over to the authorities within five days was punishable by a fine of $4.28 for every day beyond five the slave was not turned over. On the economics of adventitiously recovered property see Shavell, *Foundations*, 43. The rule effectively states that property readily recovered without much effort should be returned to the original owner because there is no need to create incentives to recover readily recoverable property. Such a rule reduces the owner's incentive to invest in too much precaution against losing the property.
76. Whitman, *Price of Freedom*, 69.
77. Franklin and Schweninger, *Runaway Slaves*, 210.
78. Blackburn, "Introduction," 9.

Chapter 6

1. Wilkerson, *Warmth of Other Suns*, 21.
2. *National Era*, October 5, 1854.
3. Bogger, *Free Blacks in Norfolk*, 113.
4. Johnson, *Black Savannah*.
5. Phillips, *Freedom's Port*, 101–102.
6. Bogger, *Free Blacks in Norfolk*, 104.
7. Alexis de Tocqueville reported that the "conjugal union" was nearly unknown among slaves in the French colonies. According to Tocqueville, slave men eschewed marriage because "a man does not marry when he cannot exercise marital authority, when his children must be born his equals; . . . when, having no power over their fate, he can neither know the duties, the privileges, the hopes, nor the cares which belong to the paternal relation." In stripping the adult male of meaningful authority over a household, slavery eliminated one of the principal motivations for men to marry. E. Franklin Frazier, *Negro Family*, considered the black family a strong institution, but one subject to disruption from any number of sources. Other studies are discussed below.
8. Quoted in Gutman, *Black Family*, xxi.
9. Bureau of Refugees, *Registers of Marriage of Freedmen*, National Archives Microfilm M826-42 (Vicksburg and Natchez, Mississippi) and Record Group 105.2 (Memphis, Tennessee).
10. Demographers label the marriage failure rate the "disruption rate," which consists of the fraction of marriages in a cohort that dissolve voluntarily through divorce, desertion, or separation. On the disruption rate in the United States among cohorts marrying between 1860 and 1940 see Cvrcek, "When Harry Left Sally."
11. William Dusinberre's, *Them Dark Days*, reconstructions of unhappy family life on the Georgia low-country Gowrie plantation are typical. He finds some lasting marriages, but he focuses on several cases like Sary's. At age 17, Sary married 22-year-old William, who left his then-pregnant wife to move in with her. William left after a year or two; a year or so after that

Sary married a man her own age named Pompey. Pompey and Sary remained married long enough to produce four children, only one of whom survived past its fifth birthday. The evidence on this and other area plantations leads Dusinberre to conclude that "so many [slave] couples split up voluntarily, that over half the women who reached the age of twenty-eight married at least twice, and not uncommonly three, four, or even five times." It is easy to attribute a large number of short marriages to planter indifference to life in the quarters or to the deliberate breaking up of families for profit. But slave marriages were often short-lived even on plantations where planters rarely sold slaves. While there are many reasons why slave marriages were transient, one often overlooked reason was the low likelihood of finding a suitable life partner from among a relatively small number of slaves on a single, or even a few neighboring plantations.

12. Wolf, "Manumission and the Two-Race System," 311.
13. US Census Office, *Population of the United States in 1860*.
14. In some Caribbean slave societies, manumitted slaves still owed specific duties to their former master—deference, obedience, and sometimes labor—but North American manumission released the slave from such formal obligations. In 1802, Caleb Bradford manumitted Anne with the statement "I this Day Mancipates her and Declares her to be a free woman and that I have no *Command* of the sd Negro from this . . . day" (quoted in Wolf, "Manumission and the Two-Race System," 313–314). Similarly, when Marylander Sarah Gray freed her slaves, her will explicitly stated that "no heir or representative of mine shall have or exercise any sort of authority or mastership over them or any of them" (quoted in Condon, "Slave Owner's Family," 346).
15. For evidence of assortative mating on different characteristics, Lee at al., "If I'm Not Hot," explore attractiveness; Williamson, "Dating Game," discusses political persuasion; Fryer, "Guess Who's Been Coming to Dinner" discusses race; Oreffice and Quintana-Domeque, "Anthropometry and Socioeconomics among Couples," find assortative mating on height and weight.
16. While identical ranking appears to be a strong (and easily violated) requirement for the existence and uniqueness of equilibrium, research reveals broad agreement on the attractiveness of potential partners (Lee et al., "If I'm Not Hot"). Gale and Shapley, "College Admissions and the Stability of Marriage," generate a sorting algorithm that yields a stable equilibrium. Eeckhout, "On the Uniqueness," derives the conditions under which the equilibrium is unique.
17. Burdett and Coles, "Marriage and Class"; Burdett and Coles, "Long-Term Partnership"; and Belding, "Nobility and Stupidity."
18. Lee et al., "If I'm Not Hot," 675, find that this may not strictly hold. From their research into online dating they conclude that although people of similar attractiveness tend to date one another, people prefer to date others slightly more attractive than themselves, but not those substantially more attractive.
19. The discussion of alternative measures of assortative matching draws heavily on Kalmijn, "Intermarriage and Homogamy," 404–405. McCaa and Schwartz, "Measuring Marriage Patterns," 711–724, also discusses the relative merits of alternative approaches to measuring intermarriage.
20. The standard error of δ_{ij} is defined as: $SE(\delta_{ij}) = (1/N_{ii} + 1/N_{ix} + 1/N_{xi} + 1/N_{xx})^{1/2}$. For a 2 x 2 interaction table, dividing the observed log odds ratio by its standard error produces a standard normal Z-score that can be used to test for statistical significance. In interaction tables larger than 2 x 2, however, this Z-score cannot be legitimately compared to the usual standard normal value (i.e., 1.96 for a two-tailed test at the 95th percentile). If there is more than one interaction of interest (that is, the relevant table is larger than 2 x 2 table), the Z-score must be adjusted to reflect the appropriate degrees of freedom. If the test of interest involves a 2 x 2 interaction (e.g., black-black) drawn from a larger R x C table, such as the interactions observed in Tables 5.2 through 5.4, then the appropriate Z-score test statistic is that corresponding to the (2.5/(R x C))th percentile (assuming a two-tailed test at the

underlying 95th percentile). Thus, if the test of interest involves the 95th percentile of a 2 x 2 match drawn from a larger 11 x 11 table, the appropriate Z-score is that corresponding to the 0.02th (2.5/121) percentile, which is 3.49, not the usual 1.96. For further information on calculating log-odds ratios and standard deviations, see Kalmijn, "Intermarriage and Homogamy," Kalmijn, "Shifting Boundaries," and Goodman, "How to Ransack Social Mobility Tables."

21. See, for example, Williamson, *New People*; and Berlin, *Slaves Without Masters*; Nicholls, "Passing Through This Troublesome World," 51, uses the term *black* in reference to all African Americans because, he contends, "Virginians did not develop the fractional distinctions of other societies to differentiate among the degrees of mixture between black and white." The available evidence suggests otherwise; African American clearly drew distinctions among themselves.

22. The description of the Freedmen's Bureau records draws on National Archives, *Marriage Records*, 1–6.

23. National Archives, *Marriage Records*, 7.

24. Caution is warranted because the Freedmen's Bureau official recording the marriages did not observe the marriage partners' parents. The partners were asked about their parents' racial heritage, which the official could not confirm. Moreover, the officials themselves sometimes introduced reporting errors into the marriage partners' information. Consider America E. Trimble, a mixed-race woman who married James Cathers in Natchez, Mississippi. She informed the official that her father was one-sixteenth white and her mother was one-half white. The Freedmen's Bureau official then labeled America as one-thirty-second white, presumably simply multiplying one-half and one-sixteenth. Using the racial proportion calculation developed by Thomas Jefferson and discussed in Chapter 2, America's racial heritage (assuming the information she provided about her parents was correct) was nine-thirty-seconds white. Thus America was closer, by racial heritage, to griff (one-quarter white) than black (one-thirty-second white).

25. Goldin, "America's Graduation," 365.

26. Some county clerks identified women as "wife of X," which simplified the matching. In other cases, matches were constructed either through the index (when available) or by reading the registers and matching on last names. If it was possible that the individuals were familial relations (brother-sister, etc.), they were excluded from the sample.

27. Stevenson, *Life in Black and White*, 64.

28. Greenwood and Guner, "Marriage and Divorce," provide a dynamic optimization model of marriage and the family.

29. Stevenson, *Life in Black and White*, 83.

30. See essays in Herndon and Murray (eds.), *Children Bound to Labor*; and Bodenhorn, "Just and Reasonable Treatment."

31. Stevenson, *Life in Black and White*, 72. There is scientific evidence consistent with the proverb that each child cost a woman a tooth. Christensen et al., "A Tooth Per Child," 204, reports the results of a study of older Danish women that low social class women lost about one additional tooth per child whereas upper class women lost about one-half tooth per child.

32. Gutman, "Persistent Myths," 182.

33. Frazier, *Negro Family in Chicago*, 33–34; Frazier, *Negro Family in the United States*, 627.

34. Moynihan's *The Negro Family* opened and continues to influence the modern debate.

35. Hershberg, "Free Blacks in Antebellum Philadelphia," 190; Gutman, "Persistent Myths," 194; Stevenson, *Life in Black and White*, 310; Nicholls, "Passing Through This Troublesome World," 70; Lammermeier, "Urban Black Family," 443.

36. Orthner, Brown, and Ferguson, "Single-Parent Fatherhood," cite maternal mortality, divorce and adoption as the principal sources of single-fatherhood. Given that as late as 1935 the maternal mortality rate was 58 deaths per 10,000 live births (compared to 3 per 10,000 in 1970), maternal mortality appears to be a factor contributing to the relatively high rates of single-fatherhood.

37. The published population census for 1860 does not differentiate blacks and mixed-race men and women by age. The overall sex ratio for black Baltimoreans was 718 males per 1,000 women; for mixed-race people it was 715. US Census Office, *Population of the United States in 1860.*

38. Hershberg, "Free Blacks in Antebellum Philadelphia," 190.

39. Hershberg, "Free Blacks," 188.

40. Stevenson, *Life in Black and White,* 310.

41. Gutman, "Persistent Myths," 194.

42. Willis, "Theory of Out-of-Wedlock Childbearing," and Neal, "Relationship."

43. Qian, Lichter, and Mellott, "Out-of-Wedlock Childbearing," show that women with out-of-wedlock children are less well matched. Their spouses are older, less educated, and of another race than are the spouses of women without children.

44. Salisbury, "Women's Income and Marriage Markets."

45. Stevenson, *Life in Black and White,* 311.

46. Again, it is important to not interpret this as a causal effect because occupation, marriage, child-bearing, and location were endogenous and jointly determined.

47. Nicholls, "Passing Through This Troublesome World," 70.

48. Stevenson, *Life in Black and White,* 308.

49. Nicholls, "Passing Through This Troublesome World," 50.

50. Letter of Peter Fontaine to Moses Fontaine, March 30, 1757, reprinted in Ann Maury, *Memoirs of a Huguenot Family,* 350.

51. Nicholls, "Passing Through This Troublesome World," 53.

Chapter 7

1. Latrobe, *Rambler in North America,* 333–334.

2. Benwell, *Englishman's Travels in America,* 191, offered a similar observation on Charleston, South Carolina's African Americans: he was "quite struck to see . . . such a disproportion of . . . the negro race, tinged in a greater or less degree with the hue.".

3. Frazier, *Black Bourgeoisie,* for example, provides a pessimistic assessment of prior black accomplishments and future prospects. Similarly, the very title of Ira Berlin's now classic study *Slaves Without Masters* leaves little doubt about his central conclusions. Juliet Walker's *History of Black Business* provides a more subtle and optimistic, though far from rosy, interpretation.

4. Franklin, *Free Negro in North Carolina,* 139.

5. Nash, *Forging Freedom,* 217, 251, 145–146.

6. Quoted in Litwack, *North of Slavery,* 154.

7. Rockman, *Scraping By,* 158–193.

8. Delany, *Condition, Elevation, Emigration,* 92–110; Walker, *History of Black Business,* I, 108–163.

9. Steffen, *Mechanics of Baltimore,* 41.

10. Quoted in Bogger, *Free Blacks in Norfolk,* 66.

11. Hanger, "Patronage, Property, and Persistence," 45.

12. Quoted in Fields, *Slavery and Freedom,* 83–84.

13. See, many among others, Arrow, "Models of Job Discrimination"; Akerlof, "Discriminatory, Status-Based Wages"; and Becker, *Economics of Discrimination.*

14. Russell, *Free Negro in Virginia,* 150.

15. Berlin, *Slaves Without Masters,* 96–97; England, "Free Negro in Antebellum Tennessee," 37–58; Franklin, *Free Negro in North Carolina,* 131.

16. Franklin, *Free Negro in North Carolina,* 136.

17. Wikramanayake, *World in Shadow,* 103.

18. Curry, *Free Black in Urban America,* 16–18.

19. Johnson, *Black Savannah,* 44–45.

20. Foner, *Life and Writings of Frederick Douglass*, 249–250; Olmsted, *Journey*, 367.

21. Berlin, *Masters Without Slaves*, 231–232; Litwack, *North of Slavery*, 165; Reinders, "Free Negro in the New Orleans Economy," 276–277; Whitman, *Price of Freedom*, 165; Hirsch, "Free Negro in New York," 436.

22. Bodenhorn, "Industrious, Sober, Good Citizens," 29 (Table 2). Multinomial logistic regression analysis of employment patterns for black, mixed-race, immigrant, and native-born men in the ten-city southern urban sample of the 1860 census described shortly reveal that blacks and mixed-race men were more likely than immigrants to work in the service industry. But black and mixed-race were more likely than immigrants to be employed as semiskilled operatives. Mixed-race men were more likely than immigrants to work at a skilled trade.

23. Schelling, "Dynamic Models" and Pryor, "Empirical Note" represent early contributions. Recent applications include Zhang, "Tipping and Residential Segregation," and Caetano and Maheshri, "School Segregation."

24. The cities are Baton Rouge (LA), Baltimore (MD), Charleston (SC), Frederick (MD), Louisville (KY), Mobile (AL), Nashville (TN), New Orleans (LA), Petersburg (VA), and Richmond (VA). No sampling weights are used because all African Americans in each city are included in the sample; the sample is observationally self-weighted.

25. Reiss et al., *Occupations and Social Status*.

26. The 33 occupations account for 83.7 percent of black male workers, 72.5 percent of mixed-race men, and 66.5 percent of white men. The "no occupation" category, which is not used in the narrow job calculations, accounts for an additional 5.8, 8.1, and 4.5 percent, respectively.

27. The Duncan Index is defined as $D = \frac{1}{2} \Sigma_j \, |b_j - w_j|$, where j indexes jobs or occupational categories, b_j is the fraction black workers in job j, and w_j is the fraction of white workers in job j. The Duncan Index takes on values betwen 0 and 1. A value of 0 implies perfect integration; a value of 1 implies perfect segregation. For discussions of the features and interpretations of the index, see Duncan and Duncan, "Methodological Analysis"; and Preston, "Occupational Gender Segregation."

28. Gleeson, *Irish in the South*.

29. The No Occupation category was dropped from the analysis.

30. Technically, the odds ratio of observing a black man, b, in occupation $j = [p_{bj} / (1 - p_{bj})] / [p_{mj} / (1 - p_{mj})]$, where p_{bj} is the probability of observing a black man in job j and p_{mj} is the probability of observing a mixed-race man in job j.

31. Rockman, *Scraping By*, and Whitman, *Price of Freedom*.

32. Horton and Horton, "Power and Social Responsibility," 330; Delany, *Condition, Elevation, Emigration, and Destiny*, 206. See also Bristol, "From Outposts to Enclaves," 594–606.

33. Franklin and Schweninger, *In Search of the Promised Land*, 64.

34. Jones's shop is listed and advertised in Baltimore city directories between 1842 and 1860.

35. Walker, *History of Black Business in America*, 140–141.

36. Franklin and Schweninger, *In Search of the Promised Land*, 69; Schweninger, "Thriving Within the Lowest Caste," 353–364; Walker, *History of Black Business*, 108. See Margo and Villaflor, "Growth of Wages," and Margo, *Wages and Labor Markets*, for evidence on contemporary wage rates for skilled and unskilled workers.

37. Jesse Garner was not atypical in this regard. In 1816 he announced that he had a "large supply of oysters prepared in any manner," available in his oyster cellar in the rear of the Washington Hotel in the District of Columbia. See Brown, *Free Negroes in the District of Columbia*, 131–132.

38. Jackson, "Negro Enterprise in Norfolk," 8, and Niehaus, *Irish in New Orleans*, 57.

39. Borjas and Bronars, "Consumer Discrimination," 582–589.

40. Fairlie, *Kauffman Index*, p. 2. Boyd, "Trends in the Occupations"; Boyd, "Race, Gender, and Survivalist Entrepreneurship"; and Koo, "Small Entrepreneurship," label this "survivalist" entrepreneurship and investigate its application to early twentieth-century blacks, Great

Depression era workers, and rural-to-urban Korean migrants. Colvin and Needleman, "Better Times," discuss a variant of necessity entrepreneurship in the post-Great Recession era.

41. Borjas and Bronars, "Consumer Discrimination"; Bernhardt, "Comparative Advantage."
42. See Appendix 7.1 for the particulars of the estimation and the results.
43. The predicted probability is calculated as $\hat{y} = \Sigma_i \left[f\left(Z_{ib}\, \beta_m\right) / N\right]$, where β_m is the vector of estimated logit coefficients, Z_{ib} is the vector of variables (for black individuals indexed by i) included in the logit regression, and N is the number of black men.
44. Real estate ownership and household size are endogenous choices in that men who expect to be self-employed may save more than those who expect to pursue wage work. But Bernhardt, "Comparative Advantage," 278, contends that a large component of wealth is inherited and not readily explained the same factors that influence self-employment. Absent one or more reasonable instruments for home ownership, which Adelino, Schoar, and Severino, "House Prices," find to be an important determinant of self-employment, no causal conclusions can be drawn.
45. Smith, "The Washerwoman," reprinted in Foner and Lewis (eds.), *The Black Worker*, v.1, 63–64.
46. Stevenson, *Life in Black and White*, 293.
47. This section draws heavily on Bodenhorn, "Complexion Gap." The data underlying that study were lost in the interval between the publication of that article and the writing of this book. I would have liked to rework some of the numbers and engaged in some additional statistical analysis that is now impossible short of reconstructing the entire data set. See Bogue, *From Prairie to Corn Belt*. See also Winters, *Farmers without Farms*, for a discussion of laboring, tenancy, and farm ownership.
48. Reid, "Antebellum Southern Rental Contracts." Jackson, *Free Negro Labor*, 102, writes that free African Americans worked as laborers, tenants and owners, and "moved from rung to rung of the farm ladder." Jackson, "Virginia Free Negro Farm Worker," 400–401, further reports that cash rental was more common in antebellum Virginia than the share tenancy that emerged in the postbellum era.
49. Winters, "Agricultural Ladder," 37.
50. Postbellum censuses explicitly enumerate land tenure, but agricultural and economic historians still debate the meaning of terms used by the census marshals. Alston and Kauffman, "Up, Down, and Off," and Irwin and O'Brien, "Where Have All the Sharecroppers Gone" offer recent reinterpretations based on alternative definitions of seemingly precise terms. A close reading of the literature reveals that the manuscript censuses are open to interpretation.
51. Any answer to this seemingly straightforward question is not straightforward. The fundamental problem facing agricultural historians using antebellum censuses is resolving the question of how to treat people identified as farmers in the population manuscripts and not enumerated in the farm manuscripts. (The opposite case of people appearing in the farm manuscript and not in the population census occurs much less frequently.) Nearly as many methods have been devised for dealing with these so-called farmers without farms as there are researchers interested in the question. Allen Bogue, *From Prairie to Corn Belt*, labeled individuals described as farmers in the population manuscripts without a corresponding entry in the farm manuscripts as hopeful farm laborers. Frederick Bode and Donald Ginter, *Farm Tenancy*, argue that some of these men were tenants. Jeremy Atack, in "Agricultural Ladder Revisited," is uncomfortable with Bogue's treatment of landless farmers as laborers, but is reluctant to classify them as tenants so he excludes them from his analysis. Bogue's method produces a lower-bound estimate of tenancy and an upper-bound estimate of laboring. Atack's estimates produce lower bounds for both tenancy and laboring. Bode and Ginter's interpretations produce intermediate estimates of both.
52. Grivno, *Gleanings of Freedom*.
53. Winters, "Agricultural Ladder"; Bode and Ginter, *Farm Tenancy*, 180–181.
54. The reported statistics do not control for state of residence or free- versus slave-born status.
55. Berlin, *Slaves Without Masters*, 318.

56. Wikramanayake, *World in Shadow*, 95.
57. Benwell, *An Englishman's Travels in America*, 56.
58. Walker, *History of Black Business*, 126.
59. Quoted in Walker, *History of Black Business*, 120.
60. Benwell, *An Englishman's Travels in America*, 57.
61. Hershberg and Williams, "Mulattoes and Blacks," 415. See also Horton and Horton, *In Hope of Liberty*, 122–123, who draw a comparable conclusion.

Chapter 8

1. Quoted in Schweninger, *Black Property Owners*, 241–242.
2. Cole, "Capitalism and Freedom," 1012; $600 in 1800 is approximately $11,000 in 2012 dollars. See EH.Net "How Much Is That?" http://eh.net/howmuchisthat/ for price level adjustment factors. The prices paid in New Orleans are comparable to the average price of $624 slaves paid for their freedom in 1850s Richmond, Virginia (see Jackson, *Free Negro Labor*, 184).
3. Emerson, *Conduct of Life*, 207
4. Brewer, "Negro Property Owners," 575.
5. Breen and Innes, *Myne Owne Ground*, 73–74.
6. Breen and Innes, *Myne Owne Ground*, 74.
7. For the evolving social implications of property ownership, market participation, and economic independence in the nineteenth century see Lamoreaux, "Rethinking the Transition," and Kulikoff, "Households and Markets."
8. Jackson, *Free Negro Labor*, 103–136.
9. Schweninger, *Black Property Owners*, 97–141.
10. Collins and Margo, "Race and Home Ownership."
11. Jackson, "Free Negro Farmer," 411; Jackson, *Free Negro Labor*, 239–246.
12. Available at https://usa.ipums.org/usa/voliii/inst1860.shtml.
13. Bodenhorn, "Complexion Gap," 60. Unfortunately, the data underlying this earlier study, which included information on nearly 3,000 African-American households, were lost and have not been reconstructed.
14. Franklin, *Free Negro in North Carolina*, 150.
15. Jackson, "Virginia Free Negro Farmer," 399; Seventh Census (1850), population manuscript Westmoreland County, Virginia, (family number 508), 65.
16. Jackson, "Virginia Free Negro Farmer," 421.
17. Wallenstein, *Tell the Court*, 162.
18. Sterkx, *Free Negro*, 179–180; Oliver and Shapiro, *Black Wealth / White Wealth*, 171; Phillips, *Freedom's Port*, 154.
19. Jackson, *Free Negro Labor*, 137–140.
20. Regression results are reported in Appendix 8.1. A more detailed discussion of the results, along with racial decompositions are reported in Bodenhorn and Ruebeck, "Colourism."
21. Quantile regression procedures estimate coefficients only above the cutoff point. Because nearly half of the sample report no personalty, coefficients cannot be estimated below the median.
22. The raw mean ($276) and median ($10) of personal wealth for mixed-race households demonstrate an even greater gap between the two for a mean and median age of 40 year-olds.
23. Phillips, *Freedom's Port*, 154–155.
24. Smith, *An Inquiry into. . . the Wealth of Nations*, 228.
25. Ehrenberg and Smith, *Modern Labor Economics*, 293; Heaton and Lucas, "Portfolio Choice," 1173. Heaton and Lucas define human capital wealth ("capitalized labor") as the discounted value of future labor income over the remainder of the expected working life.
26. See Appendix 8.4 for the derivation of human capital.

27. On low saving rates among Americans, now and in the past, see Garon, *Beyond Our Means.*
28. Phillips, *Freedom's Port,* 158.
29. The statistics discussed here are from a six-county sample (Anne Arundel, Baltimore, Frederick, Prince Georges, Somerset, and Talbot) of 116 African-American apprentices. For more on the sample and its collection see Bodenhorn, "Just and Reasonable Treatment."
30. Goldin, "Human-Capital Century," 277.
31. Bellamy, "Education of Blacks," 146. The laws allowing dues in lieu of school were originally designed to relieve masters from the burden of educating pauper apprentices, but the agreements were observed as well in a handful of parent-master contracts. See Bodenhorn, "Just and Reasonable Treatment," for a discussion of pauper apprenticeship.
32. Russell, *Free Negro in Virginia,* 140–141.
33. Franklin, *Free Negro in North Carolina,* 167.
34. Howe, "Church, State, and Education," 13.
35. Woodson, *Education of the Negro,* 140; Brigham, "Negro Education." 414.
36. Birnie, "Education of the Negro," 18.
37. Quoted in Franklin and Schweninger, *In Search of the Promised Land,* 35.
38. Sterkx, *Free Negro in Ante-Bellum Louisiana,* 269–270.
39. Franklin, *Free Negro in North Carolina,* 168–169.
40. Woodson, *Education of the Negro,* 159–169.
41. Bellamy, "Education of Blacks." 156.
42. Andrews (1787–1858) was a nineteenth-century educator who taught at University of North Carolina and authored several texts, mostly Latin textbooks. He also wrote *Slavery and the Domestic Slave Trade,* under the auspices of the American Union. His report on the free blacks of Baltimore paints a bleak and discouraging portrait of sloth, dissipation, and criminality, which he was quick to attribute to their "imperfect moral discipline" (65) rather than their poverty. Still, Andrews was favorably disposed toward the city's African Americans, though he doubted whether they might integrate into society and realize economic advancement.
43. Moehling, "Family Structure"; and Margo, *Race and Schooling.*
44. Vinovskis, "Quantification," 770.
45. Horton and Horton, "Shades of Color," 125–126.
46. Horton and Horton, *In Hope of Liberty,* 154.
47. Jordan, *White Over Black,* 133.
48. Frazier, *Black Bourgeoisie,* 147–148.
49. Frazier, *Black Bourgeoisie,* 77.
50. Margo, *Race and Schooling.*
51. Welch, "Labor-Market Discrimination," 233.
52. Russell, *Free Negro in Virginia,* 88–89; Schweninger, *Black Property Owners,* 5.
53. Breen and Innes, *Myne Owne Ground,* 92.
54. Shapiro, *Hidden Cost,* 10–11.
55. Sweat, *Free Negro in Antebellum Georgia,* 198–199.

Chapter 9

1. Schultz, "Wage Gains"; Anand, Peter, and Sen, *Public Health, Ethics and Equity,* provides a collection of essays that investigate equity and efficiency issues of health and well-being.
2. Troesken, *Water, Race and Disease.*
3. See Tanner, *History of the Study of Human Growth,* for synopses of early studies.
4. Bowditch, "Growth of Children," 65. Compare Bowditch's depiction to Tanner's, *Foetus Into Man,* 15. They are nearly identical; simply subtract one year from Bowditch's description of late nineteenth-century growth and you have Tanner's mid-twentieth-century description.
5. Tanner, *History of the Study of Human Growth,* 191.
6. Tanner, *Foetus Into Man,* 14.

7. Eveleth and Tanner, *Worldwide Variation*, 276–277.

8. Bilger, "Height Gap."

9. Voth and Leunig, "Did Smallpox Reduce Height," 542, claim that since 1980, more resources have been devoted to this broadly defined research project than any other in economic history.

10. Extensive reviews of the literature are found in Steckel, "Stature and the Standard of Living," and "Heights and Human Welfare."

11. Eveleth and Tanner, *Worldwide Variation*, 1.

12. Rona, "Impact of the Environment on Height," 112, notes the myriad factors influencing growth and height and argues that only the most carefully constructed clinical longitudinal study could ever hope to sort out the relative importance of each factor. The two-inch difference, too, may not accurately depict the actual increase in average heights. Modern heights are collected from random, nationally representative samples; nineteenth-century height samples are rarely either random, or nationally representative.

13. Eveleth and Tanner, *Worldwide Variation*, 246–247; Tanner, *Foetus Into Man*, 132–134; Mora et al., "Effects of Nutritional Supplementation."

14. Based on several studies of populations in developing countries, Tanner, *Foetus Into Man*, 132–134 reports that diarrheal and upper respiratory infections have the most pronounced detrimental effects on growth in childhood.

15. Tanner, *History of the Study*, 169–196; Eveleth and Tanner, *Worldwide Variation*, appendices.

16. See Eveleth and Tanner, *Worldwide Variation*, 238 and appendices for further information on these studies.

17. Bodenhorn, Guinnane, and Mroz, "Caveat Lector."

18. Eveleth and Tanner, *Worldwide Variation*, 2–4.

19. "Stunted" usually implies two or more standard deviations below the mean. See Burgard, "Does Race Matter?" Two standard deviations below the mean places an individual at the 2.5th centile, which is typically rounded to the 3rd centile in standard growth charts.

20. Steckel, "Growth Depression and Recovery." While plausible, the complex interactions between unmeasurable environmental factors makes any monocausal explanation problematic. It is also possible that Steckel's results are driven by changing selection on height at different ages. If more taller adolescents and adults entered the interstate market, the reported catch-up growth may be overstated. Of course, the same may be true of the free register sample. It is hard to know whether or how selection may have changed over the life cycle.

21. Rees et al., "Optimal Food Allocation"; and Liu et al., "Parental Compensatory Behavior."

22. Dusinberre, *Them Dark Days*, 181.

23. See Appendix 9 and Steckel, "Growth Depression and Recovery," 113. In most instances, the exact age at manumission is not stated in the registrations, but manumitted children were generally registered, along with their parents, when their manumissions were approved and processed by the county court (see Chapter 5 and Appendix 5.1 for discussion of manumission).

24. Tanner, *Foetus Into Man*, 3–4.

25. Coelho and McGuire, "Diets Versus Diseases," and sources cited therein provide the essentials of the debate.

26. Quoted in Dusinberre, *Them Dark Days*, 64.

27. Kiple and Kiple, "Slave Child Mortality."

28. It is important to reiterate that children who entered the sample and were measured may not have been representative of the populations of black and mixed-race children. Still, the diagram shows that at least some nineteenth-century African Americans compare favorably to historical populations.

29. Even if the selection bias overstates true height by as much as one-half inch, free-born mixed-race men were still nearly as tall as relatively privileged white men measured in the late-nineteenth century (see Table 9.2).

30. Eveleth and Tanner, *Worldwide Variation*, 34.
31. Douglass, *Educational Laws of Virginia*, 12–13. Douglass's failure to name the girl suggests an apocryphal tale; even so, given the condition of urban tenements and the extent of contemporary poverty, it not hard to imagine factual events not far removed from Douglass's recounting.
32. Bogger, *Free Blacks in Norfolk*, 120–121.
33. See Ferrie, "The Rich and the Dead."
34. Quinan, *Medical Annals of Baltimore*, 39.
35. Quinan, *Medical Annals of Baltimore*, 49.
36. Ferrie, "The Rich and the Dead," 39 (table 2A.3).
37. Kiple and Kiple, "Slave Child Mortality."
38. Coelho and McGuire, "Diets Versus Dieases."
39. Steckel, "Diets Versus Diseases."
40. The sample counties are the same as those used in the occupation and wealth studies in earlier chapters (see Appendix 8.1), except Chesterfield County, Virginia is substituted for Caroline County, Maryland. Caroline County's mortality census was incomplete. The five cities are Baltimore, Louisville, Nashville, Petersburg, and Richmond.
41. Ferrie, "The Rich and the Dead," 33 (Table 2.9).

Epilogue

1. Joseph, "The Fury Over a Cheerios Ad."
2. "White Father Furious," *Daily Mail*.
3. Buckley, "Unfixing Race," 360.
4. Hill, "Color Differences."
5. Mill and Stein, "Race, Skin Color, and Economic Outcomes."
6. Sacerdote, "Slavery," 218.
7. Hochschild and Powell, "Racial Reorganization"; Hochschild, Weaver, and Burch, *Creating a New Racial Order*; Nobles, *Shades of Citizenship*; Hickman, "Devil and the One Drop Rule."
8. The 1969 peak corresponds to Katherine Dunham's *Island Possessed*, an anthropological study of Haiti's voodoo culture, as well as the social and economic gulf separating the island nation's poor blacks and relatively wealthy mixed-race men and women.
9. Between 1890 and 1910, the word "miscegenation" appeared approximately 0.1 times per million published words; in the 1980s it appeared 0.45 times, 0.65 times in the 1990s, and 0.75 times per million words between 2000 and 2008. Google Books Ngram viewer, for "miscegenation+Miscegenation." https://books.google.com/ngrams.
10. Jordan, "More Marriages Cross," A2.
11. Fryer, "Guess Who's Been Coming," 76 (Figure 1).
12. *Loving v. Virginia*, 388 U.S. 1 (1967).
13. Harris and Sim, "Who Is Multiracial," 614.
14. Gullickson, "Significance of Color Declines."
15. Harris and Sim, "Who Is Multiracial"; see Udry, Li, and Hendrickson-Smith, "Health and Behavior Risks," and sources therein for details about the construction and administration of the survey.
16. Harris and Sim, "Who Is Multiracial," 622; the remaining 8.5 percent refused to select a best single racial identifier.
17. *Walker v. Internal Revenue Service*, 713 F. Suppl. 403 (N. D. Ga. 1989); see Jones, "Shades of Brown," 1538.
18. Drake and Cayton, *Black Metropolis*, 495.
19. Graham, *Our Kind of People*.
20. Golden, *Don't Play in the Sun*, 127–128.

21. Graham, *Our Kind of People.*
22. Reuter, *The Mulatto in the United States,* summarizes and extends the arguments Reuter advanced in a handful of articles.
23. Reuter was not along among his contemporaries in concluding that mixed-race people demonstrated greater intellectual ability. In an article appearing in the prestigious Annals of the *American Academy of Political and Social Science,* George T. Winston, president of the historically black North Carolina Agricultural and Mechanical College, wrote that "the Mulatto is quicker, brighter, and more easily refined than the Negro. There is a general opinion among Southern people that he is inferior morally; but I believe that his inferiority is physical and vital." It is remarkable how little scientific opinion has evolved between 1840 and 1900. Winston, "Relation," 108.
24. Miller, "Review of *The Mulatto in the United States,*" 219.
25. Park, "Human Migration and the Marginal Man." Park, "Mentality of Racial Hybrids," 545, argues that mixed-race personalities are restless, aggressive, ambitious, sensitive, self-conscious and serious, traits that result from the "warring ancestry in his veins."
26. Johnson, "Review of *The Marginal Man,*" 115.
27. Gordon-Reed, "Reading *White Over Black,*" 857.
28. Freeman, Armor, Ross, and Pettigrew, "Color Gradation," 368.
29. Udry, Bauman, and Chase, "Skin Color, Status, and Mate Selection."
30. Edwards, "Skin Color," 476.
31. Seltzer and Smith, "Color Differences," 284.
32. Hill, "Color Differences," 1451.
33. Gullickson, "Significance of Color Declines."
34. Goldsmith, Hamilton, and Darity, "From Dark to Light" and "Shades of Discrimination"; and Hersch, "Skin Color, Physical Appearance."
35. Hersch, "Profiling the New Immigrant Worker"; and "Skin Color."
36. Fairlie, "Can the 'One-Drop Rule,'" 460.
37. Loury, "Am I Still Too Black for You."
38. Ruebeck, Averett, and Bodenhorn, "Acting White," and Fryer et al., "Plight of Mixed-Race Adolescents."
39. Stonequist, "Problem of the Marginal Man," 12.
40. Gyimah-Brempong and Price, "Crime and Punishment," 248.

Appendices

1. Gross, "Litigating Whiteness," Appendix, 186–188.
2. Johnson, "Slave Trader," relates how abolitionists used white slavery to convince Americans of slavery's immorality.
3. Aydemir and Borjas, "Attenuation Bias," 71–79.
4. Spurr, *Economic Foundations of Law,* 166–168, offers a textbook explanation of Rubin's model.
5. Wallenstein, *Tell the Court,* 31 outlines the legal procedures followed in Virginia after 1795 in slave freedom suits. In brief, once a slave petitioned the court for freedom, the court appointed a counsel to investigate to determine whether the case had merit. If the slave convinced the court-appointed counsel and the counsel convinced the court that the slave's case had enough merit to proceed, the slave appointed a attorney to represent the slave and summoned the owner to answer the complaint.
6. *Miller v. Denman,* 16 Tenn. 233; *Morrison v. White,* 16 La. Ann. 100.
7. Menard et al., *Public Use Microdata of the Slave Population.*
8. See Stanton, *Leopard's Spots,* 54–72 for a discussion of the contemporary debate.
9. Menard et al., *Public Use Microdata of the Slave Population.*
10. Fogel and Engerman, "Explaining," 278.
11. The maximum slaveholding size in the 1860 sample is 527 slaves, so the implied maximum occurs within the observed sample size.

12. Virginia, *The Revised Code*, §C.111.67, Vol. I, 438.
13. Virginia, *The Revised Code*, §C.111.77, Vol. I, 441.
14. See Bodenhorn, Guinnane, and Mroz, "Problems of Sample-Selection Bias," 13–20, for a detailed analysis of the general problem and its application to eighteenth- and nineteenth-century English army recruits.
15. Bodenhorn, Guinnane, and Mroz, "Caveat Lector," 18–22.
16. Komlos, "Toward an Anthropometric History," 310 and Bodenhorn, "A Troublesome Caste," 983.
17. Eblen, "New Estimates," 308.
18. The test for proportional hazard assumption is a test of the null hypothesis $\ln(p) = 0$, which is equivalent to a test of $p=1$. Because the Weibull specification assumes that individual hazards are increasing or decreasing in time, a rejection of the null hypothesis indicates that the Weibull distribution assumption is appropriate for explaining individual transitions from slavery to freedom.
19. Lewis, "Transition from Slavery to Freedom," 158–159, and private correspondence.
20. Whitman, *Price of Freedom*, 110–111.
21. Babcock, "Manumission in Virginia"; Wolf, *Race and Liberty*, 71–72.
22. Fogel and Engerman, "Philanthropy at Bargain Prices," 390, estimate break-even at age 28.
23. Bodenhorn, Guinnane, and Mroz, "Problems with Sample-Selection Bias," 13–20.
24. Carter et al., *Historical Statistics*, Series Bb215–Bb216.
25. Coleman and Hutchinson, "Determinants of Slave Prices," 12. Estimates in Kotlikoff, "Structure,"501; Cole, "Capitalism and Freedom," 1022; and Calomiris and Pritchett, "Preserving Slave Families," 992 are all similar.
26. Franklin and Schweninger, *Runaway Slaves*, 177.
27. Daily wages from Margo and Villaflor, "Growth Wages," Table 6, 894; number of days worked from Rockman, *Scraping By*, 87 and Grivno, *Gleanings of Freedom*, 157.
28. Shavell, *Foundations*, 41; Landes and Posner, "Salvors, Finders, Good Samaritans," 100–108.
29. Becker, *A Treatise on the Family*, 108–135.
30. Of the several notions of social capital, the usage employed here refers to Glaeser, Laibson, and Sacerdote's, "An Economic Approach," notion that an individual's social capital is captured by the size of his or her Rolodex.
31. Kalmijn, "Intermarriage and Homogamy," 396–397, 399–400.
32. Kalmijn, "Intermarriage and Homogamy," 411–412.
33. Greenwood et al., "Marry Your Like," 348–353.
34. Burdett and Coles, "Marriage and Class," 142, 146–150.
35. Belding, "Nobility and Stupidity."
36. In this formulation, lighter complected individuals belong to groups with lower-value subscripts.
37. The lightest complected individuals, then, establish the taste parameters for their complexion peer group. As such, light individuals become trend setters, defining what is fashionable in their marriage market.
38. This is the last woman rejected by males in set C_m^1.
39. This condition is reasonable in this context because it is possible, some even contend likely, that African Americans of light enough complexion will abandon the black community by passing into the white community.
40. Burdett and Coles, "Marriage and Class," 146–150, establish the precise criteria for the sets described above to represent an equilibrium distribution of sets. Interested readers are encouraged to refer to their article for the details.
41. Steckel, "Percentiles of Modern Height Standards," Table 10 and Table 11, provides modern standards (means and standard deviations) for comparative historical studies.
42. Greenwood et al., "Marry Your Like," 348–353.
43. The economics and econometrics of the self-employment choice are discussed in Borjas and Bronars, "Consumer Discrimination," and Bernhardt, "Comparative Advantage." The discussion here follows Bernhardt, which is a simplified version of Borjas and Bronars.

44. Williamson, *New People*, 64.

45. The skip samples were created by calculating the total number of households in each city's census. A target number of white households was set equal to the number of African-American households. The total number of households was divided by the target number, to yield a skip value. A two-digit random number generator selected the starting household (say, for example, household number 54 in the city's first ward). The white sample includes that start household and every nth household thereafter as identified using the page order of the manuscript censuses, where n = total households / target households.

46. Blau, "Immigration and Labor Earnings," 28.

47. Murphy and Welch, "Empirical Age-Earnings Profiles," 208.

48. Conley and Galenson, "Nativity and Wealth," 472–478.

49. Conley and Galenson, "Nativity and Wealth," 472.

50. In the cases of small positive values of real estate and blank personal property it seems likely that census marshals mistakenly recorded personal as real property. My search of the extant secondary literature reveals no other study that makes this assumption or adjustment. Given that no one else has made such an adjustment, I follow convention and take real and personal property values at face value.

51. Steckel and Moehling, "Rising Inequality," 175.

52. Smith, *Wealth of Nations*, 228.

53. Heaton and Lucas, "Portfolio Choice," 1173.

54. As Paul Rhode notes (personal communication), there is no taxation without *mis*representation. Tax records must be used knowing that households had incentives to disguise or hide assets from the view of tax commissioners. The principal types of real and personal property were not easily hidden. It was hard to hide land, structures, slaves, livestock and carriages.

55. The tax sheets read "slaves 16 years and upwards" and "slaves 12 years and upwards," so that slave 16 years and older should be listed in each column. In practice, however, it is common for slaves to be enumerated as 16 years and older that do not appear in the 12 years and older category. It appears that the tax marshals interpreted the "12 and upwards" category to imply that 12- to 15-year-old slaves were to be separately enumerated. See Weisiger, "Using Personal Property Tax Records" 1–3, for a brief description of the source.

56. In Virginia, cities are legally autonomous and not part of the surrounding counties. Slave counts are taken from the counties that surround the relevant city. Spotsylvania County is used for Fredericksburg, Dinwiddie for Petersburg, and Henrico for Richmond. This adds more error into the calculations, because the cities and counties were not coterminous and some slaves resided in the cities and some in each city's hinterlands.

57. Hacker, "Decennial Life Tables," Table 3, Table 8.

58. Fogel and Engerman, *Time on the Cross*, Figure 8, show that male slaves continued to generate positive output up to age 70, but beyond age 55 the value of output produced (about $60/annum) earnings were not inadequate for subsistence.

59. Brush, "Risk, Discounting, and the Present Value," 270.

60. Bodenhorn, *History of Banking*, 135–136. Homer and Sylla, *History of Interest Rates*, Chapter 16, report rates on a host of government and corporate securities at mid-century. Most offered a return between 4 and 6 percent.

61. Sylla, Wilson, and Wright, *Early U.S. Securities Prices*.

62. Virginia House of Delegates, *Thirty-Sixth Annual Report*, 230, 234.

63. Komlos, "Toward an Anthropometric History," 302–304.

64. Zemel and Johnson, "Application of the Preece-Baines Growth Model," 563–570. See Onis et al., "National Center for Health Statistics Reference," for a recent application using the model. It has been used in an historical context by Mokyr and Ó Grada, "Heights of the British and the Irish."

65. Hansen, Cortina-Borja, and Ratcliffe, "Assessing Non-linear Estimation Procedures," 85.

66. Ledford and Coles, "Mathematical Models of Growth," 102, 109.

REFERENCES

Data Sources and Archival Materials

BUREAU OF REFUGEES, FREEDMEN, AND ABANDONED LANDS

Bureau of Refugees, Freedmen, and Abandoned Lands. Records of the Assistant Commissioner for the State of Mississippi. *Registers of Marriages of Freedmen.* Vol. 1 (1863–1865). National Archives and Records Administration. Series M826, Reel 42. (Natchez, Mississippi and Vicksburg, Mississippi).

Bureau of Refugees, Freedmen, and Abandoned Lands. Records of the Assistant Commissioner for the State of Mississippi. *Freedmen's Marriage Certificates* (1861–1869). National Archives and Records Administration. Record Group 105.2. (Memphis, Tennessee).

National Archives and Records Administration. *Marriage Records of the Office of the Commissioner. Washington Headquarters of the Bureau of Refugees, Freedmen, and Abandoned Lands, 1861–1869.* Washington, DC: NARA, 2002.

FREE NEGRO AND SLAVE RECORDS

Albermarle County, 1803–1864, Box 1. Library of Virginia. Richmond, Virginia.

Henrico County, 1789–1864, Box 2. Library of Virginia. Richmond, Virginia.

MARYLAND FREE BLACK REGISTERS

Komlos, John. *Height of Free African Americans in Maryland, 1800–1864.* Computer File ICPSR 03422. Ann Arbor: Inter-university Consortium for Political and Social Research. 2002.

PRICE INDICES AND WAGES

Cole, Arthur Harrison. *Wholesale Commodity Prices in the United States, 1700–1861.* Cambridge, MA: Harvard University Press, 1938.

Margo, Robert A. *Wages and Labor Markets in the United States, 1820–1860.* Chicago: University of Chicago Press, 2000.

Margo, Robert A., and Georgia Villaflor. "The Growth of Wages in Antebellum America: New Evidence." *Journal of Economic History* 47.4 (December 1987), 873–895.

Warren, George F., and Frank A. Pearson. *Prices.* New York: John Wiley & Sons, 1933.

290

RUNAWAY SLAVE ADVERTISEMENTS AND SUPPLEMENTAL DATA

Carter, Susan B., Scott Sigmund Gartner, Michael R. Haines, Alan L. Olmstead, Richard Sutch, and Gavin Wright (eds) *Historical Statistics of the United States: Millennial Edition*. New York: Cambridge University Press, 2006. Series Bb209–218.

Meaders, Daniel (ed.) *Advertisements for Runaway Slaves in Virginia, 1801–1820*. New York: Garland Publishing, 1997.

Parker, Freddie L. (ed.) *Stealing a Little Freedom: Advertisements for Slave Runaways in North Carolina, 1791–1840*. New York: Garland Publishing, 1994.

UNITED STATES DECENNIAL CENSUSES

Menard, Russell, Trent Alexander, Jason Digman, and J. David Hacker. *Public Use Microdata Samples of the Slave Population of 1850–1860*. Minneapolis: Minnesota Population Center, University of Minnesota, 2004. http://usa.ipums.org/usa/slavepums/index.html.

Ruggles, Steven, J. Trent Alexander, Katie Genadek, Ronald Goeken, Matthew B. Schroeder, and Matthew Sobek. *Integrated Public Use Microdata Series. Version 5.0*. [Machine-readable database]. Minneapolis: University of Minnesota, 2010. (1860 population census).

United States. Census Office. 8th Census. *Population of the United States in 1860*. Washington, DC: Government Printing Office, 1864.

United States. Bureau of the Census. *Negro Population of the United States, 1790–1915*. Washington, DC: Government Printing Office, 1918.

University of Virginia Library. Historical Census Browser. http://mapserver.lib.virginia.edu.

VIRGINIA FREE BLACK REGISTERS

Alleghany County: "Register of Free Negroes, 1855–1856." Alleghany County Microfilm Reel No. 17. Local Government Records, County Court Records. Library of Virginia. Richmond, Virginia.

Amelia County: "Free Negro and Slave Records, 1781–1866." Manuscript. Amelia County. Local Government Records Collection, County Court Records. Library of Virginia. Richmond, Virginia.

Amherst County: Sherrie S. McLeRoy and William R. McLeRoy. *Strangers in their Midst: The Free Black Population of Amherst County*.Virginia. Bowie, MD: Heritage Books, 1993.

Arlington County: "Free Negro Register, 1797–1861." Arlington County Microfilm Nos. 60, 62, 225. Local Government Records Collection, County Court Records. Library of Virginia. Richmond, Virginia.

Augusta County: Katherine G. Bushman, *The Registers of Free Blacks, 1810–184, Augusta County, Virginia and Staunton, Virginia*. Verona, VA: Mid-Valley Press, 1989.

Bedford County: "Registers of Free Negroes, vol. 1 (1803–1820); vol 2 (1820–1860)." Bedford County Microfilm No. 120a. Local Government Records Collection, County Court Records. Library of Virginia. Richmond, Virginia.

Botetourt County: Dorothy A. Boyd-Rush. *Free Negroes Registered in the Clerk's Office, Botetourt County, Virginia, 1802–1836*. Athens, GA: Iberian Publishing Company, 1993.

Brunswick County: Wynne, Frances Holloway. *Register of Free Negroes and of Dower Slaves, Brunswick County, Virginia, 1803–1850*. Berwyn Heights, MD: Heritage Books, 1983.

Campbell County: "Register of Free Negroes, 1801–1850." Campbell County Microfilm No. 68. Local Government Records Collection, County Court Records. Library of Virginia. Richmond, Virginia.

Charles City County: "Register of Free Negroes, 1835–1864." Charles City County Microfilm No. 22. Local Government Records Collection, County Court Records. Library of Virginia. Richmond, Virginia.

Charles City County: "Registrations of Free Negroes and Mulattoes: 1823–1864." Charles City County Historical Society (n.d.). www.charlescity.org/fnr.

Chesterfield County: "Register of Free Negroes, #1 (1804–183); #2 (1830–1853)." Chesterfield County Microfilm No. 351. Local Government Records Collection, County Court Records. Library of Virginia. Richmond, Virginia.

Cumberland County: "Register of Free Negroes, 1821–1863." Manuscripts. Cumberland County. Local Government Records Collection, County Court Records. Library of Virginia. Richmond, Virginia.

Essex County: "Free Negro Register, 1843–1861." Essex County Microfilm No. 120. Local Government Records Collection, County Court Records. Library of Virginia. Richmond, Virginia.

Fairfax County: Donald Sweig. *Registrations of Free Negroes Commencing September Court 1822, Book No. 2 and Register of Free Blacks 1835 Book 3*. Fairfax, VA: Office of Comprehensive Planning of Fairfax County, Virginia, July 1977.

Fauquier County: Karen King Ibrahim, Karen Hughes White, & Courtney Gaskins. *Fauquier County, Virginia Register of Free Negroes, 1817–1865*. Privately published, 1993.

Fluvanna County: "Register of Free Negroes, 1851–1862." Fluvanna County Microfilm No. 48. Local Government Records Collection, County Court Records. Library of Virginia. Richmond, Virginia.

Henrico County: "Register of Free Negroes and Mulattoes, 1831–1865." Henrico County Microfilm No. 113. Local Government Records Collection, County Court Records. Library of Virginia. Richmond, Virginia.

Lancaster County: "Register of Free Negroes and Mulattoes, 1803–1860." Lancaster County Microfilm No. 337. Local Government Records Collection, County Court Records. Library of Virginia. Richmond, Virginia.

Louisa County: Janice Abercrombie. *Free Blacks of Louisa County, Virginia*. Athens, GA: Iberian Publishing Company, 1994.

Loudoun County: Patricia B. Duncan. *Abstracts of Loudoun County, Virginia: Register of Free Negroes, 1844–1861*. Westminster, MD: Willow Bend Books, 2000.

Lynchburg City: "Register of Free Negroes, 1843–1865." Lynchburg City Microfilm No. 37. Local Government Records Collection, County Court Records. Library of Virginia. Richmond, Virginia.

Middlesex County: "Registers of Free Negroes and Mulattoes, 1800–1860." Middlesex County Microfilm Nos. 74, 114. Local Government Records Collection, County Court Records. Library of Virginia. Richmond, Virginia.

Montgomery County: Richard B. Dickenson. *Entitled! Free Papers in Appalachia Concerning Antebellum Freeborn Negroes and Emancipated Blacks of Montgomery County, Virginia*. Washington, DC: National Genealogical Society, 1981.

Nelson County: "Register of Free Negroes, 1853–1865." Nelson County Microfilm No. 50. Local Government Records Collection, County Court Records. Library of Virginia. Richmond, Virginia.

Norfolk County: "Register of Free Negroes, 1850–1861." Norfolk County Microfilm No. 105. Local Government Records Collection, County Court Records. Library of Virginia. Richmond, Virginia.

Northampton County: Frances Bibbins Latimer. *The Register of Free Negroes: Northampton County, Virginia, 1853 to 1861*. Bowie, MD: Heritage Books, 1992.

Northumberland County: Karen E. Sutton. *Northumberland County, Virginia, Register of Free Blacks*. Bowie, MD: Heritage Books, 1999.

Orange County: "Free Negro Papers." Orange County Microfilm No. 565. Local Government Records Collection, County Court Records. Library of Virginia. Richmond, Virginia.

Petersburg City: "Hustings Court Registry of Free Negroes and Mulattoes, 1850–1858" and "Hustings Court Registry of Free Negroes and Mulattoes, 1859–1865." Petersburg City Microfilm No. 123. Local Government Records Collection, County Court Records. Library of Virginia. Richmond, Virginia.

Pittsylvania County: Alva H. Griffith. *Pittsylvania County, Virginia Register of Free Negroes and Related Documentation*. Bowie, MD: Heritage Books, 2001.

Powhatan County: "Register of Free Negroes, 1820–1865." Powhatan County Microfilm No. 45. Local Government Records Collection, County Court Records. Library of Virginia. Richmond, Virginia.

Princess Anne County: "Register of Free Negroes and Mulattoes, 1830–1862." Princess Anne County Microfilm No. 75. Local Government Records Collection, County Court Records. Library of Virginia. Richmond, Virginia.

Roanoke County: "Free Negro Register, 1838–1864." Roanoke County Microfilm No. 312. Local Government Records Collection, County Court Records. Library of Virginia. Richmond, Virginia.

Surry County: Dennis Hudgins, *Surry County Virginia Register of Free Negroes*. Richmond, VA: Virginia Genealogical Society, 1995.

Westmoreland County: "Register of Free Negroes, etc., 1828–1849. Westmoreland County Microfilm No.75. Local Government Records Collection, County Court Records. Library of Virginia. Richmond, Virginia.

VIRGINIA TAX RECORDS

Fredericksburg City. Land Tax Records, 1860. Fredericksburg City Microfilm Reel 556. Library of Virginia. Richmond, Virginia.

Fredericksburg City. Personal Property Tax Records, 1860. Fredericksburg City Microfilm Reel 803. Library of Virginia. Richmond, Virginia.

Petersburg City. Land Tax Records, 1860. Petersburg City Microfilm Reel 591. Library of Virginia. Richmond, Virginia.

Petersburg City. Personal Property Tax Records, 1860. Petersburg City Microfilm Reel 815. Library of Virginia. Richmond, Virginia.

Richmond City. Land Tax Records, 1860. Richmond City Microfilm Rel 596. Library of Virginia. Richmond, Virginia.

Richmond City. Personal Property Tax Records, 1860. Richmond City Microfilm Rel 827. Library of Virginia. Richmond, Virginia.

Edwards, Conley L. "Using Land Tax Records in the Archives at the Library of Virginia." Research Notes Number 1. Richmond: Library of Virginia, 2001.

Weisiger, Minor T. "Using Personal Property Tax Records in the Archives at the Library of Virginia." Research Notes Number 3. Richmond: Library of Virginia, 2010.

OTHER SOURCES

Burton, William Lewis. *Annals of Henrico Parish*. Richmond, VA: privately printed, 1904.

Chamberlayne, Churchill Gibson. *The Vestry Book and Register of Bristol Parish, Virginia, 1720–1789*. Richmond, VA: Privately Printed, 1898.

Sylla, Richard E., Jack Wilson and Robert E. Wright. *Early U.S. Securities Prices*. Data set available at http://eh.net/database/early-u-s-securities-prices/.

Virginia. House of Delegates. *Thirty-Sixth Annual Report of the Board of Public Works to the General Assembly of Virginia*. Virginia House Document No. 18. Richmond: William Ritchie, public printer, 1851.

Articles, Books, Theses, and Working Papers

"Account of the Number of Souls in the Province of Maryland, in the Year 1755." *Gentlemen's Magazine and Historical Chronicle* 34 (June 1764), 261.

Acemoglu, Daron, and Alexander Wolitzky. "The Economics of Labor Coercion.t" *Econometrica* 79.2 (March 2011), 555–600.

Adelino, Manuel, Antoinette Schoar, and Felipe Severino. "House Prices, Collateral and Self-Employment." Working Paper, Duke University, 2014.

Akerlof, George A. "Discriminatory, Status-Based Wages among Tradition-Oriented, Stochastically Trading Coconut Producers." *Journal of Political Economy* 93.2 (April 1985), 265–276.

Allen, Robert C. "Pessimism Preserved: Real Wages in the British Industrial Revolution." Unpublished working paper, Nuffield College, Oxford University, April 2007.

Alston, Lee J., and Kyle D. Kauffman. "Agricultural Chutes and Ladders: New Estimates of Sharecroppers and 'True Tenants' in the South, 1900–1920." *Journal of Economic History* 57.2 (June 1997), 464–475.

Alston, Lee J. and Kyle D. Kauffman. "Up, Down, and Off the Agricultural Ladder: New Evidence and Implications of Agricultural Mobility for Blacks in the Postbellum South." *Agricultural History* 72.2 (Spring 1998), 263–279.

American Anti-Slavery Society. *The Legion of Liberty! And Force of Truth, Containing the Thoughts, Words, and Deeds, of Some Prominent Apostles, Champions and Martyrs.* 2d ed. New York: American Anti-Slavery Society, 1843.

American Colonization Society. "Amalgamation of Races." *The Colonizationist and Journal of Freedom.* (June 1833).

Anand, Sudhir, Fabienne Peter, and Amartya Sen. *Public Health, Ethics and Equity.* New York: Oxford University Press, 2004.

Anbinder, Tyler. *Five Points: The 19th-Century New York City Neighborhood That Invented Tap Dance, Stole Elections, and Became the World's Most Notorious Slum.* New York: Free Press, 2001.

Andrews, Ethan Allen. *Slavery and the Domestic Slave Trade in the United States.* Boston: Light & Stearns, 1836.

Anonymous. "Black and Mulatto Population of the South. *De Bow's Review* 8.6 (June 1850), 587–589.

Anonymous. "Progress of Population in the United States." *Hunt's Merchants' Magazine and Commercial Review* 32 (January 1855), 38–56.

Arbery, Glen Cannon. "Victims of Likeness: Quadroons and Octoroons in Southern Fiction." *Southern Review* 25.1 (January 1989), 52–71.

Arrow, Kenneth J. "Models of Job Discrimination." In *Racial Discrimination in Economic Life,* 83–102. Edited by A. H. Pascal. Lexington, MA: D. C. Heath, 1972.

Atack, Jeremy. "The Agricultural Ladder Revisited: A New Look at an Old Question with Some Data for 1860." *Agricultural History* 63.1 (Winter 1989), 1–25.

Aydemir, Abdurrahman and George J. Borjas. "Attenuation Bias in Measuring the Wage Impact of Immigration." *Journal of Labor Economics* 29.1 (January 2011), 69–112.

Babcock, Theodore Stoddard. "Manumission in Virginia, 1782–1806." Unpublished masters thesis, University of Virginia.

Bachman, John. *The Doctrine of the Unity of the Human Race Examined on the Principles of Science.* Charleston, SC: C. Canning, 1850.

Baker, Ray Stannard. *Following the Color Line: An Account of Negro Citizenship in the American Democracy.* New York: Doubleday, Page & Co., 1908.

Baldwin, Bird T. *The Physical Growth of Children from Birth to Maturity.* University of Iowa Studies in Child Welfare. Iowa City: University of Iowa, 1921.

Ballagh, James Curtis. *A History of Slavery in Virginia.* Baltimore, MD: Johns Hopkins University Press, 1902.

Barrow, John, A. A. Sandilands, and Joshua Hill. "Recent Accounts of the Pitcairn Islanders." *Journal of the Royal Geographical Society of London* 3 (1833), 156–168.

Becker, Gary S. *The Economics of Discrimination.* Chicago: University of Chicago Press, 1971.

Becker, Gary S. *A Treatise on the Family.* Cambridge, MA: Harvard University Press, 1981.

Becker, Gary S. and George J. Stigler. "De Gustibus Non Est Disputandum." *American Economic Review* 67.2 (March 1977), 76–90.

Belding, Theodore C. "Nobility and Stupidity: Modeling the Evolution of Class Endogamy." Unpublished working paper: Center for the Study of Complex Systems, University of Michigan (May 2004).

Bellamy, Donnie D. "The Education of Blacks in Missouri prior to 1861." *Journal of Negro History* 59.2 (April 1974), 143–157.

Bennett, Lerone Jr. "Miscegenation in America." *Ebony* 18.12 (October 1962), 94–104.

Bentley, Nancy. "White Slaves: The Mulatto Hero in Antebellum Fiction." *American Literature* 65.3 (September 1993), 501–522.

Benwell, John. *An Englishman's Travels in America: His Observations of Life and Manners in the Free and Slave States*. London: Binns and Goodwin, 1853.

Berlin, Ira. *Slaves Without Masters: The Free Negro in the Antebellum South*. New York: The New Press, 1974.

Berlin, Ira, and Herbert G. Gutman. "Natives and Immigrants, Free Men and Slaves: Urban Workingmen in the Antebellum American South." *American Historical Review* 88 (December 1983), 1175–1200.

Bernard, Karl. *Travels through North America, during the Years 1825 and 1826*. 2 vols. Philadelphia: Carey, Lea & Carey, 1828.

Bernhardt, Irwin. "Comparative Advantage in Self-Employment and Paid Work." *Canadian Journal of Economics* 27.2 (May 1994), 273–289.

Berzon, Judith R. *Neither White Nor Black: The Mulatto Character in American Fiction*. New York: New York University Press, 1978.

Bilger, Burkard. "The Height Gap: Why Europeans are Getting Taller and Taller—and American Aren't." *New Yorker* (April 5, 2004).

Billings, Warren M. "The Law of Servants and Slaves in Seventeenth-Century Virginia." *Virginia Magazine of History and Biography* 99.1 (January 1991), 45–62.

Birnie, C. W. "Education of the Free Negro in Charleston, South Carolina, prior to the Civil War." *Journal of Negro History* 12.1 (January 1927), 13–21.

Blackburn, Robin. "Introduction." In *Paths to Freedom: Manumission in the Atlantic World*, 1–13. Edited by Rosemary Brana-Shute and Randy J. Sparks. Columbia: University of South Carolina Press, 2009.

Blangero, John, Peter T. Katzmarzyk, Michael C. Mahaney, Robert M. Malina, and Jon-Jong Quek. "Potential Effects of Ethnicity in Genetic and Environmental Sources of Variability in the Stature, Mass and Body Mass Index of Children." *Human Biology* 71.6 (December 1999), 977–987.

Blassingame, John W. (ed.) *Slave Testimony: Two Centuries of Letters, Speeches, Interviews, and Autobiographies* Baton Rouge: Louisiana State University Press, 1977.

Blassingame, John W. *The Slave Community: Plantation Life in the Antebellum South*. New York: Oxford University Press, 1979.

Blau, Francine D. "Immigration and Labor Earnings in Early Twentieth Century America." *Research in Population Economics* 2 (1980), 21–41.

Block, Sharon. *Rape and Sexual Power in Early America*. Chapel Hill: University of North Carolnia Press, 2006.

Bode, Frederick A., and Donald E. Ginter. *Farm Tenancy and the Census in Antebellum Georgia*. Athens: University of Georgia Press, 1966.

Bodenhorn, Howard. "A Troublesome Caste: Height and Nutrition of Antebellum Virginia's Rural Free Blacks." *Journal of Economic History* 59.4 (December 1999), 972–996.

Bodenhorn, Howard. *A History of Banking in Antebellum America: Financial Markets and Economic Development in an Era of Nation-Building*. New York: Cambridge University Press, 2000.

Bodenhorn, Howard. "The Complexion Gap: The Economic Consequences of Color among Free African Americans in the Rural Antebellum South." *Advances in Agricultural Economic History* 2 (2003), 41–73.

Bodenhorn, Howard. "Just and Reasonable Treatment: Racial Differences in the Terms of Pauper Apprenticeship in Antebellum Maryland." National Bureau of Economic Research Working Paper 9752 (June 2003).

Bodenhorn, Howard. "Single Parenthood and Childhood Outcomes in the Mid-Nineteenth-Century Urban South." *Journal of Interdisciplinary History* 38.1 (Summer 2007), 33–64.

Bodenhorn, Howard. "Industrious, Sober, Good Citizens: The Occupational Choices of Antebellum Baltimore's Free Blacks." Working Paper, Clemson University, 2011.

Bodenhorn, Howard. "Manumission in Nineteenth-Century Virginia." *Cliometrica* 5.2 (June 2011), 145–164.

Bodenhorn, Howard, Timothy W. Guinnane, and Thomas A. Mroz. "Problems of Sample-Selection Bias in the Historical Heights Literature: A Theoretical and Econometric Analysis." Yale University Economic Growth Center Working Paper No 1023 (2013).

Bodenhorn, Howard, Timothy W. Guinnane, and Thomas A. Mroz. "Caveat Lector: Sample Selection in Historical Heights and the Interpretation of Early Industrializing Economies." National Bureau of Economic Research Working Paper #19955, March 2014.

Bodenhorn, Howard and Christopher S. Ruebeck. "The Economics of Identity and the Endogeneity of Race." National Burea of Economic Research Working Paper #9962, September 2003.

Bodenhorn, Howard and Christopher S. Ruebeck. "Colourism and African-American Wealth: Evidence from the Nineteenth-Century South." *Journal of Population Economics* 20.4 (Fall 2007), 599–620.

Bogger, Tommy L. *Free Blacks in Norfolk, Virginia, 1790–1860: The Darker Side of Freedom.* Charlottesville: University Press of Virginia, 1997.

Bogin, Barry, Maureen Wall, and Robert B. MacVean. "Longitudinal Analysis of Adolescent Growth of *Ladino* and Mayan School Children in Guatemala: Effects of Environment and Sex." *American Journal of Physical Anthropology* 89.4 (December 1992), 447–457.

Bogue, Allan G. *From Prairie to Corn Belt: Farming on the Illinois and Iowa Prairies in the Nineteenth Century.* Chicago: University of Chicago Press, 1963.

Bolzan, A., L. Guimarey, and A. R. Frisancho. "Study of Growth of Rural School Children from Buenos Aires, Argentina using Upper Arm Muscle Area by Height and Other Anthropometric Dimensions of Body Composition." *Annals of Human Biology* 26.2 (March 1999), 185–193.

Borjas, George J., and Stephen G. Bronars. "Consumer Discrimination and Self-Employment." *Journal of Political Economy* 97.3 (June 1989), 581–605.

Bowditch, Henry P. *The Growth of Children.* Eighth Annual Report of the State Board of Health of Massachusetts. Boston: Albert J. Wright, State Printer, 1877.

Bowditch, Henry P. *The Growth of Children: A Supplementary Investigation.* Tenth Annual Report of the State Board of Health. Boston: Rand, Abery & Co., Printers to the Commonwealth, 1879.

Bowditch, Henry P. "The Growth of Children." *Papers on Anthropometry.* Boston: American Statistical Association, 1894.

Boyd, Robert L. "Race, Gender, and Survivalist Entrepreneurship in Large Northern Cities during the Great Depression." *Journal of Socio-Economics* 34.3 (May 2005), 331–339.

Boyd, Robert L. "Trends in the Occupations of Eminent Black Entrepreneurs in the United States." *Journal of Socio-Economics* 37.6 (December 2008), 2390–2398.

Brackenridge. Hugh Henry. *Adventures of Captain Farrago.* Philadelphia: T. B. Peterson & Brothers, 1856.

Brana-Shute, Rosemary. "Sex and Gender in Surinamese Manumissions." In *Paths to Freedom: Manumission in the Atlantic World,* 175–196. Edited by Rosemary Brana-Shute and Randy J. Sparks. Columbia: University of South Carolina Press, 2009.

Brana-Shute, Rosemary, and Randy J. Sparks (eds) *Paths to Freedom: Manumission in the Atlantic World.* Columbia: University of South Carolina Press, 2009.

Breen, T. H. and Stephen Innes. *"Myne Owne Ground"*: Race and Freedom on Virginia's Eastern Shore. New York: Oxford University Press, 2005.

Brewer, James H. "Negro Property Owners in Seventeenth-Century Virginia." *William and Mary Quarterly*, 3rd Series, 12.4 (October 1955), 575–580.

Brigham, R. I. "Negro Education in Ante Bellum Missouri." *Journal of Negro History* 30.4 (October 1945), 405–420.

Bristol, Douglas Jr. "From Outposts to Enclaves: A Social History of Black Barbers from 1750 to 1915." *Enterprise & Society* 5.4 (December 2004), 594–606.

Brown, Letitia Woods. *Free Negroes in the District in Columbia, 1790–1846*. New York: Oxford University Press, 1972.

Brown, Sterling. *The Negro in American Fiction*. Port Washington, NY: Kennikat Press, 1968. Reprint of 1937 edition.

Brown, William Wells. *Clotel; Or, the President's Daughter: A Narrative of Slave Life in the United States*. London: Partridge & Oakey, 1853.

Browne, Patrick Arrell. *The Classification of Mankind, by the Hair and Wool of Their Heads, with the Nomenclature of Human Hybrids* (Philadelphia: J. A. Jones, 1852).

Brush, Brian. "Risk, Discounting, and the Present Value of Future Earnings." *Journal of Forensic Economics* 16.3 (Fall 2003), 263–274.

Buckley, Thomas E. "Unfixing Race: Class, Power, and Identity in an Interracial Family." *Virginia Magazine of History and Biography* 102.3 (July 1994), 349–380.

Budros, Art. "Social Shocks and Slave Social Mobility: Manumission in Brunswick County, Virginia, 1782–1862." *American Journal of Sociology* 110.3 (November 2004), 539–579.

Burdett, Ken, and Melvyn G. Coles. "Marriage and Class." *Quarterly Journal of Economics* 112.1 (February 1997), 141–168.

Burdett, Kenneth, and Melvyn G. Coles. "Long-Term Partnership Formation: Marriage and Employment." *Economic Journal* 109.465 (June 1999), 307–344.

Burgard, Sarah. "Does Race Matter? Children's Height in Brazil and South Africa." *Demography* 39.4 (November 2002), 763–790.

Caetano, Gregorio, and Vikram Maheshri. "School Segregation and the Identification of Tipping Behavior." Working paper, University of Houston (December 2012).

Calhoun, John C. "Who Is a Negro?" *University of Florida Law Review* 11.2 (Summer 1958), 235–240.

Calomiris, Charles, and Jonathan Pritchett. "Preserving Slave Families for Profit: Traders' Incentives and Pricing in the New Orleans Slave Market." *Journal of Economic History* 69.4 (December 2009), 986–1011.

Camerer, Colin F., and Howard Kunreuther. "Decision Processes for Low Probability Events: Policy Implications." *Journal of Policy Analysis and Management* 8.4 (Autumn 1989), 565–592.

Campbell, John. "Negro-Mania." *De Bow's Review* 12.5 (May 1852), 507–524.

Campbell, John F. "How Free is Free? The Limits of Manumission for Enslaved Africans in Eighteenth-Century British West Indian Sugar Society." In *Paths to Freedom: Manumission in the Atlantic World*, 143–159. Edited by Rosemary Brana-Shute and Randy J. Sparks. Columbia: University of South Carolina Press, 2009.

Carbado, Devon W., and Mitu Gulati. "The Law and Economics of Critical Race Theory." *Yale Law Journal* 112.7 (May 2003), 1757–1828.

Carbado, Devon W., And Rachel F. Moran. "Introduction: The Story of Law and American Racial Consciousness—Building a Canon One Case at a Time." In *Race Law Stories*, 1–36. Edited by Rachel F. Moran and Devon W. Carbado. New York: Foundation Press, 2008.

Carbado, Devon W., and Donald Weise. *The Long Walk to Freedom: Runaway Slave Narratives*. Boston: Beacon Press, 2012.

Caroll, Kenneth L. "Religious Influences on the Manumission of Slaves in Caroline, Dorchester, and Talbot Counties." *Maryland Historical Magazine* 56.2 (June 1961), 176–197.

Carson, Scott Alan. "Health, Wealth, and Inequality: A Contribution to the Debate about the Relationship between Inequality and Health." *Historical Methods* 42.2 (Spring 2009), 43–56.

Case, Anne, and Christina Paxon. "Stature and Status: Height, Ability, and Labor Market Outcomes." *Journal of Political Economy* 116.3 (June 2008), 499–532.

Catterall, Helen Tunnicliff. *Judicial Cases Concerning American Slavery and the Negro.* 5 volumes. Washington, DC: Carnegie Institute of Washington, 1926–1937.

Child, Lydia Marie. "The Quadroons." In *The Liberty Bell*, 115–141. Boston: Massachusetts Anti-Slavery Fair, 1842.

Christensen, Kaare, David Gaist, Bernard Jeune, and James W. Vaupel. "A Tooth Per Child?" *Lancet* 352 (18 July 1998), 204.

Cipolla, Carlo M. *Between Two Cultures: An Introduction to Economic History.* New York: W. W. Norton & Company, Inc., 1988.

Clark, Emily. "Atlantic Alliances: Marriage among People of African Descent in New Orleans, 1759–1830." Working paper, Tulane University (2010).

Clement, E. M. B. "Changes in the Mean Stature and Weight of British Children over the Past Seventy Years." *British Medical Journal* 2.4842 (October 24, 1953), 897–902.

Clinton, Catherine. "Caught in the Web of the Big House: Women and Slavery." In *The Web of Southern Social Relations: Women, Family, and Education*, 19–34. Edited by Walter J. Fraser Jr., R. Frank Saunders Jr., and John L. Wakelyn. Athens: University of Georgia Press, 1987.

Clover, David. "'This Horably Wicked Action': Abortion and Resistance on a Jamaican Slave Plantation." *Society for Caribbean Studies Annual Conference Papers* 8 (2007), 1–10.

Coase, Ronald H. "The Problem of Social Cost." *Journal of Law and Economics* 3 (October 1960), 1–44.

Coelho, Philip R., and Robert A. McGuire. "Diets Versus Diseases: The Anthropometrics of Slave Children." *Journal of Economic History* 60.1 (March 2000), 232–246.

Cole, Shawn. "Capitalism and Freedom: Manumissions and the Slave Market in Louisiana, 1725–1820." *Journal of Economic History* 65.4 (December 2005), 1008–1027.

Coleman, Ashley N., and William K. Hutchinson. "Determinants of Slave Prices: Louisiana, 1725 to 1820." Unpublished working paper (July 2006).

Collins, William, and Robert A. Margo. "Race and Home Ownership from the End of the Civil War to the Present." National Bureau of Economic Research Working Paper #16665 (January 2011).

Collins, William, and Robert A. Margo. "Race and Home Ownership from the End of the Civil War to the Present." *American Economic Review* 101.2 (May 2011), 355–359.

Colvin, Rhonda, and Sarah E. Needleman. "Better Times Mean Fewer Businesses." *Wall Street Journal* (9 April 2014), B2.

Condon, John Joseph Jr. *Family Strategies, Slavery and Freedom in Post-Revolutionary Rural Chesapeake: Anne Arundel County, Maryland, 1781–1831.* PhD dissertation: University of Minnesota, 2001.

Condon, Sean. "The Slave Owner's Family and Manumission in the Post-Revolutionary Chesapeake Tidewater: Evidence from Anne Arundel County Wills, 1790–1820." In *Paths to Freedom: Manumission in the Atlantic World*, 339–362. Edited by Rosemary Brana-Shute and Randy J. Sparks. Columbia: University of South Carolina Press, 2009.

Condon, Sean. "The Significance of Group Manumission in Post-Revolutionary Rural Maryland." *Slavery & Abolition* 32.1 (March 2011), 75–89.

Conley, Timothy G. and David W. Galenson. "Nativity and Wealth in Mid-Nineteenth Century Cities." *Journal of Economic History* 58.1 (June 1998), 468–493.

Conrad, Alfred H., and John R. Meyer. "The Economics of Slavery in the Ante Bellum South." *Journal of Political Economy* 66.2 (April 1958), 95–130.

Cooper, James Fenimore. *The Last of the Mohicans: A Narrative of 1757.* 3 vols. London; John Miller, 1826.

Croly, David Goodman, and George Wakeman. *Miscegenation: The Theory of the Blending of the Races, Applied to the American White Man and Negro.* New York: Trubner & Company, 1863.

Curry, Leonard P. *The Free Black in Urban America, 1800–1850: The Shadow of the Dream.* Chicago: University of Chicago Press, 1981.

Cvrcek, Tomas. "When Harry Left Sally: A New Estimate of Marital Disruption in the U.S., 1860–1948." *Demographic Research* 21.24 (November 2009), 719–758.

Dain. Bruce. *A Hideous Monster of the Mind: American Race Theory in the Early Republic.* Cambridge, MA: Harvard University Press, 2002.

Dalzell, Robert F. Jr. *The Good Rich and What They Cost Us.* New Haven, CT: Yale University Press, 2013.

Danubio, M. E., G. Gruppioni, and F. Vecchi. "Height and Secular Trend in Conscripts Born in the Central Apennines (Italy), 1865–1972." *Annals of Human Biology* 30.2 (March 2003), 225–231.

David, Paul A., Herbert G. Gutman, Richard Sutch, Peter Temin, and Gavin Wright. *Reckoning with Slavery: A Critical Study in the Quantitative History of American Negro Slavery.* New York: Oxford University Press, 1976.

Davis, F. James. *Who Is Black? One Nation's Definition.* Tenth Anniversary Edition. University Park: Pennsylvania State University Press, 2001.

De Bow, James D. B. *The Industrial Resources, Etc., of the Southern and Western States* (3 vols.). New Orleans: Office of De Bow's Review, 1852.

DeCuir, Jessica T., and Adrienne D. Dixson. "'So When It Comes Out, They Aren't That Surprised That It Is There': Using Critical Race Theory as a Tool of Analysis of Race and Racism in Education." *Educational Researcher* (June 2004), 26–31.

Degler, Carl N. *Neither Black Nor White: Slavery and Race Relations in Brazil and the United States.* New York: Macmillan, 1971.

De la Fuente, Alejandro, and Ariela J. Gross. "Comparative Studies of Law, Slavery and Race in the Americas." University of Southern California Law School working paper No. 56 (2010).

Delany, Martin. *The Condition, Elevation, Emigration, and Destiny of the Colored People of the United States.* New York: Arno Press, 1968 (reprint of 1852 edition).

De Onis, Mercedes, Parasmani Dasgupta, Syamal Saha, Debasis Sengupta, and Monika Blössner. "The National Center for Health Statistics Reference and the Growth of Indian Adolescent Boys." *American Journal of Clinical Nutrition* 74.2 (August 2001), 248–253.

Dittmar, Jeremiah, and Suresh Naidu. "Contested Property: Fugitive Slaves in the Antebellum U.S. South." Working paper, Columbia University (September 2012).

Domínguez, Virginia R. *White By Definition: Social Classification in Creole Louisiana.* New Brunswick: Rutgers University Press, 1986.

Douglass, Frederick. *My Bondage and My Freedom.* New York: Miller, Orton and Mulligan, 1855.

Douglass, Frederick. *The Life and Times of Frederick Douglass, From 1817 to 1882, Written by Himself.* Edited by John Lobb. London: Christian Age Office, 1882.

Douglass, Margaret. *Educational Laws of Virginia: The Personal Narrative of Mrs. Margaret Douglass, A Southern Woman Who Was Imprisoned for One Month in the Common Jail of Norfolk, Under the Laws of Virginia, for the Crime of Teaching Free Colored Children to Read.* Boston: John P. Jewett & Co., 1854.

Drake, St. Clair, and Horace R. Cayton. *Black Metropolis: A Study in Negro Life in a Northern City.* New York: Harcourt, Brace and Company, 1945.

Duncan, Otis Dudley, and B. Duncan. "A Methodological Analysis of Segregation Indices." *American Sociological Review* 20.2 (1955), 200–217.

Dunglison, Robley. *Human Physiology.* 7th edition. 2 vols. Philadelphia: Lea and Blanchard, 1850.

Dunham, Katherine. *Island Possessed.* Chicago: University of Chicago Press, 1969.

Dusinberre, William. *Them Dark Days: Slavery in the American Rice Swamps.* Athens: University of Georgia Press, 1996.

Eblen, Jack Ericson. "New Estimates of the Vital Rates of the United States Black Population during the Nineteenth Century." *Demography* 11.2 (May 1974), 301–319.

Edwards, Ozzie L. "Skin Color as a Variable in Racial Attitudes of Black Urbanites." *Journal of Black Studies* 3.4 (June 1973), 473–483.

Eeckhout, Jan. "On the Uniqueness of Stable Marriage Matchings." *Economics Letters* 69.1 (2000), 1–8.

Ehrenberg, Ronald G., and Robert S. Smith. *Modern Labor Economics.* 3d ed. Glenview, IL: Scott, Foresman, and Company, 1988.

Elliott, Michael A. "Telling the Difference: Nineteenth-Century Legal Narratives of Racial Taxonomy." *Law & Social Inquiry* 24.3 (Summer 1999), 611–636.

Emerson, Ralph Waldo. *The Conduct of Life, Nature & Other Essays.* New York: E. P. Dutton & Co., 1911.

Encyclopædia Perthensis, or Universal Dictionary of Knowledge. Vol. XV. Perth: C. Mitchel and Co., no date.

Engels, Friedrich. *The Condition of the Working Class in England.* Edited by David McLellan. Oxford: Oxford University Press, 1993.

England, J. Merton. "The Free Negro in Antebellum Tennessee." *Journal of Southern History* 9.1 (February 1943), 37–58.

Eveleth, Phyllis B. and James M. Tanner. *Worldwide Variation in Human Growth.* New York: Cambridge University Press, 1990.

Fairlie, Robert W. "Can the 'One-Drop Rule' Tell Us Anything about Racial Discrimination? New Evidence from the Multiple Race Question on the 2000 Census." *Labour Economics* 16.4 (September 2009), 451–460.

Fairlie, Robert W. *Kauffman Index of Entrepreneurial Activity, 1996–2013.* Kansas City, MO: Ewing Marion Kauffman Foundation, April 2014.

Ferrie, Joseph P. "The Rich and the Dead: Socioeconomic Status and Mortality in the United States, 1850–1860." In *Health and Labor Force Participation over the Life Cycle: Evidence from the Past,* 11–50. Edited by Dora L. Costa. Chicago: University of Chicago Press, 2003.

Fields, Barbara Jeanne. *Slavery and Freedom on the Middle Ground: Maryland during the Nineteenth Century.* New Haven, CT: Yale University Press, 1985.

Findlay, Ronald. "Slavery, Incentives, and Manumission: A Theoretical Model." *Journal of Political Economy* 83.5 (October 1975), 923–933.

Finkelman, Paul. "Jefferson and Slavery: Treason against the Hopes of the World." In *Jeffersonian Legacies,* 182–221. Edited by Peter S. Onuf. Charlottesville: University Press of Virginia, 1993.

Floud, Roderick, Kenneth Wachter, and Annabel Gregory. *Height, Health and History: Nutritional Status in the United Kingdom, 1750–1980.* Cambridge: Cambridge University Press, 1990.

Fogel, Robert William, and Stanley L. Engerman. *Time on the Cross: The Economics of American Negro Slavery.* Boston: Little, Brown, 1974.

Fogel, Robert William, and Stanley L. Engerman. "Philanthropy at Bargain Prices: Notes on the Economics of Gradual Emancipation." *Journal of Legal Studies* 3.2 (June 1974), 377–401.

Fogel, Robert W., and Stanley L. Engerman. "Explaining the Relative Efficiency of Slave Agriculture in the Antebellum South." *American Economic Review* 67.3 (June 1977), 275–296.

Foner, Philip S. *The Life and Writings of Frederick Douglass.* Vol. II. New York: International Publishers, 1950.

Foner, Philip S., and Ronald L. Lewis (eds) *The Black Worker: A Documentary History from Colonial Times to the Present. Volume 1: The Black Worker to 1869.* Philadelphia: Temple University Press, 1978.

Ford, Paul Leicester (editor). *The Works of Thomas Jefferson.* Vol. 12. New York: G. Putnam's Sons, 1905.

Francis, Andrew M. "The Economics of Sexuality: The Effect of HIV/AIDS on Homosexual Behavior in the United States." *Journal of Health Economics* 27.3 (May 2008), 675–689.

Franklin, John Hope. *The Free Negro in North Carolina, 1790–1860.* Chapel Hill: University of North Carolina Press, 1995.

Franklin, John Hope, and Loren Schweninger. *Runaway Slaves: Rebels on the Plantation.* New York: Oxford University Press, 1999.

Franklin, John Hope, and Loren Schweninger. *In Search of the Promised Land: A Slave Family in the Old South*. New York: Oxford University Press, 2006.

Franklin, John Hope, and Loren Schweninger. "The Quest for Freedom: Runaway Slaves and the Plantation South." In *Slavery, Resistance, Freedom*, 21–39. Edited by Gabor Boritt and Scott Hancock. New York: Oxford University Press, 2007.

Frazier, E. Franklin. *The Negro Family in Chicago*. Chicago: University of Chicago Press, 1932.

Frazier, E. Franklin. *The Negro Family in the United States*. Chicago: University of Chicago Press, 1939.

Frazier, E. Franklin. *Black Bourgeoisie*. New York: Free Press, 1997 [1957].

Frederickson, George M. *The Black Image in the White Mind: The Debate on Afro-American Character and Destiny, 1817–1914*. New York: Harper & Row, 1971.

Freeman, Howard E., David Armor, J. Michael Ross, and Thomas F. Pettigrew. "Color Gradation and Attitudes among Middle-Income Negroes." *American Sociological Review* 31.3 (June 1966), 365–374.

Fryer, Roland G. Jr. "Guess Who's Been Coming to Dinner? Trends in Interracial Marriage over the 20th Century." *Journal of Economic Perspectives* 21.2 (Spring 2007), 71–90.

Fryer, Roland G. Jr., Lisa Kahn, Steven D. Levitt, and Jörg L. Spenkuch. "The Plight of Mixed Race Adolescents." *Review of Economics and Statistics* 94.3 (August 2012), 621–634.

Gale, D., and L. S. Shapley. "College Admissions and the Stability of Marriage." *American Mathematical Monthly* 69.1 (January 1962), 9–15.

Garon, Shedon. *Beyond Our Means: Why America Spends While the World Saves*. Princeton, NJ: Princeton University Press, 2011.

Gatewood, Williard B. *Aristocrats of Color: The Black Elite, 1880–1920*. Fayetteville: University of Arkansas Press, 2000.

Genovese, Eugene. *Roll Jordan Roll: The World the Slaves Made*. New York: Pantheon, 1974.

Gillmer, Jason A. "Suing for Freedom: Interracial Sex, Slave Law, and Racial Identity in the Post-Revolutionary and Antebellum South," *North Carolina Law Review* 82.2 (2004), 535–620.

Glaeser, Edward L., David Laibson, and Bruce Sacerdote. "An Economic Approach to Social Capital." *Economic Journal* 112.483 (November 2002), 437–458.

Gleeson, David T. *The Irish in the South, 1815–1877*. Chapel Hill: University of North Carolina Press, 2000.

Golden, Marita. *Don't Play in the Sun: One Woman's Journey through the Color Complex*. New York: Doubleday, 2004.

Goldin, Claudia D. *Urban Slavery in the American South, 1820–1860: A Quantitative History*. Chicago: University of Chicago Press, 1976.

Goldin, Claudia. "America's Graduation from High School: The Evolution and Spread of Secondary Schooling in the Twentieth Century." *Journal of Economic History* 58.2 (June 1998), 345–374.

Goldin, Claudia. "The Human-Capital Century and American Leadership: Virtues of the Past." *Journal of Economic History* 61.2 (June 2001), 263–292.

Goldsmith, Arthur, Darrick Hamilton, and William Darity Jr. "Shades of Discrimination: Skin Tone and Wages." *American Economic Review* 96:2 (May 2006), 242–245.

Goldsmith, Arthur, Darrick Hamilton, and William Darity Jr. "From Dark to Light: Skin Color and Wages among African Americans." *Journal of Human Resources* 42:4 (month 2007), 701–738.

Goodman, Alan. "Comment." *Current Anthropology* 50.6 (December 2009), 807–808.

Goodman, Leo A. "How to Ransack Social Mobility Tables and Other Kinds of Cross-Classification Tables." *American Journal of Sociology* 75.1 (July 1969), 1–40.

Gordon-Reed, Annette. "Logic and Experience: Thomas Jefferson's Life in the Law." In *Slavery and the American South*, 3–20. Edited by Winthrop D. Jordan. Jackson: University Press of Mississippi, 2003.

Gordon-Reed, Annette. *The Hemingses of Monticello: An American Family.* New York: W. W. Norton & Company, 2008.

Gordon-Reed, Annette. "Reading *White Over Black*." *William and Mary Quarterly* 69.4 (October 2012), 853–857.

Gould, Stephen Jay. *The Mismeasure of Man.* New York: Norton, 1996.

Graham, Lawrence Otis. *Our Kind of People: Inside America's Black Upper Class.* New York: Harper Collins, 2009.

Greenwood, Jeremy, and Nezih Guner. "Marriage and Divorce since World War II: The Role of Technological Progress on the Formation of Households." *NBER Macroeconomics Annual 2008* 23 (2009), 231–276.

Greenwood, Jeremy, Nezih Guner, Georgi Kocharov, and Cezar Santos. "Marry Your Like: Assortative Mating and Income Inequality." National Bureau of Economic Research Working Paper #19829, 2014.

Grinberg, Keila. "Freedom Suits and Civil Law in Brazil and the United States." *Slavery & Abolition* 22.3 (December 2001), 66–82.

Grivno, Max. *Gleanings of Freedom: Free and Slave Labor along the Mason-Dixon Line, 1790–1860.* Urbana: University of Illinois Press, 2011.

Gross, Ariela J. "Litigating Whiteness: Trials of Racial Determination in the Nineteenth-Century South." *Yale Law Journal* 108.1 (October 1998), 109–188.

Gross, Ariela J. *What Blood Won't Tell: A History of Race on Trial in America.* Cambridge, MA: Harvard University Press, 2008.

Guillory, Monique. "Some Enchanted Evening on the Auction Block: The Cultural Legacy of the New Orleans Quadroon Balls." PhD dissertation, New York University, 1999.

Gullickson, Aaron. "The Significance of Color Declines: A Re-analysis of Skin Tone Differentials in Post-Civil Rights America." *Social Forces* 84.1 (September 2005), 157–180.

Gutman, Herbert G. "Persistent Myths about the Afro-American Family." *Journal of Interdisciplinary History* 6.2 (Autumn 1975), 181–210.

Gutman, Herbert G. *The Black Family in Slavery and Freedom, 1750–1925.* New York: Vintage Books, 1977.

Gutman, Herbert G. and Richard Sutch. "Victorians All? The Sexual Mores and Conduct of Slaves and Their Masters." In *Reckoning With Slavery*, 134–162. Edited by Paul A. David, Herbert G. Gutman, Richard Sutch, Peter Temin, and Gavin Wright. New York and Oxford: Oxford University Press, 1976.

Gyimah-Brempong, Kwabena, and Gregory N. Price. "Crime and Punishment: And Skin Hue Too?" *American Economic Review* 96.2 (May 2006), 246–250.

Hacker, J. David. "Decennial Life Tables for the White Population of the United States, 1790–1900." *Historical Methods* 43.2 (April 2010), 45–79.

Hadden, Sally E. *Slave Patrols: Law and Violence in Virginia and the Carolinas.* Cambridge, MA: Harvard University Press, 2001.

Hamermesh, Daniel, and Jeff E. Biddle. "Beauty and the Labor Market." *American Economic Review* 84.5 (December 1994), 1174–1194.

Handlin, Oscar, and Mary F. Handlin. "Origins of the Southern Labor System." *William & Mary Quarterly* 7.2 (April 1950), 199–222.

Haney Lopez, Ian F. "The Social Construction of Race: Some Observations on Illusion, Fabrication, and Choice." *Harvard Civil Rights-Civil Liberties Law Review* 29.1 (Winter 1994), 1–62.

Hanger, Kimberly S. "Patronage, Property, and Persistence: The Emergence of a Free Black Elite in Spanish New Orleans." In *Against the Odds: Free Blacks in the Slave Societies of the Americas*, 44–64. Edited by Jane G. Landers. London: Frank Cass, 1996.

Hansen, B., M. Cortina-Borja, and S. G. Ratcliffe. "Assessing Non-linear Estimation Procedures for Human Growth Models." *Annals of Human Biology* 30.1 (January 2003), 80–96.

Harris, Cheryl I. "Whiteness as Property." *Harvard Law Review* 106.8 (June 1993), 1707–1791.

Harris, David R. and Jeremiah Joseph Sim. "Who is Multiracial? Assessing the Complexity of Lived Race." *American Sociological Review* 67.4 (August 2002), 614–627.

Harris, Marvin D. "Racial Identity in Brazil." *Luso-Brazilian Review* 1.2 (Winter 1964), 21–28.

Hartley, L. P. *The Go-Between* (1953). New York: New York Review of Books, 2002 (reprint).

Hauspie, R. C., S. R. Das, M. A. Preece, and James M. Tanner. "A Longitudinal Study of the Growth in Height of Boys and Girls of West Bengal (India) Aged 6 Months to 20 Years." *Annals of Human Biology* 7.5 (1980), 429–441.

Heaton, John, and Deborah Lucas. "Portfolio Choice and Asset Prices: The Importance of Entrepreneurial Risk." *Journal of Finance* 55.3 (June 2000), 1163–1198.

Heck, J. G. *Iconographic Encyclopedia of Science, Literature, and Art.* 4 vols. Translated by Spencer F. Baird. New York: Rudolph Garrigue, 1852.

Heinegg, Paul. *Free African Americans of North Carolina, Virginia and South Carolina: From the Colonial Period to About 1820.* Fourth Edition. Clearfield Company, 1997.

Henry, H. M. *The Police Control of the Slaves in South Carolina.* PhD dissertation, Vanderbilt University, 1913.

Herndon, Ruth Wallis, and John Muuray. *Children Bound to Labor: The Pauper Apprentice System in Early America.* Ithaca, NY: Cornell University Press, 2009.

Hersch, Joni. "Skin Color, Immigrant Wages, and Discrimination." In *Racism in the 21st Century: A Question of Color,* 77–90. Edited by Ronald E. Hall. New York: Springer, 2008.

Hersch, Joni. "Profiling the New Immigrant Worker: The Effects of Skin Color and Height." *Journal of Labor Economics* 26.2 (April 2008), 345–386.

Hersch, Joni. "Skin Color, Physical Appearance, and Perceived Discriminatory Treatment." *Journal of Socio-Economics* 40.5 (October 2011), 671–678.

Hershberg, Theodore. "Free Blacks in Antebellum Philadelphia: A Study of Ex-Slaves, Freeborn, and Socioeconomic Decline." *Journal of Social History* 5.2 (Winter 1971), 183–209.

Hershberg, Theodore, and Henry Williams. "Mulattoes and Blacks: Intra-Group Color Differences and Social Stratification in Nineteenth-Century Philadelphia." In *Philadelphia: Work, Space, Family, and Group Experience in the Nineteenth Century: Essays Toward an Interdisciplinary History of the City.* Edited by Theodore Hershberg. New York: Oxford University Press, 1981.

Hickman, Christine B. "The Devil and the One Drop Rule: Racial Categories, African Americans, and the U.S. Census." *Michigan Law Review* 95.5 (March 1997), 1161–1265.

Higginbotham, A. Leon Jr. *In the Matter of Color: Race and the American Legal Process, The Colonial Period.* New York: Oxford University Press, 1978.

Higginbotham, A. Leon Jr. *Shades of Freedom: Racial Politics and Presumptions of the American Legal Process.* New York: Oxford University Press, 1996.

Higginbotham, A. Leon Jr., and Barbara K. Kopytoff. "Racial Purity and Interracial Sex in the Law of Colonial and Antebellum Virginia." *Georgetown Law Journal* 77.6 (August 1989), 1967–2030.

Hill, Mark E. "Color Differences in the Socioeconomic Status of African American Men: Results of a Longitudinal Study." *Social Forces* 78.4 (June 2000), 1437–1460.

Hirsch, Leo H Jr. "The Free Negro in New York." *Journal of Negro History* 16 (October 1931), 415–453.

Hitchcock, Edward. "Anthropometric Statistics of Amherst College." *Papers on Anthropometry.* Boston: American Statistical Association, 1894.

Hochschild, Jennifer L., and Brenna Marea Powell. "Racial Reorganization and the United States Census 1850–1930: Mulattoes, Half-Breeds, Mixed Parentage, Hindoos, and the Mexican Race." *Studies in American Political Development* 22.1 (March 2008), 59–96.

Hochschild, Jennifer L., Vesla M. Weaver, and Traci R. Burch. "Destabilizing the American Racial Order." *Daedalus* 140.2 (Spring 2011), 151–165.

Hochschild, Jennifer L., Vesla M. Weaver, and Traci R. Burch. *Creating a New Racial Order: How Immigration, Multiracialism, Genomics, and the Young Can Remake Race in America.* Princeton, NJ: Princeton University Press, 2014.

Hollinger, David A. "Amalgamation and Hypodescent: The Question of Ethnoracial Mixture in the History of the United States." *American Historical Review* 108.5 (December 2003), 1363–1390.

Homer, Sidney and Richard Sylla. *A History of Interest Rates*. New York: John Wiley & Sons, 2011.

Hopkins, Pauline E. *Contending Forces: A Romance Illustrative of Negro Life North and South*. Reprint. Oxford: Oxford University Press, 1988.

Horsman, Reginald. *Josiah Nott of Mobile: Southerner, Physician, and Racial Theorist*. Baton Rouge: Louisiana State University Press, 1987.

Horton, James Oliver and Lois E. Horton. *In Hope of Liberty: Culture, Community, and Protest Among Northern Free Blacks, 1700–1860*. New York: Oxford University Press, 1997.

Horowitz, Donald L. "Color Differentiation in the American Systems of Slavery." *Journal of Interdisciplinary History* 3.3 (Winter 1973), 509–541.

Horton, James Oliver, and Lois E. Horton. *In Hope of Liberty: Culture, Community and Protest among Northern Free Blacks, 1700–1860*. Oxford: Oxford University Press, 1997.

Horton, Lois, and James Oliver Horton. "Power and Social Responsibility: Entrepreneurs and the Black Community in Antebellum Boston." In *Entrepreneurs: The Boston Business Community, 1700–1850*. Edited by Conrad E. Wright and Katheryn P. Viens. Boston: Northeastern University Press, 1997.

Howe, David Walker. "Church, State, and Education in the Young American Republic." *Journal of the Early Republic* 22.1 (Spring 2002), 1–24.

Howe, Daniel Walker. *What Hath God Wrought: The Transformation of America, 1815–1848*. New York: Oxford University Press, 2009.

Howells, William Dean. *An Imperative Duty*. New York: Harper & Brothers, 1892.

Huston, James L. *Securing the Fruits of Labor: The American Concept of Wealth Distribution, 1765–1900*. Baton Rouge: Louisiana State University Press, 1998.

Irmscher, Chritophe. *Louis Agassiz: Creator of American Science*. Boston: Houghton Mifflin Harcourt, 2013.

Irwin, James R. "Explaining the Affinity of Wheat and Slavery in the Virginia Piedmont." *Explorations in Economic History* 25.3 (July 1988), 295–322.

Irwin, James R. and Anthony Patrick O'Brien. "Where Have All the Sharecroppers Gone? Black Occupations in Postbellum Mississippi." *Agricultural History* 72.2 (Spring 1998), 280–297.

Jackson, Luther P. "Free Negroes of Petersburg, Virginia." *Journal of Negro History* 12.3 (July 1927), 365–388.

Jackson, Luther P. "Manumission in Certain Virginia Cities." *Journal of Negro History* 15.3 (July 1930), 278–314.

Jackson, Luther P. "Negro Enterprise in Norfolk during the Days of Slavery." *Quarterly Journal of the Florida A&M University* 8.2 (April 1939), 3–14.

Jackson, Luther P. "The Virginia Free Negro Farmer and Property Owners, 1830–1860." *Journal of Negro History* 24.4 (October 1939), 390–439.

Jackson, Luther P. *Free Negro Labor and Property Holding in Virginia, 1830–1860*. New York: D. Appleton-Century Company, 1942.

Jacobs, Harriet [nom de plume Linda Brent]. *Incidents in the Life of a Slave Girl*. Edited by L. Maria Child. Boston, private printing, 1861.

James, Charles. *A New and Enlarged Military Dictionary, or, Alphabetical Explanation of Technical Terms*. Second edition. London: T. Egerton, Printer, 1805.

Jefferson, Thomas. *Notes on the State of Virginia*. London: John Stockdale, 1787.

Jefferson, Thomas. *The Writings of Thomas Jefferson: Being His Autobiography, Correspondence, Reports, Messages, Addresses, and Other Writings, Official and Private*. Edited by H. A. Washington. New York: H. W. Derby, 1861.

Jefferson, Thomas. *The Works of Thomas Jefferson*. Vol. IV. Edited by H. A. Washington. New York: Townsend Maccoun, 1884.

Jefferson, Thomas. *The Works of Thomas Jefferson*. Vol. V. Edited by Paul Leicester Ford. New York: G. P. Putnam's Sons, 1904.

Jennings, Thelma. "'Us Colored Women Had to Go through a Plenty': Sexual Exploitation of African-American Slave Women." *Journal of Women's History* 1.3 (Winter 1990), 45–74.

Johnson, Charles S. "Review of *The Marginal Man* and *Jamaica: The Blessed Land.*" *American Sociological Review* 3.1 (February 1938), 115–116.

Johnson, Lyman L. "Manumission in Colonial Buenos Aries, 1776–1810." *Hispanic American Historical Review* 59.2 (May 1979), 258–279.

Johnson, Paul and Stephen Nicholas. "Male and Female Living Standards in England and Wales, 1812–1867: Evidence from Criminal Height Records." *Economic History Review* 48.3 (August 1995), 470–481.

Johnson, Walter. "The Slave Trader, the White Slave, and the Politics of Racial Determination in the 1850s." *Journal of American History* 87.1 (June 2000), 13–38.

Johnson, Whittington B. *Black Savannah 1788–1864*. Fayetteville: University of Arkansas Press, 1996.

Johnston, James Hugo. *Race Relations in Virginia and Miscegenation in the South, 1776–1860*. Amherst: University of Massachusetts Press, 1970.

Jones, Alice Hanson. *Wealth of a Nation to Be: The American Colonies on the Eve of the Revolution*. New York: Columbia University Press, 1980.

Jones, Bernie D. "'Righteous Fathers,' 'Vulnerable Old Men,' and 'Degraded Creatures': Southern Justices on Miscegenation in the Antebellum Will Contest." *Tulsa Law Review* 40.4 (Summer 2005), 699–750.

Jones, Norrece T. Jr. "Rape in Black and White: Sexual Violence in the Testimony of Enslaved and Free Americans." In *Slavery and the American South*, 93–108. Edited by Winthrop D. Jordan. Jackson: University Press of Mississippi, 2003.

Jones, Trina. "Shades of Brown: The Law of Skin Color." *Duke Law Journal* 49.6 (April 2000), 1487–1557.

Jordan, Miriam. "More Marriages Cross Race, Ethnicity Lines." *Wall Street Journal*, February 17, 2012, A2.

Jordan, Winthrop D. "American Chiaroscuro: The Status and Definition of Mulattoes in the British Colonies." *William & Mary Quarterly*, Third Series 19.2 (April 1962), 183–200.

Jordan, Winthrop D. *White Over Black: American Attitudes toward the Negro, 1550–1812*. Chapel Hill: University of North Carolina Press, 1968.

Jordan, Winthrop D. *The White Man's Burden: Historical Origins of Racism in the United States*. New York: Oxford University Press, 1974.

Joseph, Ralina L. "The Fury Over a Cheerios Ad and An Interracial Family." *Seattle Times* (June 24, 2013).

Joseph, Ralina. *Transcending Blackness: From the New Millennium Mulatto to the Exceptional Multiracial*. Durham, NC: Duke University Press, 2013.

Kalmijn, Matthijs. "Intermarriage and Homogamy: Causes, Patterns, Trends." *Annual Review of Sociology* 24 (1998), 395–421.

Kemble, Frances Anne. *Journal of a Residence on a Georgian Plantation in 1838–1839*. New York: Harper & Brothers, 1863.

Kinney, James. *Amalgamation! Race, Sex, and Rhetoric in the Nineteenth-Century Novel*. Westport, CT: Greenwood Press, 1985.

Kiple, Kenneth F., and Virginia H. Kiple. "Slave Child Mortality: Some Nutritional Answers to a Perennial Puzzle." *Journal of Social History* 10.3 (Spring 1977), 284–309.

Klebaner, Benjamin Joseph. "American Manumission Laws and the Responsibility for Supporting Slaves." *Virginia Magazine of History and Biography* 63.4 (October 1955), 443–453.

Klooster, Willem Wubbo. "Manumission in an Entrepôt: The Case of Curaçao." In *Paths to Freedom: Manumission in the Atlantic World*, 161–174. Edited by Rosemary Brana-Shute and Randy J. Sparks. Columbia: University of South Carolina Press, 2009.

Knox, Robert. *The Races of Men: A Fragment*. Philadelphia: Lea & Blanchard, 1850.

Komlos, John. "The Height and Weight of West Point Cadets: Dietary Change in Antebellum America." *Journal of Economic History* 47.4 (December 1987), 897–927.

Komlos, John. "Toward an Anthropometric History of African-Americans: The Case of the Free Blacks in Antebellum Maryland." In *Strategic Factors in Nineteenth Century American Economic History: A Volume to Honor Robert W. Fogel*, 297–329. Edited by Claudia Goldin and Hugh Rockoff. Chicago: University of Chicago Press, 1992.

Komlos, John. "Shrinking in a Growing Economy? The Mystery of Physical Stature during the Industrial Revolution." *Journal of Economic History* 58.3 (September 1998), 779–802.

Komlos, John. "Access to Food and the Biological Standard of Living: Perspectives on the Nutritional Status of Native Americans." *American Economic Review* 93.1 (March 2003), 252–255.

Koo, Hagen. "Small Entrepreneurship in a Developing Society: Patterns of Labor Absorption and Social Mobility." *Social Forces* 54.4 (June 1976), 775–787.

Kotlikoff, Laurence J. "The Structure of Slave Prices in New Orleans, 1804 to 1862." *Economic Inquiry* 17.2 (October 1979), 496–518.

Kotlikoff, Laurence J. "Quantitative Description of the New Orleans Slave Market, 1804 to 1862." In *Without Consent or Contract: Technical Papers*. Vol 1, 31–53. Edited by Robert William Fogel and Stanley L. Engerman. New York: W. W. Norton & Company, 1992.

Kotlikoff, Laurence J., and Anton J. Rupert. "The Manumission of Slaves in New Orleans, 1827–1846." *Southern Studies* 19.2 (Summer 1980), 172–181.

Kulikoff, Allan. "Households and Markets: Toward a New Synthesis of American Agrarian History." *William and Mary Quarterly* 50.3 (April 1993), 340–355.

Lachance, Paul F. "The Formation of a Three-Caste Society: Evidence from Wills in Antebellum New Orleans." *Social Science History* 18.2 (Summer 1994), 211–242.

Lammermeier, Paul J. "The Urban Black Family of the Nineteenth Century: A Study of Black Family Structure in the Ohio Valley, 1850–1880." *Journal of Marriage and the Family* 35.3 (August 1973), 440–456.

Lamoreaux, Naomi R. "Rethinking the Transition to Capitalism in the Early Northeast." *Journal of American History* 90.2 (September 2003), 437–461.

Landes, William M., and Richard A. Posner. "Salvors, Finders, Good Samaritans, and Other Rescuers: An Economic Study of Law and Altruism." *Journal of Legal Studies* 7.1 (January 1978), 83–128.

Latrobe, Charles Joseph. *The Rambler in North America: 1832–1833*. 2 vols. London: R. B. Seeley and W. Burnside, 1835.

Lawrence, William. *Lectures on Physiology, Zoology, and the Natural History of Man, Delivered at the Royal College of Surgeons*. London: 1822.

Ledford, A. W., and T. J. Cole. "Mathematical Models of Growth in Stature throughout Childhood." *Annals of Human Biology* 25.2 (1998), 101–115.

Lee, Leonard, George Lowenstein, Dan Ariely, James Hong, and Jim Young. "If I'm Not Hot, Are You Hot or Not?" *Psychological Science* 19.7 (2008), 669–677.

Lehrer, Jonah. "When We See What We Want." Wall Street Journal (June 25, 2011), C12.

Lewis, Frank D. "The Transition from Slavery to Freedom through Manumission: A Life-Cycle Approach Applied to the United States and Gaudeloupe." In *Slavery in the Development of the Americas*, 150–177. Edited by David Eltis, Frank D. Lewis, and Kenneth L. Sokoloff. New York: Cambridge University Press, 2004.

Lewis, Jan Ellen, and Peter S. Onuf. *Sally Hemings & Thomas Jefferson: History, Memory, and Civic Culture*. Charlottesville: University Press of Virginia, 1999.

Litwack, Leon F. *North of Slavery: The Negro in the Free States, 1790–1860*. Chicago: University of Chicago Press, 1965.

Liu, Haiyong, Linda Adair, and Thomas Mroz. "Parental Compensatory Behaviors and Early Child Health Outcomes in Cebu, Phillipines." *Journal of Development Economics* 90.2 (November 2009), 209–230.

Longfellow, Henry Wadsworth. *The Poetical Works of Henry Wadsworth Longfellow: Household Edition*. Boston: James R. Osgood & Company, 1874.

Loury, Linda Datcher. "Am I Still Too Black for You? Schooling and Secular Change in Skin Tone Effects." *Economics of Education Review* 28.4 (August 2009), 428–433.

Maier, Frank H., Sheridan T. Maitland, and Gladys K. Bowles. *The Tenure Status of Farmworkers in the United States*. Washington, DC: United States Department of Agriculture Technical Bulletin No. 1217, July 1960.

Margo, Robert A. *Race and Schooling in the South, 1850–1950*. Chicago: University of Chicago Press, 1990.

Margo, Robert A. *Wages and Labor Markets in the United States, 1820–1860*. Chicago: University of Chicago Press, 2000.

Margo, Robert A. "Civilian Occupations of Ex-Slaves in the Union Army, 1862–1865." In *Without Consent or Contract: Technical Papers*. Vol. 1, 170–185. Edited by Robert William Fogel and Stanley L. Engerman. New York: W. W. Norton & Company, 1992.

Margo, Robert A., and Richard H. Steckel. "The Heights of American Slaves: New Evidence on Slave Nutrition and Health." *Social Science History* 6.4 (Autumn 1982), 516–538.

Margo, Robert A., and Richard H. Steckel. "Heights of Native-Born Whites during the Antebellum Period." *Journal of Economic History* 43.1 (March 1983), 167–174.

Margo, Robert A., and Georgia C. Villaflor. "The Growth of Wages in Antebellum America: New Evidence." *Journal of Economic History* 47.4 (December 1987), 873–895.

Marryat, Frederick. *A Diary in America with Remarks on Its Institutions*. 2 vols. Philadelphis: Carey & Hart, 1839.

Martin, Waldo E. Jr. *The Mind of Frederick Douglass*. Chapel Hill: University of North Carolina Press, 1984.

Martineau, Harriet. *Society in America*. 2 vols. Paris: A. & W. Galignani & Co., 1837.

Matison, Sumner Eliot. "Manumission by Purchase." *Journal of Negro History* 33.2 (April 1948), 146–167.

Maury, Ann. *Memoirs of a Huguenot Family*. Translated by James Fontaine. New York: G. P. Putnam & Sons, 1872.

McCaa, Robert, and Stuart B. Schwartz. "Measuring Marriage Patters: Percentages, Cohen's Kappa, and Log-Linear Models." *Comparative Studies in Society and History* 25.4 (October 1983), 711–724.

McFeely, William S. *Frederick Douglass*. New York: W. W. Norton & Company, 1991.

McLaurin, Melton A. *Celia, A Slave*. Athens: University Press of Georgia, 1991.

Michel, Jean-Baptiste, Yuan Kui Shen, Aviva Presser Aiden, Adrian Veres, Matthew K. Gray, William Brockman, The Google Books Team, Joseph P. Pickett, Dale Hoiberg, Dan Clancy, Peter Norvig, Jon Orwant, Steven Pinker, Martin A. Nowak, and Erez Lieberman Aiden. "Quantitative Analysis of Culture Using Millions of Digitized Books." *Science* 14.331 (January 2011), 176–182.

Mill, Roy and Luke C. D. Stein. "Race, Skin Color, and Economic Outcomes in Early Twentieth Century America." Working Paper, Stanford University, November 2012.

Miller, Kelly. "Review of *The Mulatto in the United States*." *American Journal of Sociology* 25.2 (September 1919), 218–224.

Moehling, Carolyn. "Family Structure, School Attendance, and Child Labor in the American South in 1900 and 1910." *Explorations in Economic History* 41.1 (January 2004), 73–100.

Mokyr, Joel, and Cormac Ó Gráda. "The Heights of the Britich and the Irish c. 1800–1815: Evidence from Recruits to the East India Company's Army." In *Stature, Living Standards, and Economic Development*, 39–59. Edited by John Komlos. Chicago: University of Chicago Press, 1994.

Mora, J.O., M. G. Herrera, J. Suescun, L. de Navarro, and M. Wagner. "The Effects of Nutritional Supplementation on Physical Growth of Children at Risk of Malnutrition." *American Journal of Clinical Nutrition* 34.9 (September 1981), 1885–1892.

Morgan, Philip D. "Interracial Sex in the Chesapeake and the British Atlantic World, c. 1700–1820." In *Sally Hemings & Thomas Jefferson: History, Memory, and Civic Culture*, 52–84. Edited by Jan Ellen Lewis and Peter S. Onuf. Charlottesville: University Press of Virginia, 1999.

Morris, Thomas D. *Southern Slavery and the Law, 1619–1860*. Chapel Hill: University of North Carolina Press, 1996.

Morton, Samuel George. *Crania Ægyptiaca; Or, Observations on Egyptian Ethnography, Derived from Anatomy, History and the Monument*. Philadelphia: John Pennington, 1844.

Moynihan, Daniel Patrick. *The Negro Family: The Case for National Action*. In *The Moynihan Report and the Politics of Controversy: A Transaction Social Science and Public Policy Report*. Edited by Lee Rainwater and William L. Yancey. Cambridge, MA: MIT Press, 1967.

Mullin, Gerald W. *Flight and Rebellion: Slave Resistance in Eighteenth-Century Virginia*. New York: Oxford University Press, 1974.

Mumford, Kevin. "After Hugh: Statutory Race Segregation in Colonial America, 1630–1725." *American Journal of Legal History* 43.3 (July 1999), 280–305.

Murphy, Kevin and Finis Welch. "Empirical Age-Earnings Profiles." *Journal of Labor Economics* 8.2 (April 1990), 202–229.

Murray, Charles. "The Diversity of Life: A Scientific Revolution in Under Way—Upending One of Our Reigning Orthodoxies." *Wall Street Journal* (May 3, 2014), C5.

Nasar, Sylvia. *Grand Pursuit: The Story of Economic Genius*. New York: Simon & Schuster, 2011.

Nash, Gary B. *Forging Freedom: The Formation of Philadelphia's Black Community, 1720–1840*. Cambridge, MA: Harvard University Press, 1991.

The New Encyclopedia; or Universal Dictionary of Arts and Sciences. 23 vols. Vol. 15. London: R. Morrison, Printer, 1807.

Neal, Derek. "The Relationship between Marriage Market Prospects and Never-Married Motherhood." *Journal of Human Resources* 39.4 (Autumn 2004), 938–957.

Nicholas, Stephen, and Richard H. Steckel. "Heights and Living Standards of English Workers during the Early Years of Industrialization, 1770–1815." *Journal of Economic History* 51.4 (December 1991), 937–957.

Nicholls, Michael L. "Passing Through This Troublesome World: Free Blacks in the Early Southside." *Virginia Magazine of History and Biography* 92.1 (January 1984), 50–70.

Nicholson, William. *The British Encyclopedia: or, Dictionary of Arts and Sciences; Comprising an Accurate and Popular View of the Present Improved State of Human Knowledge*. Vol. IV (I- N) London: C. Whittingham, Printer, 1809.

Niehaus, Earl F. *The Irish in New Orleans, 1800–1860*. Baton Rouge: Louisiana State University Press, 1965.

Nott, Josiah Clark. "The Mulatto A Hybrid—Probable Extermination of the Two Races if the Blacks and Whites are Allowed to Intermarry." *American Journal of the Medical Sciences* 6.11 (July 1843), 252–256.

Nott, Josiah Clark. "Nature and Destiny of the Negro." *De Bow's Review* 10.3 (March 1851), 329–332.

Nott, Josiah Clark, George R. Gliddon, Samuel George Morton, Louis Agassiz, William Usher, and Henry S. Patterson. *Types of Mankind: Or, Ethnological Researches: Based Upon the Ancient Monuments, Paintings, Sculptures, and Crania of Races, and Upon Their Natural, Geographical, Philological and Biblical History, Illustrated by Selections from the Inedited Papers of Samuel George Morton and by Additional Contributions from L. Agassiz, W. Usher, and H.S. Patterson*. Philadelphia: Lippincott, Grambo & Co., 1854.

Nott, Josiah Clark, and George R. Gliddon. *Indigenous Races of the Earth; Or, New Chapters of Ethnological Inquiry*. Philadelphia: J. B. Lippincott & Co., 1857.

Nobles, Melissa. *Shades of Citizenship: Race and the Census in Modern Politics*. Redwood City, CA: Stanford University Press, 2000.

Oliver, Melvin L., and Thomas M. Shapiro. *Black Wealth / White Wealth: A New Perspective on Racial Inequality*. New York: Routledge University Press, 1995.

Olmsted, Frederick Law. *A Journey in the Back Country*. New York: Mason Bros., 1860.

Olmsted, Frederick Law. *A Journey in the Seaboard Slave States, With Remarks on Their Economy*. New York: Mason Brothers, 1861.

Olmsted, Frederick Law. *The Cotton Kingdom: A Traveller's Observations on Cotton and Slavery in the American Slave States*. 2 vols. New York: Mason Brothers, 1861.

Olson, John F. "The Occupational Structure of Southern Plantations during the Late Antebellum Era." In *Without Consent or Contract: Technical Papers*. Vol. 1, 137–169. Edited by Robert William Fogel and Stanley L. Engerman. New York: W. W. Norton & Company, 1992.

Olwell, Robert. "Becoming Free: Manumission and the Genesis of a Free Black Community in South Carolina, 1740–90." *Slavery & Abolition* 17.1 (March 1996), 1–19.

Onis, Mercedes de, Parasmani Dasgupta, Syamal Saha, Debasis Sengupta, and Monika Blössner. "The National Center for Health Statistics Reference and the Growth of Indian Adolescent Boys." *American Journal of Clinical Nutrition* 74.2 (August 2001), 248–253.

Onwuachi-Willig, Angela. "Multiracialism and the Social Construction of Race: The Story of *Hudgins v. Wrights*." In *Race Law Stories*, 147–174. Edited by Rachel F. Moran and Devon W. Carbado. New York: Foundation Press, 2008.

Oreffice, Sonia, and Climent Quintana-Domeque. "Anthropometry and Socioeconomics among Couples: Evidence in the United States." *Economics and Human Biology* 8.3 (December 2010), 373–384.

Orthner, Dennis K., Terry Brown, and Dennis Ferguson. "Single-Parent Fatherhood: An Emerging Family Life Style." *The Family Coordinator* 25.4 (October 1976), 429–437.

Page, Lisa. "High Yellow White Trash." In *Skin Deep: Black Women and White Women Write about Race*, 13–23. Edited by Marita Golden and Susan Richards Shreve. New York: Doubleday, 1995.

Park, Robert E. "Human Migration and the Marginal Man." *American Journal of Sociology* 33.6 (May 1928), 881–893.

Park, Robert E. "Mentality of Racial Hybrids." *American Journal of Sociology* 36.4 (January 1931), 534–551.

Parra, Flavia C., Roberto C. Amado, José R. Lambertucci, Jorge Rocha, Carlos M. Antunes, and Sergio D. J. Pena. "Color and Genomic Ancestry in Brazilians." *Proceedings of the National Academy of Sciences of the United States of America* 100.1 (January 2003), 177–182.

Patterson, Orlando. "Three Notes of Freedom." In *Paths to Freedom: Manumission in the Atlantic World*, 15–29. Edited by Rosemary Brana-Shute and Randy J. Sparks. Columbia: University of South Carolina Press, 2009.

Patton, James W. "The Progress of Emancipation in Tennessee, 1796–1860." *Journal of Negro History* 17.1 (January 1932), 67–102.

Phillips, Christopher. *Freedom's Port: The African American Community of Baltimore, 1790–1860*. Urbana: University of Illinois Press, 1997.

Pimenta, Juliana R., Luciana W. Zuccherato, Adriana A. Debes, Luciana Maselli, Rosângela P. Soares, Rodrigo S. Moura-Neto, Jorge Rocha, Sergio P. Bydlowski, and Sergo D. J. Pena. "Color and Genomic Ancestry in Brazilians: A Study with Forensic Microsatellites." *Human Heredity* 62.4 (November 2006), 190–195.

Posner, Richard A. *Sex and Reason*. Cambridge, MA: Harvard University Press, 1992.

Preece, M. A., and M. J. Baines. "A New Family of Mathematical Models Describing the Human Growth Curve." *Annals of Human Biology* 5.1 (July–August 1978), 1–24.

Preston, Jo Anne. "Occupational Gender Segregation: Trends and Explanations." *Quarterly Journal of Economics and Finance* 39.5 (1999), 611–624.

Price, Richard, and Sally Price (eds) *Narrative Account of Five Years Expedition against the Revolted Negroes of Surinam*. Baltimore, MD: Johns Hopkins University Press, 1988.

Pritchett, Jonathan B. "The Interregional Slave Trade and the Selection of Slaves for the New Orleans Market." *Journal of Interdisciplinary History* 28.1 (Summer 1997), 57–85.

Proctor, Frank III. "Gender and the Manumission of Slaves in New Spain." *Hispanic American Historical Review* 86.2 (May 2006), 309–336.

Provine, Dorothy. "The Economic Position of the Free Blacks in the District of Columbia, 1800–1860. *Journal of Negro History* 58.1 (Jan 1973), 61–72.

Pryor, Frederic L. "An Empirical Note on the Tipping Point." *Land Economics* 47.4 (1971), 413–417.

Qian, Zhenchao, Daniel T. Lichter, and Leanna M. Mellott. "Out-of-Wedlock Childbearing, Marital Prospects, and Mate Selection." *Social Forces* 84.1 (2005), 473–491.

Quinan, John R. *Medical Annals of Baltimore from 1608 to 1880, Including Events, Men and Literature.* Baltimore, MD: Isaac Friedenwald, 1884.

Rees, R., John Komlos, Ngo V. Long, and Ulrich Woitek. "Optimal Food Allocation in a Slave Economy." *Journal of Population Economics* 16.1 (February 2003), 21–36.

Reid, Joseph B. "Antebellum Southern Rental Contracts." *Explorations in Economic History* 13.1 (February 1976), 69–83.

Reid, Thomas Mayne. "Oceola: A Romance of the History of Florida and the Seminole War." In *The American Freemason: A Monthly Masonic Magazine.* Vol. IV. New York: J. F. Brennan, 1859.

Reinders, Robert C. "The Free Negro in the New Orleans Economy, 1850–1860." *Louisiana History* 6 (1965),

Reiss, Albert J., Otis Dudley Duncan, Paul K. Hatt, and Cecil C. North. *Occupations and Social Status.* Glencoe, IL: Free Press, 1965.

Reuter, Edward Byron. *The Mulatto in the United States: Including a Study of the Role of Mixed-Bloods throughout the World.* Boston: Gorham Press, 1918.

Ridley, Matt. "Basic Human Nature: Can It Be Changed?" *Wall Street Journal* (November 5–6, 2011), C4.

Rockman, Seth. *Scraping By: Wage Labor, Slavery, and Survival in Early Baltimore.* Baltimore, MD: Johns Hopkins University Press, 2008.

Rona, Roberto J. "The Impact of the Environment on Height in Europe: Conceptual and Theoretical Considerations." *Annals of Human Biology* 27.2 (March 2000), 111–126.

Rothman, Joshua D. "James Callender and Social Knowledge of Interracial Sex in Antebellum Virginia." In *Sally Hemings & Thomas Jefferson: History, Memory, and Civic Culture,* 87–113. Edited by Jan Ellen Lewis and Peter S. Onuf. Charlottesville: University Press of Virginia, 1999.

Rothman, Joshua D. *Notorious in the Neighborhood: Sex and Families across the Color Line in Virginia, 1787–1861.* Chapel Hill, NC: University of North Carolina Press, 2003.

Rubin, Paul H. "Why Is the Common Law Efficient?" *Journal of Legal Studies* 6.1 (January 1977), 205–233.

Ruebeck, Christopher S., Susan Averett, and Howard Bodenhorn. "Acting White or Acting Black: Mixed-Race Adolescents' Identity and Behavior." *B.E. Journal of Economic Analysis and Policy* 9.1 (March 2009), Article 9.

Russell, John Henderson. *The Free Negro in Virginia, 1619–1865.* Baltimore, MD: Johns Hopkins University Press, 1913.

Russell, Kathy, Midge Wilson, and Ronald Hall. *The Color Complex: The Politics of Skin Color among African Americans.* New York: Anchor Books, 1993.

Sacerdote, Bruce. "Slavery and the Intergenerational Transmission of Human Capital." *Review of Economics and Statistics* 87.2 (May 2005), 217–234.

Salisbury, Laura. "Women's Income and Marriage Markets in the United States: Evidence from the Civil War Pension." Working paper, Boston University (November 2012).

Salmond, Anne. *Bligh: William Bligh in the South Seas.* Berkeley: University of California Press, 2011.

Santos, Ricardo Ventura, Peter H. Fry, Simone Montiero, Marcos Chor Maio, José Carlos Rodrigues, Luciana Bastos-Rodrigues, and Sergio D. J. Pena. "Color, Race and Genomic Ancestry in Brazil: Dialogues between Anthropology and Genetics." *Current Anthropology* 50.6 (December 2009), 787–819.

Schwartz, Stuart B. "The Manumission of Slaves in Colonial Brazil: Bahia, 1684–1745." *Hispanic American Historical Review* 54.4 (November 1974), 603–635.

Schelling, Thomas C. "Dynamic Models of Segregation." *Journal of Mathematical Sociology* 1.2 (1971), 143–186.

Schiller, Reuel E. "Conflicting Obligations: Slave Law and the Late Antebellum North Carolina Supreme Court." *Virginia Law Review* 78.5 (August 1992), 1207–1251.

Schlesinger, Arthur M. Jr. *The Age of Jackson.* Boston: Little Brown, 1945.

Schultz, T. Paul. "Wage Gains Associated with Height as a Form of Health Human Capital." *American Economic Review* 92.2 (May 2002), 349–353.

Schwarz, Philip J. "Emancipators, Protectors, and Anomalies: Free Black Slaveowners in Virginia." *Virginia Magazine of History and Biography* 95.3 (July 1987), 317–338.

Schweninger, Loren. "Thriving Within the Lowest Caste: The Financial Activities of James P. Thomas in the Nineteenth-Century South." *Journal of Negro History* 63.4 (October 1978), 353–364.

Schweninger, Loren. *Black Property Owners In the South, 1790–1915.* Urbana: University of Illinois Press, 1997.

Seaver, Jay W. *Anthropometry and Physical Examination.* New Haven, CT: O. A. Dorman, Co., 1896.

Seltzer, Richard and Robert C. Smith. "Color Differences in the Afro-American Community and the Differences They Make." *Journal of Black Studies* 21.3 (March 1991), 279–286.

Senese, Donald J. "The Free Negro and the South Carolina Court, 1790–1860." *South Carolina Historical Magazine* 68.3 (July 1967), 140–153.

Shapiro, Thomas M. *The Hidden Cost of Being African American: How Wealth Perpetuates Inequality.* New York: Oxford University Press, 2004.

Sharfstein, Daniel J. "The Secret History of Race in the United States." *Yale Law Journal* 112.6 (April 2003), 1473–1509.

Sharfstein, Daniel J. "Crossing the Color Line: Racial Migration and the One-Drop Rule, 1600–1860." *Minnesota Law Review* 91.3 (Fall 2007), 592–656.

Shavell, Steven. *Foundations of Economic Analysis of Law.* Cambridge, MA: Belknap Press of Harvard University Press, 2004.

Silventoinen, Karri. "Determinants of Variation in Adult Body Height." *Journal of Biosocial Science* 35.2 (April 2003), 263–285.

Singhal, Atul, Peter Thomas, Robert Cook, Klaas Wierenga, and Graham Serjeant. "Delayed Adolescent Growth in Homozygous Sickle Cell Disease." *Archives of Disease in Childhood* 71.5 (May 1994), 404–408.

Sollors, Werner. *Neither Black Nor White Yet Both: Thematic Explorations of Interracial Literature.* New York: Oxford University Press, 1997.

Smedley, Audrey. *Race in North America: Origin and Evolution of a Worldview.* Boulder, CO: Westview Press, 1993.

Smith, Adam. *An Inquiry into the Nature and Causes of the Wealth of Nations.* C. J. Bullock, editor. New York: P. F. Collier & Son Company, 1909.

Spurr, Stephen J. *Economic Foundations of Law.* Mason, OH: Thomson: Southwestern, 2006.

Stampp, Kenneth M. *The Peculiar Institution: Slavery in the Ante-Bellum South.* New York: Alfred A. Knopf, 1967.

Stanton, William R. *The Leopard's Spots: Scientific Attitudes toward Race in America, 1815–59.* Chicago: University of Chicago Press, 1960.

Steckel, Richard H. "Miscegenation and the American Slave Schedules." *Journal of Interdisciplinary History* 11.2 (Autumn 1980), 251–263.

Steckel, Richard H. "Growth Depression and Recovery: The Remarkable Case of American Slaves." *Annals of Human Biology* 14.2 (March/April 1987), 111–132.

Steckel, Richard H. "Stature and the Standard of Living." *Journal of Economic Literature* 33.4 (December 1995), 1903–1940.

Steckel, Richard H. "Percentiles of Modern Height Standards for Use in Historical Research." *Historical Methods* 29.4 (Fall 1996), 157–166.

Steckel, Richard H. "Diets Versus Disease in the Anthropometrics of Slave Children: A Reply." *Journal of Economic History* 60.1 (March 2000), 247–259.

Steckel, Richard H. "What Can Be Learned from Skeletons that Might Interest Economists, Historians, and Other Social Scientists." *American Economic Review* 93.2 (May 2003), 213–220.

Steckel, Richard H. "Heights and Human Welfare: Recent Developments and New Directions." *Explorations in Economic History* 46.1 (January 2009), 1–23.

Steckel, Richard H., and Carolyn M. Moehling. "Rising Inequality: Trends in the Distribution of Wealth in Industrializing New England." *Journal of Economic History* 61.1 (March 2001), 160–183.

Steckel, Richard H., and Joseph M. Prince. "Tallest in the World: Native Americans of the Great Plains in the Nineteenth Century." *American Economic Review* 91.1 (March 2001), 287–294.

Stedman, John Gabriel. *Narrative of Joanna, An Emancipated Slave of Surinam.* Boston: Issac Knapp, 1838.

Steffen, Charles G. *The Mechanics of Baltimore: Workers and Politics in the Age of Revolution, 1763–1812.* Urbana: University of Illinois Press, 1984.

Sterkx, H. E. *The Free Negro in Ante-Bellum Louisiana.* Rutherford, NJ: Fairleigh Dickinson University Press, 1972.

Stevenson, Brenda E. *Life in Black and White: Family and Community in the Slave South.* New York: Oxford University Press, 1996.

Stewart, John. *An Account of Jamaica, and Its Inhabitants by a Gentleman, Long Resident in the West Indies.* London: Longman, Hurst, Rees & Orme, 1808.

Stocking, George W. Jr. *Race, Culture, and Evolution: Essays in the History of Anthropology.* New York: The Free Press, 1968.

Stonequist, Everett V. "The Problem of the Marginal Man." *American Journal of Sociology* 41.1 (July 1935), 1–12.

Stowe, Harriet Beecher. *Uncle Tom's Cabin; or, Negro Life in the Slave States of America.* London: Richard Bentley, 1852.

Suarez-Kurtz, Guilherme, Daniela D. Vargens, Claudio J. Struchiner, Luciana Bastos-Rodrigues, and Sergio D. J. Pena. "Self-Reported Skin Color, Genomic Ancestry and the Distribution of GST Polymorrphisms." *Pharmacogenetics and Genomics* 17.9 (2007), 765–771.

Sullivan, Edward. *Rambles and Scrambles in North and South America.* London: Richard Bentley, 1852.

Sweat, Edward F. *The Free Negro in Antebellum Georgia.* Ph.D. Dissertation, Indiana University, 1957.

Talty, Stephan. *Mulatto America: At the Crossroads of Black and White Culture, A Social History.* New York: Harper Collins Publishers, 2003.

Tanner, J. M. *Foetus Into Man: Physical Growth from Conception to Maturity.* Cambridge, MA: Harvard University Press, 1978.

Tanner, J. M. *A History of the Study of Human Growth.* Cambridge: Cambridge University Press, 1981.

Tanner, J. M., and R.H. Whitehouse. "Clinical Longitudinal Standards for Height, Weight, Height Velocity, Weight Velocity, and Stages of Puberty." *Archives of Disease in Childhood* 51.3 (March 1976), 170–179.

Tanner, J. M., R. H. Whitehouse, and M. Takaishi. "Standards from Birth to Maturity for Height, Weight, Height Velocity, and Weight Velocity: British Children, 1965 Part II." *Archives of Disease in Children* 41.220 (December 1966), 613–635.

Tasistro, Louis Fitzgerald. *Random Shots and Southern Breezes, Containing Critical Remarks on the Southern States and Southern Institutions, with Semi-Serious Observations on Men and Manners.* 2 vols. New York: Harper & Brothers, 1842.

Telles, Edward E. "Racial Ambiguity among the Brazilian Population." California Center for Population Research, UCLA working paper, 2001.

Templeton, Alan R. "Human Races: A Genetic and Evolutionary Perspective." *American Anthropologist* 100.3 (September 1998), 632–650.

Tenzer, Lawrence R. *The Forgotten Cause of the Civil War: A New Look at the Slavery Issue.* Madison, Wisc.: Scholar's Publishing House, 1997.

Tocqueville, Alexis de. *Democracy in America*. Harvey C. Mansfield and Debra Winthrop, translators. Chicago: University of Chicago Press, 2000.

Tocqueville, Alexis de. *Report Made to the Chamber of Deputies on the Abolition of Slavery in the French Colonies*. Translation. Boston: James Munroe & Company, 1840.

Toplin, Robert Brent. "Between Black and White: Attitudes toward Southern Mulattoes, 1830–1861." *Journal of Southern History* 45.2 (May 1979), 185–200.

Troesken, Werner. *Water, Race, and Disease*. Cambridge, MA: MIT Press, 2004.

Turner, Edward Raymond. *The Negro in Pennsylvania: Slavery—Servitude—Freedom, 1639–1861*. Washington, DC: American Historical Association, 1911.

Turtle, George B. "Slave Manumission in Virginia, 1782–1806: The Jeffersonian Dilemma in the Age of Liberty." Masters thesis, University of Alberta, 1991.

Tversky, Amos, and Daniel Kahneman. "The Framing of Decisions and the Psychology of Choice." *Science* 211 (January 30, 1981), 453–458.

Udry, Richard, Karl E. Bauman, and Charles Chase. "Skin Color, Status, and Mate Selection." *American Journal of Sociology* 76.4 (January 1971), 722–733.

Udry, J. Richard, Rose Maria Li, and Janet Hendrickson-Smith. "Health and Behavior Risks of Adolescents with Mixed-Race Identity." *American Journal of Public Health* 93.11 (November 2003), 1865–1870.

Van Evrie, John H. *Negroes and Negro "Slavery": The First an Inferior Race: The Latter Its Normal Condition*. New York: Van Evrie, Horton & Co., 1863.

Vinovskis, Maris A. "Quantification and the Analysis of American Antebellum Education." *Journal of Interdisciplinary History* 13.4 (Spring 1983), 761–768.

Voth, Hans-Joachim, and Timothy Leunig. "Did Smallpox Reduce Height? Stature and the Standard of Living in London, 1770–1873." *Economic History Review* 44.3 (August 1996), 541–560.

Wade, Nicholas. *A Troublesome Inheritance: Genes, Race, and Human History*. New York: Penguin Press, 2014.

Wade, Nicholas. "Race Has a Biological Basis. Racism Does Not." *Wall Street Journal* (June 23, 2014), A13.

Walker, Alice. *In Search of Our Mother's Gardens*. New York: Harcourt Brace Jovanovich, 1983.

Walker, Juliet E. K. *The History of Black Business in America: Capitalism, Race, Entrepreneurship*. 2d Edition. 2 vols. Chapel Hill: University of North Carolina Press, 2009.

Wallenstein, Peter. *Tell the Court I Love My Wife: Race, Marriage, and Law—An American History*. New York: Palgrave Macmillan, 2002.

Ward, Richard, Janet Schlenker, and Gregory S. Anderson. "Simple Method for Developing Percentile Growth Curves for Height and Weight." *American Journal of Physical Anthropology* 116.3 (2001), 246–250.

Welch, Finis. "Labor-Market Discrimination: An Interpretation of Income Differences in the Rural South." *Journal of Political Economy* 75.3 (June 1967), 225–240.

West, Emily. *Family or Freedom: People of Color in the Antebellum South*. Lexington: University Press of Kentucky, 2012.

White, Deborah Gray. *Ar'n't I a Woman? Female Slaves in the Plantation South*. New York: W. W. Norton & Company, 1999.

"White Father Furious after Being Accused of Kidnapping His Own Biracial Daughters after Family Trip to Walmart." *Daily Mail*, May 21, 2013.

Whitman, T. Stephen. "Diverse Good Causes: Manumission and the Transformation of Urban Slavery." *Social Science History* 19.3 (Autumn 1995), 333–370.

Whitman, T. Stephen. *The Price of Freedom: Slavery and Manumission in Baltimore and Early National Maryland*. Lexington: University Press of Kentucky, 1997.

Wikramanayake, Marina. *A World in Shadow: The Free Black in Antebellum South Carolina*. Columbia: University of South Carolina Press, 1973.

Wilentz, Sean. *The Rise of American Democracy: Jefferson to Lincoln*. New York: W. W. Norton & Company, 2005.

Williamson, Elizabeth. "The Dating Game Gets Partisan, with Politics a Deal Breaker." *Wall Street Journal* 260.101 (October 29, 2012), A1.

Williamson, Joel. *New People: Miscegenation and Mulattoes in the United States*. New York: The Free Press, 1980.

Willis, Robert J. "A Theory of Out-of-Wedlock Childbearing." *Journal of Political Economy* 107.S6 (December 1999), S33–S64.

Wilkerson, Isabel. *The Warmth of Other Suns: The Epic Story of America's Great Migration*. New York: Random House, 2010.

Winston, George T. "The Relation of the Whites to the Negroes." *Annals of the American Academy of Political and Social Science* 18.1 (July 1901), 105–118.

Winterbottom, Thomas. "Account of the Native Africans in the Neighborhood of Sierra Leone," *African Repository and Colonial Journal* 1.7 (September 1825), 193–204.

Winters, Donald L. *Farmers Without Farms: Agricultural Tenancy in Nineteenth-Century Iowa*. Ames: Iowa State University Press, 1978.

Winters, Donald L. "The Agricultural Ladder in Southern Agriculture, 1850–1870." *Agricultural History* 61.3 (Summer 1987), 36–52.

Wolf, Eva Sheppard. *Race and Liberty in the New Nation: Emancipation in Virginia from the Revolution to Nat Turner's Rebellion*. Baton Rouge: Louisiana State University Press, 2006.

Wolf, Eva Sheppard. "Manumission and the Two-Race System in Early National Virginia." In *Paths to Freedom: Manumission in the Atlantic World*, 309–337. Edited by Rosemary Brana-Shute and Randy J. Sparks. Columbia: University of South Carolina Press, 2009.

Wolff, Georg. "A Study of Height in White School Children from 1937 to 1970 and a Comparison of Different Height-Weight Indices." *Child Development* 13.1 (March 1942), 65–77.

Woodson, Carter G. "The Beginnings of the Miscegenation of the Whites and Blacks." *Journal of Negro History* 3.4 (October 1918), 335–353.

Woodson, Carter G. *The Education of the Negro prior to 1861: A History of the Education of the Colored People of the United States from the Beginning of Slavery to the Civil War*. Second edition. Washington, DC: Associated Publishers. 1919.

Woodson, Carter G. "Review of *The Mulatto in the United States*." *Mississippi Valley Historical Review* 7.2 (September 1920), 175–176.

Wright, Frances (An Englishwoman). *Views of Society and Manners in America; In a Series of Letters from that Country to a Friend in England, during the Years 1818, 1819, and 1820*. London: Longman, Hurst, Rees, Orme, and Brown, 1821.

Wright, James M. *The Free Negro in Maryland, 1634–1860*. Baltimore, MD: Johns Hopkins University Press, 1921.

Wright, Luther Jr. "Who's Black, Who's White, Who Cares: Reconceptualizing the United States's Definition of Race and Racial Classifications." *Vanderbilt Law Review* 48.2 (March 1995), 513–570.

Young, Robert J. C. *Colonial Desire: Hybridity in Theory, Culture and Race*. London: Routledge, 1995.

Zanger, Jules. "The 'Tragic Octoroon' in Pre-Civil War Fiction." *American Quarterly* 18.1 (Spring 1966), 63–70.

Zemel, B. S., and F. E. Johnston. "Application of the Preece-Baines Growth Model to Cross-Sectional Data: Problems of Validity and Interpretation." *American Journal of Human Biology* 6.5 (1994), 563–570.

Zhang, J. "Tipping and Residential Segregation: A Unified Schelling Model." *Journal of Regional Sciences* 51.1 (February 2011), 167–193.

Case Law, Legal Treatises, Statutes, and Compilations

Adelle v. Beauregard, 1 Mart. 183 (La. 1810) [1810 La. Lexis 24].

Anderson v. Martin, 375 U.S. 399.

Anderson v. Millikin and Others, 9 Ohio St. 568 [1859 Ohio Lexis 229].

Bryan v. Wadsworth, 18 N.C. 384 [1835 N. C. Lexis 49].

Bolling v. Sharpe, 347 U.S. 497.

Cobb, Thomas R. R. *An Inquiry into the Law of Negro Slavery in the United States of America*. Vol. I. Philadelphia: T. & J. W. Johnson & Co., 1858.

The Code of Virginia: With the Declaration of Independence and the Constitution of the United States; and the Declaration of Rights and Constitution of Virginia. Richmond: William F. Ritchie, Public Printer, 1849.

Daniel v. Guy, 19 Ark. 121 [1857 Ark. Lexis 15].

Dean v. Commonwealth, 45 Va. (4 Gratt.) 541 [1847 Va. Lexis 51].

[Jane] Doe v. State of Louisiana, 479 So. 2d 369 [1985 La. App. Lexis 10022].

Doe on demise of Frances Howard v. Sarah Howard, et al. 51 N.C. 235 [1858 N.C. Lexis 160; 6 Jones Law 235].

Fisher's Negroes v. Dabbs et al.,14 Tenn. 119 at 126 [1834 Tenn. Lexis 59].

Gaines v. Ann, 17 Tex. 211 [1856 Tex. Lexis 152].

Gentry v. McMinnis, 33 Ky. (3 Dana) 382 [1835 Ky. Lexis 109].

Gobu v. Gobu, 1 N.C. 188 (N.C. 1802) [1802 N.C. Lexis 1].

Gray v. Ohio, 4 Ohio 353 [1831 Ohio Lexis 169].

Gregory v. Baugh, 25 Va. (4 Rand.) 611 [1827 Va. Lexis 4].

Guild, June Purcell. *Black Laws of Virginia: A Summary of the Legislative Acts of Virginia Concerning Negroes from Earliest Times to the Present*. Whittet & Shepperson, 1936. (Reprint New York: Negro Universities Press, 1969).

Hook v. Nanny Pagee and Her Children, 16 Va. 379; 2 Munf. 379 [1881 Va. Lexis 80].

Hudgins v. Wrights (11 Va. 134; 1 Hen. & M. 134, 1806) [1806 Va. Lexis 58].

James, Benjamin. *A Digest of the Laws of South-Carolina, Containing the Public Statute Law of the State, Down to the Year 1822*. Columbia, SC: Telescope Press, 1822.

Jeffries v. Ankeny et al., 11 Ohio 372 [1842 Ohio Lexis 98].

Korematsu v. United States, 323 U.S. 214.

Lane v. Baker et al., 12 Ohio 237 [1843 Ohio Lexis 80].

Loving v. Virginia, 388 U.S. 1 [1967 U.S. Lexis 1082].

M'Cutchen et al v. Marshall et al., 33 U.S. 220 at 238 [1834 U.S. Lexis 579].

McLaughlin v. Florida, 379 U.S. 184.

Medway v. Natick, 7 Mass (7 Tyng) 88 [1810 Mass. Lexis 111].

Miller v. Denman, 16 Tenn. (8 Yer.) 233 [1835 Tennessee Lexis 85].

Morrison v. White, 16 La. Ann. 100.

O'Neall, John Belton. *The Negro Law of South Carolina*. Columbia, SC: John G. Bowman, 1848.

Perry & Van Houten v. Beardslee & Wife, 10 Mo. 568 (March 1847) [1847 Mo. Lexis 147].

Plessy v. Ferguson, 163 U.S. 537 [1896 Lexis 3390].

Rawlings v. Boston, 3 H. & McH. 139 (Md 1793) [1793 Md. Lexis 12].

Snethen, Worthington G. *The Black Code of the District of Columbia, In Force September 1st, 1848*. New York: William Harned, 1848.

State v. Cantey, 20 S.C. Law 614 (1835).

State v. Chavers, 50 N.C. (5 Jones) 11 [1857 N.C. Lexis 5].

State v. Henry Kimber, [1859 Ohio Misc. Lexis 58].

Stephenson, Gilbert Thomas. *Race Distinctions in American Law*. New York: D. Appleton & Co., 1910.

Thacker v. Hawk et al., 11 Ohio 376 [1842 Ohio Lexis 99].

Thurman v. State, 18 Ala. 276 [1850 Lexis 186].

Vaughan v. Phebe, 8 Tenn (1. Mart.) 5 [1827 Tenn. Lexis 1].

Virginia. *The Revised Code of the Laws of Virginia: Being a Collection of All Such Acts of the General Assembly, of a Public and Permanent Nature, as Are Now in Force*. Richmond: Thomas Ritchie, Printer to the State, 1819.

Waddill v. Martin, 3 Iredell Eq. 562 (N. C. 1845).

Walker v. Internal Revenue Service, 713 F. Suppl. 403 (N. D. Ga. 1989).

INDEX

abolitionists, 36, 54, 55, 56
Acemoglu, Daron, 77
adolescent growth spurt, 169
advertisements, runaway, 91, 92, 93, 95, 96,
    223–229
Agassiz, Louis, 40, 44, 45, 46, 48
age structure, 203–207
agricultural ladder, 17, 138, 140, 141
Alvord, John, 99
amalgamation, 45, 46, 47, 48, 51, 53, 60, 121
    antiamalgamation law, 53
    and slavery, 208–211
American Union for the Relief and Improvement
    of the Colored People, 161
Anderson, Meriwether L., 81
Andrews, Ethan Allen, 161
anthropometrics, 168, 170, 214, 253
apprenticeship, 159, 160
    pauper, 113
Ashley, Moses, 46
assortative mating, 61, 98, 106, 195, 229–236
    marriage, 232–236
    matching, 60, 101, 102, 104, 105, 110, 111,
        119, 120, 232, 233, 234
Atack, Jeremy, 141
Atwell & Hutt, 152
Audubon, John J., 46
Auld, Hugh, 88
Auld, Thomas, 70, 71
Averett, Susan, 196

Babcock, Theodore Stoddard, 222
Bachman, John, 46
Bailey family, 2, 3, 11
    Edith, 9
    John Scott, 1, 5, 7, 9
    Joseph, 9

Bailey, Abram, 32
Bailey, Frederick Augustus, 50, 88
Bailey, Lucy Ann Bee, 32
Baker, Ray Stannard, 19
Bayley, Richard Drummond, 76
Beardslee, Mr., 91
Belding, Theodore C., 100, 230, 231, 232
Bell, Grimble, 160
Benwell, John, 63, 142
Berlin, Ira, 25, 26, 30, 32, 125, 126, 142
Bernhardt, Irwin, 135, 238
Berzon, Judith, 195
Blasingame, John, 64
Block, Sharon, 59
Boasman, Mary Elizabeth, 4
Boasman, Virginia Ann, 4
Bode, Frederick, 139
Bogger, Tommy, 98
Bogue, Alan, 139
Bonneau, Thomas, 160
Booker, James, 32
Booker, Nancy Harris, 32
Borgas, George, 133, 241
bound servant, 32
    Bidde, 32
    Dol, 52
Bowditch, Henry Pickering, 168, 169, 170, 172
Brackenridge, Hugh Henry, 40, 41
Brana-Shute, Rosemary, 74, 87
Brandon, Ida Mae, 98
Breen, T. H., 165
Brewer, James, 145
Bronars, Stephen, 135, 241
Brown, Peter A., 12
Brown, William Wells, 36, 37
Bryan, Andrew, 144
Bryan, Seaborn, 34
Burch, Traci R., 7

Burdett, Kenneth, 100, 230, 232
Burghard, 179, 181
Burton, Francis C., 1, 9
Burton, Sarah M., 1, 9
Byrd, William II, 55

Callender, James, 50
Camerer, Colin, 80
Campbell, John, 45
capitalized wages and human capital, 247–253
Carey, Thomas, 153
Carter, Landon, 71
Carter, Robert "Councilor" III, 141, 217
carting, 17
Cayton, Horace, 193
Chambers, Eliza, 106
Chambers, Isaac, 106
Charles, Jethro, 216
Chestnut, Mary Boykin, 57, 63
Childs, Lydia Marie, 36
church school, 34
Cippola, Carlo, 14
Clark, Josiah, 42
Clark, Robert, 79
Coase Theorem, 30
Cole, Aggy, 32
Cole, Shawn, 67, 144
Coles, Melvyn G., 100, 230, 232
Collins, William, 148
color factor, 149
color line, 19, 32, 125, 182, 188
color ordering, 3
colorism, 3, 98, 193
complexion, 98
Conley, Timothy, 243
Conrad, Alfred, 249
Conrad, Nancy, 113
Conway, Moncure, 46
Cooley, Charles, 14
Cowling, Richard, 98
critical race theory, 27, 28, 29, 30,
     31, 34, 201
Cross, Albert, 129
Crow, Jim, 189
Curry, Leonard, 126

Darity, William, 196
Davidson, Polly, 188, 189
Davis, Hugh, 52
Davis, James, 196
Degler, Carl, 15, 31
Delany, Martin, 125, 132
Dittmar, Jeremiah, 90
Dominguez, Virginia, 195

Douglas, Stephen, 48
Douglass, Frederick, 50, 51, 63, 70, 71, 88,
     126, 161
     Frederick Augustus Bailey, 50, 88
Douglass, Margaret, 182
Drake, St. Clair, 193
DuBois, W. E. B., 62
Dumford, Annette, 146
Duncan Index, 129, 130
Duncan, Otis Dudley, 127
Dusinburre, William, 68, 69

Eblen, Jack, 217
economic well-being and assortative marriage,
     234–236
Edwards, Ozzie, 195
Eltonhead, Jane, 145
Emerson, Ralph Waldo, 144
Engerman, Stanley, 60

Fairlie, Robert, 196
fancy girls, 67, 68
farm laborers, 17
Fawcett, Sarah, 33
Ferrie, Joseph, 183, 184, 185, 186
field hand, prime, 249
Fogel, Robert, 60
Franklin, John Hope, 92, 124, 126,
     151, 197, 227
Frazier, E. Franklin, 113, 114, 118, 164, 194
Frederickson, George, 37
Freedmen's Bureau, 99, 105, 106, 107, 110
freedom suits, 201–203
Freeland, Mrs., 70
Freeman, Howard, 195
Frick, Charles, 183
Fryer, Roland, 191, 196, 197
Fuller, Nancy, 98

Gaines, George, 27
Galenson, David, 243
Gallemore, Elizabeth, 121
genes, 5
Genovese, Eugene, 64, 65, 66
Gibbes, Robert W., 45
Gilchrist, Seraphine, 14
Gilliam, Elizabeth, 216
Ginter, Donald, 139
Gladney, George, 98
Gliddon, George R., 42, 45
Godsey, Mary, 188
Golden, Marita, 193
Goldin, Claudia, 159

Goldsmith, Arthur, 196
Gordon-Reed, Annette, 195
Gough, Harry Dorsey, 89
Gowrie Plantation, 55
Graham, Lawrence Otis, 164, 196
Green, Eliza, 32
Green, William, 32
Greenwood, Jeremy, 229, 236
griff, 106, 107, 108
Gross, Ariela, 26, 28, 29, 199
growth model, Preece-Baines, 173, 177, 181,
    254, 256
Guillory, Monique, 36
Guinnane, Timothy, 172, 214, 215
Gullickson, Aaron, 191, 196
Guner, Nezih, 229
Gutman, Herbert, 64, 113, 117, 118
Gyimah-Brempong, Kwabena, 197

Hamilton, Darrick, 196
Hammond, Leroy, 144
Hanger, Kimberly, 125
Harris, David, 192
Harris, Marvin, 5
Hartley, L. P., 8
health human capital, 167
heights, estimated, 253–262
Hemings, Betty, 50
Hemings, Sally, 36, 50, 51, 55, 68
Henry, Patrick, 71
Henshaw, Philip, 58
Herbert, Butler, 53
Herring, Cedric, 196
Hersch, Joni, 196
Hershberg, Theodore, 113, 117, 143
Higginbotham, Leon, 23
Hill, Mark, 189, 196
Hirsh, Leo, 127
Hobbes, Thomas, 186
Hochschild, Jennifer, 3, 7, 189
Hodge, Willis Augustus, 99
homogamy, 16, 17, 98, 102, 110,
    195, 229, 230, 231, 232
hookworm, 183
Horseman, Reginald, 42, 43
Horton, George, 79
Horton, James, 132, 163
Horton, Lois, 132, 163
households, county rural sample of,
    245–247
Howe, Daniel Walker, 160
Howe, Samuel Gridley, 47
Howell, William Dean, 48
huckstering, 17
human capital and capitalized wages,
    247–253

hybridity, 43, 45, 46, 47, 48
hypodescent, 7, 19

Index of Dissimilarity, 129, 130, 137
infant mortality, 185, 186
Innes, Stephen, 165
interracial marriage, 7, 8, 52
Irish, 7, 8
Irmscher, Christophe, 45

Jackson, Andrew, 12
Jackson, James, 81, 87
Jackson, Luther Porter, 17, 146, 148, 149, 152,
    153, 194, 220
Jackson Square, 123
Jacobs, Harriet, 62
Jarrett, Alexander, 98
Jefferson, Sally, 50
Jefferson, Thomas, 11, 12, 36, 38, 50, 68, 71, 73,
    166, 171
Johnson, Richard, 8
Johnson, Samuel, 72
Johnson, Walter, 28
Johnson, Whittington, 98
Johnson, William, 132, 133
Johnston, James Hugo, 23, 194
Jones, Bernie, 56, 58
Jones, John A., 132
Jones, Henry, 121
Jordan, Winthrop, 64, 163, 194, 195
jury service, 34

Kalmijn, Mattijs, 229
Keith, Verna, 196
Kemble, Frances Ann (Fanny), 39, 64
Kendall, William, 59
Kennedy, Joseph, 45
Kidd, Ben, 54, 55
Kimber, Henry, 33
Kiple, Kenneth, 183
Kiple, Virginia, 183
Kneeland, Samuel, 45
Kochardkov, Georgi, 229
Komlos, John, 215, 253, 254
Kotlikoff, Lawrence, 66, 67, 68
Kunreuther, Howard, 80

Lacroix, François, 142
Lacroix, Julian, 142
Lafayette College, 12
Lammermeier, Paul, 113
Latrobe, Charles Joseph, 123
Lawrence, William, 41, 43

Lewis, David, 54
Lewis, Ruby, 192
life table, 205
Lincoln, Abraham, 48
Litwack, Leon, 126
Lloyd, Daniel, 51
Lloyd, Edward, 51, 53
Logan, Peter, 32
Long, Edward, 87
Lookado, Jordin, 173
Loury, Linda Datcher, 196

Madison, James, 171
malaria, 183
Manigault, Chares, 55, 63, 64, 67, 176
Manigault, Elizabeth Heyward, 63
Manigault, Gabriel, 178
Manigault, Louis, 63, 67
manumission, 16, 27, 30, 31, 71, 72, 73, 74, 76, 77, 78,
    81, 82, 83, 84, 85, 87, 89, 96, 97, 141, 177, 203,
    212, 215, 216, 217, 218, 219, 220, 222, 223
    deeds, 76, 81
    delayed, 76, 89, 215
    economics of, 145
    and prospect theory, 80
    rates, 80
    self-purchase, 74, 79, 84, 144, 201
    term slavery, 76, 89
    Virginia register samples, 215–223
    wills, 76
marginal man, 194, 197
Margo, Robert, 65, 148, 252
marriage market, 16
Marshall, John, 71
Martineau, Harriet, 39, 57
Mason, George, 71
Maxwell, Patrick, 32
Maxwell, Sophia Lazenberry, 32
McIntosh, David, 98
meamelouc, 9
mental disabilities, 203–207
Meyer, Joseph, 249
Mill, Roy, 189
Miller, Kelly, 194
miscegenation, 48, 51, 117, 190, 191
Mitchell, John, 40
monogenesis, 40, 41, 42
Morgan, Morman, 173
Morrison, Alexina, 28, 29
mortality rates, 183, 184, 185, 186
    infant, 185, 186
Morton, Samuel George, 7, 45, 47
Mroz, Thomas, 172, 214, 215
mulattin, 12
mulatto, 1, 3, 4, 5, 6, 8, 9, 11, 13, 14, 21, 22, 23,
    24, 25, 27, 30, 31, 32, 33, 34, 35, 37, 39, 42,

46, 47, 57, 64, 65, 67, 85, 96, 98, 106, 108,
    110, 111, 119, 121, 123, 165, 173, 189, 190,
    194, 203, 206, 212, 215, 222, 227
    as-hybrid, 13, 42
Murray, Anna, 88

Naidu, Suresh, 91
Napoleon, 12
Nash, Gary, 125
negro, 9, 11, 13, 14, 19, 20, 23, 52, 54, 57, 72, 123,
    160, 212, 222
Newsome, Robert, 55
Nicholls, John, 120, 145, 146
Nott, Josiah Clark, 7, 43, 44, 45, 46, 47, 48, 194
Nuñez, Joseph, 34, 35, 49
Nutt, Haller, 57

Oblate Sisters of Providence Convent, 160
occupational segregation, 125, 127, 137
    Duncan Index, 129, 130
    Index of Dissimilarity, 129, 130, 137
octoroon, 9, 11, 14, 37, 48, 106, 108, 110, 190
old-age hypothesis, 159, 167
Oldham, Mary J., 81
Olmsted, Frederick Law, 9, 47, 57, 66, 126
one-drop rule, 15, 19, 21, 31, 33, 48, 181,
    192, 193
origin of the races, 40

Park, Robert, 194, 197
Parrish, Frank, 132
partus sequitur ventrem, 22, 28, 29, 56, 58
passing, 25, 32
patrol, slave, 93, 94
pauper apprentices, 113
Paxton, John D., 64
Payne, Francis, 165
pellagra, 183
Phillips, Christopher, 98, 159
Phipps, Suzy, 20
plaçage, 38, 59, 117
placée, 38
Plessey, Homer, 20, 21, 22, 33
Plessey v Ferguson, 19, 20, 21, 33
polygenesis, 40, 41, 42, 44, 45, 46
Posner, Richard, 56
Powell, Brenna, 3
Preece-Baines model, 173, 177, 181, 254, 256
Price, Gregory N., 197

quadroon, 9, 11, 14, 27, 37, 39, 63, 64, 65, 67, 106,
    108, 123, 190
quadroon ball, 38, 117

quarterón, 9
quinteroon, 44

race, definition of, 29
race mixing, 12, 15, 16, 23, 43, 44, 47, 48, 54, 61, 63, 74, 172, 191, 208, 209
racial determination, 199–201
racial ordering, 3, 8
Ragsdail, Godfrey, 52, 53
Randolf, Henry, 53
real-estate ownership, 241–245
Redmond, Daniel, 225
Reggio, A., 142
Reid, Mayne, 36, 37
Reinders, Robert, 126
residential segregation, 8
Reuter, Edward Bryon, 14, 190, 193, 195
Richardson, Dorothea, 50
Richardson, John, 50
Rippon, John, 144
Rix, Polly, 4
Rix, Wager, 4
Roberts, Charles, 172
Rock, Chris, 193
Rockman, Seth, 125, 132
Rogers, Mary, 34
romantic racialist tradition, 37
Rothman, Joshua, 59
Royall, Henry, 53
Rubin, Paul, 29, 201
Ruebeck, Christopher, 196
runaways, 71, 89, 90, 91, 92, 93, 94, 95, 96, 97, 203, 223–229
    advertisements, 91, 92, 93, 95, 96, 223–229
    running away, 16
Russell, John, 126
Rutledge, John, 80

Sacerdote, Bruce, 189
Santos, Cezar, 229
Schultz, T. Paul, 167
Schweninger, Loren, 92, 146, 227
selection bias, 214, 215, 253
self-employment, 17, 134, 135, 137, 236–241
self-purchase, 74, 79, 84, 144, 201
Sen, Amartya, 167
Shapiro, Thomas, 166
sharecroppers, 138
Sharfstein, Daniel, 31
Shavell, Steven, 93, 94
Sim, Jeremiah Joseph, 192
Simon Legree, 36
single parenthood, 114, 115, 116, 117, 118, 119
Sisters of the Sacred Heart, 160
slave patrol, 93, 94

slaves, 50
    Anthony Chase, 89, 96
    Celia, 55, 56, 57, 62
    Chloe Matilda, 87
    Cinderilla, 225
    David, 91
    Dick, 87
    Dolly, 63
    Edmund, 50
    Eliza, 87
    Fanny, 81
    Francis Payne, 145
    Frank, 225
    Henry, 70
    Henry Francis, 144
    John Izard, 68
    John (MD), 70
    John (VA), 225
    J. W. Lindsay, 54, 55
    Kit, 81
    Madison Jefferson, 54, 91
    Martha, 67
    Pat, 87
    Peter, 87
    Polly, 216
    Sachel, 81
    Sally (GA), 64
    Sally (SC), 80
    Sylvia, 188
    Sylvie, 58
    Tom, 87
    Will Bates, 89
    William, 87
    Willis, 87
slavery and amalgamation, 208–211
slavery, term, 76, 89, 216, 254
Smith, Adam, 158, 247
Smith, Braxton, 1, 2, 3, 5, 7
Smith, James McCune, 136, 137
Smith, Jonathan, 32
Smith, Lucy Ann Davenport, 32
Smith, Milly, 1
social construction of race, 7, 31
Soller, Werner, 15, 196
Somerhill, George, 173
Soulie, Alvin, 142
Soulie, Bernard, 142
Southampton insurrection, 84
Stampp, Kenneth, 55
Stanton, William, 42
State v Kimber, 33
Steckel, Richard, 60, 175, 177, 208
Stedman, John, 38
Stein, Luke, 189
Stephenson, George, 9, 10, 11
Stephenson, Gilbert, 19
Stevenson, Brenda, 112, 113, 117, 119, 121, 137

Stewart, Daniel, 4
Stewart, John, 58
Stocking, George, 43
Stonequist, Everett V., 194, 197
Stowe, Harriet Beecher, 36, 37, 69
Stowe, Joseph, 165
Sullivan, Edward, 39, 67
survivalist entrepreneurship, 134
Sweet, Robert, 52

talented tenth, 189
Tanner, J. M., 177
Tate, Anderson, 152
Tate, Campbell, 152
Tate, Julia, 152
Tate, Mary, 152
tenancy, 138, 139, 140, 141, 152
    tenant farmers, 16
    tenants, 138, 140, 142
tercerón, 9
term slavery, 76, 89, 216
Toplin, Robert, 66
tragic mulatta, 37, 38, 48
tragic, mulatto, 15, 35, 36
Tucker, George, 46
Turner, Nat, 84, 161, 220

Udry, Richard, 195
urban residence and assortative marriage,
    232–234

Van Evrie, John, 7
Vaughan, Thomas, 81
Vesey, Denmark, 79
Villaflor, Georgia C., 252

Vinoskis, Maris, 162
Virginia register sample, 211–215
    manumission, 215–223

wages, capitalized, 247, 250, 251
Walker, Juliet E. K., 125, 132
Walker, Tracy, 192
Wall, Ann, 54
Washington, George, 12, 77, 78, 217
Wayles, James, 50
Weaver, Vesla M., 7
White, Daniel, 3
White, Deborah, 58
White, James, 28
Whitehead, Arthur, 81
Whitman, T. Stephen, 74, 126,
    132, 218, 220
Whitman, Walt, 37
Wikramanayake, Marina, 126, 142
Wilks, William, 63
Williams, Henry, 143
Williamson, Joel, 23, 24, 31, 195
wills, 76
Wilson, John, 45
Winters, Donald, 139, 141
Winthrop, John IV, 40
Wolf, Eva Sheppard, 74, 222
Wolitzky, Alexander, 77
Woodson, Carter, 54
Wright, Robert, 58, 188, 189
Wright, Thomas, 58, 188

yellow, 14

Zealy, Joseph T., 45

Printed in the USA/Agawam, MA
July 21, 2020

758491.108